The Sports 100

THE ONE HUNDRED MOST IMPORTANT PEOPLE
IN AMERICAN SPORTS HISTORY

Brad Herzog

To Larry,
one helluva guy

— Brad Herzog

3-21-96

MACMILLAN • USA

MACMILLAN
A Simon & Schuster Macmillan Company
1633 Broadway
New York, NY 10019-6785

Library of Congress Cataloguing-in-Publication data

Herzog, Brad
    The sports 100 : the one hundred most important people
in American sports history / Brad Herzog.
        p.   cm.
    Includes bibliographical references.
    ISBN 0–02–860402-4
        1. Sports—Biography.   2. Athletes—Biography.
    3. Sports—History.   I. Title.
    GV697.A1H397   1995
    796'.092'2—dc20
    [B]   95–40968
                                                          CIP

Manufactured in the United States of America
10 9 8 7 6 5 4 3 2 1

Book Design by George J. McKeon

*Cover photos courtesy of (from top) the National
Baseball Library and Archives, Bill Smith, and TeamTennis, Inc.*

Contents

Acknowledgments

The Sports 100 is the product of both extensive historical research and intensive soul-searching. It is one man's ranking, but it is actually the compilation of dozens of perspectives, those of some of the most respected observers of American sport. The profiles are both biographical and explanatory in nature, and every effort has been made to convey the importance of each figure through the words of the people best qualified to do so—contemporary athletic figures and journalists, biographers and sports historians. Please take a moment to peruse the names listed in the acknowledgments and bibliography. In writing each of the 100 profiles, I relied immensely on these respected scholars and studies of the games and their participants.

The authorities whose opinions and reflections were vital to compiling *The Sports 100* come from all over the athletic, academic and journalistic spectrum, and I thank them for taking the time to offer their perspective about their area of expertise and, in some cases, about themselves. In particular, I would like to thank Lamar Hunt; Bill Rasmussen; Jim Bouton; Ray Meyer; Dr. Richard Lapchick, director of Northeastern University's Center for the Study of Sport in Society; Donna Lopiano (executive director) and Marjorie Snyder (associate executive director) of the Women's Sports Foundation; Wayne Wilson, vice-president (research) at the Amateur Athletic Foundation of Los Angeles; Rick Korch, editor of *Pro Football Weekly*; football historians Jim Campbell and Bob Carroll; baseball historians John Thorn and Tom Gilbert; hockey historian Stan Fischler; basketball historian Bill Himmelman; Wayne Patterson, research specialist at the Naismith Memorial Basketball Hall of Fame; *Chicago Tribune* basketball columnist Sam Smith; Roy S. Johnson, senior editor at *Money* magazine; Bob Sullivan, senior editor at *Life* magazine; *Sports Illustrated* senior writers and/or editors Paul Fichtenbaum, Jack McCallum and Alex Wolff; former *Sports Illustrated* senior writers Robert W. Creamer, Andrew Crichton and Robert H. Boyle; Bob Brown, former editor-in-chief of *Car and Driver* and currently deputy editorial director of *Outdoor Life*; Craig Neff, managing editor of *Sports Illustrated For Kids*; Neil Cohen, editorial director of *Sports Illustrated For Kids* Books; Steve

Farhood, editor-in-chief of *The Ring* magazine; Herbert Warren Wind, sports historian and former golf writer for *The New Yorker*; Frank Hannigan, former executive director of the U.S. Golf Association; NASCAR media coordinator Kevin Triplett; Mark Young, librarian at the International Tennis Hall of Fame; Steve Nidetz, radio and television columnist for the *Chicago Tribune*; Arthur A. Fleisher III, associate professor of economics at Metropolitan State College in Denver; and Andrew Zimbalist, professor of economics at Smith College and co-founder of the U.S. Baseball League.

Thanks also to all those who helped in the search for information about Charles McNeil, including Arne Lang, Mort Olshan and Howard Schwartz from the Gambler's Book Club. I also would like to express my appreciation to Mark Goldberg, Steve Madden, J. B. Morris, Liza Landsman and my colleagues and mentors at the Cornell University Sports Information Office, the *Ithaca Journal* and *Sports Illustrated For Kids* for their guidance and support. And finally, my gratitude goes to my editor, Jeanine Bucek, who had the foresight and courage to turn a casual lunchtime conversation into a bona fide book.

The Sports 100 is dedicated to my parents—from my father I inherited an appreciation of sport, and from my mother a tendency to make lists; the end product is a tribute to both—and to my wife, Amy, always and forever my number-one inspiration.

Introduction

In any walk of life, there are those who make their mark and those who just mark time. Greatness is measured not only by one's contemporary feats, but by one's historical impact. History has presented us with outstanding figures—from Thomas Jefferson to Albert Einstein to Martin Luther King, Jr.— whose pioneering words and deeds have influenced generations after them, touching millions and perhaps billions of lives in one way or another.

American sport, a significant part of American history, also has witnessed its share of influential figures, men and women who have had a profound effect on the course of the games and sometimes, through the far-reaching nature of sport, on society itself. What would baseball be like without Babe Ruth's influence? Football without George Halas? Golf without Arnold Palmer? What if the early NBA hadn't enjoyed the services of a star like George Mikan or if the modern NBA hadn't hitched its star to Michael Jordan? What if Jackie Robinson and Arthur Ashe had been disappointments as athletes and as role models?

Clearly, there are some sports figures who stand out from the rest, people whose actions have impacted the games beyond the moment and often beyond the playing fields. This book honors—or at least spotlights—those people. The list, and particularly its ordering, is bound to be somewhat controversial. After all, sports aficionados enjoy nothing more than debating the relative merits of something. But such is its purpose: to arouse debate and reflection about the big picture of sports through a healthy dose of hindsight.

You may be disappointed (or perhaps intrigued) by the omission of many of the biggest names in sports. But this is a list, in many respects, of tangible contributions. Pick any sports figure and then quickly try to describe why he or she was important. If all you can say about someone is that he was the greatest quarterback ever, or he hit this many home runs or he collected that many victories, that is not enough. There are just too many stars in the world of sports to have included people for star power alone. *The Sports 100* is an attempt to show that there are a handful of unknowns or behind-the-scenes figures who left more of an imprint than a great many legends. You'll find Nike CEO Phil Knight, but not Bobby Knight; famed sportswriter Grantland Rice, but not Jerry Rice; Pete Rozelle, but not Pete Rose.

If, as many readers will contend, this list MUST include Pete Rose, must it also include Hank Aaron and Willie Mays, Joe DiMaggio and Ty Cobb, Nolan Ryan and Walter Payton, Joe Montana and Gordie Howe, Wilt Chamberlain and Carl Lewis, Jimmy Connors and Casey Stengel, Adolph Rupp, Ben Hogan and Rocky Marciano? Where does one draw the line?

In fact, just to make it easy on the critics, the following is a list of 100 sports figures (in addition to the aforementioned) who are *not* profiled in *The Sports 100*. Many, undoubtedly, were tremendously important—they just didn't quite make the cut: Kareem Abdul-Jabbar, Phog Allen, Mario Andretti, Bob Arum, Ernie Banks, Red Barber, Charles Barkley, Sammy Baugh, Elgin Baylor, August Belmont, Yogi Berra, Bonnie Blair, Barry Bonds, Lou Brock, Bear Bryant, Dick Butkus, Dick Button, Frank Calder, Clarence Campbell, Bob Cousy, Al Davis, Dizzy Dean, Eric Dickerson, Ken Dryden, Dale Earnhardt, Phil Esposito, Chris Evert, Jim Fixx, Peggy Fleming, George Foreman, Rube Foster, Lou Gehrig, Josh Gibson, Dorothy Hamill, Eric Heiden, Rickey Henderson, Hank Iba, Bo Jackson, Joe Jackson, Reggie Jackson, Jackie Joyner-Kersee, Don King, Sandy Koufax, Bowie Kuhn, Jack LaLanne, Tom Landry, Greg LeMond, Ray Leonard, Nancy Lopez, Sid Luckman, Connie Mack, Mickey Mantle, Pete Maravich, Dan Marino, Billy Martin, Christy Mathewson, John McEnroe, John McGraw, Jim McKay, Cheryl Miller, Earl Monroe, Helen Wills Moody, Edwin Moses, Stan Musial, Bronko Nagurski, Byron Nelson, James Norris, Shaquille O'Neal, Joe Paterno, Roger Penske, Mary Lou Retton, Maurice Richard, Pat Riley, Oscar Robertson, Eddie Robinson, Frank Robinson, Ray Robinson, Deion Sanders, Gale Sayers, Willie Shoemaker, Don Shula, O. J. Simpson, Dean Smith, Red Smith, Conn Smythe, Sam Snead, Mark Spitz, Roger Staubach, George Steinbrenner, Fran Tarkenton, Lawrence Taylor, Ted Turner, Mike Tyson, Johnny Unitas, Honus Wagner, Bill Walsh, Jerry West, Lenny Wilkens, Ted Williams and Cy Young.

The Sports 100 represents an ever-evolving collection of sports figures. A revised edition fifteen years from now might include a handful of new names. Perhaps African-American golf prodigy Tiger Woods will prove to have an enormous impact; or Hispanic basketball star Felipe Lopez might merit inclusion. Or possibly Donald Fehr and Bud Selig, the forces behind the 1994 baseball strike. Perhaps, once the dust settles, O. J. Simpson may find himself somewhere among *The Sports 100*.

Each of the above people has the potential to make a significant imprint on American athletics, to represent an important aspect of sport itself or of sport's influence on society. And, indeed, one of the primary aims of the book is to put sport into historical perspective, to show how sport's cultural influence is often manifest in a handful of significant individuals. It also highlights the many cases in which one person was largely responsible for introducing a new and eventually monumental element of sport into the world—be it free agency, the point spread, the NCAA, artificial turf, the minor league farm system, the forward pass or the jump shot. In fact, the book is not only a study of 100 remarkable individuals, but also of 100 components of sport's evolution. It is as much a history of the games as a profile of the participants.

In compiling the list, each person's impact was judged according to several criteria. The following questions and answers concern the premise of the book and, consequently, the ranking of each sports figure:

•How is "important" defined?

In the context of *The Sports 100*, "important" does not mean outstanding, nor does it necessarily mean famous. This is, by no means, a list of the greatest figures in American sports. If it were, you would find Mays and Howe and Chamberlain and Hogan and Montana. Brilliant performances and even legendary status aren't enough to be included—unless they translated into influence.

"Important," in this case, means influential, impacting, pioneering. The book profiles 100 people without whom American sports would not be the same. How would the person's sport—or sports in general—have unfolded had he or she not existed? Did the person's actions alter the course of sports history or simply run the course? These are the central questions. Consider football without Pete Rozelle, for example. It would likely be vastly different. But football without Walter Payton, though his greatness on the field is unquestioned, could actually be very much the same. Rozelle is ranked #25; Payton is unranked.

•Did the person have an impact beyond the playing fields?

The Sports 100 profiles the people who were most important within American sport, but also the most important sports figures, period. In fact, the handful of men and women who transcended the games—who used sport as a stage for entry into the national consciousness and as a platform for social change—tend to be ranked at the high end of the list.

For the most part, they are members of minority groups, like Joe Louis (#7), Arthur Ashe (#36) and Roberto Clemente (#78); and women, like Billie Jean King (#8), Babe Didrikson Zaharias (#23) and Martina Navratilova (#73). This is primarily because sport, like other forms of entertainment, has occasionally been more progressive than the rest of society in providing opportunities. While their sporting feats themselves may have little significance to American culture, the symbolic statements occasionally accompanying such feats have been resounding because of the visibility sport affords these figures.

Of course, the fact that there are only a handful of women on the list is the unfortunate product of a sports society which, for the most part, has only provided high-profile opportunities for females in tennis, golf and a handful of Olympic events. Were history more inclusive of female athletes, the list certainly would be, too.

•What was the person's long-term impact?

Compare Curt Flood and Gary Davidson. In the mid-1970s, Davidson, having founded three new professional sports leagues, was described as "one of the most influential figures in the history of professional sports." And Flood? He was just a talented former baseball player who had challenged baseball's reserve clause in 1970 and lost. Had *The Sports 100* been published in 1974, Davidson might have ranked among the elite, while Flood might not have been ranked at all.

But then things changed. One of Davidson's leagues folded; the other two were absorbed into existing leagues. Although Davidson's legacy remains impressive, it certainly failed to meet its potential. Meanwhile, as it turned out, Curt Flood won a moral victory. Free agency arrived in 1975, and no athlete was more responsible for that than Flood. Time has reordered the rankings. Flood is #39; Davidson is #75.

•Must the person have made a positive impact?

Absolutely not. Early baseball star Cap Anson (#89) was the most public crusader for the creation of baseball's color barrier in the nineteenth century. Kenesaw Mountain Landis (#30) perpetuated the barrier as the game's first commissioner a half-century later. Jack Johnson (#13) was a sports pioneer as the first black heavyweight champion, yet his behavior was so contrary to public expectations at the time that his championship was also viewed as a *negative* influence on the cause. *The Sports 100* includes all types.

•What was the person's role in a particular momentous event?

This question deals with what became a recurring chicken-and-egg dilemma. Who is more important—Jackie Robinson or the man who had the courage to sign him, Branch Rickey? Red Grange or his employer, George Halas? Who deserves more credit for the success of the AFL—its founder, Lamar Hunt, or its biggest star, Joe Namath? Such decisions were generally decided on an individual basis, taking into account the role each person played in a watershed event and the importance of that event. Sometimes the athlete was deemed more influential; sometimes the executive. Usually, both figures are included. Incidentally, Robinson is #1 and Rickey #10; Halas #14 and Grange #20; Hunt #35 and Namath #40.

•What was the relative contribution of the person?

Early baseball star Cap Anson is profiled in *The Sports 100* primarily because he was an important force in the emergence of baseball's color barrier. Sonja Henie is included for spawning figure skating's fan base. Few would argue that skating is more important than a 60-year ban on black athletes. However, Henie's contribution to her sport's emergence far outdistanced Anson's role in the creation of the color barrier. Thus, Henie is ranked #87, two steps ahead of Anson.

•How does the person's influence within the sport compare to the popularity and historical importance of that sport?

Bobby Jones was more important to golf than Red Auerbach was to basketball. Should Auerbach be ranked higher because basketball is more popular? Not necessarily. In each case, a person's impact on a sport was weighed against the overall prominence of the sport. Jones is #27; Auerbach is #84.

However, the list is, to some extent, the product of a quota system. Baseball figures make up more than twenty percent of the list, followed closely by football and basketball. But this is a book covering the entire spectrum of sports, and so there are also representatives from tennis, golf, boxing, hockey, the Olympics, auto racing and other endeavors. Occasionally, a moderately important figure in one of the "big three" sports was omitted to allow the inclusion of a seminal figure in one of the lesser sports. Thus, the sixth most important golf figure (Walter Hagen, #80) appears; the fifteenth most important basketball figure does not. The fourth most important auto racing figure (A. J. Foyt, #96) is included; the twenty-second most important baseball figure is not. The most important soccer figure (Pelé, #90) is included; the seventeenth most important football figure is not.

•**Where is the line between sports and society?**
While Bill France, Sr., founder of NASCAR and the Daytona 500, is ranked #41, that does not necessitate the inclusion of a man like Henry Ford—though without the automobile, there would be no automobile racing. Nor, of course, does this book pay homage to the anonymous inventor of the wheel. Likewise, while ESPN founder Bill Rasmussen (#57) is on the list, that does not mean that John Lawson, the first man to hook up a primitive cable-TV system in the 1940s, must appear as well. This is a book about sports figures, though it is not limited to people associated only with sports. President Theodore Roosevelt, for example, played a pivotal role in saving football from itself and spurring the creation of the NCAA. He is ranked #65.

•**It is a book about American sports, so must it be about Americans?**
No. Certainly, there are several non-Americans on the list, many of them prominent figures. In fact, much of *The Sports 100* is made up of people born outside the U.S.—from basketball inventor James Naismith (#4) to Knute Rockne (#28) to Bobby Hull (#77). In fact, every hockey figure on the list is Canadian. In addition, a handful of the people profiled, such as Sonja Henie (#87), made their most pronounced athletic feats representing foreign countries. But they still played significant roles in the evolution of U.S. sports.

The end result, after all these questions, is a list of sports figures as diverse as sports itself. There are names you would expect (Babe Ruth), names you might not expect (William Randolph Hearst), and names you may never have seen (Charles McNeil). There are legendary figures (Jim Thorpe) and contemporary figures (Wayne Gretzky); famous figures (Michael Jordan) and infamous figures (Walter O'Malley). There are athletes and innovators, activists and academics, executives and inventors, journalists and judges, agents and outcasts, pioneers, producers, promoters and presidents—all of whom made a lasting impact, in one way or another, on American sports.

Of course, you are bound to disagree with many of the selections and omissions. But, like the old argument about New York's greatest center fielder in the 1950s, it's all a matter of perspective.

Jackie Robinson

Through the force of his personality, the personification of his skills and a fateful combination of time, place and unstoppable talent, Jackie Robinson became the most important person in the history of American sports and, indeed, one of the most significant figures in American history.

America's racial climate was at a crossroads when Robinson burst onto the scene in the mid-1940s. For the most part, the overt racial violence that had permeated the country a few decades earlier had been replaced by entrenched Jim Crowism. Baseball was no exception. The game's executives had long been devising various excuses for segregated playing fields, but by the end of World War II, Brooklyn Dodgers president Branch Rickey had begun to create his blueprint for the removal of the color barrier. He had planned how and when it would happen, but the most important question was: Whom would he find to bear the burden? Rickey's standard-bearer had to merit close scrutiny, and he had to pass with flying colors.

In his definitive study of the momentous event, *Baseball's Great Experiment*, Jules Tygiel reveals Rickey's standards: "The candidate did not have to be the best black ballplayer, though he naturally needed superior skills. Rather, he had to be the most likely to maintain his talents at a competitive peak while withstanding pressure and abuse. He needed the self-control to avoid reacting to his tormentors without sacrificing his dignity."

Even Rickey himself admitted his scouts faced an imposing task. "There were," he said, "just not very many such humans."

Jack Roosevelt Robinson was born in Cairo, Georgia, on January 31, 1919, the youngest of five children. His grandfather had been a slave. His father was a sharecropper who deserted the family when Jackie was six months old. Eight

1

months later, his mother moved the family from the deep South to the Far West, settling in Pasadena, California.

Robinson attended junior college and then transfered to UCLA, where baseball was actually a secondary interest of his. One coach called him "the best basketball player in the United States," as he twice led the Pacific Coast Conference in scoring. He averaged eleven yards per carry as a junior running back, leading another writer to call him "probably the greatest ball carrier on the gridiron today." He won swimming championships, a golf championship and a national Negro tennis tournament. Robinson even broke his brother's national long jump record. He was, said a third writer, "the Jim Thorpe of his race."

But Robinson was financially strapped. He dropped out of UCLA during his senior year, obtained a job as an assistant athletic director in the National Youth Administration, and barnstormed with the Los Angeles Bulldogs football team. He was drafted by the Army early in 1942, and when Lieutenant Robinson refused a bus driver's command to sit in the back of the bus two years later, he found himself in a courtroom facing a court-martial for insubordination. Justice prevailed, and Robinson received an honorable discharge in November 1944, but he later admitted, "I learned I was in two wars, one against a foreign enemy, the other against prejudice at home."

In 1945, Robinson turned his attention to baseball, joining the Kansas City Monarchs of the Negro National League. Though he was not the league's best player, he was certainly one of its stars. More important, Robinson had the character Branch Rickey was searching for. Rickey liked the fact that Robinson was college- and military-educated, a man accustomed to integrated athletics on the field, yet thoughtful and intelligent off of it. All that remained was a face-to-face interview.

That fateful meeting occurred on August 28, 1945. After three hours of hypothetical challenges in the form of racial epithets and characterizations of hostile fans, teammates and opponents, as well as lectures about the importance of Robinson's behavior and the momentousness of his task, Rickey was satisfied he had found his man.

On October 23, 1945, Hector Racine, president of the International League's Montreal Royals, the Dodgers' top farm club, announced that the organization had signed an African-American, triggering front-page exultation in the black press, which was eager to attach profound significance to Robinson's quest. One writer proclaimed that Robinson "has the hopes, aspirations and ambitions of thirteen million black Americans heaped upon his broad, sturdy shoulders." Another wrote, "Alone, Robinson represents a weapon far more potent than the combined forces of all our liberal legislation."

Major League Baseball executives kept remarkably quiet on the subject, but behind the scenes they condemned Rickey for his move, and so Robinson not only carried the burden of black America's hope, he also faced the specter of the baseball establishment's disapproval.

Soon, talk turned from the event's significance to its feasibility. Could Robinson handle the job after only one season of professional baseball? "We would like to see him make good, but it is unfair to build up hopes and then dash them down," wrote Jimmy Powers in the *New York Daily News*. "Robinson is a 1,000–1 shot to make the grade." *The Sporting News* predicted "the waters of competition in the International League will flood far over his head," and many black athletes began to fear that Rickey had chosen Robinson suspecting that he would not succeed, thus assuring the failure of integration. It was up to Robinson to win over the nonbelievers.

He began to do that at spring training, where he competed for a spot on the team with another black player, pitcher John Wright, whom Rickey had signed to keep Robinson company. After overcoming some early Florida bigotry, and some nervousness, Robinson displayed his major league talent and earned a spot in Montreal's starting lineup.

Montreal couldn't have been a better place for Robinson to start his minor league career, although one *Chicago Defender* editorial found it ironic that "America, supposedly the cradle of democracy, is forced to send the first two Negroes in baseball to Canada in order for them to be accepted." The city's French-Canadians genuinely welcomed the arrival of Robinson, but it was up to him to produce results on the field.

On April 18, 1946, in front of more than 50,000 spectators in Jersey City, New Jersey, Robinson broke baseball's color barrier as the second batter in the first inning. When Robinson's name was announced, he was greeted by muted applause, but he avoided looking at the crowd "for fear I would see only Negroes applauding." After letting five pitches go by for a full count, Robinson grounded out to the shortstop, undoubtedly the most dramatic 6-3 put-out in baseball history.

But the drama was only beginning. In his second at-bat, Robinson clouted a three-run home run, and he would go on to collect four hits, four runs, three runs batted in and two stolen bases that day. One newspaper headline stated the impact succinctly: "JIM CROW DIES AT SECOND."

Opening Day was the beginning of a two-week road trip for the Royals, including games in Baltimore and Syracuse, where fans threw racial slurs—and even a black cat—at Robinson in a relentless display of intolerance. Yet Robinson refused to succumb to the pressure. By the time the Royals returned home, Robinson was batting .372 with 17 runs and 8 steals in only 12 games. And as the season wore on, he became the biggest drawing card in the history of the International League.

By the middle of the summer, Robinson had won his originally reluctant teammates over, though he continued to dodge spikings at second base and beanballs at the plate. But he remembered Rickey's advice about keeping his composure and channelled his anger into aggressiveness. By the end of the summer, he had topped the league in hitting (.349) and runs scored (113), while placing second in stolen bases. Four other African-Americans had also played in the Dodgers minor leagues system that season, including future stars Roy Campanella and Don Newcombe, but as Campanella explained, "Jackie made things easy for us. I'm just another guy playing baseball."

Robinson's accomplishments are even more remarkable when one considers that he missed thirty games with various injuries, and he was often unable to eat or sleep because of the enormous pressure on him. In fact, as close as he was to the major leagues, he was even closer to a nervous breakdown. "There were the stresses of just knowing that you were pulling a big weight of a whole lot of people on your back," Robinson's wife, Rachel, explained. "I think Jackie really felt, and I agreed, that there would be serious consequences if he didn't succeed and that one of them would be that nobody would try again for a long time."

Robinson's Royals won the league pennant by nineteen and a half games and then played their way into the Little World Series, where they faced the American Association's Louisville Colonels. As did many southern stadiums, Louisville's Parkway Field had a blacks-only section, but it held only 466 people. Yet hundreds more blacks found a way to watch the game, sitting atop freight cars, clinging to sloped roofs, and climbing telephone poles.

The Royals lost two of the first three games, but Robinson starred in the final three contests, as Montreal won them all to capture the championship. When Robinson emerged from the clubhouse after the final game, he was surrounded by delirious Montreal fans, who kissed him, hugged him, and finally chased him for three blocks as he tried to leave. As one writer observed, "It was probably the only day in history that a black man ran from a white mob with love, instead of lynching, on its mind."

Yet Robinson's historic journey was only beginning, and the big question following his unprecedented 1946 campaign concerned where he would play in 1947. Was Robinson ready for the big leagues? Were the big leagues ready for Robinson? Was America ready for the integration of the two?

As David Halberstam wrote, in a 1986 tribute to Robinson in *Sport* magazine, there was "a sense among even the most tepid fan and the least socially aware citizen that something profound was taking place, that one lone black man was being judged, and as he was being judged so was the sport, and indeed the nation."

When Robinson arrived for spring training in 1947, he faced an even bigger challenge than the year before. The Dodger players were more secure in their positions than their minor league counterparts, and thus they were more willing to express their misgivings about Rickey's experiment. Rumors circulated that the players were passing around an anti-Robinson petition. But respected shortstop Pee Wee Reese refused to sign, and Dodger manager Leo Durocher announced, "I don't care if a guy is yellow or black, or if he has stripes like a fuckin' zebra. I'm the manager of the team, and I say he plays." And so he did, batting .519 over 11 crucial games against the big league squad, and by the time Opening Day rolled around, Robinson was a Dodger. One black newspaper announced, "TRIUMPH OF WHOLE RACE SEEN IN JACKIE'S DEBUT IN MAJOR LEAGUE BALL."

Atypically, Robinson managed only one bunt single in his first two big league games. But he hit a home run in front of 37,000 fans at the Polo Grounds in his third game and went 3-for-4 in front of 52,000 the following day. When the Dodgers returned to Brooklyn to take on Philadelphia, however, the Phillies bench spewed the ugliest parade of racial taunts Robinson had yet heard, and for a moment he considered striking back. "For one wild and rage-crazed minute," he wrote in 1972, "I thought, 'To hell with Mr. Rickey's noble experiment.'"

In the next few weeks, Robinson was refused acceptance at a Philadelphia hotel, suffered through rumors of an impending anti-integration players' strike, and watched as opposing players pointed bats at him and made machine-gun noises, a prelude to the many death threats he would receive over the years. He also went hitless in 20 straight at-bats, and in early May, writer Jimmy Cannon described him as "the loneliest man I have ever seen in sports."

But the ensuing days, perhaps more than any others, gave notice that Robinson would not be denied his place in the sports pantheon of heroes. Other men would have crumbled; Robinson thrived. By the end of June, he was batting .315 and leading the league in steals. He had been accepted by his teammates even faster than in the minors, and he was touted as baseball's biggest draw since Babe Ruth. In fact, in 1947 National League attendance increased by nearly 800,000 over the all-time record set a year earlier.

By the end of the season, even the most skeptical observers allowed that the Jackie Robinson experiment was an unqualified success. He had batted .297 with 125 runs and a league-best 29 steals. *The Sporting News* honored him as the Rookie of the Year, assuring that "the sociological experiment that Robinson represented, the trail blazing that he did, the barriers that he broke down, did not enter into the decision."

Robinson also realized a financial windfall. On September 23, Rickey staged a "Jackie Robinson Day" at Ebbets Field, and Robinson received $10,000 worth of gifts from admirers. After the season, he added to his income by performing in a vaudeville act and guesting on radio. He also signed contracts to write an autobiography and star in a movie. His season salary had been only $5,000, but it is likely he made more money in his rookie season than all but a handful of major leaguers.

At the end of the year, a public opinion poll named him the second most popular man in America. Bing Crosby sure must have been popular.

Robinson's legacy on the playing fields was obviously considerable, even though baseball took its time fully integrating the game. Larry Doby had signed with the Cleveland Indians in July 1947 as the American League's first black player, and he was soon joined by Hank Thompson and Willard Brown on the St. Louis Browns, and pitcher Dan Bankhead on the Dodgers. Though Doby would go on to be a star, all four were first-year failures, which led one black writer to comment, "Remember, all our boys can't be a Robinson."

In the following season, there were four black major leaguers—Robinson and Roy Campanella on the Dodgers, and Doby and Satchel Paige on Cleveland. But teams began to sign Negro League players to minor league contracts, and soon black players were excelling in the lower circuits. In the major leagues, Robinson, Doby, Campanella and Don Newcombe each played in the 1949 All-Star Game, and Robinson batted .342 to win the National League Most Valuable Player Award.

As late as 1953, only six of sixteen major league teams fielded blacks, but the emergence of exciting players like Willie Mays, Minnie Minoso and Ernie Banks helped accelerate the process. And in 1959, Elijah "Pumpsie" Green joined the Boston Red Sox, the last team to integrate. Other sports quickly followed baseball's lead. After Robinson signed his first professional contract in 1945, four black players joined professional football teams. By 1950, the NBA had integrated, and by 1957 black golfer Charlie Sifford had won a PGA tournament and tennis star Althea Gibson had won at Wimbledon.

But Robinson's impact was equally remarkable away from the playing fields, in part because he felt the need to carry the torch further. Wrote Jules Tygiel, "Others viewed the integration of baseball as an end in itself; Robinson envisioned the baseball experience as the stepping stone to more significant advances."

By the end of 1948, Robinson felt comfortable enough to declare independence from Rickey's "turn the other cheek" admonition, and in 1949 he announced at spring training, "They better be prepared to be rough this year, because I'm going to be rough on them." From then until his retirement following the 1956 season, Robinson met with his share of controversy. On the field, he turned into an umpire's nightmare. Off of it, he denounced discrimination at every opportunity. In fact, he became so bold in his accusations against baseball that even black writers and teammates like Campanella began to criticize him.

But baseball, thanks to Robinson, had helped induce the rumblings of a racial revolution below the Mason-Dixon line. Southern towns, captivated by integrated baseball's economic possibilities, began begging Branch Rickey to stage games there—and to bring his black players. "For more than a decade before the explosion of sit-ins and freedom rides of the 1960s challenged Jim Crow accommodations in the deep South, black athletes had desegregated playing facilities, restaurants and hotels in many areas across the country," Tygiel explains. "Baseball was one of the first institutions in modern society to accept blacks on a relatively equal basis."

"The most important black person in American history is Martin Luther King," said political columnist and baseball fan George Will. "A close second, I would argue, is Jackie Robinson, who came before Martin Luther King and began the consciousness raising of whites and blacks that resulted in Martin Luther King's career." Even King himself appreciated the impact that the breaking of the color barrier had on the civil rights movement, telling Don Newcombe one night, "You'll never know what you and Jackie and Roy did to make it possible to do my job."

As for Robinson, he remained an outspoken symbol in the fight for racial equality. On October 15, 1972, he accepted an invitation to throw out the first ball at a World Series game in Cincinnati. Nine days later he would be dead of a heart attack. But on national television, the 53-year-old had one last chance to reach into America's social conscience. His last public words: "I'd like to live to see a black manager."

So why rank Jackie Robinson as the most important person in American sports history? Why not Branch Rickey? While it is true that without Rickey's efforts Robinson would never have had the chance to make his impact, it is also true that

Rickey's grand design placed the burden squarely on the success or failure of one man. Had that man been a .220 hitter with a chip on his shoulder larger than the courage in his heart, the game's first modern attempt at integration might have gone up in flames.

Would someone else have broken baseball's color barrier if Robinson hadn't? Certainly, but that doesn't diminish Robinson's impact, because it is just as certain that nobody would have done it as well. "I couldn't have done it," Robinson's early Dodger teammate Joe Black admitted. "I might have taken it for a few days, or maybe a week but then I'd have grabbed one of them in the dugout runway or outside the ballpark and popped him . . . and right there Mr. Rickey's whole program would have gone down the drain."

Still, does the integration of baseball supersede any other event in sports history? Why rank Robinson ahead of James Naismith, the inventor of basketball, or Walter Camp, football's first true pioneer? Why place him before one of America's other truly transcendental heroes like Babe Ruth or Muhammad Ali? The answer lies not only in the depth of Robinson's accomplishments, but in the breadth as well.

The Sports 100 contains three types of sports figures. First, there are those who changed the way the games were played, like basketball's Bill Russell and hockey's Bobby Orr. Then there are the men and women whose presence and performance forever altered the sporting scene in a fundamental manner—such as Roone Arledge and television's influence, or Red Grange's impact on professional football. And, finally, there are the handful of sports figures whose influence transcended the playing fields and impactedAmerican culture, like Ali and Billie Jean King. Robinson, to a greater extent than anybody else, was all three types in one.

His impact on the way baseball was played came largely because he brought the Negro League version to the major leagues, reintroducing speed, baserunning and a brand of aggressive play to a game that had come to rely on muscle. The National League, quicker to integrate than its American League counterpart, went on to dominate World Series and All-Star competition in the late '50s and '60s.

As for fundamentally altering American sports, is there any greater impact than that of the African-American athlete in the twentieth century? Since Robinson won his Most Valuable Player Award in 1949, nearly half of baseball's MVPs have been black. By 1995, seventeen of the past twenty-one Heisman Trophy winners had been African-Americans, as had every NFC and AFC rushing leader since 1978. Black players make up more than three-fourths of the NBA and all but eight of the league's first forty-one MVP Award recipients. Essentially, American sports can be divided into two eras—before Jackie Robinson and after Jackie Robinson.

Finally, Robinson's influence beyond the playing fields was incomparable. Sportswriter Leonard Koppett observed that Robinson's crusade "compelled millions of decent white people to confront the fact of race prejudice—a fact they had been able to ignore for generations before . . . The consequences of the waves his appearance made spread far beyond baseball, far beyond sports, far beyond politics, even to the very substance of culture."

In the crucial years leading up to the civil rights movement, Robinson was the most salient symbol of impending change. "The Supreme Court decision of 1954, *Brown v. The Board of Education*, desegregating public schools, was about the law of the nation," explained Halberstam, "but the coming of Jackie Robinson into organized baseball in 1946 and 1947 was about the very soul of the nation."

2

Muhammad Ali

The original Cassius Marcellus Clay was a Southern abolitionist, professing anti-slavery at a time and place in which to do so was as courageous as it was unpopular. He was big; he was loud; he was fearless. At an abolitionist rally, he was said to have proclaimed, "For those who respect the laws of God, I have brought a Bible. For those who respect the laws of man, I have a copy of the state constitution. For those who believe in neither, I have these." He then revealed a pair of pistols.

The same fire could be seen in another man named Cassius Marcellus Clay some two centuries later, a man who himself was very much an original and who discarded what he considered his "slave name" in favor of one that became one of the most well-known in history—Muhammad Ali. Calling him a "spiritual heir" to the original Clay, sports historian Wells Twombly writes in *200 Years of Sports in America*, "Ali fought with religion, with law, and with his fists, and he won against great odds with all three."

He was America's foremost athletic figure for nearly two decades. In 1987, *The Ring* magazine ranked him as the greatest heavyweight boxing champion of all time, a status Ali had been claiming for himself for years. He gained the heavyweight championship a record three times and successfully defended it nineteen times; he was both the third-youngest and the third-oldest heavyweight champion; his career spanned seven U.S. presidents. He earned more money in the ring, an estimated $60 million, than every other heavyweight champion before him combined.

In the process, according to Ali biographer Thomas Hauser he "altered the consciousness of people all over the world." Ali was probably the most photographed, interviewed, chronicled and talked about athlete in history; the most

9

loved and the most hated; one of the most triumphant and tragic; perhaps the most recognizable person on earth, and, as it turned out, a surprisingly important figure in American history. Essentially, he had Babe Ruth's charisma, Jackie Robinson's courage, Bill Russell's agenda, Arthur Ashe's sense of priority, Michael Jordan's fame and Charles Barkley's mouth. It all combined to form perhaps the most compelling figure in sports history.

As George Plimpton wrote at the peak of Ali's career, "I would think that anyone with young granchildren coming along had better be prepared one day to answer, 'Tell me about Muhammad Ali.'"

Born January 17, 1942, in Louisville, Kentucky, and raised under the specter of segregation, Cassius Clay was the son of Marcellus and Odessa Clay and the great-great-grandson of a slave and a slave owner. His boxing career began in October 1954 when his beloved Schwinn bike was stolen. The 89-pound 12-year-old threatened revenge, and Joe Martin, a local policeman who taught boxing, suggested he learn how to fight first. Six weeks later, he made his ring debut, winning a three-round split decision.

Clay went on to win 100 of 105 amateur bouts, taking six Kentucky Golden Gloves championships and two National Golden Gloves titles by the time he was eighteen years old. Then, a few weeks after graduating high school, he won the light heavyweight gold medal at the 1960 Summer Olympics in Rome. Along with Wilma Rudolph, Clay was America's most lionized Olympic hero. He talked a lot, but for most Americans, he said the right things. In response to a Soviet reporter's question asking how it felt to represent a country that still treated him like a second-class citizen, Clay said, "Tell your readers we got qualified people working on that problem, and I'm not worried about the outcome. To me, the USA is the best country in the world, including yours." He would soon change his tune.

Clay turned professional soon after, signing a promotional contract with the Louisville Sponsoring Group and finding a man who would serve as his trainer for two decades, Angelo Dundee. He won a six-round decision in his pro debut, and as he continued to win, he developed boxing and bragging into an art form. He was articulate, intelligent, remarkably handsome and uncommonly accessible, all of which made him even more famous than his early success would seem to dictate. He was, said former *New York Times* columnist Robert Lipsyte, "the journalistic equivalent of an easy lay."

When he began successfully to predict in which round he would knock out his opponents ("This boy likes to mix, he must fall in six"), his popularity grew even more. Clay became the first young professional to have his fights televised nationally, and certainly the first to have an entire poem published in *Life* magazine. He was as much entertainer as fighter. Said John Condon, director of publicity at Madison Square Garden, which began to feature Clay, "He did everything except grab the microphone during the prefight introductions. And I'm sure, if he'd thought of it, he'd have done that too."

Clay's explanation seemed to make sense, though it hinted at the principles behind the brash exterior. "Where do you think I'd be next week if I didn't know how to shout and holler and make the public take notice?" he asked. "I'd be poor and I'd probably be down in my home town, washing windows or running an elevator and saying, 'yes suh' and 'no suh' and knowing my place. Instead of that, I'm one of the highest paid athletes in the world. Think about that. A southern colored boy has made one million dollars."

But Clay had his detractors. Many writers soon became disenchanted with the temerity of the "Louisville Lip," including Arthur Daley of *The New York Times,* who wrote, "The exceedingly likable Clay is lousing up his public relations by his boasting, and it's high time he eased off." And so, naturally, after a dramatic victory over British heavyweight champion Henry Cooper, Clay recorded an album of monologues and poems about himself and said, "I'm not the greatest. I'm the double greatest . . . I'm the boldest, the prettiest, the most superior, most scientific, most skillfullest fighter in the ring today." So much for easing off.

By February 25, 1964, Clay was still talking and still backing it up. But there was a formidable obstacle to Clay's actually being "the greatest" in the form of fearsome heavyweight champion Sonny Liston. This was a man who had been arrested dozens of times, was managed by organized crime, hadn't lost in ten years, and had knocked out his last three challengers in the first round. Many thought Clay was crazy to enter the ring with Liston, and his build-up to the fight was based on making Liston believe just that.

The odds were 7-to-1 in Liston's favor, nearly every sportswriter in Miami Beach agreeing with Daley's assessment that the "irritatingly confident Cassius enters this bout with one trifling handicap. He can't fight as well as he can talk."

Even worse for Clay, during the fight something got into his eyes, and for much of the fifth round he could barely see. Somehow, he managed to survive the round, leading fight doctor Ferdie Pacheco to remark, "Beethoven wrote some of his greatest symphonies when he was deaf. Why couldn't Cassius Clay fight when he was blind?" Clay's eyes were better by round six, which he dominated, and when the bell for round seven rang, Liston refused to come out, claiming a shoulder injury. Clay, the new heavyweight champion, could only repeat, "I shook up the world! I shook up the world! I shook up the world!" He was right, but there was more to come.

A month before the Liston fight, it had become known that Clay had travelled with Malcolm X and addressed a rally of the Nation of Islam, then popularly known as the "Black Muslims." It was a page-one story in the *New York Herald Tribune,* which noted that Clay was "the first nationally famous Negro to take an active part in the Muslim movement." Two days after the Liston fight, Clay officially announced his conversion to Islam.

The Nation of Islam, led by the prophet Elijah Muhammad, taught that God's true name was Allah and that Islam was Allah's true religion. But the movement differed considerably from the teachings of the ancient Islamic prophet, Muhammad, in that it revolved around the notion that whites were a genetically engineered "devil race" on the eve of destruction. The movement had gained momentum when Malcolm X took over leadership of one of its sectors, and though

Clay professed deep religious convictions, the Nation of Islam was considered by many to be more of a social and political phenomenon.

As the country entered one of its most divisive eras, few movements were more divisive than the Nation of Islam, so Clay's announcement sent shockwaves throughout the country. About one week later, the conversion took tangible form in a new name. Elijah Muhammad, who was originally named Elijah Poole, announced that he would henceforth call Clay "Muhammad Ali," Muhammad meaning "one worthy of praise" and Ali being a cousin of the prophet Muhammad. Nobody had complained when Joe Louis Barrow had become Joe Louis, but this change was viewed as un-Christian, un-American, unacceptable. Virtually every member of the media refused to call him by his new name. The typical reaction reflected the sentiment that the heavyweight champion shouldn't be preaching at all, or that he certainly shouldn't be preaching what was considered a "hate religion."

Ali, who still embraces Islam, would later explain, "Elijah Muhammad was trying to lift us up and get our people out of the gutter . . . I think he was wrong when he talked about white devils, but part of what he did was make people feel it was good to be black. So I'm not apologizing for what I believed. I'm wiser now, but so are a lot of people."

Indeed, with Ali's lead, athletics would soon become a platform for social revolt, but at the time, it was entirely new ground for sports journalists. "Sports figures were supposed to be one-dimensional quasi-cartoon characters," writes Hauser. "Reporters were used to fighters telling them how much they weighed and what they ate for breakfast." And here was Ali saying, "I don't have to be what you want me to be; I'm free to be me."

Promoters shied away from his rematch with Liston in 1965, leading to the remarkable occurrence of a heavyweight title bout in front of only a few thousand spectators, at a youth center in Lewiston, Maine. The fight took place three months after Malcolm X was assassinated, amid rumors that Ali was going to suffer the same fate. On top of that, Liston was once again the favorite, but the former champion never even made it through the first round, succumbing to what some have termed Ali's "phantom punch."

Ali defended his title a second time six months later against former heavyweight champ Floyd Patterson following vicious pre-fight banter in which Patterson vowed to defeat the "Black Muslims' scourge" and Ali called Patterson an "Uncle Tom." Having proved himself in the ring, Ali was in for far greater battles out of it. He was in the most public position—with the most public disposition—in sports; he had embraced a widely condemned movement; and now, with the war in Vietnam beginning to spiral out of control, he would jump from the frying pan straight into the fire.

Ali had registered for the draft back in 1960 and had been classified 1-A (available for the draft) in 1962, but he had scored in only the sixteenth percentile on the mental aptitude portion of the military qualifying examination in 1964. At the time, the passing grade was the thirtieth percentile, so he didn't qualify. But by 1966, the war had led the military to lower the qualifying percentile to 15, making the 24-year-old Ali eligible. When pushed repeatedly for a statement, Ali responded with one as simple as it was profound: "I ain't got no quarrel with them Viet Cong."

Ali's contention that he was a conscientious objector made him even more of a lightning rod for 1960s-era emotions. *Sports Illustrated*'s Mark Kram wrote that Ali was "the first symptom of a national nervous breakdown." Ali himself said, "I've left the sports pages. I've gone to the front pages." For the anti-Ali forces, it was enough to put them over the edge. A typical reaction was reflected in an announcement by a congressman from Pennsylvania: "The heavyweight champion of the world turns my stomach."

Ali defended his title seven times in 1966 and early 1967, but his bout on March 22, 1967, would be his last fight for more than three years. On April 28, he appeared at the U.S. Armed Forces Examination and Entrance Station in Houston for his scheduled induction into the Army. Along with twenty-five others, he was placed in a line and told to take one step forward as his name was called, which would constitute his induction into the military. With each name, each would-be soldier stepped forward. When "Cassius Marcellus Clay" was called, he didn't move. "You can't condemn a man for wanting peace," Ali had said. "If you do, you condemn peace itself. A rooster crows only when it sees the light . . . I have seen the light and I'm crowing."

In a prepared statement to the press, after refusing induction, Ali explained, "I strongly object to the fact that so many newspapers have given the American public and the world the impression that I have only two alternatives in taking this stand—either I go to jail or go to the Army. There is another alternative, and that alternative is justice."

It took a while in coming, if it ever really came at all. One hour after Ali's refusal to step forward, the New York State Athletic Commission suspended his boxing license and stripped him of his title. Every boxing commission soon did the same. Said a still-disgusted Howard Cosell more than two decades later, "Due process of law hadn't even begun, yet they took away his livelihood because he had failed the test of political and social conformity."

Ten days later, a federal grand jury indicted Ali. The trial took place almost six weeks later, the jurors returning a guilty verdict after twenty minutes of deliberation and the judge imposing the maximum sentence—a $10,000 fine and five years in prison. "So I'll go to jail," said Ali. "We've been in jail for 400 years."

Ali the loudmouth was becoming, to many, Ali the martyr. African-American athletes and activists, in particular, admired his stand and his principles. In fact, when black athletes threatened to boycott the 1968 Olympics, listed first among their demands was the restoration of Ali's titles.

A court of appeals upheld Ali's conviction one year later, and his case moved to the U.S. Supreme Court. For forty-one months, Ali was banned from boxing. But those forty-one months were some of the most turbulent in American history, and in that time a large percentage of the nation came to agree with Ali's perspective of the war. Writes Hauser, "Ali might not have been an intellectual, but he'd correctly perceived history's bend."

As the tide turned against support of the war, support for Ali grew immeasurably, but Ali himself played no small part in turning that tide. As comedian/activist Dick Gregory explained, "There were a lot of us against the war in our way, but nobody heard us, because we didn't command the worldwide attention that Ali enjoyed. Then he stood up and said, 'War is wrong; people get killed in wars.' And when he did that, he didn't embarrass the United States. He embarrassed armies all over the world."

It is often stated that Ali returned to the ring after the Supreme Court unanimously reversed his conviction on June 28, 1971, exactly fifty months after his refusal of induction. But, in fact, he returned some eight months earlier, after his promoters finally arranged a fight in Georgia, where there was no state athletic commission. On October 26, 1970, he defeated Jerry Quarry in Atlanta. Six weeks later, on Pearl Harbor Day, he returned to Madison Square Garden, beating Oscar Bonavena in fifteen rounds. Ali was back.

Then came what has been described as boxing's biggest-ever event and the beginning of sport's greatest rivalry—undefeated former champion Muhammad Ali versus undefeated champion Joe Frazier. "It was a classic matchup between boxer and slugger," Hauser explains. "It was Ali the draft-dodger versus patriotic Joe; Ali the loudmouth versus softspoken Joe; Ali the Muslim against honest Bible-reading Baptist Joe." Frazier, primarily because he was Ali's foil, came to represent, ironically, the white Establishment. Ali was everything but that.

The fight resulted in unprecedented numbers. Each fighter received $2.5 million; 760 press credentials were awarded and 500 more were rejected; thirty-five foreign countries broadcast the fight live. Everyone who was anyone could be found in Madison Square Garden, including Frank Sinatra, whose press pass announced that he was photographing the fight for *Life* magazine.

Four years earlier, Ali had been a hated champion with awe-inspiring boxing talent. Now, though he was an increasingly beloved figure, his skills had diminished somewhat. On March 8, 1971, with Frazier able to catch him, Ali lost a 15-round decision.

Ali had fought to reenter the ring, but his loss to Frazier set him upon a new mission—to regain his title. After a proposed bout with 7-foot-2 Wilt Chamberlain fell through (thankfully, for Ali's self-respect and Chamberlain's health), Ali fought and won ten times over the next two years until his quest was detoured by a 12-round loss to little-known Ken Norton. Ali had trained for only three weeks.

George Foreman had beaten Frazier to become heavyweight champion; Frazier had beaten Ali; and Norton had beaten Ali. Such was the triple-challenge facing the world's most popular athlete in his attempt to return to sport's pinnacle. First, he dispatched Norton by capturing the twelfth and final round of a close battle. Then, after a pre-fight brawl in a television studio, Ali-Frazier II went Ali's way by unanimous decision. Finally, more than three years after failing in his first attempt to win back his title, seven years after being stripped of it, and ten years after grabbing it in the first place, Ali would have another chance to make history, this time against Foreman in Zaire—the "Rumble in the Jungle."

"In 1974," writes Hauser, "the spirit of the sixties was very much alive. Indeed, within the span of twelve weeks, two events seemed to vindicate the decade." As Ali put it, "You think the world was shocked when Nixon resigned? Wait till I whup George Foreman's behind."

Foreman was considered as invincible as Sonny Liston had been a decade earlier. He was 40-0 with 37 knockouts, the last 8 in the first or second round. And, unlike his '90s persona, he was perceived as being downright mean. Some people even feared for Ali's life, but they didn't fear for his bank account. Ali received a record $5.45 million for stepping into the ring, more than any heavy-weight champion before him had earned in an entire career.

Going toe-to-toe with Foreman inside the ring was as inadvisable as matching wits with Ali outside it, yet Ali surprised everyone by doing just that. He had lost his leg speed, but he had discovered that he owned an iron chin. Fighting out of a defensive posture for most of the fight, his famous "rope-a-dope" strategy, he traded punches with perhaps the hardest puncher in heavyweight history. By the seventh round, Foreman had tired. In the eighth round, Ali knocked him out. He had shocked the world again.

Ali had become America's darling. The most vilified athlete of the '60s be-came the most heroic of the '70s. A man denounced as anti-American in 1967 was invited to the White House in 1974. Of course, Ali was still far from perfect. In fact, he occasionally crossed the line from brash to vicious in pre-fight hype, doing just that before Ali-Frazier III, the "Thriller in Manila," which took place eleven months later.

Each man had triumphed over the other once, and this would be the most hard fought of their three battles. Indeed, it has been called the best fight in box-ing history. Ali dominated the early rounds, Frazier took over control in the middle rounds, and Ali came back late in the fight. By the end of round 14, both men were battered and exhausted; both seemed on the verge of collapse. Frazier's cor-ner simply threw in the towel first.

As Ali would later recall, "Of all the men I fought in boxing, Sonny Liston was the scariest; George Foreman was the most powerful; Floyd Patterson was the most skilled as a boxer. But the roughest and toughest was Joe Frazier. He brought out the best in me, and the best fight we fought was in Manila."

Ali had become the best-known person on the globe. He had survived the tumultuous '60s—thus escaping the fate of the rest of the decade's icons—and he had conquered the '70s. But the latter part of the decade moved Ali closer to the tragedy that seems to have afflicted not only the giants of the '60s, but the giants of boxing throughout the ages.

He would successfully defend his title six times over the next two years, but he had clearly lost a step, and four of those bouts would go the maximum fifteen rounds. Still, he enjoyed unprecedented fame. A movie about his life was released, entitled simply *The Greatest*; a special edition comic book was created, called *Superman vs. Muhammad Ali*; a 15-round decision over Ernie Shavers was watched by seventy million national television viewers.

On February 15, 1978, Ali was confronted with one of the easiest fights of his career—against an inexperienced pro named Leon Spinks. Ali barely trained, entered the ring weighing 242 pounds, and left it having lost a split decision. It marked the only time Ali lost his title by losing a fight.

In the rematch, seven months later, the roles were reversed. Ali was the challenger who had trained harder than ever; Spinks hardly trained at all. In front of a record crowd of 63,532 in the New Orleans Superdome, paying a record gate of more than $4.8 million, Ali was even worse the second time around. But he was better than Spinks. For a record third time, at the age of thirty-six, he was crowned heavyweight champion.

A few months after the fight, Ali announced his retirement. He was going to go out on top. Had the saga ended there, tragedy might have been averted. But it didn't. By 1979, excessive generosity, business failures and exploitation by hangers-on and had left him in financial straits. When he was offered $8 million to fight new heavyweight champion Larry Holmes in the autumn of 1980, the 38-year-old reentered the ring and attracted a new record gate of nearly $5.8 million.

Amid controversy over Ali's health, whispers that he was speaking slowly, and financial scandal that saw a bogus promoter use Ali's name to defraud others of $21 million, Holmes crushed the former champion in eleven rounds. "It wasn't a fight; it was an execution," Hauser explains. "Most of the world might have been rooting for Ali, but in the ring, like every other fighter, he was alone."

When Ali chose to fight again, more than a year later, against Trevor Berbick, it was too much for most observers. No American arena would host it; no television network would broadcast it; many writers simply refused to cover it. Berbick won by decision in the Bahamas, leading Ali to finally admit it was the end of the line. "Father Time caught up with me," he said. "We all lose sometimes. We all grow old."

But Ali seemed to grow old before his time. In 1984, it was discovered that he had Parkinson's disease, a neurological syndrome characterized by tremors, rigidity of muscles and slowness of speech and movement. He has since faded from the limelight, but not from the memory of those who watched him become the Babe Ruth of boxing, the Moses of black dignity, the Elvis of sports.

Parkinson's disease has left the Ali of the '90s a shadow of his former self. The man who took more punches than any other, inside and outside of the ring, finally seems to have suffered from too many blows. Commented Howard Cosell, "The irony is that Ali has become a victim of the sport he saved."

But while Ali's boisterous shell is gone, his principled core remains, and the adulation of legions of fans worldwide remains with it. As Dr. Richard Lapchick, director of Northeastern University's Center for the Study of Sport in Society, explained, "You may have to lean to hear what he has to say, but that is a good excuse to get closer to hear him speak."

3

Babe Ruth

Arthur Daley of *The New York Times* once claimed that writing about Babe Ruth was like trying to paint a landscape on a postage stamp. He was—and remains—bigger than life; the most mythical athlete ever to step on a playing field, the ultimate American sports celebrity.

In Robert W. Creamer's biography, *Babe Ruth: The Legend Comes to Life*, the author calls his subject "a unique figure in the social history of the United States. For more than any other man," he continues, "Babe Ruth transcended sports, moved far beyond the artificial limits of baselines and outfield fences and sports pages." There have been others with equally remarkable impacts on the American psyche. Jackie Robinson and Joe Louis made social commentary with each stolen base and uppercut, but even Ruth became somewhat of a hero to black America, thanks in part to persistent rumors that he carried some African-American blood. Muhammad Ali and Michael Jordan have become world-wide cultural icons, but Ruth's fame nearly matched theirs in an era before technology made the world a global village.

Ruth was far from perfect. He was a prima donna, an adulterer, a man who fought with umpires and managers and who treated responsibility like a hanging curveball. In 1922 alone he was suspended five times for various indiscretions. But he single-handedly reshaped the most American of sports while representing the most American of pursuits—excess. As Ruth himself explained, "I swing big, with everything I've got. I hit big or I miss big. I like to live as big as I can."

No athlete has become such a symbol of supremacy, not only in sports but in every facet of American culture. As Creamer points out, *The New York Times* once called Enrico Caruso "the Babe Ruth of operatic tenors." *Time* magazine called Willie Sutton "the Babe Ruth of bank robbers." At Michael Jordan's retirement press conference in 1993, Chicago Bulls owner Jerry Reinsdorf called him "the Babe Ruth of basketball." It was as much a tribute to Ruth as to Jordan.

Indeed, while Jordan perfected and greatly expanded the concept of the one-man endorsement conglomerate, Ruth did it first. He earned as much money off the field as on it, performing in movies and vaudeville routines, barnstorming around the world, and endorsing any number of products—from Babe Ruth gum, Babe Ruth underwear and Bambino Tobacco to Wheaties, Louisville Slugger bats and Remington shotguns. Even today, Ruth's heirs still earn quite an income through the licensing of his name and image—much like the family of another American icon, Elvis Presley.

Not that Ruth needed to pad his income. His first professional salary, with the International League's Baltimore Orioles in 1914, was $600. By 1930, he was making $80,000 a year. To put it in perspective, when Ruth was earning $70,000 on the great 1927 New York Yankees, the next highest salary was Herb Pennock's $17,500. Lou Gehrig made $8,000. Pitcher Wilcy Moore, a 19-game winner, made $3,000. Even more than a decade later, after Ruth retired, Gehrig's $30,000 salary was the game's highest.

While it is true that Ruth requested a $52,000 salary in 1922 because "I've always wanted to make a grand a week," much of the Ruth legend is just that—legend, misinformation turned into myth. Did he miraculously cure a dying kid in the hospital by hitting a World Series home run? Well, the promise came by word-of-mouth, and the kid wasn't dying. Did Ruth really hit a ball so hard it went through the pitcher's legs and over the center field fence? No, but the ball bounced over the center fielder's head for a double.

Did Ruth really call his shot at Wrigley Field in the 1932 World Series? There are so many versions of the tale that it will never be verified one way or another. The pitcher, Charlie Root, and catcher, Gabby Hartnett, adamantly denied it, and only one of the following day's newspaper accounts interpreted Ruth's gestures as pointing toward center field, but the notion caught on and soon took on a life of its own. Yet the simple fact that the legends survive is testament to Ruth's status. When was the last time you were mesmerized by an apocryphal tale about Elmer Flick?

One of the most enduring myths about Ruth was that he was an orphan, but George Herman Ruth was the son of George Herman Ruth, Sr., and Katherine Schamberger of Baltimore. Ruth—who claimed to have been born on February 7, 1894, even though forty years later he discovered (and ignored) a birth certificate announcing February 6, 1895, as his date of birth—was a hyperactive boy who took to the streets at an early age. He was placed in St. Mary's Industrial School for Boys at age eight, not because he was an orphan, but because he was "incorrigible." He remained there, off and on, until the age of twenty, when he signed as a pitcher with the Orioles.

When Ruth first arrived in the big leagues, he was a strapping 6-foot-2, 190-pound lefthander, at a time when typical players averaged about 5-foot 9 and 168 pounds. Eventually, due to his insatiable appetite for food and drink, Ruth ballooned to as high as 260 pounds. In fact, it was reportedly because of Ruth's bulk that Yankees owner Jacob Ruppert decided to dress his team in their now-traditional pinstripes, believing it would make his star appear slimmer. But Ruth's size only fed his legend, and his peformance on the field was equal to his stature.

Ruth dominated baseball in a manner matched only, perhaps, by Ty Cobb, but Ruth did it as a pitcher *and* a slugger. His absurd hold on the record books can be compared to the totals of basketball's Wilt Chamberlain and hockey's Wayne Gretzky. But Chamberlain met his equal in Michael Jordan, and Gretzky encountered nearly the same talent in Mario Lemieux. No baseball player has since towered over his contemporaries as did Ruth. Said former teammate Harry Hooper, "I saw a man transformed from a human being to something pretty close to a god."

He started out with the Red Sox in 1914, becoming the American League's best pitcher, winning 94 of 140 decisions with a career earned run average of just 2.28. In fact, he always claimed to be proudest of one record in particular—his 29 consecutive shutout innings in World Series competition, a record that lasted longer than his single-season home run mark. Had Ruth continued to pitch regularly, he would be mentioned in the same breath as Walter Johnson and Lefty Grove. Instead, he began to terrorize them at bat.

Ruth hit four home runs in only 92 at-bats in 1915, and that was twice as many as any other teammate. He tied for the league lead with 11 homers in only 317 at-bats in 1918. By then, he was already being called the Home Run King—even though he was nearly 700 home runs from retirement. In 1919, he shattered the major league record with 29 homers, and the following year he nearly doubled that total. His 54 homers in 1920 were 35 more than runner-up George Sisler's total and his .847 slugging percentage remains a major league record.

From 1918 through 1934, he averaged 40 homers per season. From 1926 through 1931, he averaged 50 home runs, 147 runs, 155 runs batted in and a .354 average. In 1927, his 60 homers were 13.7 percent of the league total and more than the home run total of twelve different teams. When he hit his 700th home run in 1934, only two others had even reached the 300-homer mark. Hank Aaron was only a few months old.

But with Ruth, it wasn't only the quantity that captured the imagination of the sporting public, it was the quality. He had a flair for the dramatic. In 1916, he hit three home runs all season, but he created a sensation by hitting them in three consecutive games. He had only one home run through August of 1917, but it was the first ball ever hit into Fenway Park's centerfield bleachers. In 1918, after returning from a week-long stay in the hospital, he hit four homers in four games. Of his 29 clouts in 1919, four were grand slams, a record that lasted forty years.

Ruth hit the first home run in Yankee Stadium, in 1923, and the first home run in All-Star Game history in 1933. Just days before he made his last appearance with the Boston Braves, in 1935, he hit three homers in one game. The third homer of the game, the 714th and final blast of his career, was the first ball ever hit over the roof at Pittsburgh's Forbes Field.

Ruth's mighty swing simply transformed baseball. Before Ruth, the home run was considered nothing special, just a long hit, omitted from weekly batting statistics. It was even scorned by purists who treasured "inside baseball"—single, steal second, take third on a sacrifice, score on a fly ball. Explains Creamer, "In sum, when Babe Ruth hit his first one, a home run was not an occasion for exploding scoreboards—or even handshakes . . . But all this changed after the war, after Ruth's breakthrough in 1919. It was not a gradual evolution but sudden and cataclysmic."

The end of World War I meant a burst of interest in baseball and a dramatic rise in attendance. Baseball's new breed of fans reveled in Ruth's feats and asked for more. As Harold Seymour writes in *Baseball: The Golden Age*, "He attracted people who might be untutored in the subtleties and refinements of inside baseball but who could understand and respond to the clear, uncomplicated drama and beauty of one of his towering drives, which had the directness and impact of one of Jack Dempsey's knockout punches and which inspired the neologism 'Ruthian.'"

Baseball executives were happy to oblige their customers, boosting hitting by outlawing trick pitches, such as the spitball, and by assuring that clean baseballs always remained in play. In addition, a whole class of power hitters began to copy Ruth's thin-handled bat and full swing. Tactics such as protecting the plate, sacrificing and stealing grew obsolete. *Baseball Magazine* wrote that Ruth "has not only slugged his way to fame, but he has got everyone else doing it. The home run fever is in the air. It is infectious."

And so the 1-0 game turned into the 10-9 slugfest. From 1905–1919, the major league batting average was about .250 and the typical ERA was around 2.85. By 1921, batters were hitting .285 and the typical ERA was over 4.00. There were 384 home runs hit in 1915, but 1,565 hit in 1930.

In 1920, seven clubs established attendance records and Ruth's new team, the Yankees, became the first to draw one million people. Ruth had been sold (by the Red Sox) to the Yankees for what amounted to about $400,000 in cash and credit. It was a match made in baseball heaven. "It has been said that where youth sees discovery, age sees coincidence, and perhaps the retrospect of years makes Ruth's arrival in Manhattan, in 1920, seem only fortuitous juxtaposition of man and place in time," writes Creamer. "Nonetheless, Ruth in that place at that time was discovery. And adventure. And excitement."

Within three years, the Yankees had a new $2.5 million stadium, the House That Ruth Built, and the makings of a dynasty. The Red Sox had won five World Series in the previous seventeen years before selling Ruth. The Yankees hadn't won one. Since the sale, Boston has failed to win even one world championship. The Yankees have won twenty-two. This is no accident. Ruth's reign in America's largest city was so successful that it created the dynasty that served as baseball's backbone for half a century, setting the stage for generations of pinstriped icons—from DiMaggio to Mantle to Reggie.

Ruth didn't create professional baseball, as several earlier figures did. And he didn't make perhaps the most symbolic cultural statement of the last century simply by stepping onto a field, as Jackie Robinson did. But Ruth, who died of cancer on August 16, 1948, left his lasting imprint on the game. As baseball historian Lee Allen explained, "For almost two decades he battered fences with such regularity that baseball's basic structure was eventually pounded into a different shape."

And so Ruth deserves to rank among the elite of *The Sports 100*, batting third, as usual.

4

James Naismith

No list of important American political figures would place, say, John F. Kennedy over George Washington. Without Washington, the executive branch of the United States, and, indeed, the very notion of democratic rule, might not exist at all. Without Kennedy, they would exist, perhaps only in a different manner. In the world of sport, such is the thinking as well, and so *The Sports 100* is dominated by many of the games' original pioneers. Without most of the names in this book, sports would have evolved in a rather different manner. Without some, certain enormous sporting ventures might not exist at all. There can be no greater measure of a person's influence.

For the most part, sport in America is not a product of invention, but adoption. Just as this country is a mosaic of the world's cultures, the great majority of its most popular pastimes are offshoots of games developed elsewhere. There is, however, one dramatic exception. "Unlike other sports, basketball is considered to be the purest American sport, invented in America for Americans," writes Dave Anderson in *The Story of Basketball*. "Baseball evolved from rounders, a British game. Football evolved from soccer and rugby, other British games. Golf is believed to have been developed by Scottish shepherds, tennis by French clerics, hockey by Canadian soldiers. Horse racing, track and field, swimming and boxing are as old as mankind. But the beginning of basketball has been documented by its inventor."

Organized basketball is played by more than 250 million people worldwide, and the game is threatening to overtake even soccer as the most popular sport on the globe. The basketball hoop is the centerpiece of the inner-city playground, the focus of the farmland, the staple of every high school gymnasium. The NCAA Tournament and the NBA Finals have taken their places next to the Super Bowl and the World Series as mega-events. Various basketball figures rank among the most publicized and lionized icons in American sports. Yet before James Naismith posted his original set of thirteen rules on December 21, 1891, basketball simply did not exist.

Of all the major sports in America, only one was invented in America by a single man with a singular vision. The inventor of this American game, ironically, was a Canadian born on November 6, 1861, in Almonte, Ontario. Naismith was orphaned in 1869, the year of professional baseball's arrival and college football's first game (on Naismith's eighth birthday). He dropped out of high school for four years before graduating in 1883 and then decided to become a minister, studying for three years at Montreal's McGill University, where he was twice named the university's "outstanding all-around athlete."

He received a theology degree from Presbyterian College in 1890, three years after graduating from McGill. He then set his sights on promoting Christianity through physical education, moving to Springfield, Massachusetts, and studying to become a physical director. By late 1891, Naismith was a 30-year-old P.E. instructor at the School for Christian Workers, which became the International YMCA Training School, which, in turn, became Springfield College. The town is now home to the Naismith Memorial Basketball Hall of Fame.

Naismith was quite content teaching swimming, canoeing, boxing and wrestling to his students in the fall and spring, but when winter arrived he was suddenly faced with what *Sports Illustrated*'s Alexander Wolff has called "the Phys-Ed Class from Hell." Two other instructors had been unable to satisfy a group of eighteen men studying to be YMCA general secretaries, and so Naismith was given the job. Football and baseball had been the students' sports of choice when the weather was good, but the men had become impatient with the traditional indoor winter activities of calisthenics, gymnastics and various children's games. Dr. Luther Gulick, a pioneer in physical education in his own right, gave Naismith two weeks to come up with a suitable alternative. As the inventor himself explained, "Invention of the game of basketball was not an accident. It was developed to meet a need."

He began to search for a new game that was "easy to learn and easy to play in the winter and by artificial light." At first, he tried to modify outdoor games like rugby, soccer and lacrosse to the small gymnasium with little success. With one day left before his deadline, he decided to carefully analyze the problem. His game had to be simple enough to be easily understood, difficult enough to be challenging and safe enough for the 30-by-50-foot gym.

Naismith decided that a large ball should be used because a small ball generally required other, more complicated equipment. He decided a running sport would result in the kind of rough play he wanted to avoid, so passing became an integral part of the game. The safety factor also precluded having the players aim at a ground level goal. Therefore, he settled on a horizontal goal, which would also promote finesse over force.

On December 21, 1891, Naismith posted his thirteen rules. He grabbed a soccer ball and asked the school's superintendent of buildings, James "Pop" Stebbins, to find a pair of boxes to be used as goals. Stebbins, in a bit of fate destined to become anecdotal legend, was only able to scrounge up a pair of peach baskets. Naismith nailed the baskets to the balcony surrounding the gym, which happened to be ten feet off the floor, divided the class into two teams, and tossed up history's first center jump. "It was the start of the first basketball game," he said, "and the finish of the trouble with that class."

The earliest, crudest form of the game was obviously a far cry from today's modern, streamlined, airborn, acrobatic version. The first game ended with a score of 1–0, and the early rules made no mention of dribbling or backboards or free throws. Though nine men per team was considered the optimum number, anywhere from three to forty was acceptable. The peach baskets were soon replaced by 15-inch cylindrical wire baskets, but open-bottom baskets didn't even appear for another two decades. Yet, it was the genius of the game, and the very fact that it came to be regarded as a sort of modern sports invention, that provided the opportunity for subsequent improvement.

Basketball spread like wildfire following its invention, sprouting up at YMCA gymnasiums around the country. Many of the students took it back to their hometowns and even to other countries through missionary work. Within a decade, the game could be found in more than a dozen nations. The first public game of basketball occurred on January 15, 1892, when a group of Springfield students beat their instructors 5-1. Naismith's students and colleagues at Springfield would go on to spread the game all over the East and Midwest, introducing it at the University of Chicago, Iowa, Temple and Hamline University in Minnesota (the school involved in the first officially recorded intercollegiate game, in 1895).

Naismith was also instrumental in making basketball widely accepted among women, who have enjoyed a rich history in basketball over the years, particularly at the high school level. In fact, Naismith met his future wife while organizing a game in March 1892 between Springfield women and a team of female teachers. Senda Berenson, director of physical training at Smith College, twenty miles north of Springfield, organized the first women's college basketball game in late 1892. Three years later, a woman named Clara Baer published the first set of women's rules. However, using a diagram created by Naismith, she mistook dotted lines as restraining lines, ushering in an era of limited movement in women's basketball that lasted more than seventy-five years.

In 1895, Naismith moved to Colorado, where he earned his medical degree from Denver's Gross Medical College. But, again, he turned back to sports, teaching physical education at the University of Kansas. He coached the Kansas team for nine years (eventually being replaced by the legendary Phog Allen), and he remained a Kansas faculty member until his retirement in 1937.

Naismith died on November 28, 1939. Three years before his death, the game had become an Olympic sport, and Naismith had been honored in Berlin as its creator. Exactly three months after his death, the first television broadcast of a basketball game was a minor success. In recent years, of course, television has emerged as the perfect vehicle for such a fast-paced game, taking Naismith's invention to unprecedented levels of popularity.

Ironically, James Naismith probably would be a household name if several of the game's original competitors had been successful in their attempts to christen it "Naismith ball." But the inventor declined the honor. After all, it may not have been his only invention. Legend has it that, as a 160-pound center on Spingfield's football team, Naismith placed a cut-up rugby ball and ear muffs on his head—possibly creating the very first football helmet. . .

WILLIAM MORGAN

When James Naismith recruited a 22-year-old named William Morgan to play for the football team at Springfield College in the early 1890s, he had no idea he was recruiting another innovative mind. By 1895, Morgan had completed his coursework in Springfield and had become physical director at the Holyoke (Massachusetts) YMCA. Basketball had already caught on at YMCAs across the East. However, Morgan was teaching a class of middle-aged men, and he believed the game seemed "suited to the younger men, but there was need of something for the older ones not quite so rough and severe."

And so he combined elements of baseball, basketball, tennis, handball and badminton into a new game. It was patterned primarily after a game called minton, which a YMCA director had brought back from India earlier in the year. Morgan's invention, which he called "mintonette," made its first appearance on December 2, 1895. The sport would eventually be played by an estimated thirty-five million Americans, and it would soon by known by a new, more appropriate name—volleyball.

5

Albert G. Spalding

It can be argued that the rise of American sports came about due to various intertwining factors: the drama of athletic display, the opportunity for participation, the organizational principle behind the business of professionalism, publicity, innovation, historical account and the creation of mythical heroes. Only one person, Albert Goodwill Spalding, had a hand in every one of those factors.

Spalding did a little bit of everything, and just about everything he did made an impact. Any one of about a half-dozen Spalding influences would have been enough to earn him a spot among *The Sports 100*. Taken as a whole, he ranks among sport's elite figures.

It was A. G. Spalding, the pitcher, who became one of professional baseball's earliest stars and the most important athlete involved with the formation of the National League. It was Spalding, the manager and then owner of the Chicago White Stockings, who became the most visible and powerful figure in baseball in the late nineteenth century. Spalding, the showman, organized baseball's first world tour and nurtured the myth of baseball's creation. Spalding, the publisher, created guide books that served as a source for the history of the game for sixty-five years and published a history of baseball, *America's National Game*, in 1911.

Finally, and perhaps most important, Spalding, the businessman, joined his younger brother in forming a company that became the largest sporting goods empire in the world, publicizing the benefits of sport throughout the nation while manufacturing enough equipment to give everyone an opportunity to play the games.

"Able to recognize the possibilities for personal gain and social purpose inherent in the promotion of sport, Spalding acted on them in a manner that encouraged the commercialization of sport and its transformation into a significant social institution in America," writes Peter Levine, in his biography, *A. G. Spalding and the Rise of Professional Baseball.* "For better or worse, the place of sport in contemporary American society owes a good deal to a man who creatively shaped the culture of his own time."

Though he liked to characterize himself as a rags-to-riches story, Spalding was born (September 2, 1850) into money, his parents owning a 320-acre estate in Byron, Illinois. At age twelve, he moved to Rockford, Illinois, where he soon pitched for the local baseball team. Between 1867 and 1870, Spalding led Rockford to 45 wins in 58 games, including a victory over the first all-professional team, Harry Wright's Cincinnati Red Stockings.

Spalding's performance spurred Wright to sign him in 1871 to play for his new team, the Boston Red Stockings, in the first year of the game's first professional league, the National Association of Professional Base Ball Players. In five years with Boston, Spalding batted .320 and posted a 207-56 record, including 57 wins in 1875, when the Red Stockings won their fourth straight pennant.

Spalding was the league's best player and among its most respected, but the league itself had attracted a reputation for unsavory characters and disorganized leadership, which led Chicago White Stockings owner William Hulbert to attempt to form a new and improved league. He started by convincing Spalding to join him, and Spalding convinced three of his teammates and Philadelphia star Cap Anson to do the same.

Not only had Hulbert matched Spalding's $2,000 contract, he also promised twenty-five percent of the club's gate receipts for the coming season and the opportunity to become captain and manager of the team. He knew Spalding gave the league instant credibility. Spalding's first responsibility, however, was to help Hulbert draft a constitution and gain support for his new league, the National League of Professional Baseball Clubs. Spalding wrote that he would do all he could for the new league, "for in my judgment on the success of this movement depends the future of baseball."

The primary difference between the old league and the new was the notion that it was an organization of clubs, not players. Spalding had enough good sense and timing to be a player in a players' league, then an owner in an owners' league. He led the National League with 47 wins in 1876, as Chicago won the pennant. But, in the following year, he handed Anson the reins of the club and retired from active play. It was not necessarily that his skills were fading (he was just twenty-seven); it was that he had more pressing matters to attend to—his sporting goods business and the business of sport.

Spalding served as the White Stockings' secretary under Hulbert until his boss's death in 1882, after which he became the team's president and one of its principal owners. Throughout the remainder of the century, he was the league's most dominant voice, playing a major role in every important event in professional baseball. He claimed to act in the interests of the fans, but often his behavior was directed at padding his pocketbook. Although he was a former player, he came to represent the ruthlessness of management.

Spalding's ego—and his obsession with attracting middle-class customers—made him a moralist who often fined or traded players for drinking. His greed made him the league's top spokesman on behalf of the reserve rule, a contract clause allowing clubs to renew expired contracts, thus binding players to one team and preventing free agency. His efforts in this regard were so successful that the rule lasted nearly a century.

Within the league, Spalding aimed to maintain management's power over its players. And within organized baseball, his goal was to maintain the league's monopoly of the professional game. "It is not surprising that, in an age that transformed robber barons into cultural heroes, A.G. emerged as the most recognizable man in American sports," Levine writes.

In 1881, a rival major league, the American Association, was formed. It soon became an established rival of the National League. But two years later, when Spalding's power had greatly expanded, another league attempted to intrude on the National League's control of players and markets. Spalding joined with National League president Abraham G. Mills in assuring its demise after only one season.

But Spalding would play a much bigger role in a more significant confrontation in 1889, when the Players' National League of Base Ball Clubs was formed. While the club owners in the Players' League were still capitalists hoping for a profit, they agreed to suspend the reserve clause, offer three-year contracts, and divide team profits among themselves and the players. By the end of the year, as many as seventy-one National League players had jumped to the new circuit, setting up what Spalding called "the battle royal for control of professional baseball."

National League owners appointed a three-man "War Committee," headed by Spalding, who told a reporter from the *Chicago Herald,* "We will spend all the money that is necessary to win this fight. From this point out it will simply be a case of dog eat dog, and the dog with the bull dog tendencies will live the longest."

That turned out to be Spalding. The Players' League actually outdrew the National League in 1890, and Spalding was forced to engineer a deal to save the New York Giants franchise (a move which he later characteristically described as having "saved the National League and by saving it, the future of professional baseball in this country"). But by the end of the season, each of baseball's three major leagues had suffered severe financial losses, primarily due to saturation of fan interest. Spalding, knowing the Players' League was least able to survive the losses, negotiated the "surrender" of the league, putting an end to the so-called Players' Rebellion.

Within a year, one baseball peace had led to another baseball war, as the National League and American Association squared off. This time, Spalding and his National League colleagues once again prevailed, and four Association teams were absorbed into a new 12-team league. The National League—and the reserve system—had survived. "Spalding's efforts reaffirmed his continual desire to have monopolistic control of professional baseball rest in the hands of competent businessmen with full power and authority to regulate its every aspect, including the potential competition of other capitalists and the careers of its players," Levine explains. "Although hardly perfected in his lifetime, his approach to the game set the tone for the development of professional sport in the twentieth century."

Spalding stepped down as White Stockings president in 1891, though he remained the team's primary stockholder. Upon retiring, Spalding said, "I have always tried to do that which I believed to be for the best interests, advancement and elevation of professional baseball. In my efforts in this direction, my thoughts have been first, the National Game, then the National League, then my club, and lastly my personal interests."

Yet, as Levine explains, ". . . when proposals to reorganize professional baseball to make it more competitive and profitable surfaced in 1901 that were not to his liking, he returned to the baseball wars in characteristic style to oppose them."

New York Giants owners Andrew Freedman and others were attempting to establish what they called the National League Baseball Trust. All franchises and players would be part of one large syndicate, and talent and teams would be relocated each year to generate the most profit. Spalding, who had always been an admirer of baseball profiteers, attacked Freedman's "inordinate greed" and warned that his plan would destroy the league.

The Freedman faction supported the nomination of incumbent Nick Young for the league presidency, but Spalding emerged from baseball retirement to run against him. The voting was at a standstill until Young's supporters withdrew. In the end, neither candidate wound up in the president's seat, but Freedman was forced to sell the Giants. Chalk it up as another victory for Spalding.

Had A. G. Spalding been merely the most important figure in professional baseball's transition from infancy to adulthood and nothing more, he still would have to be ranked among the twenty most important people in American sports history. But Spalding's most important contribution to sport came on an even more basic level—in the form of bats and balls and gloves and skates and bicycles and golf clubs . . . and every other imaginable means of providing opportunities for athletic participation.

In February 1876, Spalding and his younger brother, Walter, decided to parlay the pitcher's popularity into a sporting goods venture, A. G. Spalding & Brother. Their entire starting capital of $800 was advanced by their mother, Harriet. When their sister, Mary, married a man who provided capital for the Spaldings to open their first bat factory in 1879, the company name was changed to A. G. Spalding & Bros. By then, it was off and running.

Spalding began by securing a contract to provide the National League with baseballs for all league games. He turned that relationship with baseball into a lucrative endorsement of his products, doing the same with just about every sporting craze that hit America in the late nineteenth century.

Among the pieces of equipment first manufactured by Spalding were the first American-made football, basketball, tennis ball, golf club and golf ball. Spalding's company developed the first automatic umpire indicators, the first shoe designed for cross-country running, the first dimpled golf ball, the first steel-shafted clubs and the first set of matched woods and irons. By the turn of the century, when Spalding was named commissioner of the 1900 Olympic Games, he had monopolized the sporting goods industry in much the same fashion he did professional baseball—by merging with or absorbing his competitiors. An $800 investment had become a multimillion dollar empire.

But A. G. Spalding & Bros. represented more than just athletic equipment. It was also a publishing house, by which Spalding could promote not only his sporting goods, but his sporting philosophy. From 1876 to 1942, *Spalding's Official Baseball Guide* published player records, descriptions of the previous season, how-to-play instructions and editorial opinions.

In 1908, the *Boston Herald* announced, "Next to Abraham Lincoln and George Washington, the name of A. G. Spalding is the most famous in American literature. It has been blazing forth on the cover of guides to all sorts of sports, upon bats and gloves . . . for many years. Young America gets its knowledge of the past in the world of athletics from something that has Al Spalding on it in big black letters, and for that reason as much as any other, he is one of the national figures of our time."

But Spalding didn't only chronicle sports and meet the demands of various sporting crazes. Often he helped create them, as well. In 1900, for instance, he arranged for the world's best golfer, British star Harry Vardon, to undertake a 20,000-mile tour across the country to promote a new golf ball—the Vardon Flyer. Aside from propelling Spalding & Bros. into a dominant position in the golf equipment industry, it also greatly enhanced America's growing golf boom.

Spalding was among the first to realize that what was good for sports was good for the sporting business. He also believed that it was good business to promote baseball as purely American in origin, which is why he orchestrated a special commission's decision to erroneously tab Abner Doubleday as the inventor of the game (see page 314).

Spalding semiretired, with his fortune, to California in 1901, failing in a bid for a seat in the U.S. Senate nine years later. Seven days after his 65th birthday, on September 9, 1915, he suffered a fatal stroke. As the tributes poured in, the National League honored him as baseball's "first and greatest missionary and propagandist . . . in many respects the greatest man the National Game has produced."

CONQUERING THE WORLD

A. G. Spalding was one of baseball's more innovative minds, pioneering the notion of a farm system and night games played under electric lights long before their time came. In 1883, he supervised construction of Chicago's Lake Front Park, a 10,000-seat palace which boasted eighteen private boxes above the grandstand, each furnished with curtains and comfortable chairs—essentially the world's first skyboxes.

But perhaps Spalding's most successful venture, aside from his sporting goods empire, was his world baseball tour from October 1888 to April 1889, which was called by one reporter "the greatest event in the history of athletic sports." In an effort to promote baseball and his business, Spalding collected thirty-five major leaguers. The group was sent off by President Grover Cleveland, at the White House, and the 38-year-old Spalding pitched the opening exhibition.

Over the next six months, the teams played forty-two games before an estimated 200,000 people. They travelled west to California and then to Hawaii, Australia, Egypt (where they played a game at the Pyramids), Italy (where Spalding tried to book the Colosseum), France and the British Isles. The trek concluded with a parade through the streets of Chicago in front of some 150,000 people.

Spalding actually lost $5,000 on the trip, but he felt it was well worth it. "Having completed a virtual monopoly of the sporting goods market in the United States," claims Bill James in *The Bill James Historical Baseball Abstract,* "He was quite intent upon spreading the game of baseball to every corner of the earth where a man might have two nickels to spend on a bat or glove."

6

Walter Camp

American football was an evolutionary phenomenon. The game essentially evolved from soccer, an ancient game, and rugby, which was invented in 1823, supposedly when a student at England's Rugby school took it upon himself to pick up the soccer ball and run with it. Had it not been for Walter Camp, however, the American version of the game would likely be little different from the brand of football preferred by the rest of the world. Indeed, were it not for him, the game might not have evolved much at all.

Time was Camp's business—he was president of the New Haven Clock Company for two decades—but time has also been rather unkind to Camp's legacy. As the "Father of American Football," the most important figure in the history of what many believe has become America's national game, he should be far better known to the layperson than he is. If football can be considered a Frankenstein-like combination of sports, Camp is the doctor (he did attend Yale Medical School) responsible for the brain, the heart and a limb or two.

History records America's first intercollegiate football game as having taken place on November 6, 1869, when Princeton and Rutgers battled in front of 100 spectators on a frigid afternoon in New Brunswick, New Jersey. But today's gridiron performers would be hard-pressed to recognize their game in its original form. Each side had twenty-five players, and though the use of hands was permitted, the ball could be advanced only by kicking it or heading it. In the end, Rutgers won six goals to four in what was essentially the soccer-style forerunner to football.

Four years later, four universities—Rutgers, Princeton, Columbia and Yale—met to form a football organization. They invited Harvard to join them, but in a fateful decision destined to alter the course of American sports, Harvard declined the offer. At the time, the Crimson was playing its own version of the game, which it called the "Boston Game." Their game bore more resemblance to rugby, with players being allowed to pick up the ball and run with it, and teams limited to fifteen men instead of twenty-five.

Harvard's only problem was that no other American university preferred its version, and so it turned to McGill University in Montreal, scheduling a pair of games in May 1874. The first game was played under "Boston" rules and the second under Canadian rules, which included a rectangular field, an oval ball and drop kicks. The Harvard players preferred the latter form, and the *Harvard Advocate* agreed, declaring, "Football will be a popular game here in the future."

By 1876, the Harvard-McGill version had become the accepted style of the game, and the Intercollegiate Football Association was born. It was in that same year that Walter Camp first took up the sport, and he would transform the game. Camp was a 17-year-old freshman on the 1876 Yale squad. Born in New Haven, Connecticut, on April 7, 1859, he was an outstanding athlete, excelling in baseball, track, tennis and crew, as well as the fledgling sport of football, which he would play at Yale for six full seasons and part of a seventh. At the time, there were no rules limiting eligibility, and Camp had continued to compete while studying for his medical degree. Only a knee injury early in the 1882 campaign put an end to his football career.

A halfback, Camp captained the Yale team in three separate seasons at a time when team captains were essentially player-coaches. During his playing career, the Elis went 25-1-6, losing only to Princeton by a 1-0 margin, in 1878. Shortly after his playing career ended, his medical career followed suit. After failing his senior exams in anatomy and surgery, Camp dropped out of medical school and went to work for the New Haven Clock Company as a salesman, eventually rising to the position of president, where he served for two decades. Camp's office at the clock company doubled as Yale's athletic headquarters.

After leaving school, Camp was awarded the position of "chief football advisor" at Yale, a somewhat ambiguous role in the years preceding full-time coaches but one that allowed him to remain at the forefront of the game. He also founded and served as treasurer of the Yale Financial Union, under which he consolidated each of the school's athletic teams under university control.

By the time Camp stepped down from both positions in 1910, Yale had produced eleven undefeated national champions, turning the university into the Mecca of college football in the sport's infancy. He had also spawned dozens of protégés, many of them (like Amos Alonzo Stagg) becoming the first full-time football coaches at other universities. By the turn of the century, there were approximately 5,000 teams of one form or another and an estimated 120,000 players across the country, and Camp was being called the "coach of coaches."

In addition, Camp was the game's most important publicist. As a student and promoter of the game, he wrote hundreds of newspaper and magazine articles, edited Spalding's *Official Intercollegiate Football Guide*, and wrote nearly thirty books, including several works of football fiction and the first-ever book of football strategy. It was Camp who made "All-America" a household expression, selecting (or at least lending his byline to) the All-America teams from 1889 through 1924 and further turning the game into a national passion.

But even Camp's contributions as progenitor and publicist pale in comparison to his impact as an innovator. In fact, by the time he left medical school, he had almost single-handedly removed the game from its muddled roots and set it on a path toward its modern form. In his first visit to the Intercollegiate Football Rules Committee meeting, as a junior in 1878, Camp suggested reducing the number of players per side from fifteen to eleven. It was only the beginning.

Camp next focused his attention on eliminating the "scrum," a rugby-originated, mass-movement, free-for-all battle for possession. At Camp's suggestion in 1880, the rules committee adopted the notion of one team's holding undisputed possession of the ball. Thus came the birth of the "scrimmage" line and the center snap marking the start of each new play. "If Walter Camp had contributed not a single thing else to football, his name would still rest secure on the scrimmage, perhaps the greatest single invention in any game," claim John McCallum and Charles Pearson, authors of *College Football U.S.A.* "From the scrimmage evolved the set play, the sequence of plays, the strategy."

Indeed, the scrimmage was the most significant development in the history of American football. Until then, the game had been continuous, with play rarely stopping. However, it soon became evident that the scrimmage made it possible for one team to control the ball for the entire contest, and some dreary games followed. So Camp simply came up with football's second most important concept two years later. He suggested that teams should have three opportunities, or "downs," to gain five yards, or surrender possession (it later became four downs and ten yards). Camp decided to enforce the rule by painting lines across the field at five-yard intervals. Hence, the gridiron.

Camp continued to father some of the game's most substantial innovations and became the game's uncontested authority. He was particularly interested in standardizing football's scoring system. In the early days, scoring depended on where the game was played, with each university forming its own rules, goals often counting as much or more than touchdowns. But Camp, as usual, was at the forefront of changing the philosophy of the game by altering its rules. "It is my thinking that the future of the game lies in running rather than kicking," he explained. "If that comes about, then we shall have to award more points for a touchdown and less for field goals. If the running aspect dominates, we will see the day when a touchdown counts twice as much as a field goal."

But he wasn't finished yet. Loss-of-yardage penalties came along in 1885, along with the suggestion of a neutral zone for lineman, which, since Camp was ahead of his time, wasn't officially adopted for another twenty-one years. In 1888, he pushed through a rule as basic as permitting tackling below the waist, in an attempt to curb the game's increasingly violent bent.

Camp remained the game's foremost figure and continued to play a significant role at every Intercollegiate Football Rules Committee convention until his death. In fact, on the morning of May 14, 1925, Camp was in New York City for his forty-eighth trip to football's meeting of the minds when the convention was delayed because the dean of the game had not yet arrived. Discussing rules without the presence of Camp would be like celebrating Christmas Mass without the Pope, so the rulesmakers waited.

Camp had attended the previous night's meeting, returning to his room at the Hotel Belmont at around midnight. But after some time elapsed the following morning, and he was still a no-show, Princeton coach Bill Roper was sent to search for him. When there was no response at Camp's room, Roper had a hotel employee open the door. There they found the "Father of Football" lying on his bed, having died of heart failure in his sleep, undoubtedly dreaming about football and any rules that needed refining.

Joe Louis

Many educated observers have scoffed at the notion that athletes can be heroes, particularly when a mostly-white media is talking about the idols of African-American youths. And so, when former heavyweight boxing champion Joe Louis died in 1981, syndicated columnist Carl Rowan took umbrage with the widespread praise Louis received as a hero to black America. Rowan explained, "White people who would never compare the achievements of Jack Dempsey or Rocky Marciano with those of Jonas Salk or Franklin D. Roosevelt glibly tell us that an uneducated boxer was the most meaningful of Black men . . ."

In theory, Rowan may be right. The athletic fields are far removed from the fields of cultural, political and intellectual achievement. As shown by the O. J. Simpson saga, superficial heroism can be easily tainted. But in practice, Rowan chose the wrong man. Through some magic mix of time, place, talent, fame and courage, a handful of athletic figures—black athletes in particular—have made more of a difference, in a short span of success, than other role models have made in a lifetime of achievement. Jackie Robinson was foremost among them; Joe Louis was close behind. Few people were more significant national figures in the transition of race relations that occurred between the 1930s and the 1960s. It was Joe Louis who cracked the door open for Jackie Robinson, and together they heralded the integration of professional sports.

"Louis was the first black man to achieve lasting fame and popularity in the twentieth century," explains Chris Mead in Champion—Joe Louis, Black Hero in White America. "When he began to box professionally in 1934, there were no blacks who occupied positions of public prominence, no blacks who commanded attention from whites." Yet within two years, Louis would star in a movie, publish an autobiography and be named the Associated Press Athlete of the Year. He was not yet twenty-five years old, but sportswriter Damon Runyon would estimate that "more has been written about Louis in the past two years than about any living man over a similar period of time, with the exception of Lindbergh."

Like the three other outstanding black sport pioneers in the first half of the twentieth century—Jackie Robinson, Jesse Owens and Jack Johnson—Joseph Louis Barrow had his roots in the South. He was born on May 13, 1914, in Lafayette, Alabama, the son of sharecroppers Munroe and Lillie Barrow, and the seventh of eight children. His father was committed to a state hospital for the mentally ill less than two years after Joe arrived, and his mother, hearing her husband had died, remarried to a man named Pat Brooks, who had six kids of his own. Unbeknownst to all of them, Munroe Barrow was still alive and would live another twenty years in the Searcy State Hospital for the Colored Insane.

For a while, the Barrow-Brooks clan slept three to a bed in Alabama, but the automobile industry brought the family to a Detroit ghetto, where, despite being hit hard by the Depression, Lillie Barrow scraped up enough money to send her son to violin lessons in an attempt to keep him off the streets. But he soon began using the money to pay for boxing lessons, adopting the name Joe Louis so that his mother wouldn't find out. It would be a household name within three years.

In 1933, Louis won 50 of 54 amateur fights, including Golden Gloves and Amateur Athletic Union titles. He gained the attention of John Rox-borough, king of the numbers rackets in Detroit's black neighborhoods, and by June of 1934, Roxborough was convinced it was time for Louis to turn professional. He called on Chicago-based trainer Jack Blackburn, who told Louis that his challenge was not only his opponent, but prejudice. "You can't get nowhere these days trying to outpoint fellows in the ring," he said. "Let your right fist be the referee." On July 4, 1934, Louis competed in his first professional fight. He knocked out his opponent in the first round.

By the spring of 1935, Louis had won all twenty-two of his pro fights, and his managers felt he was ready for New York and Madison Square Garden. But Blackburn cautioned, "Yeah, he's ready for New York, but New York ain't ready for him." He was proved right when a Garden promoter told Roxborough, "Well, you understand he's a nigger, and he can't win every time he goes into the ring."

But Louis's manager found a New York connection in the person of Mike Jacobs. Along with three New York sportswriters, Jacobs had formed the 20th Century Sporting Club to compete with Madison Square Garden for control of boxing. According to Louis, he had "no prejudice about a man's color so long as he could make a green buck for him." And so Jacobs made the momentous decision to sign Louis.

Louis's first New York fight was against 6-foot-6, 275-pound former heavyweight champion Primo Carnera of Italy. The fact that Italy was threatening to invade Ethiopia, one of the world's few independent black countries, only increased the fight's significance. In front of 60,000 fans and 400 sportswriters at Yankee Stadium, Louis knocked Carnera out in the sixth round. "Many Americans saw something very unusual on the morning of June 26, 1935—a black man's name in the headlines across the front page of their newspapers," Mead explains.

In becoming one of the most famous athletes in America, he was saddled with the same burden that would later fall to Jackie Robinson: for better or for worse, and with all the stereotypical inferences that came with it, whites saw him as a symbol of his race, and African-Americans found hope in the image of a black man climbing into a ring with a white opponent and enjoying equal opportunity for success.

Louis was exhorted by all not to act as the first and only black heavyweight champion, Jack Johnson, had a generation earlier. Johnson had refused to bow to convention and had thus incurred the wrath of white America. However successful he had been as a boxer, he had failed as a symbol of black America. Louis was being asked to do, all over again, what Johnson had not been able to do. He was told never to brag, never to criticize an opponent, never to smile after beating a white man, never to have his picture taken with a white woman. And he was told to keep winning, which he did until he met German fighter Max Schmeling.

On June 19, 1936, Louis took on the man who would come to represent the lowest and highest points of his early career. However, this first bout between the two had little of the accompanying pathos that the rematch provided two years later. Schmeling was not yet cast as the symbol of an evil empire; Louis was not yet heavyweight champion. Yet Louis was a prohibitive favorite, which is why it came as such a surprise when he experienced his first defeat in twenty-eight pro fights.

Nazi propagandists took advantage of the upset, one German magazine commenting that the result "clearly demonstrated . . . the superiority of white intelligence." And many in the African-American community took the loss hard. But for his part, Louis shrugged off the social significance of the event. "I didn't hurt my people," he said. "There are just as many Negro doctors, lawyers and politicians as before I was whupped. And none of the poor ain't suddenly rich either."

Had Louis's career then embarked on a downward slide, his legacy would have been one of fleeting success; his impact similar to that of Jesse Owens, with his four gold medals at the Berlin Olympics only weeks later. Indeed, Owens, who temporarily replaced Louis as a vicarious symbol to black America, and a lesson to white racists, later recalled that "inwardly many of us were trying to atone for Joe's loss." But Louis returned with a vengeance to become one of sport's most enduring and influential figures.

On June 22, 1937, Louis finally earned a shot at the heavyweight championship, the first such opportunity given an African-American in nearly three decades. Of the 45,000 spectators at Chicago's Comiskey Park, there to see if Louis could take the title away from Jim Braddock, nearly half of them were black. As Louis began to dominate the fight, the black spectators' delight began to turn into delirium.

Louis became the youngest champion in history, yet everyone seemed to point to the rematch with Schmeling as the true bout for supremacy—in every sense of the word. The rematch was scheduled for exactly one year later, and the lead-up to the fight was unlike that of any sporting event in American history. Jack Johnson's brawl with "Great White Hope" Jim Jeffries, in 1910, had been labelled the "Fight of the Century," but the Louis-Schmeling rematch added another significant wrinkle, besides the race issue.

Nazi Germany had been reluctant to back Schmeling in the first fight, for fear he would lose. But after his victory, Hitler had largely tied his twisted views in with Schmeling's success, particularly after being embarrassed by Owens at the Olympic Games. As Mead puts it, "The swastika hugged Schmeling like flypaper."

Germany and the United States were on a collision course in 1938, and the boxing match took on the form of a preamble to war. It was not only a test of might but a battle of philosophies—alleged American tolerance against aggressive Aryan dogmas. Even President Franklin Roosevelt added to the pressure by telling Louis, "Joe, we need muscles like yours to beat Germany." Suddenly, and for the first time, a lone black man was pitted against a white man, and Americans were backing the former. When Louis was asked if he was scared, he was quoted as saying, "Yeah, I'm scared. I'm scared I might kill Schmeling."

The fight lasted 124 seconds—a first-round knockout. Less than a year earlier, Jesse Owens had run the notion of Aryan supremacy into submission; here Louis had done it with one resounding punch. He had earned nearly $350,000, but he also had earned acceptance as an American hero. As Heywood Broun wrote in the *New York World-Telegram*, "One hundred years from now some historian may theorize, in a footnote at least, that the decline of Nazi prestige began with a left hook . . ."

But if Louis had become a hero to whites, he was a godsend to blacks. Explains Arthur Ashe, in *A Hard Road to Glory*, "No political happening, no other sports occasion, no war, no imminent passing of any law could compare with the possibility of a Louis victory. Ask any black person who was alive and over ten years of age when Joe Louis fought Schmeling, and he or she would remember it clearly. Neither Jesse Owens' four Olympic gold medals nor Jackie Robinson's signing with the Brooklyn Dodgers equaled the elation of this night."

Louis defended his title eight times in 1939 and 1940, followed by a parade of challengers in 1941 that came to be known as the "bum-of-the-month" club. But he was still stereotyped to an extent that would seem remarkable, had it not been so typical of the times. Virtually any news account of Louis would not only mention his color, but dwell on it. Writers stereotyped the way he talked, the way he looked, the way he lived his life. They constantly pointed out how "well-behaved" he was, how he was "as different from Jack Johnson as Lou Gehrig is from Al Capone." Louis had enough nicknames to start a football team. Not only was he the "Brown Bomber," he was the "dark destroyer," the "chocolate chopper," the "shufflin' shadow," even "Mike Jacobs's pet pickaninny."

Writers described Louis in the ring as if he were one step up from savagery. After he beat Carnera, the lead for one story read, "Something sly and sinister and perhaps not quite human came out of the African jungle last night . . ." Clearly, there was one more step for Louis to take. He had made it possible for America to accept the black athlete, but it remained for him to gain respect for the black man.

World War II made it possible. One month after Pearl Harbor, Jacobs convinced Louis to risk his heavyweight championship in a charity bout for the Navy Relief Society. He knocked out his opponent in the first round, and his public relations, in the time of patriotic fervor, grew by leaps and bounds. The day after the bout, Louis enlisted in the Army, and he soon fought another exhibition; this one for the Army Relief Fund. When Louis told a crowd, "We will win because we are on God's side," it become one of the most popular phrases surrounding the war effort, and Louis became one of the most appealing symbols of the good fight. Explains Mead, "The same papers that had once called him an African called him a good American . . ."

Louis became a propaganda tool for the armed forces. He embarked on a morale-boosting tour through the U.S. and Europe, travelling more than 70,000 miles and fighting ninety-six exhibitions in his forty-six months of army duty. After the war, the white press treated Louis differently. There was less condescension, less reference to color. Yet, while Louis's public image had improved, his personal life was on the verge of disaster. He had divorced his first wife, and his free-spending ways had caught up with him. After going four years without a substantial prizefighting purse, he owed some $300,000 in back taxes to the IRS and debts to Mike Jacobs. Though Louis received $600,000 for knocking out Billy Conn in June 1946, between paying his managers, his ex-wife and his debts, he was left with virtually nothing, and he hadn't yet paid taxes on this new income. It was becoming a vicious financial circle.

He defended his title against aging Jersey Joe Walcott in 1947 and 1948, announcing after the latter bout that he would not fight again. But in 1950, owing more than $500,000 in back taxes, Louis came out of retirement to fight Ezzard Charles, who had beaten Walcott for the heavyweight crown. Charles won by unanimous decision, though Louis won eight more bouts against mediocre competition over the next ten months. Finally, on October 26, 1951, Rocky Marciano put an end to Louis's career with an eighth-round knockout and then apologized to him through tears.

As an athletic figure over the previous seventeen years, Louis had ranked second in popularity only, perhaps, to Joe DiMaggio. As a boxer, he had become the greatest gate attraction since Jack Dempsey, reviving a moribund sport. But his role as a barrier breaker is what places him among the most important figures in sports history. Louis had been a lone pioneer in 1934, but when he retired, his handpicked successors to his heavyweight crown, Charles and Walcott, were both black men. Color barriers had been broken in baseball, football and basketball, and Jackie Robinson was saying, "I'll try to do as good a job as Joe Louis has done."

White America was finally opening its eyes to the injustices it had heaped on black America, in and out of sports, and Louis was given a great deal of credit for the awakening. An open letter to Louis in the *Pittsburgh Courier* in 1948 read, "You made white America realize that Negroes were Americans, too. You let them see that Negroes had feelings . . . had patriotism . . . had loyalty . . . had decency . . . had a sense of humor. You shamed White America into realizing that they had to do better by their 'forgotten tenth.'"

And, of course, his impact on African-Americans was immense. Martin Luther King, Jr., told a story about how a young man's last words before execution were, "Save me, Joe Louis." And Malcolm X admitted, "Every Negro boy old enough to walk wanted to be the next Brown Bomber." Indeed, in the thirty-five years after Louis's retirement black boxers made more money than all other black professional athletes combined.

So if Louis made Muhammad Ali and Jackie Robinson possible, why rank them ahead of Louis in *The Sports 100?* Essentially, it is because while Louis opened the door for black athletes, Robinson opened the floodgates. While Louis yearned to be welcomed, Ali yearned to be heard.

Louis's pioneering efforts came in a sport that had always existed along the fringes of respectability in American culture; Robinson's came in the national pastime. And Robinson, more articulate and introspective than Louis, followed his deeds with words, becoming a relentless voice against racial injustice. "Sometimes," Louis once admitted to a reporter, "I wish I had the fire of a Jackie Robinson to speak out and tell the black man's story." Yet when Ali tried to do just that, Louis was critical of him.

In fact, Louis was conspicuous in his silence concerning the civil rights movement, becoming a conservative voice of assimilation amid a new generation promoting black empowerment. Many even branded Louis an "Uncle Tom" and a pathetic figure, in view of his financial failure and dramatic spiral into personal tragedy. But in truth, Louis was simply a product of his generation and no longer necessary as a public icon. There were others—Robinson, Ali, Ashe—who carried the torch with the bearing required in their era—just as Louis had.

FALL FROM GLORY

Incredibly, Joe Louis's fall from glory was even more pronounced than his rise to prominence. He was married and divorced three times, and by 1956 he owed the government more than $1 million, had attempted a career as a professional wrestler, and was living hand-to-mouth. He turned to drugs and prostitutes and eventually became so severely paranoid and delusional that he spent time in a psychiatric hospital. By the late 1970s, he had signed an agreement with Caesar's Palace in Las Vegas, which paid him $50,000 a year to be a "greeter." In 1977, at the age of sixty-three, Louis suffered a heart attack and a cerebral hemorrhage, which left him almost unable to speak and confined to a wheelchair.

But Joe Louis's name still meant something. When he was wheeled in just before the Larry Holmes–Trevor Berbick title fight on April 11, 1981, just hours before he would die of a heart attack, he received a standing ovation. Soon after, the Reverend Jesse Louis Jackson, eulogizing his namesake, remarked, "Usually the champion rides on the shoulder of the nation and its people, but in this case, the nation rode on the shoulders of its hero."

8

Billie Jean King

"Was there ever tennis before her?" sportscaster Lesley Visser once asked while considering the impact of Billie Jean King. "Were there ever equal rights?"

There, arguably, has been no sports figure who actively did more to further one cause more often, and with more success, than King has done in her fight for financial and social respect for women in athletics. In the struggle for equal rights in the 1970s, on and off the tennis court, she served as a symbol, an advocate, an educator, a promoter, a lightning rod and a role model.

Consider her résumé. She led a boycott to protest inequitable prize money on the professional tennis tour; she was a pivotal force behind the launch of the separate women's pro circuit; she successfully pressured the United States Lawn Tennis Association into providing equal prize money for men and women at the U.S. Open; she became a symbol of financial independence and potential in female professional athletes; she founded and presided over the infancy of the Women's Tennis Association.

King defeated a man—and recorded a resounding political triumph for women—in history's most anticipated tennis spectacle; she was a vital force in fueling the tennis explosion of the 1970s; she became a vocal advocate for equality in collegiate sports; she created TeamTennis, as well as a magazine and a nonprofit organization devoted to women athletes; she brought the issue of sexual preference to the forefront with honesty and dignity; she has been called "the first truly successful role model in women's sports."

In 1967, the Associated Press voted her Female Athlete of the Year, an honor she received again six years later; in 1972, *Sports Illustrated* selected King its Sportswoman of the Year; in 1974, *Esquire* magazine named her, along with Muhammad Ali, one of the two most recognizable athletes in the world; in 1976, *Time* magazine tabbed her Woman of the Year; in 1977, *Harper's Bazaar* called her one of the ten most powerful women in America; and in 1990, the same year in which she was inducted into the National Women's Hall of Fame, *Life* magazine chose her as one of the 100 most important Americans of the twentieth century.

Consider her record. She won 695 matches in her lengthy career on the court, which spanned, roughly, the years between Althea Gibson in the late 1950s and Steffi Graf in the mid-1980s. She recorded 39 Grand Slam championships, a total trailing only Margaret Court Smith and Martina Navratilova, including 12 singles titles. She won a record 20 Wimbledon crowns (six singles, 10 doubles and four mixed doubles) and four U.S. Open singles titles. King ranked first in the world five times between 1966 and 1972, and held a top ten ranking for a total of seventeen years, beginning in 1960. She retained the number-one doubles ranking for twelve years. She is the only woman to have won U.S. singles titles on grass, clay, carpet and hard court.

These accomplishments were a product of King's attacking serve-and-volley game, an aggressive style that mirrored her personality. "When in doubt, she charged," wrote Sally Jenkins in *Sports Illustrated*, "and with that philosophy she shifted the spectrum of female possibilities from the decorative to the active."

Said Chris Evert, "She put money in my pocket and the pockets of all women tennis players." Added Martina Navratilova, "She was a crusader fighting a battle for all of us. She was carrying the flag: it was all right to be a jock, a competitor, to be tough, to question the officials. Chris did it her way, I did it mine, but Billie Jean did it first." King's two most renowned American contemporaries are quick to admit that all that they have received from the game stems from what she gave to it.

Billie Jean Moffitt was born on November 22, 1943, in Long Beach, California. Her father was a firefighter, her mother a homemaker, her younger brother, Randy, a future major league pitcher. She, herself, was a star softball shortstop until she turned to tennis, at age eleven, partly because it was suggested she take up a more "ladylike" sport, and partly because she sensed there was little future for her in team sports.

King was barely over 5-foot-4 and terribly nearsighted, but she had the desire, which she stated more than once, to become the world's best tennis player. The dream appeared increasingly possible, particularly when she won the Southern California 15-and-under girls' championship in 1958. By 1960, she was America's fourth-ranked player.

In 1961, at the age of seventeen, she and Karen Hantze-Susman became the youngest tandem ever to win the women's All-England doubles title at Wimbledon. In 1962, King defeated top-seeded Margaret Court in the Wimbledon singles competition, and though she failed to win the title, she did manage to repeat her doubles victory. But King's career stalled a bit when she entered Los Angeles State College, where she met and married law-student Larry King. She spent three years as a history major who seemed to minor in tennis before deciding to devote herself completely to tennis—and making history.

King won her first Wimbledon singles title in 1966, repeating as champion the following year. In 1968, she made it three in a row in what was a particularly significant tournament. The era of "open tennis" had arrived that year with tournaments finally being opened up to professionals as well as amateurs. But in this, the first open Grand Slam event, King found that the prize money she received as winner was barely one-third as much as that awarded the men's winner.

As the months went by, more and more amateur players were attracted to the financial benefits of professionalism. In particular, they were attracted to a pair of pro circuits that had been formed in 1967: oil tycoon Lamar Hunt's World Championship Tennis and promoter George MacCall's National Tennis League (NTL), which King, and four other women, joined before Hunt absorbed the NTL and cut the women loose. The arrival of open tennis heralded a financial boom for all concerned—or almost all concerned. But by the time 1970 rolled around, a rather distinct pattern had emerged.

"When the decade opened, tennis was expanding everywhere in the world. New sponsors were coming into the game, and prize money was on the rise," King writes in her history of women's tennis, *We Have Come a Long Way*. "Tournaments were making more money. Promoters were making more money. Male tennis players were making more money. Everybody was making more money except the women, who were actually losing ground."

Promoters were increasingly inclined to concentrate their efforts on attracting the male stars, leaving the women out in the cold and leading King, Rosie Casals and a handful of other women to become more disenchanted and outspoken with each successive snub.

By 1970, they had had enough. They decided to form their own tour, which had its origins in disgust. They were furious that legendary pro and promoter Jack Kramer, himself a seminal figure in tennis history, was offering men about ten times the prize money he was offering women at his Pacific Southwest tournament, and they proposed a boycott of the event. But Gladys Heldman, founder, editor and publisher of *World Tennis* magazine, went them one better. She formed her own $5,000 tournament in Houston to compete against Kramer's event.

King and eight others elected to risk their careers by signing with Heldman, who sought out her friend Joe Cullman, CEO of Philip Morris, to provide backing for the tournament. And, thus, the tournament became sponsored by a new brand of cigarette, designed primarily for women and marketed with the slogan, "You've Come a Long Way, Baby"—Virginia Slims.

By 1971, the Virginia Slims circuit had evolved into a $250,000, 24-tournament bonanza. Philip Morris poured unprecedented amounts of money into the tour, as did Heldman, who ran it without compensation and used her magazine to provide free advertising. But it was King's personality and talent that provided the most important publicity. "She was the star," Heldman would say, "and everyone wanted to talk to her."

But King also made statements on the court. She finished 1971 by becoming the first woman athlete to exceed $100,000 in prize money in one year, but the men's money leader, Rod Laver, had won nearly $300,000 in about one-third as many tournaments. Clearly, there was a long way to go.

In 1973, after a few years of haggling, the USLTA tour and the Virginia Slims tour were merged into one. In that same year, King finally convinced her colleagues to form a players' union, and the Women's Tennis Association was born, with King as its first president. The association would spawn the WTA Tour, which by 1995 had grown from a handful of players, a few thousand dollars and some maverick tournaments to a 62-tournament, 22-country, $35 million odyssey, drawing an estimated five million fans.

Having revolutionized women's tennis already in 1973, King's luck ran out when poor health forced her to withdraw from the U.S. Open. But even then she could claim a victory. Upon winning the title the previous year, she had received $15,000 less than male winner Ilie Nastase. In no uncertain terms, she informed the tournament chairman, through the press, that "if it isn't equal next year, I won't play, and I don't think the other women will either." The following year, the U.S. Open became the first major tournament to offer equal prize money for men and women.

But King's greatest triumph was still to come. Bobby Riggs had won Wimbledon and the U.S. title in 1939; by 1973 he was, as Rosie Casals told *Sports Illustrated*, "an old, obnoxious has-been . . . who can't hear, can't see, walks like a duck, and is an idiot besides." Riggs was famous for betting lesser opponents that he could beat them while under a severe, if peculiar, handicap—like being forced to hold a suitcase during the match. Usually, he won.

At the age of fifty-five, he decided to take his penchant for self-promotion to a new level. He was out to prove that women didn't deserve prize money equal to the men, so he challenged King to a $5,000 winner-take-all match. Scornful of Riggs's sideshow tendencies, King declined, and he turned instead to Margaret Court.

Court's views on women's liberation were the antithesis of King's. The Australian star had won all four Grand Slam tournaments in 1970, but she had defended her choice not to join King's fight for a new tour at the time by saying simply, "I'm a happily married woman and I've no wish to wear the pants." Yet she was lured by a guarantee of $10,000, and, despite her views, the match loomed as a battle of philosophies. It turned out to be an ignominious defeat for the women's movement. On Mother's Day, in front of a national television audience, Riggs annihilated Court 6-2, 6-1. A few days later, Riggs issued another challenge to King. She promptly accepted.

The combination of King's agenda, Riggs's mouth, a healthy dose of hype and the emergence of the women's movement turned the "Battle of the Sexes" into one of the most widely anticipated events in modern sports history. This time it would, per Riggs's suggestion, be best three out of five sets, the winner raking in a cool $100,000. The victor would also receive $200,000 in fees from television rights, the loser taking home half as much.

The match would be played in the Astrodome in Houston, the city where women's tennis had begun its revolution three years earlier. More than 30,000 people would fill the stadium, joined by a worldwide television audience of nearly 50 million people. Howard Cosell, at the peak of his fame, would announce what amounted to the most watched tennis match in history. "With Bobby's unwitting help," King writes, "we took women's tennis to the masses."

On September 20, 1973, King was brought into the stadium on a throne carried by four men dressed as ancient slaves; Riggs, the self-proclaimed "male chauvinist pig," entered on a rickshaw pulled by five scantily clad women. The oddsmakers had made Riggs the favorite; King won 6-4, 6-3, 6-3.

A victory over a man twenty-six years her senior may have provided little athletic solace, and some considered the whole event tacky, silly, even pointless. But, as writer Frank Deford has said, "It meant something because she won." It was an embarrassingly overhyped made-for-TV event, but it turned out to be surprisingly powerful, becoming, according to the *London Sunday Times*, "the drop shot and volley heard around the world."

To King—and to millions of other women—it was an incomparable psychological and political conquest, firmly connecting women's sports with the women's movement. "Ridiculous as this may sound, her victory helped validate the idea that women could hang in there, not just on the tennis court, but on the job or in the home. It was proof not so much of physical prowess but of mental toughness," explained Grace Lichtenstein, former executive editor of *World Tennis* magazine. "Feminists had not yet reached out to the masses. Billie Jean reached out, grabbed them by the hair, and made them take notice."

King capitalized on the publicity by putting the finishing touches on her image as the symbol of athletic self-empowerment, with a series of contributions to women's sports. In 1974, she founded *WomenSports* magazine, a monthly publication for and about women athletes which evolved into *Women's Sports and Fitness*. That same year, she started the Women's Sports Foundation, a non-profit organization dedicated to promoting and enhancing athletic opportunities for girls and women, which has grown into a powerful advocate with a 200-member advisory board and more than 3,000 voting members.

Also in 1974, King became the first woman to coach male professional athletes when she took over the Philadelphia Freedoms of the World Team Tennis league, a concept created by King and her husband. A decade later, she made history once more by becoming the league's commissioner, the first female czar in professional athletics. King has also worked as a television commentator, organized a women's professional softball league, and co-authored several books on tennis technique, two autobiographies and her history of women's tennis.

But even as her career wound down, she continued to find herself in the headlines, treading where nobody had tread before. Even her private life had a public impact. In 1981, three years before she officially retired from competitive tennis, King chose to admit her bisexuality amid a palimony suit brought by a former lover. Avon Products dropped its sponsorship of women's tennis in the wake of the scandal, and King lost an estimated $1.5 million in endorsements, but she remained NBC's Wimbledon announcer. Yet another social barrier had been broken.

King feared she would only be remembered for her sexuality and not her accomplishments, but her athletic feats and the social implications of her conquests assure her a legacy as the most important person in the history of women's sports. As *Life* magazine explained, "She did more than show 51 percent of Americans they could win—she put them in the game."

9

Roone Arledge

Sports and American television first encountered one another on May 17, 1939, when W2XBS in New York City broadcast a college baseball game to little interest, and with little success. With only 400 television sets in the country, and just one camera at the game, *The New York Times* reported that it was "difficult to see how this sort of thing can catch the public fancy." Observers wondered whether sports and television could co-exist at all.

By the mid-1950s, however, Americans had come to rely on television, and by the late 1960s, sports had come to rely on it as well. The sports television industry was, then, still in its somewhat formative years, but it had already become the foundation of American sport. As *Sports Illustrated* stated in 1969, "Some view it as a godsend and others as a monster, but a decade of television has created more changes in sport—and the interests of its fans—than anything in the history of play."

How did television transform the games? Sport's regional flavor dissipated and big league teams sprouted from coast to coast; franchises shifted when community loyalty became secondary to television revenue; spiralling salaries and TV endorsement bonanzas turned athletes into corporations, as performance on the playing fields became an athletic means to a financial end; events and seasons were designed around television schedules, rather than vice-versa; and sportswriting became less a matter of chronicling events and more an analytical enterprise. Even the essence of the games was altered—golf championships went from match play to medal play; TV timeouts disrupted the pace of the games, and perhaps the outcomes; the opening kickoff of the second half of the first Super Bowl was actually re-kicked because the first one had occurred during a commercial.

Television has created modern sports heroes. Indeed, a great many of the figures in *The Sports 100*—Michael Jordan, Magic Johnson, Arnold Palmer,

Howard Cosell, Pete Rozelle, David Stern, Phil Knight, Bill Rasmussen, Mark McCormack—are there largely because their performance was recorded by television, or because they learned how to best make use of the medium.

No single person is solely responsible for the success of televised sports and its myriad peripheral influences, but one man does tower above all others in his contributions to the industry—technically, aesthetically and financially—and so he must rank among the elite figures in sports. He has been called the "creator of the electronic sports revolution". . . a man who "established TV sports as an industry" and "transformed the financial infrastructure of amateur and professional sports." That man is Roone Arledge.

"When I got into it in 1960," said Arledge, "televising sports amounted to going out on the road, opening three or four cameras and trying not to blow any plays. They were barely documenting the game, but just the marvel of seeing a picture was enough to keep the people glued to their sets."

Indeed, in those days, television was still largely considered somewhat of an enemy of sport, a threat to attendance figures. It was widely believed that no little picture tube should give fans a better view of the game than the worst seat in the stadium, and so television production was largely governed by such principles. Arledge arrived and changed the focus, transforming how sporting events were covered, what was covered, where they were covered and how much money was involved.

"Television is largely responsible for having made sports the global and moneyed enterprise that it is," wrote Steve Rushin in *Sports Illustrated* in 1994, "and Roone Arledge is largely responsible for having made sports on television look and sound and succeed the way it does."

Born July 8, 1931, in Forest Hills, New York, Roone Pinckney Arledge, Jr., grew up farther east, in the town of Merrick, amid what he described as "a typical Long Island childhood—affluence masquerading as the middle class." He graduated from Columbia University, worked for the DuMont network as a production assistant, and was then drafted into the Army for twenty-one months, where he produced and directed radio programs. In 1955, Arledge took a job at NBC. He worked his way up to producer-director, and, in 1959, he won an Emmy for "Hi, Mom," a children's puppet show starring Shari Lewis. He also won a job producing sports telecasts for ABC.

At first glance, it isn't quite the background one would expect of the man who would become the most important person in sports television. But as Rushin pointed out, "There was really little hope of competing with him when you think back on it; after all, the man had won an Emmy producing a *puppet* show. What could he do with the Olympic Games?"

Of the three networks in 1960, ABC was indisputably third, desperate enough to tolerate mavericks and experimenters, the Fox of the '60s. Arledge seemed to fit right in, as evidenced by a memo he circulated to his bosses shortly after he was hired. "Heretofore, television has done a remarkable job of bringing the game to the viewer—now we are going to take the viewer to the game!" it began. "We will utilize every production technique that has been learned in producing variety shows, in covering political conventions, in shooting travel and adventure series . . . we will have cameras mounted in jeeps, on mike booms, in risers on helicopters, anything necessary . . . In short—WE ARE GOING TO ADD SHOW BUSINESS TO SPORTS!"

Arledge was able to put his ideas into action, in part, because the network was willing to experiment with its college football broadcasts, and with its newly acquired AFL telecasts, which required some gimmickry to challenge NFL games on rival stations. And that's just what Arledge's innovations were derisively described as—gimmicks. They would soon become staples of sports broadcasting.

Television sports had been as bland as oatmeal; Arledge spiced it up. He was the first to utilize a platoon of TV cameras surrounding the field to capture all of the game's sights and sounds from various angles. He was the first to use cranes, blimps and helicopters to offer the TV audience a panoramic view of the stadium and the first to have cameras wander just as spectators' eyes would—to the nervous coach, the backup quarterback, the eccentric spectator, the cheerleader.

"His telecasts were characterized by an intensely intimate, personal look and feel—the athletes' faces flooded the screen, and the athletes themselves became almost like fictional characters in the ABC announcers' ongoing 'story line,'" wrote Ron Powers in *Sport* magazine. "Games looked different on ABC—more intense, more personal, more intimate."

Arledge introduced, or perfected, the use of halftime highlights, pre-recorded biographies and interviews, superimposed graphics, split screens, isolation cameras, hand-held cameras and field microphones. He also pioneered slow-motion instant replay. It was first used on Thanksgiving Day in 1961 during an uneventful Texas–Texas A&M game. But its first important usage came a week later when Boston College quarterback Jack Concannon escaped a handful of Syracuse tacklers during a 70-yard touchdown dash. Instant replay revealed every minute detail of the dramatic run. "Nobody had ever seen anything like that before, and the impact was unbelievable," Arledge later recalled. "That moment changed TV sports forever."

While transforming the way America watched the game, Arledge proceeded to influence what America chose to watch. Since the other networks owned the rights to most of the major sporting events, Arledge flew around the world purchasing rights to somewhat obscure, and sometimes outrageous, sporting endeavors to fill airtime. He called his weekly, year-round program "Wide World of Sports," and it remains the longest-running and most successful sports anthology show in television history. According to Powers, the show "established a truth that had never been tested before: that instead of telecasting events because people were already interested in them (the World Series, the Rose Bowl), clever programmers could make people interested in events *because they were on television*."

Since its inception in 1961, the show has, indeed, spanned the globe, visiting virtually every U.S. state and even more countries. It presented an American viewing audience the 24 Hours of Le Mans, the British Open, the Tour de France, the Little League World Series. Whereas it was once suspected that television audiences would only respond to big events in major sports, Arledge managed to get them to watch surfing and snowmobiling, wrist-wrestling and midget-car racing, demolition derby and barrel jumping. The show's extensive coverage of gymnastics and figure skating, among other sports, not only fueled interest in the Olympic Games but also took the female athlete further into the public consciousness.

"Wide World of Sports" delivered "the thrill of victory and the agony of defeat," a phrase, punctuated on the screen by the dramatic spill of immortalized skier Vienko Bogatej, that Arledge first wrote on the back of an airline ticket. It has become one of television's most enduring sports expressions, along with "Do you believe in miracles?" The latter, of course, was a phrase uttered on an ABC Olympic telecast, one of ten between 1964 and 1984. Arledge's impact in that arena was such that the *Atlanta Journal-Constitution* called him "the man most responsible for transforming the Olympic Games from an athletic competition for sports aficionados into an entertainment spectacular enjoyed by billions the world over."

Arledge turned the Games into a collection of dramas. Most notable were the 1972 Summer Games in Munich. Not only was it the first Olympiad telecast in prime time, it also changed the relationship between television and news. After Palestinian terrorists kidnapped eleven Israeli athletes, Arledge produced eighteen hours of coverage, which earned ABC twenty-nine Emmy awards. Ever since, Americans have expected to get the news while it was happening.

But Arledge also made his mark on the Olympics as an executive producer, when spearheading the evolution of television rights fees from a pittance into millions. Arledge paid less than $600,000 for the rights to the 1964 Winter Games in Innsbruck. By 1972, the Munich Games had set ABC back $13.5 million; and by 1988, a fierce bidding war led Arledge to pay an unfathomable $309 million for the Calgary Winter Olympics.

By then, of course, Arledge had profoundly changed the viewing habits of the nation, not only with each Olympiad and each cliff-diving competition, but on Monday nights as well. In 1970, ABC's prime-time lineup was the laughingstock of the business, so much so that Milton Berle announced that the best way to end the Vietnam War would be to put in on ABC, explaining, "It'll be canceled in three weeks." But that was before Arledge introduced the nation to "Monday Night Football," which became the longest-running prime-time series on one network and which would transform American culture as no TV show had since, well, since Milton Berle in the '50s.

CBS had broadcast five Monday night games in the late '60s with no particular success. But as the decade came to a close, Arledge approached NFL commissioner Pete Rozelle about a weekly Monday night telecast, and Rozelle was intrigued. Yet Rozelle first offered the idea to the other networks, which already had a relationship with the NFL. They weren't interested—CBS had "Here's Lucy" on Mondays, NBC had "Laugh-In." Before ABC signed on, however, Arledge refused to allow the usual practice of league approval of the announcing team. He then hired a man nobody would ever approve of: Howard Cosell.

Cosell had worked as a boxing analyst for ABC for several years, and had earned fame as Muhammad Ali's straightman, but he owned a reputation for being long-winded and opinionated. The other networks had blacklisted him; Arledge decided to build his new program around him. "In truth," wrote Rushin, "[Arledge] was giving viewers what they wanted—candor—before they knew they wanted it, a talent of his that is uncanny."

Arledge eventually settled on a three-man team of Cosell, Don Meredith and Frank Gifford, and the game became somewhat secondary to the evolving story line and the traveling circus that was the announcer's booth. Within a year, "Monday Night Football" was drawing some 30 million viewers. Prime-time football had succeeded, and the Olympics, the World Series and the Super Bowl soon followed suit.

As for Arledge, he had risen from ABC's vice-president in charge of sports to president of ABC Sports when the department became a separate division in 1968. In 1977, he also became president of ABC News, where he continued his pioneering ways, developing, among other programs, "Nightline." In 1986, he was named group president of ABC News and Sports, commanding a salary well into seven figures.

Thanks primarily to Arledge's efforts and the network's strategy of cross-promoting sports and prime-time programming, ABC, once the perennial doormat, reached No. 1 in the mid-'70s for the first time in its history. Sports, it seems, had become as important to television as television was to sports.

10

Branch Rickey

He often has been described as a remarkable contradiction in terms. Historian Jules Tygiel claims he displayed "a strange mixture of moralist and mountebank." *Time* magazine called him a combination of "Phineas T. Barnum and Billy Sunday." And David Halberstam characterized him as "part preacher, part carnival barker, part Shakespearean actor."

It took a talented man like Red Smith to capture Branch Rickey's divergent traits in one breath. Smith simply called him "a player, manager, executive, lawyer, preacher, horsetrader, spellbinder, innovator, husband and father and grandfather, farmer, logician, obscurantist, reformer, financier, sociologist, crusader, sharper, father confessor, checker shark, friend and fighter."

Rickey was the kind of man who honored his Methodist upbringing by never attending Sunday games, but who always collected profits from Sunday doubleheaders. He never drank or smoked or swore, but he always seemed to hire talented people known for that kind of behavior. Historian Harold Seymour writes that Rickey was "so adept at bargaining with players over salaries that they sometimes came away thanking him for a pay cut." Yet few men inspired more loyalty among their employees than Rickey did.

Rickey's sporting legacy is simple yet monumental—the expansion of baseball's grasp, the expansion of its opportunities and the expansion of the game itself.

By almost single-handedly designing the concept of the farm system in the 1920s and 1930s, Rickey turned his imaginative scheme into the blueprint for modern professional baseball, likely saving the minor leagues in the process. By signing Jackie Robinson to a professional contract in 1945 and then carefully planning each step of the integration process over the next few years, Rickey choreographed the most momentous development in the history of the game. And finally, by presiding over the attempt to form a third major league late in his career, Rickey scared Major League Baseball executives into an expansionist mode, which translated to new franchises from Montreal to Miami, from Seattle to San Diego.

Indeed, it is likely there has never been a sports figure who has profoundly affected one game in so many different ways. Trace the careers of many current major leaguers, and you can see Rickey's influence in every step. Take Tony Gwynn, for instance—a black man who rose through a farm system to begin his career with the once-expansion San Diego Padres. What would his baseball opportunities have been if Branch Rickey hadn't dreamed about tomorrow?

Born on December 20, 1881, in Stockdale, Ohio, Wesley Branch Rickey's path to adulthood consisted of a constant quest for education and a yearning for athletics. After starting his working career as a country schoolteacher, he put his $35-a-month salary toward classes at Ohio Wesleyan University, where he coached and competed on the baseball team before graduating in 1904. He continued to teach and coach in various places over the next several years, even spending some time as a catcher and outfielder with the American League's St. Louis Browns and the New York Highlanders. In parts of four seasons, he batted .239. His playing career is perhaps most remembered for the day he allowed a record 13 stolen bases in one game.

After his playing days ended, Rickey worked his way through law school at the University of Michigan by coaching college baseball. After struggling to make it as a lawyer, his big break in baseball came in 1913, when Browns owner Robert Hedges hired him as his personal assistant. By the end of the season, he was managing the team. Rickey moved across town to the St. Louis Cardinals' front office in 1917, becoming the Cardinals' manager two years later. After limited success, he moved permanently to the team's front office in 1925, serving as the Cardinals' vice-president and business manager through the 1942 season.

Rickey has been credited with many baseball creations while working in St. Louis, including sliding pits, batting tees and the practical use of batting cages. But the farm system was his most important contribution to the game—at least until he moved to Brooklyn.

In the early 1900s, minor league clubs were independently owned propositions that depended greatly on player sales to the major leagues in order to survive. Major league clubs could draft players in the off-season, paying a set sum for each, but shrewd minor league executives often sold their best players to the highest bidder before the draft. In fact, from 1909 to 1913 the major leagues spent nearly $2 million purchasing minor league prospects.

Early rules prevented major league clubs from having minor league holdings, but by 1921 there were no restrictions on minor league involvement. Rickey made the most of his opportunity. Annoyed that wealthier clubs would often outbid him for a prospect that he had discovered, Rickey took action. "Starting the Cardinal farm system was no sudden stroke of genius," he later explained. "It was a case of necessity being the mother of invention."

Rickey pioneered the notion of succeeding due to preparation instead of profits. "He believed that the power of wealth to create winning teams should be minimized and emphasis be placed instead on work, planning and good judgment," writes Seymour. "Good farmer that he was, Rickey decided to grow his own crop on his own land."

Rickey's revolutionary contribution was the idea of linking clubs together at various classification levels, assuring a steady supply of talent by weeding out the best players at each stop. He started by purchasing 50 percent of the Fort Smith, Arkansas, club, following that by buying into the Houston franchise of the Texas League, a step above Fort Smith. Then it was Syracuse, a Class-AA team. Within a few years, it was a minor league empire. By the time World War II arrived, the Cardinals owned or had working agreements with thirty-two clubs at various levels.

Baseball's most powerful figures, including commissioner Kenesaw Mountain Landis, were dead set against Rickey's system, believing it destroyed the independence of the minor league clubs. But it soon became so successful that every major league team copied the concept. Without the farm system, minor league baseball, at least at its lower levels, might not have survived the Great Depression, the second World War and the emergence of television.

When Rickey first created the scheme in the 1920s, its detractors dubbed it the "chain gang." But St. Louis won the 1926 pennant and finished first or second fourteen times in the next twenty seasons. The success, ironically, was as much a product of profit as preparedness. Even though the Cardinals drew fewer fans than their counterparts in bigger cities, between 1925 and 1950 they took in more than twice the profit of those clubs, most of it coming from the sale of surplus players to other teams. In 1949, it was estimated that three out of eight major leaguers were the product of Rickey's farm systems.

After turning the Cardinals into the National League's most successful franchise, Rickey did the same with the Brooklyn Dodgers. He became president and general manager of the Dodgers in 1942, and while most teams were reluctant to sign young talent during World War II, Rickey continued to do so with an eye toward the future. As a result, between 1946 and 1956, Brooklyn won six pennants and placed second four times.

But the Dodgers became as much a symbol as a success story. Organized baseball's unwritten ban against African-American players had been in effect for more than half a century when Rickey took over the Dodgers. Over the years, there had been only a few clandestine attempts at crossing the color line. In 1901, Baltimore Orioles manager John McGraw attempted to disguise black second baseman Charlie Grant as an American Indian, renaming him Chief Tokohoma, but the scheme was exposed. Ten years later, the Cincinnati Reds signed two light-skinned Cubans to big league contracts, heralding the grudging acceptance of Latin Americans, but only as long as their skin wasn't too dark. In 1916, pitcher Jimmy Claxton even pitched in the Pacific Coast League after being introduced to the owner of the Oakland Oaks as a Native American. But he was released six days later when it was discovered he had African-American ancestry, as well.

The color barrier was stronger than ever by the 1940s, but there were signs of a crack in the wall. Two of baseball executives' most consistent rationalizations for the barrier concerned geography. One-third of the game's players were from the South, and the owners feared negative reactions to integration. In addition, three-fourths of the country's black population lived in the South, while every big league franchise existed in the North. The owners were reluctant to court a handful of black fans and risk losing their white customers.

However, during the 1940s, black population in the northern states increased by 50 percent, and one poll revealed that four out of five National League players and managers had no objections to integrating the game. Soon, the owners even began to recognize the inevitability of integration. In 1938, Washington Senators owner Clark Griffith had said, "There are few big league magnates who are not aware of the fact that the time is not far off when colored players will take their places beside those of the other races in the major leagues."

But the owners' statements still reeked of passivity, and "If only you were white" was still their common refrain to Negro League stars. It was Rickey who took on the role of aggressor in the good fight.

For twenty-one years, Landis had privately prevented integration, despite public statements to the contrary. But when he died, in 1944, and was replaced by former Kentucky governor A. B. "Happy" Chandler, Rickey's opportunity arrived. Though rumored to be a staunch segregationist, Chandler surprised many by announcing, "I don't believe in barring Negroes from baseball just because they are Negroes."

In April 1945, black sportswriter Joe Bostic arrived at the Dodgers' training camp with two black players, demanding tryouts. Though he allowed them to perform for forty-five minutes, Rickey was enraged. "I'm more for your cause than anybody else you know, but you are making a mistake using force," he told Bostic. "You are defeating your own aims." Bostic was all but certain Rickey's words were hollow, but only because he had no idea that Rickey had constructed a careful plan.

Less than a month later, Rickey called a press conference to criticize Bostic's actions and the manner in which the Negro Leagues were run. He then announced the formation of the new all-black United States League, which many observers interpreted as his way of assuring baseball's continued segregation. In reality, it was his way of secretly scouting African-American athletes for the Dodgers.

Rickey had first approached Dodgers owners about his plan in 1943, and by 1945 his scouts had been examining black players for two years, thinking they were searching for athletes for a new team, the Brown Dodgers. The creation of the U.S. League simply allowed them to scout more openly. Meanwhile, Rickey attempted to cover every base, even consulting historians and sociologists in order to make the transition as smooth as possible. The signing of Jackie Robinson represented the culmination of Rickey's careful search for the perfect pioneer.

Rickey meticulously planned every phase of Robinson's journey to the big leagues. He signed him to play for the Montreal Royals, knowing that the team would have to venture no farther south than Baltimore. He signed another black player, pitcher John Wright, to accompany Robinson in spring training in Florida and even launched a behind-the-scenes program to prepare Daytona Beach residents for Robinson's arrival. Finally, he selected 44-year-old Mississippian Clay Hopper to manage the Montreal club, trusting his integrity and hoping his southern roots would mute dissension.

Before Robinson and Wright arrived at spring training, Rickey gathered the players together and replaced his usual talk on baseball fundamentals with a lecture on race relations. He explained that he had not been forced into signing Robinson and that winning was his only goal. "I would have signed an elephant to play shortstop," he announced, "if the elephant could have done it better than anybody else."

Rickey tended to explain his actions in spiritual terms, saying, "I couldn't face my God much longer knowing that His black creatures are held separate and distinct from His white creatures in the game that has given me all I own." Yet there are other possible reasons why he attacked the color line, each representative of his paradoxical personality. He certainly believed that by signing the game's first African-Americans he would be giving the Dodgers an advantage on the field, and he may have believed the club would benefit off the field in the form of increased attendance. It has even been suggested that Rickey may have hoped to crush two all-black teams competing with him for spectators in the New York area.

But regardless of his motives, his actions were obviously enormously influential. As Robinson himself explained, "I really believe that in breaking down the color barrier in baseball, our 'national game,' he did more for the Negroes than any white man since Abraham Lincoln."

Certainly, just as slavery would likely have ended eventually even if Lincoln hadn't forced its hand, baseball probably would have integrated with or without Rickey. Likewise, it has been suggested that Rickey's preparations may have been overly elaborate. But hindsight cannot diminish the fact that it was Rickey, and only Rickey, who had the courage to sign a black player. Indeed, many years later, Happy Chandler claimed that baseball's owners had condemned Rickey for breaking the color barrier by a 15-1 vote. And it was a full two years before any other major league owner would sign an African-American. While Rickey's grand designs may seem extreme, they were, after all, successful.

The influx of black talent on the Dodgers—including Robinson, Roy Campanella and Don Newcombe—would propel the club to its first world championship in 1955. But by then, Rickey had been squeezed out of a job by new Brooklyn owner Walter O'Malley. After selling his Dodgers stock for $1 million, Rickey was named vice-president and general manager of the Pittsburgh Pirates in 1951, becoming chairman of the team's board of directors five years later, an association that lasted until 1959.

It was then that Rickey moved to the forefront of the first attempt in four decades to establish a third major league, the Continental League. Major League Baseball fought off the attempt, but Rickey's league was the key force in spurring expansion, resulting in what are now the Mets, Astros, Angels and Twins. The league also announced that within several years four additional clubs would be added. In fact, of the eight cities originally planned for the Continental League, seven of them have major league franchises today.

Rickey returned to the St. Louis Cardinals as an advisor for a short while in the mid-1960s, but by then his health was waning. He died eleven days before his eighty-fourth birthday, on December 9, 1965. He had been in a coma for twenty-six days after suffering a heart attack during an acceptance speech following his induction into the Missouri Sports Hall of Fame. Among his last words were the following: "Now I'm going to tell you a story from the Bible about spiritual courage . . ."

Marvin Miller

In the past thirty years, there have been four major developments in American sports: the impact of television, the full flowering of sports marketing, the arrival of the women's sports revolution and the explosion of athletes' salaries. What all four have in common is an icon, a person who aggressively propelled sports toward the twenty-first century. Television had Roone Arledge; sports marketing had Mark McCormack; the women's movement had Billie Jean King. And the dramatic inflation of sports salaries—in baseball, in particular, which has always served as a model to the other games—was largely caused by a man who never made it much past the sandlots.

"If baseball ever buys itself a mountain and starts carving faces in it," claims baseball historian Bill James, "one of the first men to go up is sure to be Marvin Miller." As the first executive director of the Major League Baseball Players' Association (MLBPA), a position he held for what *Sports Illustrated* called "17 undefeated years," Miller reversed nearly 100 years of owner-dominated, legally backward virtual-slavery. The owners weren't ready for his energy and expertise, and so the players prospered.

Miller brought to baseball such basic notions as a grievance system, impartial arbitration and a free market—concepts that the game's earliest powers fought hard to prevent. He handed the players, around whom the game revolves, an equitable part of the spoils of the business. In bringing legitimate labor relations to the game, he also ushered in significant labor confrontations. To some, this is just an example of the monster he created. But others claim he simply opened the athletes' eyes to the inequity of it all. Writes Studs Terkel, "Marvin Miller . . . not only changed the rules of the game but brought an end to the age of innocence: for some of our finest athletes, it was a liberating experience. They discovered that 'union' was not a dirty word."

Before Miller, no attempt at forming a players' union had been entirely successful. In 1946, lawyer Robert F. Murphy had tried to form the American Baseball Guild, but the union quickly folded. Eight years later, the MLBPA was formed, with pitching great Bob Feller as its first president, but it was not a bargaining unit and it was still far from being the owners' adversary. In fact, Robert Cannon, a circuit court judge who served as the Association's advisor in the early 1960s, often reminded the players how lucky they were to be playing ball. Cannon was openly supportive of the reserve clause, and in 1964 he told Congress that the players "have it so good we don't know what to ask for next."

When the players formed a search committee (consisting of Robin Roberts, Jim Bunning, Harvey Kuenn and Bob Friend) in 1965 to find a full-time executive director and establish an MLBPA office in New York City, it came as no surprise that Cannon emerged as the owners' favorite for the job. He was actually elected to the position, but the players became disenchanted with his conditions for taking the job, so they turned to Miller. He turned out to be the most successful pinch-hitter the game has seen.

Miller was born on April 14, 1917, in the Bronx, but he grew up in Brooklyn, near Ebbets Field. After graduating from New York University in 1938, with a degree in economics, he worked for the New York City Department of Welfare, the National War Labor Board (during World War II) and the International Association of Machinists. By 1966, he was the chief economist and assistant to the president of the United Steelworkers of America, the country's third-largest union, and a member of President Lyndon B. Johnson's National Labor-Management Panel. But the baseball offer was too intriguing to pass up.

"The more I thought about the Players' Association, the more I figured I could make a difference. I loved baseball, and I loved a good fight, and, in my mind, ballplayers were among the most exploited workers in America," Miller writes in his memoirs, *A Whole Different Ball Game*. "Considering that major league players represented the very top of their profession, salaries were bad—no, not just bad: pitiful."

The average major league salary in 1966 was $19,000, with only a few of the biggest stars reaching the $100,000 plateau. The major league minimum was $6,000, having been raised by only $1,000 since World War II. Indeed, the combined payroll of all major league clubs that year was less than the combined salaries of Roger Clemens and Dwight Gooden twenty-five years later.

Miller has described Major League Baseball in 1966 as being "as lawless, in its own way, as Dodge City in 1876." Baseball executives had a "policy" of never dealing with agents, and salaries were rarely released publicly, so players who were told they were the fourth-highest paid on the team would later find out they ranked eighth. In fact, the balance of power was so distorted when Miller took over that one of his first responsibilities was to assure that players at least be given copies of every document that became a part of their contract.

His election as executive director made the MLBPA the first legitimate union in organized sports, but it had, he says, "the financial stability of a third world nation." The Association had total assets of less than $6,000 and an insufficient dues system. More importantly, and despite the inequities of the times, it had very little support among those it was created to protect. "Here's what we had: no money, no office, no staff, and no union consciousness," Miller explains. "Players were not only ignorant about unions, they were positively hostile to the idea: They didn't know what a union was, but they knew they didn't want one."

Miller toured spring training in his first year in an attempt to explain his role, expound on his philosophy, and drum up support. Of the first 119 players who voted on Miller's nomination, only 17 supported him. But as they got to know him, they got to like him. Of the next 506 votes, 472 were pro-Miller. The newspapers reported his election as executive director on April 12, 1966, a date that might serve as the beginning of the modern age of player-management relations.

Miller then set his sights on the owners, who viewed the union with as much disinterest as disdain. "To the owners, the union in 1966 was an aberration, a temporary irritation. Surely, they thought, once they applied pressure, the players would give up and I would be gone, and in a very short time," he claims. "And who could blame them for such beliefs? They had ridden over every single challenge to their absolute authority and control for almost a century." One of Miller's first moves was to develop a licensing arrangement to help fund the Association, a step toward making it financially secure.

In December 1966, a benefit plan agreement between the Association and the owners marked the first agreement in organized sports resulting from collective bargaining. The first Basic Agreement, in any sport, followed two years later, and included the creation of a formal grievance procedure, an agreement that the Uniform Player's Contract could not be changed unilaterally, and a raise of the minimum salary to $10,000. Miller's efforts so began to threaten the owners that they fired the commissioner, General William Eckert, and hired Bowie Kuhn, who would become Miller's nemesis (or patsy) for more than a decade.

The second Basic Agreement, signed in 1970, guaranteed a minimum salary of $15,000. More importantly, Miller secured binding, impartial arbitration for players' grievances, instead of arbitration by the owner-hired commissioner. Ultimately, he considered it the MLBPA's most significant victory, explaining, "Before 1970, baseball was like one of those tiny towns in which a stranger passing through gets arrested by the sheriff, who also turns out to be the judge and the mayor."

The first mass strike in professional sports history occurred in early April 1972, when the players walked out for fourteen days, forcing the cancellation of eighty-six games. Though the players voted 663-10 to support a strike, the media critics focused on Miller. Columnist Dick Young wrote, "Clearly, to the owners, the enemy is not the players, whom the owners regard merely as ingrates, misled ingrates. The enemy is Marvin Miller, general of the Union. The showdown is with him. It is not over a few more thousand dollars . . . it is over the principle of who will run their baseball business, they, the Lords, or this man Miller."

As it turns out, Miller seems to have won the war. Certainly, he won the hearts and minds of the players. Pete Rose, for instance, complained that he had lost $7,000 during the 1972 strike. He later changed his tune, became a free agent, signed a $3.2 million contract with the Philadelphia Phillies and earned more than $7,000 a day.

The 1972 season also marked the culmination of the Curt Flood saga. Flood had refused a trade to Philadelphia in 1969, saying he deserved the right to "consider offers from other clubs before making a decision." With Miller's support, he took Major League Baseball to court, challenging the reserve clause, which supposedly bound players for life to the team that signed them. Flood lost his case, but the reserve clause lost its luster. The case also led to a decision by Miller to forego the courts and challenge baseball's executives at their own game.

When Miller had first examined the Uniform Player's Contract upon taking over the MLBPA, he was struck by the information he found in paragraph 10a. "The first time I read it, I did a double take," he explains in his memoirs. "What I had been told—and what the *players believed*—was that once a player signed his first contract, he no longer had control over his career. But the plain words of this section of the contract, as I read it, gave a club a one-year option on a player's services after his contract expired. *Nothing more*. It provided that if a club and player did not agree on a new contract to replace the old one that had terminated, the club could renew the old contract for *one additional year*." What would happen if a player refused to sign a contract and then played out his option?

Jim "Catfish" Hunter had become baseball's first free agent following the 1974 season, but only because Oakland A's owner Charlie Finley had violated his contract by neglecting to direct half of his salary toward an annuity during the season. Miller took Hunter's complaint to arbitrator Peter Seitz, who ruled that Hunter was a free agent. After making $100,000 with the A's, Hunter signed a five-year $3.75 million contract with the New York Yankees. Suddenly, the players discovered what they would be worth in an open market.

Having repeatedly heard of teams coercing their players to sign, Miller realized the clubs didn't believe an unsigned contract could be renewed beyond one year. It was his chance to challenge the wording of the reserve clause. In 1975, two players—Andy Messersmith of the Dodgers and Dave McNally of the Expos—refused to sign their contracts. Their teams exercised their right to renew the contracts for an option year without their signature. And then, on the last day of the season, Messersmith and McNally claimed that by playing out their options they were now free agents.

Bowie Kuhn called free agency "nothing more than one of those myths Miller spent so much time inventing," and he and the owners believed it would result in chaos, the disruption of competitive balance and the bankruptcy of the league.

Seitz was, once again, the arbitrator, and after three days of testimony, he knew the players had a case. He tried to get baseball's executives to settle the issue peacefully, but to no avail. "I begged them to negotiate," he later told Miller. "The owners were too stubborn and stupid. They were like the French barons in the twelfth century. They had accumulated so much power they wouldn't share it with anybody." More than a month later, on December 23, Seitz released a 61-page document stating that the two players were free to negotiate and sign with other teams. The owners promptly fired him.

Though the owners' appeals of the decision were shot down in court, Miller was in a mood to negotiate. He shrewdly realized that free agency rights, after one year, would mean a flooded market, which would hold salaries down. But if free agency were staggered, bidding wars would develop. The owners locked the players out of spring training for seventeen days in 1976, but the negotations continued for weeks. Finally, it was announced at the All-Star break that any player with six years of big league experience was eligible for free agency.

The end result was the most rapid salary growth in any industry in history. Miller explains, "In 1966, Bobby Bonds was a twenty-year-old rookie making $6,000 a year. Had I told him that his son, if he made it to the major leagues, would make as a rookie what Bobby's teammate Willie Mays was paid—he would have rightly told me to take a hike. And had I added that his son, if he became an outstanding player, would be guaranteed millions of dollars a year—more in one season than the great Willie Mays would make during his entire career—Bobby Bonds would have concluded that I needed psychiatric help."

Yet, the players' gains have been accompanied by similarly spectactular growth in the owners' revenue and unprecedented parity throughout the league. "What happened with free agency turned out to be exactly the opposite of what the owners said," Miller contends. "Teams could no longer stockpile talent, perennial cellar dwellers could improve themselves. Competition became keener, pennant races became more exciting, attendance increased, TV revenues went up, players were finally rewarded as the professionals they were, and everyone was happy. Everyone, that is, except the owners."

The average player's salary tripled between 1976 and 1980, and the owners' attempt to reverse the trend resulted in a 50-day players' strike in 1981, and what will forever be known as the split season. Miller retired at the end of 1982, but returned to set the house in order after the players fired his replacement, Ken Moffet. In 1984, Miller became a consultant to Donald Fehr, giving him sage advice—and reminding all who asked about the history of labor relations in baseball—right up through the 1994 strike.

Many observers point to the recent bitter confrontations and a lack of loyalty on the part of the players, and blame Miller for robbing the game of its innocence. But there are also those who claim the age of innocence was really an era of naiveté. "And that is what makes Miller special to the history of the game," Bill James explains, "that he was the man who saw the absurdity inherent in The Natural Order of Things and took the trouble to expose it."

Peter Seitz himself wrote a letter to *The New York Times* in 1982, just before his death, calling Miller "the Moses who had led Baseball's Children of Israel out of the land of bondage." *Sports Illustrated*'s Tom Verducci preferred a more secular analogy, writing: "Having established for the players both purpose and freedom, he is the association's George Washington and Abraham Lincoln in one."

But perhaps one baseball executive's perspective, though biased, is most apt. "If Marvin wants to be fair," he said during Miller's reign, "once he retires he then should go and work for the owners; it would help even things up."

12

Mark McCormack

"No one stands above the sports compost the way Mark Hume McCormack does," *Los Angeles Times* columnist Jim Murray wrote in 1991. "You look at the billion-dollar business sports has become in this country, you look at the multimillion-dollar salaries and ancillary takes of the players and, if you had one man to thank (or curse), that man would be Mark McCormack."

McCormack is, for all intents and purposes, the father of sports marketing; the man who generated the merger of sports and business to such an extent that what were once simple playing fields and players have grown to become vast corporate playgrounds and playthings. Sports has always been driven by money, but thanks largely to McCormack, modern competition has become a virtual afterthought. Starting with one office, and one marketable client, McCormack turned his company, International Management Group, into a multinational force with more than five dozen offices in more than two dozen countries, some 1,500 employees and revenues close to $1 billion annually. IMG's influence can be found, in one form or another, in virtually every aspect of sport.

As *Sports Illustrated*'s E. M. Swift explained in a 1990 profile of McCormack and his company, "It is more or less routine for athletes represented by IMG to play in IMG-promoted tournaments that are sponsored by corporations to which IMG serves as consultant, with the TV coverage produced by a company that IMG owns."

And it all began with a skull fracture, a friendship and a handshake. McCormack, the son of a farm journal publisher, was born during the Depression, on November 6, 1930, in Chicago. One of his earliest memories concerns an understanding of the value of a dollar. "Every week, my grandfather would give me a dollar to take a cab home from his house," McCormack once recalled, "and

I would get out a block and a half from my house, just before the meter clicked. That way, I saved twenty cents." Already McCormack was taking a percentage, only now IMG keeps twenty-*five* percent of a client's income.

After suffering a skull fracture in an automobile accident at age six, McCormack took up golf as therapy. He eventually became good enough to win the city golf championship, star at William and Mary, and qualify for several U.S. and British amateur championships. He attended Yale Law School, spent two years in the Army, and then joined a Cleveland law firm.

Through his amateur golf experience, McCormack had become acquainted with several golfers who went on to become pro stars. Before long, he was booking exhibition appearances for them, and the players were asking him to review their endorsement contracts. Among those players was Arnold Palmer, who soon asked McCormack to take over his finances. In 1959, he became Palmer's manager. McCormack described his move into agentry as "a way to keep me in golf and a law library at the same time." But, as Jim Murray pointed out, "Mark McCormack didn't want to be a 10-percenter. He wanted to be—well, he wanted to be Arnold Palmer."

He became even bigger. In 1960, McCormack started IMG, the first company devoted solely to managing and marketing pro athletes, with Palmer as his only client. "The deal," explained Bill Shirley of the *L.A. Times*, "sealed by a handshake, made both men millionaires and changed the face of sports agentry and merchandising."

Within two years, Palmer would rank as the supreme athlete-as-pitchman, his income jumping from $60,000 to $500,000 through lucrative endorsements and exhibitions. Within three decades, Palmer, with career PGA Tour earnings of less than $3 million, would be making four times that each year, even past the age of sixty, and he would own a financial empire worth hundreds of millions. After taking up Palmer's cause, McCormack quickly signed to manage the remaining two faces among golf's Big Three, Jack Nicklaus and Gary Player. IMG was off and running. One man's vision would evolve into a sporting revolution.

"Virtually everything being done today in the management and corporate sponsorship of athletic events, in merchandise licensing and in made-for-TV sports started with McCormack," Swift wrote. "McCormack convinced the business world that sports was an ideal marketing vehicle—high in visibility, positive in image and international in scope."

The rise of IMG was the product of recognition, understanding and timing. McCormack recognized the possibilities inherent in merging sporting ventures and corporate goals, understood the best ways to market that merger, and timed his creation to coincide with the explosion of television sports. His focus was international from the beginning, and he realized that by signing a country's top athlete, he would create opportunities for corporations around the globe. Besides Americans Palmer and Nicklaus, McCormack's early stable of stars included Player, from South Africa; golfer Tony Jacklin, from England; racecar driver Jackie Stewart, from Scotland; skier Jean-Claude Killy, from France; and Swedish tennis star Bjorn Borg.

Today, IMG is still based in Cleveland, but its tentacles reach into every country with an interest in sports and a dollar to spend. As Shirley explained, "If the chief executive officer of a corporation, say in Japan, wishes to market his company's product through a sports promotion in Great Britain, chances are he will probably call an office in Cleveland, Ohio."

The list of athletes who have signed up with sport's largest athlete management and representation firm includes Greg Norman, Nick Faldo, Curtis Strange, Bernhard Langer, Nancy Lopez, Rod Laver, Chris Evert, Martina Navratilova, Ivan Lendl, Monica Seles, Aranxta Sanchez Vicario, Kristi Yamaguchi and Alberto Tomba. And that's just in individual sports.

Throughout most of its existence, IMG placed little emphasis on team sports because McCormack felt individual sport stars were international figures, while team sport stars were regional celebrities. But the salary explosion in team sports caused McCormack to rethink that notion, and in typical fashion, IMG entered the team sports arena by buying the businesses of several well-stocked player agents. The firm quickly grabbed ahold of more team sport athletes—from Joe Montana and Herschel Walker to Wayne Gretzky and Mario Lemieux—than anyone else in the business.

Though the heart of IMG is client representation, in recent years the firm has devoted itself to event management, as well. Among the events it has tapped into: Wimbledon, the U.S. Open, the British Open, the Italian Open and the ATP Tour in tennis; and the Masters, the U.S. Open, the British Open, the Ryder Cup and the European PGA Tour in golf. McCormack summed up the thinking behind IMG's evolution by pointing out, "Bjorn Borg can break a leg; Wimbledon cannot."

In short, IMG has a grip on virtually every connection between sport and business. McCormack's creation has made athletes wealthy through commercial endorsements and financial planning; it has made events and organizations like Wimbledon and the Albertville Olympic Committee wealthy through licensing and television contracts; and it has made companies happy to sponsor IMG-run events and hire IMG clients. The firm can create and run tournaments, peddle sponsorships and television rights, provide the television commentary, and supply the stars.

IMG even bought Nick Bollettieri's Tennis Academy in 1987 for an estimated $8 million, creating a virtual minor league system that helped the firm snare young players like Andre Agassi and Jim Courier. Like the Nike Corporation scouring the high schools, this type of client recruitment tends to rankle many observers. But it remains just another example of McCormack's growing power over the sports world.

In fact, McCormack hasn't stopped at sports. Besides event and client management, there is an IMG Artists division, IMG Models, IMG Publishing, IMG Licensing, IMG Promotions, IMG Recreational Real Estate Services and IMG Financial Services. The firm has counted among its clients violinist Itzhak Perlman, Universal Studios, Ringling Brothers, the Mayo Clinic, the Nobel Foundation,

Rolex and Harvard University. In 1982, IMG promoted Pope John Paul II's tour of the British Isles. The television and film branch of IMG, Trans World International (TWI), is touted as the largest independent source of televised sports, producing more than 100 shows annually from the World Professional Figure Skating Championship to made-for-TV events like the Skins Game and American Gladiators.

So can anyone compete with the power of IMG? According to McCormack, "Stacking us up against our competition is like comparing General Motors to a garage." And IMG is still growing. The company's revenues grew 430 percent during the 1980s; a $25 million take in 1975 is now nearly forty times that. According to Swift, IMG represents "quite simply, the most powerful, farsighted, far-reaching (some would say grabby) corporation in the world of sport . . . the company that people love to hate."

Indeed, critics of the monster formed by McCormack—and there are many of them—call IMG too big, too impersonal and too arrogant. IMG, they say, stands for International Money Grabbers or I. M. Greedy. "To a lot of people," Curtis Strange once admitted, "IMG is a four-letter word."

Several clients have left McCormack's firm because of what they considered its impersonal treatment, among them Nicklaus, Tom Watson and Jimmy Connors. Others, like golfer Bill Rogers and tennis phenom Jennifer Capriati, have burned out quickly, due, according to some critics, to IMG's tendency to send its clients chasing money all around the globe.

However, while the question of whether or not McCormack has had a positive influence on sport is certainly valid, there is no doubt about the enormity of his impact. What started with a handshake with Arnold Palmer became an industry that transformed the world's athletic scene. While both men deserve credit for starting the process, McCormack's vision and aggressive control must be given more weight than Palmer's name. Thus he ranks higher among *The Sports 100*.

Jack Johnson

No figure in the history of American sports has a more divergent legacy than Jack Johnson. Perhaps only Muhammad Ali has been more criticized and more lionized than America's first black heavyweight boxing champion. But Ali was first loathed and then loved; Johnson was both at the same time.

He broke free from the shackles of racial barriers, yet, largely because his behavior was so contrary to what was expected of him, he strengthened those shackles just the same. His arrival gave African-Americans a place in the pantheon of sports heroes, yet his behavior may have temporarily hindered their hopes for more. Jack Johnson represented and evoked both the best and the worst in black America's struggle for recognition and equality. He was a pioneer in the fight, yet also a pawn—a 6-foot-2, 200-pound paradox.

The best of Jack Johnson is that he was essentially the first. Soon after he was born, on March 31, 1878, in Galveston, Texas, a handful of black boxers would gain fame in the ring, some even winning championships in lighter weight classes. But, for the most part, the heavyweight division was all that the public cared about. Horse racing was the sport most open to African-American participation, and black jockeys actually dominated in the latter part of the nineteenth century. Fourteen of the 15 jockeys at the first Kentucky Derby in 1875 were ex-slaves, and black jockeys won 15 of the first 28 Derby crowns. But, by the time Johnson reached celebrity status, the Jockey Club of New York had taken over the licensing of jockeys, and had instituted Jim Crow policies.

Johnson's skills would change the rules; his antics would throw them into chaos. By 1903, he was considered the world's best black boxer, yet he had no opportunity to win the heavyweight title. Jim Jeffries, like every heavyweight champion before him, refused to fight a black man for the crown. Jeffries retired undefeated in 1905, and a Canadian named Tommy Burns became the top heavy-weight.

Johnson set his sights on Burns, chasing him around the globe. Only when he was offered $35,000, and allowed to use his own manager as referee, did Burns finally agree to fight Johnson. In front of some 26,000 spectators in Australia, on December 26, 1908, Johnson knocked out Burns in the fourteenth round. The facts, as Arthur Ashe explains in *A Hard Road to Glory*, spoke for themselves: "John Arthur Johnson, a descendant of the Koromantee tribe of West Africa, was the new world heavyweight champion."

Yet, the sporting press gave little respect to Johnson, and, instead, embarked on a search for a "Great White Hope" to dethrone the champion. "Had the first black man to win the heavyweight championship of the world been less powerful as a boxer and a personality, the white-controlled boxing world might have been able to forgive his triumph. But Jack Johnson was not one to pander to the sensibilities of threatened Caucasians," writes Marc Pachter in *Champions of American Sport*.

Johnson defended his title five times in 1909 against the country's best white challengers. The white public saw Jim Jeffries, now four years retired, overweight, and living the life of a quiet farmer, as their only hope. The "Great White Hope" craze became a national obsession, led, in part, by former champion John L. Sullivan, the man who had fostered boxing's segregationist bent. Author Jack London even got into the act, writing, "Jim Jeffries must emerge from his alfalfa farm and remove the golden smile from Jack Johnson's face."

The "Fight of the Century" was set for Reno, Nevada, on Independence Day, 1910. It boasted boxing's largest ever guaranteed purse ($101,000) and became the most eagerly awaited sporting event in American history. As Ashe would later explain, "Nothing that Frederick Douglass did, nothing that Booker T. Washington did, nothing that any African-American had done up until that time had the same impact as Jack Johnson's fight against Jim Jeffries."

Jeffries was no match for Johnson, who also had the hopes of an entire race riding on him. Sullivan himself was at ringside, covering the bout for *The New York Times*. Afterward, he wrote that Jeffries "wasn't in it from the first bell tap to the last, and as he fell bleeding, bruised, and weakened in the twenty-seventh second of the third minute of the fifteenth round no sorrier sight has ever gone to make pugilistic history."

White superiority, it seems, was a poor loser. Next to fight stories covered on page one of newspapers all over the country were accounts of race rioting, with thirteen blacks being killed and hundreds wounded everywhere from Georgia to New York City. As one writer explained, "Not until the sinking of an unsinkable Titanic two years later would public confidence receive such a shock."

As for the man who shocked the nation, in an era when lynchings were far more common than title fights, Johnson enjoyed wealth beyond the imagination of most Americans and became an immutable symbol of black success in a white world. That was his positive impact.

His negative impact, however, was one of such dimensions that it counteracted his pioneering accomplishments. This was due partly to Johnson's erratic behavior and partly to a nation's ignorance and insecurities. The combination was powerfully unfortunate, and, in one of sport's most intriguing developments, America's first black sports superstar actually set civil rights efforts—in and out of sports—back several steps.

Johnson was cocky and arrogant in the ring, even more so out of it. Today, much of his behavior might be called eccentric, even somewhat appealing, in the mold of Muhammad Ali or Charles Barkley or Deion Sanders. But in those days, many considered it downright blasphemous. As Nelson George, author of *Elevating the Game*, explains, "There had never been a widely known Black man, much less an athlete, who was as bold and openly contemptuous of the tenets of white male supremacy as this fighter."

Johnson married white women, traveled openly with white prostitutes, drank prodigiously, spent lavishly, and purposefully reinforced sexual stereotypes about black men. Similar behavior was swept under the rug when Babe Ruth did it a decade later. When Johnson did it, however, the critics pounced. Clearly, as much as Jackie Robinson represented the kind of man Branch Rickey was looking for to break baseball's color barrier with class and dignity, Johnson—particularly according to the racist public of the time—broke boxing's barrier with a complete lack of the same.

The more the white public saw of Johnson, the less he was appreciated, particularly after he married a white woman in 1911. He continued to carouse with prostitutes, which may have caused his wife to shoot herself in September 1912. One month later, Johnson was charged with violating the Mann Act, a law passed in 1910 making the interstate transportation of women for "immoral purpose" illegal. It was meant to stop organized crime; it was used to stop Johnson.

It was a trumped-up charge, but it further fanned the flames of bigotry. One national newspaper, the *Police Gazette*, called Johnson "the vilest, most despicable creature that lives." Even among black observers, Johnson was condemned for his public image. The *Baltimore Afro-American Ledger* declared that he was "anything but a credit to his race," and the *New York Age* stated, "As a black champion he has given the Negro more trouble by his scandals than he did in twenty years as a black tramp."

Johnson was charged with three counts of prostitution, one count of inducement to prostitution, three counts of unlawful sexual intercourse, two counts of debauchery and two counts of crimes against nature. Judge Kenesaw Mountain Landis, who would become baseball's first commissioner, presided over the trial. The all-white jury returned a guilty verdict, and Johnson was sentenced to a year and a day in prison, but he fled to Canada and began nearly seven years as a fugitive from "justice."

By late 1913, Johnson was in Paris, where he defeated Jim Johnson (no relation) in the first heavyweight title fight between two black men. Two years later, in London, a promoter offered him $30,000 to fight 6-foot-6, 250-pound Jess

Willard. Johnson dominated the first twenty-five rounds of the fight. But during the twenty-sixth round, Johnson reportedly signaled for his wife to leave, stuck his chin out and all but dared Willard to knock him out. Willard complied.

Johnson remained prone and motionless during the ten-count, then immediately stood up and left the ring. "Willard was just too much for me," he said after the fight. More accurately, the money Johnson was probably offered to lie down proved too much to resist. He later admitted he had thrown the fight.

No longer heavyweight champion of the world, but still a man without a country, Johnson traveled to England, Spain and Mexico before finally being persuaded to turn himself in. On July 20, 1920, almost seven years after leaving American soil, he surrendered to American authorities and was sent to Leavenworth Prison for eight months. Following his release, he remarried (for the fourth time) and made speeches for a living. He later worked in vaudeville and circuses, and even attempted a short ring comeback before dying in an automobile accident on June 10, 1946.

Jackie Robinson was in the midst of breaking baseball's color barrier when Johnson died. Joe Louis had been heavyweight champion for nine years. The question surrounding Johnson's legacy—and his ranking among *The Sports 100*—is whether those accomplishments came because of him or, to some extent, despite him. He is ranked below the aforementioned athletes simply because his role as a black pioneer was all but cancelled out—and probably overwhelmed—by his role as ammunition in support of unenlightened racial attitudes.

Of course, to many African-Americans during Jack Johnson's reign, and even to some modern athletes, like Ashe and Ali, Johnson represented a sort of appealing self-worth. Said Ali, "He came along at a time when black people felt they had nothing to be proud of, and he made them proud."

14

George Halas

The contributions of the people profiled in *The Sports 100* essentially fall under three categories—creation, transformation and long-term guidance. Among the 100 sports figures, no one combined all three to the extent of George Halas, a player, coach and owner with the Chicago Bears for sixty-three years and the most important person in the history of professional football.

Halas was a founder of the National Football League, its most successful publicist, its most willing innovator and its most powerful executive. No figure in any sport has ever been associated with one team for a longer period of time, nor been more enduring and influential within the confines of one league, than Halas. He has the distinction among the people in *The Sports 100* of being there at the beginning and still being there deep into the modern age, from the era of Jim Thorpe to the days of Jim McMahon.

Halas spent ten years as the Bears' right end and forty seasons as head coach—coincidentally divided into four ten year periods (1920–1929, 1933–1942, 1946–1955, 1958–1967). His coaching record (325-151-31, seven NFL titles and only six losing seasons) is matched only by Don Shula. In his sixty-three years as "Papa Bear," he was constantly among the most forceful voices in league affairs, from the maturation of football rules and the league's association with television to the AFL-NFL merger and the selection of NFL executives. In fact, it has been suggested that while the league's commissioners held the fancy titles, Halas always wielded the most power.

Though he was instrumental in the birth of the NFL, Halas was not, as he has been called, the "father of professional football." Pay-for-play had been around, in one form or another, since shortly after Halas was born in Chicago on February 2,

1895. The last of eight children (four died in infancy) born to Bohemian immigrants, he was an excellent athlete, lettering in baseball, football and basketball at
the University of Illinois.

After graduating in 1918, Halas played football at the Great Lakes Naval
Training Station, starring in the 1919 Rose Bowl by catching two touchdown
passes and returning an interception 77 yards. But Halas's first attempt at professionalism came in baseball. He earned a tryout with the New York Yankees in
1919 and made the team, but he managed only two hits in 22 at-bats and spent
the rest of the summer in the minor leagues.

It was Halas's failure on the diamond that led him to the gridiron. Up to that
point, professional football had been a comparatively primitive phenomenon. The
first organization to call itself the National Football League had been founded in
1902, when three baseball teams—the Philadephia Athletics, Philadelphia Phillies
and Pittsburgh Pirates—backed football squads, but pro football was a disorganized venture through the early part of the century.

By the autumn of 1919, Halas was playing pro football with the Hammond
Pros. The following spring, A. E. Staley of Decatur, Illinois, offered Halas a job
as player-coach of the Decatur Staleys, a semiprofessional football squad used
to promote his cornstarch products. It was the start of a 63-year relationship
between Halas and the team.

Disenchanted with pro football's haphazard methods, Halas sent a letter to
Ralph Hay, manager of the Canton (Ohio) Bulldogs, suggesting formation of a
viable professional league. On September 17, 1920, Halas and representatives
from nine other teams met in Hay's automobile showroom in Canton, where they
formed the American Professional Football Association and named gridiron legend Jim Thorpe the league's figurehead president. Only two teams from the original meeting, Halas's club and the Cardinals, are still in business, but the league
plays on.

"I knew we had a great game right from the start, but I never dreamed we
would wind up with anything like this," Halas recalled. "It was just a matter of
surviving in the early days. There wasn't much time to look beyond."

Two vital transitions occurred in 1921. Columbus team manager Joe Carr
took over for Thorpe and began an 18-year reign as league president, and Halas
took over complete control of the Decatur Staleys. Regardless, Halas took on a
partner, former Illinois halfback Dutch Sternaman, moved the club to Chicago
and signed a lease to play in Wrigley Field. By the close of 1922, the APFA had
been renamed (at Halas's suggestion) the National Football League and the Staleys
had been renamed the Bears, an attempt to link the team with baseball's Cubs.

The Bears and the NFL faced myriad challenges—from dozens of
semipro teams fragmenting the market, from the immense popularity of the college game and from criticism of professionalism from sportswriters and college
coaches, including college football's most acclaimed coach, Amos Alonzo Stagg,
of the University of Chicago. And so, despite topping the league in 1921, Halas's
team reported a net loss of $71.63.

Soon, Halas's prospects began to improve. In November 1925, he found the pro football Pied Piper he had been hoping for when Red Grange, an already legendary halfback from Illinois, signed an agreement with Halas which would prove to be remarkably lucrative to both parties. Over the next two months, Grange and the Bears barnstormed from coast-to-coast, playing seventeen games in seventeen cities in front of some 300,000 fans. It was, said Halas, the "box-office shot in the arm pro football needed."

Though the Grange tours had catapulted the sport into the public consciousness, NFL ownership still meant financial instability, particularly as the Depression came on. As a result, Sternaman sold his half of the team to Halas in 1933 for $38,000. By then, Halas had already set the stage for another revolution in the game, this one being a transformation in strategy.

Halas had retired as a player and stepped down as head coach in 1929, replacing himself with yet another University of Illinois product, Ralph Jones. During the 1920s, while most teams had switched to Pop Warner's single-wing offense, the Bears had stuck with football's old T-formation. With Halas's blessing, Jones redesigned the old T, splitting the ends two yards away from the tackles, spacing the halfbacks wider apart and converting one of them to a man-in-motion. By spreading the defense, Jones's formation made the Chicago running attack more mobile and opened up the passing game. Halas took over again, in 1933, and led the Bears to the league championship using what became known as the modern T-formation. It remains the basic offensive formation in football.

In the late 1930s, Halas also refined the game from his position as head of the league rules committee. He returned the goal posts to the goal lines, boosting the kicking game until it came of age some four decades later, requiring a return to the back of the end zone. He insisted that any time a ball was downed within five yards of the sideline, it was to be moved ten yards toward the center of the field, resulting in the creation of hash marks. And he proposed that passes be permitted from anywhere behind the line of scrimmage, instead of at least five yards behind where the ball was snapped.

All three rules injected life into the game, particularly the passing rule, which made football a far less predictable affair. The passing game also found benefit in the slimming down of the ball some two inches, and in the infusion of talent into the league, such as Green Bay end Don Hutson and Washington quarterback Sammy Baugh.

The maturation of the forward pass and the advent of the new and improved T-formation formed the foundation of modern football. In addition, as Red Grange put it, "Playing football became a lot more fun." When University of Chicago coach Clark Shaughnessy became an advisory coach to Halas in 1937, he perfected the new formation, developing the basic signal-calling system and blocking combinations. The following year, Halas obtained Columbia University halfback Sid Luckman—whom he thought to be the perfect T-formation player—in a pre-arranged draft-day trade, and converted him to quarterback. In the NFL championshp game two years later, thanks to Shaughenessy's innovations,

Luckman's arm and Halas's orchestration of it all, the Bears beat the Washington Redskins 73-0.

The Bears followed with three more titles in the next six years, but soon age began to catch up with Halas, at least in the eyes of many in the sporting public. In 1956, at the age of sixty-one, he yielded to pressure and let old friend and teammate Paddy Driscoll, who was but one year younger, take over the team for two years. But Halas, who had pulled the strings behind Driscoll anyway, officially took over again in 1958.

By 1963, there were whispers that Halas had been out-innovated by the likes of Paul Brown and Vince Lombardi. According to biographer George Vass, he "symbolized stagnation and the reluctance of age and entrenched authority to relinquish its faltering grip." But Halas adapted enough to lead his 1963 Bears to their first championship in seventeen years, and the 68-year-old was named Coach of the Year only months after he became a charter member of the Pro Football Hall of Fame.

Halas won the award again following the 1965 season, when Chicago, led by rookies Gale Sayers and Dick Butkus, won nine of its final eleven games. But his most important contribution to pro football in the 1960s came in relations with the upstart American Football League. As chairman of the NFL's expansion committee in 1959, Halas had rebuffed Texas millionaire Lamar Hunt's attempts to buy the Chicago Cardinals and move the team to Dallas. Hunt went on to form the AFL, while Halas and his committee responded by expanding into what were to be two AFL strongholds, Dallas and Minneapolis, effectively stealing the latter city away from Hunt's league.

But after being at the forefront of the war against the new league, Halas soon became a major player in the move toward a merger. "Halas seemed to be the NFL man most interested in peace. He had been in the game a long time, and he hated to see expenses spiraling the way they were," explained Hunt, who reportedly met with Halas several times in the years preceding the 1966 agreement. Though Halas's involvement in the actual agreement was rather indirect, his behind the scenes maneuvering and support were vital. In 1970, when the leagues officially merged, Pete Rozelle remained as NFL commissioner, Hunt became president of the American Conference and Halas was named the first president of the National Conference.

But by then Halas had finally put an end to his coaching career. Said his wife of forty-four years, Minnie, "He used to promise he'd retire when he was fifty-five, but when he got there he changed it to sixty. Later it became seventy." Finally, in May 1968, at the age of seventy-three, he made it official. Suffering from arthritis in both hips, Halas explained that he just couldn't keep up with the referees along the sidelines anymore. "I began to wonder," he said, "whether the officials were speeding up or I was slowing down."

Halas died on October 31, 1983, one of his last moves being the hiring of head coach Mike Ditka. Papa Bear missed out on Chicago's only Super Bowl trophy by less than twenty-seven months. But as Vass explains, "He will never need a monument as long as pro football endures. The Bears and the National Football League are his giant markers."

FATE AND FAME

Where would professional football be without George Halas? We almost found out. On July 24, 1915, the excursion boat *Eastland* capsized alongside its dock on the Chicago River. Among the nearly 1,000 names listed as missing persons was "Halas, G. S." Several days later, two men showed up at the Halas home, prepared to mourn the loss of their fraternity brother—until Halas, who had missed the boat, answered the door.

But Halas wasn't the only legendary sports figure to cheat fate. While driving his car in 1920, Babe Ruth was unable to negotiate a turn, spun off the road, and flipped over. He and his companions limped from the scene, spent the night in a nearby farmhouse, and finally made their way to Philadelphia the next day. There they were met with a newspaper headline: "RUTH REPORTED KILLED IN CAR CRASH." The corpse went on to hit about 650 more home runs.

At about the same time, an Illinois high school student named Red Grange was run over by a truck loaded with three tons of ice, and an Alabama youth named Jesse Owens survived being run over by a cotton drag. In 1943, six-year-old Richard Petty barely escaped as his North Carolina house was engulfed in flames. As a youngster growing up in Pennsylvania in the 1950s, Joe Namath once had to hold on to a railing to escape from the path of an oncoming train on a bridge.

As a senior at Wake Forest, Arnold Palmer refused a friend's exhortations to come along to the homecoming dance. Driving back from the dance, his friend was killed when his car careened off the road. Less than two decades later, Magic Johnson suffered through much the same experience when his best friend was killed by a drunk driver on a trip the two usually took together.

Two days before Muhammad Ali won the heavyweight boxing title for the first time, he was riding in a speedboat despite the fact that he couldn't swim. The boat capsized, and Ali was saved by a stranger. And finally, in 1970, a seven-year-old boy, who had nearly been electrocuted when he was three, narrowly escaped drowning. The boy grew up to be Michael Jordan.

15

Michael Jordan

Larry Bird considered him "God disguised as Michael Jordan." *Boston Globe* columnist Bob Ryan anointed him "the highest order of a basketball evolutionary chain." And *Sports Illustrated*'s Jack McCallum said he was "unquestionably the most famous athlete on the planet and one of its most famous citizens of any kind."

In short, technology and talent have combined to make Michael Jordan probably the most successful—in every sense of the word—athlete in sports history. As a result, he also is one of the most important. Said Roy S. Johnson, senior editor at *Money* magazine and former basketball correspondent for *The New York Times* and *Sports Illustrated*, "Jordan set the standard of how athletes are perceived by the general public. The notion of celebrity in athletics has been redefined."

Jordan's legacy is one of dimension, of reaching new heights—aesthetically, athletically and financially. Julius Erving revealed basketball's potential for aerial artistry; Jordan raised it higher. Magic Johnson and Larry Bird turned the NBA into a national phenomenon; Jordan made it a global passion. Arnold Palmer demonstrated the marketability of the athlete; Jordan showed how to dominate the market. Muhammad Ali emerged as a worldwide superstar; Jordan, thanks to television's impact, advertising's influence and basketball's ascension, may even have surpassed him.

Jordan's childhood offered few hints of his impending triumph. He was born on February 17, 1963, in Brooklyn, New York, moving to Wilmington, North Carolina, soon after. He was a good baseball player, but as a 5-foot-9 sophomore in high school, he was cut from the varsity basketball team. However, by his junior season he had grown to 6-foot-3, and as a senior he became an all-state guard. He then became an All-American in college, averaging 17.7 points per game at North Carolina and earning Player of the Year honors as a sophomore and junior.

Still, few realized he was a legend in the making. In fact, two centers—Hakeem Olajuwon and Sam Bowie—were picked ahead of Jordan in the 1984 NBA draft, before the lowly Chicago Bulls drafted the player who would turn their team into one of sport's premier franchises. Before Jordan, Chicago had difficulty filling one-third of Chicago Stadium, averaging just over 6,000 spectators per home game; Jordan's arrival led to 294 straight sellouts and construction of a new $175 million stadium.

There are any number of reasons for Jordan's high ranking among *The Sports 100*, perhaps the least of which is this: He is considered by many to be the greatest athlete of all time. His numbers are remarkable. Two Olympic gold medals, an NCAA championship as a freshman at North Carolina, three NBA championships, seven consecutive scoring titles and three MVP awards. In 1988, he was named league MVP, All-Star MVP, Defensive Player of the Year and slam-dunk champion. In 1992, he was league MVP, All-Star MVP and playoff MVP. Jordan has exceeded 60 points in a game five times; he has reached 50 points nearly three dozen times. His NBA records include a career average of more than 32 points per game, an even better playoff average, a 1993 NBA Finals average of 41.0 and an All-Star Game average of 21.0. In one game in 1987, #23 scored a record 23 straight points.

There have been countless dramatic moments—a 16-foot jumper with seventeen seconds remaining to give North Carolina the 1982 title; a 63-point performance against the Boston Celtics in the 1986 playoffs, after Jordan had missed most of the season with a broken foot; a last-second, dagger-in-the-heart swish to eliminate the Cleveland Cavaliers from the 1989 playoffs; a 35-point first half against Portland in the 1992 NBA Finals, during which Jordan twice hit three straight three-pointers.

Judged by quality and quantity, there was never a better basketball player than Jordan. Of course, greatness is not necessarily a criterion for inclusion in this book. But in Jordan's case, it was his greatness that led to his influence, in and out of sports. It was his talent that opened doors to places no athlete has gone before and perhaps no athlete will go ever again.

Jordan's actual impact on the NBA basketball court was probably significantly less than that of others such as Hank Luisetti, George Mikan, Bill Russell—men whose innovative styles profoundly changed the way the game was played. Jordan's style left room for only pale imitations in the NBA, but on the playgrounds, young boys all over the world have tried to emulate his high-flying, gravity-defying style. Jordan became a cultural icon unlike any athlete in history. Baggy pants, shaved heads, wagging tongues—what Dorothy Hamill was to haircuts, Jordan was to any number of cultural trends.

"The only person in my lifetime I can compare to Michael is Elvis Presley," said Bulls owners Jerry Reinsdorf. "He wasn't just a singer, and Michael isn't just an athlete. They are cult figures, bigger than life." Playing with Jordan was compared to touring with the Beatles. In sports, perhaps only Ali and Pelé were recognized on such a worldwide scale. Both had Jordan's charisma, but neither had his timing, arriving just as TV technology shrunk the world and sports marketing turned athletes into money trees. In a *Sports Illustrated* piece about Jordan, David Halberstam wrote, "The last great export of America in the postindustrial international economy may be entertainment and media"—which made Jordan into an international treasure.

Ironically, as much as Jordan courted fame, he became a prisoner of it, too. Jealous teammates, led by Isiah Thomas, refused to pass Jordan the ball at the 1985 All-Star Game. The media pounced on allegations that Jordan had a gambling problem, turning a golf wager and a one-night jaunt to Atlantic City before a playoff game into an assault on his sainted status. Jordan also was frequently criticized for being apolitical, taking few stands on social issues, and speaking out (as in his 1995 attempt to decertify the NBA players' union) only when his bank account was threatened. This seems to be the case (one reason Ali is ranked above him), but it was only because Jordan had earned so much fame that he was saddled with so much obligation.

When Jordan's father was murdered in the summer of 1993, a random victim of violence, Jordan finally decided he'd had enough. He retired at the top of his game at a press conference broadcast live throughout the world. How famous had he become? "They don't ask Barry Bonds to flip the coin at the Super Bowl," wrote *USA Today* columnist Tom Weir, "and they don't drag out Joe Montana for a ceremonial tipoff at the NBA Finals." Yet, nobody flinched when Jordan threw out the first pitch of the 1993 American League Playoffs. And the Chicago White Sox? There were more than happy to offer Jordan a baseball contract.

When a Chicago cable station, SportsChannel, presented its tenth anniversary show in 1994, its host opened the show by saying, "Welcome to SportsChannel's 10th anniversary show, or as we call it here at the studio, 'Thank You, Michael. Thank You, Michael. Thank You, Michael.'" When Chinese schoolchildren were surveyed about the most famous men in world history, they chose revolutionary hero Chou-En-lai and Michael Jordan. At a press conference, a Japanese reporter once asked, "Mr. Jordan, how does it feel to be God?"

Even Jack Nicholson was known to pass up a Lakers game so he could watch Jordan play the crosstown Clippers. Jordan's athletic pursuit of a hobby (golf) and a childhood passion (baseball) received more ink than most all-stars' sporting careers. His return to basketball, in 1995, was billed as the Second Coming, even pushing the O. J. Simpson double-murder trial off the front pages and eliciting the same type of media frenzy that was thought to have driven him out of the game in the first place.

Halberstam wrote that Jordan "has given us, among other things, a new definition of male beauty." In fact, he became the marketing world's first truly successful crossover athlete, an African-American beloved by blacks and whites alike, by taking Magic Johnson's beloved stature to a level of acclaim unprecedented in American team sports. As *Sports Illustrated*'s E. M. Swift explained, ". . . until

Jordan arrived on the scene, only a handful of African-American athletes were able to parlay their multicultural popularity into anything more bankable than goodwill."

And Jordan has been paid accordingly. For several years, his income has been estimated at well beyond $30 million annually, less than one-eighth of it coming from his NBA salary. He has become the single most important spokesperson for several corporate giants, especially the Nike Corporation, which has become one of the most powerful voices in sports. In fact, on the day Jordan retired, the business section of the *Chicago Tribune* devoted nearly three pages to the story, and Nike stock dropped nearly a point.

Jordan's value as a commercial spokesman may never be matched, in or out of the athletic arena. But corporate America took note of the Jordan marketing phenomenon, and as a financial entity and an entertainment product, sports will never again be the same. "Though there is no one close to being as good as he is, he leaves the National Basketball Associaton, at least for now, with many who are nearly as leveraged," wrote Harvey Araton in *The New York Times* when Jordan first retired. "He leaves behind a new breed of American team-sports athlete, the one-man corporate powerhouse."

With Jordan leading the way, athletes are now corporate images. Charles Barkley, Andre Agassi, Deion Sanders and dozens of others have essentially become Madison Avenue creations. Shaquille O'Neal, with his Pepsi commercials, rap songs, movie roles and even his own logo, is a testament to the Jordan legacy. Said *Chicago Tribune* basketball columnist Sam Smith, author of *The Jordan Rules*, "They say Shaq has already eclipsed him, but Michael was the first. And the first man on the moon is always remembered more than the guy who stayed up there longer."

Yet, when all is said and done, Jordan's most enduring legacy is not about dollars and cents, but about the game of basketball. The Jordan image led to a cavalcade of individual stars in the NBA and spurred the league to places where only the NFL and Major League Baseball once ruled supreme. Indeed, when he retired for the first time, the question actually was posed: Was Michael Jordan bigger than the NBA? Most observers said no, but they hesitated. That's an impact.

16

Harry Wright

It was 1858, and an American sports manual described a bat-and-ball sport as "the leading game played out of doors . . . the favorite game of the country town, as well as the larger commercial cities." The name of this game, the most popular team sport of the early 19th century? Not baseball—cricket. The manual devoted four times as many pages to cricket as to the fledgling game of baseball. A cricket match between England and the United States one year later drew 24,000 fans.

But it was also in 1858 that Harry Wright joined up with—and starred for—baseball's premier club, the amateur New York Knickerbockers. Wright (his real name was William Henry Wright) would go on to play a monumental role in the development of baseball as the manager of the first all-professional team, but his background was steeped in cricket. Born in Sheffield, England, on January 10, 1835, he immigrated with his family to New York a year later. His father was a talented cricket player, and Harry began his athletic career with the local St. George Cricket Club, becoming one of the game's outstanding players.

Wright's sporting evolution would mirror that of the country. In the 1850s and 1860s, baseball moved from its purely amateur origins to a state descied by historian Harold Seymour in *Baseball: The Early Years*, as "a twilight zone between amateurism and professionalism, a semi-professional period in which hypocrisy reigned."

Teams soon began playing for a share of gate receipts, a practice spurred by a man named William H. Cammeyer, who enclosed a field in Brooklyn, built a clubhouse, and began to charge admission in 1862. In an attempt to produce successful teams, communities began to offer inducements, often in the form of jobs and salaries, to the best players they could find. Soon teams went as far as creating phantom jobs in an effort to reimburse their stars. Players for the New

York Mutuals, controlled by "Boss" Tweed, were on the city's payroll. When George Wright, Harry's brother, played for the Washington Nationals, he was listed as a clerk at 238 Pennsylvania Avenue, which happened to be a public park.

Professionalism was creeping into baseball, but it was clandestine and rather chaotic. Bidding for players led to an activity called "revolving," in which players would accept payment in advance from one team, then accept a better offer from another. It was in this environment that Harry Wright (and George) became nearly as important to baseball as Orville and Wilbur Wright were to air travel.

By 1865, Harry Wright moved to Cincinnati as a player and instructor for the Union Cricket Club. Meanwhile, Aaron Champion, a Cincinnati entrepreneur, believed a winning baseball team would be good for business. He built a new baseball grounds and, late in 1867, hired Wright to run it—at a salary of $1,200. Wright hired the best team money could buy, ignoring local amateurs and putting together a virtual all-star collection of players from all over the East. In fact, only one member of the club was actually from Cincinnati. By 1869, the Cincinnati Red Stockings were the first admittedly all-professional baseball club. The team's total payroll for the eight-month season, led by star shortstop George Wright's $1,400 contract, was $9,300.

The Red Stockings toured the country, travelling nearly 12,000 miles by train, playing before an estimated 200,000 people and popularizing the game immensely. The season began with a month-long, 20-game road trip through the Northeast. By the time the club was eight games into the trip, the players were national figures. Averaging more than 42 runs per game, Cincinnati finished 20-0 on the road trip, 57-0 on the season. When the Reds returned home to Cincinnati and paraded past cheering throngs, Champion exuberantly declared that he would rather be president of the Cincinnati Base Ball Club than President of the United States.

During the 1870 campaign, the club was visited by several distractions: drinking problems, jealousy among the players, injuries and newspaper criticism. The Reds even raised ticket prices from 25 cents to 50 cents, causing a drop in attendance. Yet, Cincinnati continued to dominate, proving the superiority of professional teams. After increasing their winning streak to 81 games, they finally met their match in the Brooklyn Atlantics. Some 20,000 paying spectators watched as the game was tied 5-5 after nine innings. Harry Wright then suggested a novel concept to extend what many called the finest game ever played—extra innings. Cincinnati took a 7-5 lead, but Brooklyn came back to win 8-7.

With the streak over, the club lost spectators and investors, and the Cincinnati Red Stockings disbanded following the 1870 season. But the team's success was soon widely copied, and in 1871, a group of ten professional clubs met in New York to form the National Association of Professional Base Ball Players. Wright—who had taken his brother, two other teammates and the Red Stockings name to Boston—headed a steering committee that drew up the league's constitution. "Baseball is business now," Wright explained, "and I am trying to arrange our games to make them successful and make them pay, irrespective of my feelings and to the best of my ability. If I shall fail then I will try and do better next time."

After losing the league's first title to the Philadelphia Athletics, Boston won the next four in a row. The National Association folded following the 1875 season—due, in part, to league-wide drunkenness and game-fixing rumors, in part to the formation of the National League, and in part to competitive imbalance created by Boston's domination. Wright's managerial record over the five seasons was 225-60, including a 71-8 mark in 1875.

Had Wright fallen off the face off the earth following the National Association's demise, he would still own a lofty spot among *The Sports 100*, but he continued to play a major role in baseball for eighteen more seasons. Wright served as secretary during the fateful meeting on February 2, 1876, that resulted in the formation of the new National League. He managed three teams over eighteen years, collecting 1,042 victories and winning pennants with Boston in 1877 and 1888. Though he never won another championship, his six titles in seven seasons is a managerial feat matched only by Casey Stengel.

By the early 1870s, Wright was widely known as the "Father of the Game," a man who the *Cincinnati Enquirer* claimed "eats base-ball, breathes base-ball, thinks base-ball, dreams base-ball, and incorporates base-ball into his prayers." Though Wright insisted that his players retain the spirit of amateurism, he himself, by introducing professionalism, ushered in an age of win-at-all-costs baseball, an era of on-field trickery that lasted through the end of the century.

But many of Wright's innovations have lasted as long as the game. As a manager, he dressed his Reds in knickers, instead of the old-style long pants. He also introduced pregame batting practice, coaches' hand signals and the concept of one fielder backing up another. As a sometime pitcher, he is credited as being one of the first to make use of the change up. And, in the late 1870s, he helped revolutionize pitching by moving the pitcher's box back, making every pitch count as a ball or a strike, eliminating restrictions on the pitcher's delivery and proposing that the batter no longer be allowed to call for a high or low pitch.

Clearly, Wright's influence—on and off the field—was remarkable. When Wright finally retired from the game, in 1893, a tribute in *Sporting Life* said of him, "Every magnate in the country is indebted to this man for the establishment of base ball as a business, and every patron, for furnishing him with a systematic recreation. Every player is indebted to him for inaugurating an occupation by which he gains livelihood."

A major league job, Chief of Umpires, was created for Wright—ironically, as his vision was failing—and he held the post until his death two years later. On the day he died, October 3, 1895, major league owners held a Harry Wright Day to raise funds for a monument to the man most responsible for the emergence of professional baseball.

Yet, Wright was virtually overlooked when it came time to enshrine the game's eminent figures in Cooperstown. George Wright, who was the better player, was inducted into the Hall of Fame in 1937. But Harry Wright, just a .263 hitter, wasn't elected until 1953.

PIONEERING PAYROLL

The payroll of the 1869 Cincinnati Red Stockings, listing each player with their professions on and off the field, was as follows:

- George Wright (engraver, shortstop) $1,400
- Harry Wright (jeweler, center field, manager) $1,200
- Asa Brainard (insurance, pitcher) $1,100
- Fred Waterman (insurance, third base) $1,000
- Calvin A. McVey (piano maker, right field) $800
- Andrew J. Leonard (hatter, left field) $800
- Charles H. Gould (bookkeeper, first base) $800
- Charles Sweasy (hatter, second base) $800
- Douglas Allison (marble cutter, catcher) $800
- Richard Hurley (trade unknown, substitute) $600

*source: Harold Seymour, *Baseball: The Early Years*

17

William Hulbert

Until 1995, there was a plaque missing from Cooperstown. As the man who founded the National League, the most enduring circuit in professional sports, William Hulbert must be considered one of the twenty most influential figures in the history of American athletics. Yet, more than 200 figures in baseball history were immortalized before Hulbert. In fact, in a case of mistaken identity, Hulbert's handpicked choice as the first National League president—Morgan Bulkeley, who served for only one year—was elected to the Hall of Fame in 1937. Hulbert had to wait another fifty-eight years.

Hulbert's aggressive actions essentially created Major League Baseball as we know it today, and the organizational theory behind his actions has had an equally resounding effect on the business of sport. As baseball historian Harold Seymour explains, "In the years to come, the League would bring professional baseball both stability and the disruption of bitter trade wars. It would bring both a superior brand of ball playing and trouble with the ball players. It would build up public confidence in baseball, yet at times create public disillusionment." Hulbert had set the stage for highs and lows of modern professional sports.

Hulbert was born on October 23, 1832, in a small town in Otsego County, New York, not too far from Cooperstown. He grew up in Chicago, attended Beloit College, and then spent fifteen years as a member of the Chicago Board of Trade. By 1875, he owned the Chicago White Stockings of baseball's first professional league, the National Association of Professional Base Ball Players. The disorganized NAPBP would fold following the season—with the help of Hulbert, and his plan.

Hulbert was a businessman who aimed to incorporate business principles into organized professional baseball. Seeing the chaos in the National Association caused by gambling, player disloyalty, weak franchises and competitive imbalance, he sensed his opportunity. His first bold act was a carefully choreographed bit of anarchy. He strengthened his own ballclub by raiding the most dominant team in the National Association, the Boston Red Stockings."

During the 1875 season, Hulbert convinced Boston's star pitcher, Albert Spalding, to switch his Stockings and sign with Chicago for the following season, reportedly telling him, "I'd rather be a lamppost in Chicago than a millionaire in any other city." With Spalding's help, he then brought three more Boston standouts—Cal McVey, Deacon White and Ross Barnes—into the fold, and he also signed future Hall of Famer Cap Anson away from the Philadelphia Athletics. By raiding the other clubs, Hulbert defied National Association rules, making him open to expulsion from the league. But he knew what he was doing. He told his new stars they were "bigger than the Association" and promised to pay their salaries even if they were expelled.

Hulbert followed piracy with publicity. Using *Chicago Tribune* sports editor Lewis Meacham as his mouthpiece, he outlined a set of proposals to solve professional baseball's problems, and then incorporated them into the concept behind his new venture. His plan was to put a stronger organization in place of the existing one, a league of only selected clubs, from East and West (or at least Midwest), with solid foundations that would translate into greater and more stable gate receipts.

Hulbert convinced one western team from the National Association, in St. Louis, and two independent western teams, in Cincinnati and Louisville, to join his Chicago club in the power play. He then concentrated on the franchises that would form the eastern half of his eight-team league, calling on four more National Association teams—Hartford, New York, Philadelphia and even the Boston team he had plundered. Each team sent representatives to a meeting in New York City, on February 2, 1876, and 100 years after the Declaration of Independence, the impact of the meeting on baseball was much the same.

The National League of Professional Baseball Clubs was born.

The operative word there is "Clubs." The previous league had been the National Association of Professional Base Ball *Players*, a profound distinction. Indeed, every previous league had been an association of players, but the National League separated talent from management, distinguishing the men who played the game from the men who profited from it. Said baseball historian John Thorn, "Hulbert's great contribution to sports history is the idea of a professional league that was controlled by capitalists, rather than by players. He was the first one to apply that idea to sports."

In later years, Hulbert and his colleagues often claimed that their primary goals in starting the new league were to make the game respectable and save it from corruption. But the league was actually an obvious attempt to monopolize the game. The National League constitution allowed only one club to a city, and new clubs only would be accepted if they represented cities with populations of at least 75,000. The elitist nature of the league would eventually result in several challenges by upstart collections of franchises, league wars that would greatly affect the course of professional baseball.

Hulbert served as National League president from the league's second season until his death on April 10, 1882. His dual role as president of the league and the Chicago White Stockings occasionally left him open to charges of pushing through policies for his own club's benefit. In fact, under Hulbert's guidance, the league experienced anything but smooth sailing.

Gambling problems that had haunted the National Association didn't exactly avoid the National League. Indeed, the parity in the new league actually appealed to gambling interests, and an owner-controlled league meant declining salaries, which translated to players who were easier targets for game-fixing schemes. But, much like Judge Kenesaw Mountain Landis when faced with the 1919 Black Sox scandal, Hulbert acted quickly and decisively in such situations. Most dramatically, in the league's second season, Hulbert expelled four Louisville players for throwing games.

It took a while for the National League to achieve financial and geographic stability. Only the Boston and Chicago franchises lasted through the league's formative years. Of course, the fact that the National League has endured for so long is a tribute to Hulbert's vision, though professional baseball's pitfalls can be traced to him, as well.

Hulbert's declaration in 1879, for example, that salaries were growing dangerously high, translated into the reserve clause to restrict competition among teams for players' services. Essentially, players were all but bound to a team for life, an often-challenged, much-maligned concept that survived for nearly a century.

Hulbert's blueprint for the organization of professional baseball has amounted to more than a century of player-management confrontations, with perhaps its nadir being the cancellation of the 1994 World Series. In fact, nearly a century before baseball's work stoppage, the first man to organize players into a union, John Montgomery Ward, admitted, "What was formerly a pastime has now become a business." Hulbert's legacy continues to impact the games, for better or worse.

18

John L. Sullivan

As a young boy, John Lawrence Sullivan supposedly penned a note to his classmates: "My name is John L. Sullivan . . . I can whip every kid in this room. I'm going to do it, too. Read this and pass it on." The note, apocryphal or not, represents not only the character of the boy who became the most famous man in America, but also the character of boxing in the nineteenth century. It was a haphazard succession of boasts and brawls—at least until John L. Sullivan came along.

When Sullivan first began boxing, in the late 1870s, he was a poor, indistinctive member of a downtrodden ethnic minority who was taking up an activity that the great majority of Americans considered one step above thuggery. There was a significant social stigma against his Irish American ancestry, and his so-called un-American sport. But within a decade, boxing matches were drawing thousands of spectators and Sullivan was the most recognizable man in the country, a figure approaching mythical proportions and the first of countless athletic icons to follow.

"John L. Sullivan emerged as the first significant mass cultural hero in American life," Michael T. Isenberg writes in *John L. Sullivan and His America*. "He was not merely a celebrity, a person known for being known . . . Sullivan was, like earlier heroic figures, famed for his deeds. But his deeds were controversial and conversational at the same time. People *talked about* John L. Sullivan in ways that they had not talked about, say, Lincoln."

While Abraham Lincoln and Stephen A. Douglas were involved in a war of words in Illinois in 1858, Sullivan was born in Boston, on October 12. He grew up surrounded by the trappings of urban life and anti-Irish prejudice. His father was a laborer, and though Sullivan always claimed he attended Boston College, no record of that exists. His formal education probably ended at about age fifteen.

Sullivan's first love was baseball, but he was already nearly 200 pounds by age seventeen, enormous for a baseball player in those days. He soon earned a neighborhood reputation as the Strong Boy, a nickname that would last through his celebrity. Though he had never been taught to box, Sullivan fought his first exhibition match in an opera house in 1878 and won handily. He came from an environment in which distinction was all but impossible, and saloons were the traditional means of escape. Indeed, he was an alcoholic by his early twenties. But in boxing, he had found an opportunity to separate himself from his peers.

Sullivan's name first appeared in print in March 1879, and soon after, he made the decision to become a prizefighter. "He might as well register to be a professional criminal, according to the lights of the law. No one in American history—no one—had ever made a living as a prizefighter," Isenberg explains.

Prizefighting had been brought to the colonies by British soldiers during the Revolutionary War. By 1838, the London Prize Ring Rules were standard boxing regulations in both England and the United States. The rules authorized bare-knuckle bouts and an unlimited number of rounds, each one ending when a fighter's knee touched the ground. The fighter then had thirty seconds to arise and walk to the center of the ring, or the fight was over.

In 1866, Englishman Henry Sholto Douglas, eighth marquis of Queensberry, drew up a set of twelve rules dictating a prescribed number of rounds, each three minutes long, and ten seconds for a fighter to regain his feet after a knockdown. The Queensberry Rules required gloved fights, ranging from skintight to 15-ounce gloves, with 8-ounce ones becoming most common. Sullivan fought in both types of bouts, and though he preferred Queensberry Rules, he eventually became known as the last of the bare-knuckle brawlers.

In some areas, especially New York City, boxing received widespread coverage through the mid-1800s. However, its popularity began to wane, and, by 1880, prizefighting was illegal in thirty-eight states, a typical statute mandating up to a $1,000 fine and a two-year prison sentence. As a sport, it was scorned, particularly the gloveless variety. As a commercial spectacle, it was outlawed. Fights in remote locales, staged a step ahead of the law, were commonplace as Sullivan began his career. No one, not even Sullivan himself, would have bet that he would become America's first bona fide athletic hero.

In early 1881, Sullivan met Billy Madden, who became his first manager and quickly designed an unprecedented tour to showcase his fighter's skills. Sullivan offered to knock out all comers, backing up the boast with $50. Though Sullivan toured from Philadelphia to Louisville, he found no challengers and only sparred with Madden in front of larger and larger exhibition crowds. But over the course of the tour he earned more than $6,000—more than triple what he would have made outside the ring.

Sullivan's growing reputation earned him a bout in early 1882 with Paddy Ryan, the self-proclaimed "champion," in Mississippi, under the London Rules. It was the first American prizefight to draw "informed" opinions in advance, the talk of barrooms and barbershops across the country. Every major newspaper covered the event, as Sullivan knocked Ryan out in eleven minutes to become the 23-year-old champion of the world. He had earned $4,500 in the fight, as well as the attention of the middle class and the "respectable" press. Boxing was making inroads to mainstream America, and the legend of John L. had officially begun.

Sullivan defended his title ten times in the next eighteen months, earning over $40,000, a sum matched by few men in the country. He also realized he could use his fame to make money in additional endeavours, such as the theater, baseball exhibitions and even product endorsements.

His relationship with Madden had dissolved by late 1883, but a new manager, Al Smith, conceived a tour never attempted by any American in any field: an eight-month trip featuring 195 exhibitions in twenty-six states. Every major city and dozens of small towns would have the opportunity to see the great John L., who was confident enough to announce that, along the way, he would fight anyone for four rounds, with gloves, for $250. "John L.," writes Isenberg, "was literally challenging all of America to fight."

The tour featured Sullivan at his alcoholic worst, drinking and carousing almost uncontrollably, and at his athletic best, knocking out a total of eleven challengers, including one in two seconds. The exhibitions allowed him to net an estimated $80,000, about four times what the President of the United States earned at the time and about sixteen times the salary of the next most famous athlete in the country, Mike "King" Kelly of the Boston Beaneaters.

Sullivan continued the highs and lows through the mid-1880s. He drank prodigiously, displayed an unpredictable temper, became overweight, was involved in a messy public divorce case and saw his 2-year-old son die of diptheria. Yet in 1887, he could be found shaking hands with President Grover Cleveland at the White House. Soon after, a group of admirers presented him with a 30-pound, 14-carat gold championship belt encrusted with 256 diamonds.

"He was the most prominent sporting hero America had produced, and neither he nor anyone else knew quite how to handle the novelty of his fame," Isenberg explains. "He had won no elections, no military victories; he was not in the forefront of any crusade. Yet there he was, arguably the most popular man in the United States."

There were poems and songs written about him, and dozens of nicknames awarded to him, from the Boston Hercules to His Fistic Highness. Growing innovations, such as photography and the emergence of newspaper sports staffs, only added to his celebrity, which peaked on July 8, 1889, in what happened to be the last bare-knuckle championship fight in the United States.

Overweight and considered over the hill, Sullivan managed to knock out Jake Kilrain in a dramatic, 136-minute, 75-round outdoor epic in Mississippi. After the bout, Sullivan announced he would not fight again. He turned to an acting career, becoming the first of many athletes to star on the stage or screen, but his efforts were less than successful. By mid-1892, though he was thirty-four years old and sporting a noticeable paunch, he set his sights once again on the ring. On September 7, the largest crowd ever to see a prizefight gathered in New Orleans to watch Sullivan take on "Gentleman Jim" Corbett.

Sullivan had begun his career with clandestine brawls on barges and in backrooms. Now, he was fighting in front of thousands in a specially built arena, his actions to be relayed across the country by dozens of specially employed telegraph operators and newspaper reporters. His goal was a $45,000, winner-take-all purse. It was the only fight he ever lost, as a 21st-round knockout by Corbett finally stopped the great John L.

Though the bout did, essentially, mark the beginning of a new era in boxing—a transition to science and skill, not to mention gloves—it was not the defeat of Sullivan that caused the change; rather, it was the feats of Sullivan that made it possible. As for Corbett, though he was also Irish American, he never received nearly the measure of adulation accorded Sullivan. "You can't destroy a public hero," he said later in life, "without it being resented."

While prizefighters before Sullivan tended to fall into pathetic obscurity, Sullivan was still able to find fame and fortune beyond the ring. But the first half of his retirement was a succession of alcohol-related assaults and financial disasters. "BOSTON BOY STILL BOOZES" and "SULLIVAN IS STILL DRUNK" were typical headlines. His weight ballooned to 350 pounds, and though he had earned nearly $1 million, he saved very little, giving his fortune to friends, saloons, charities, prostitutes, total strangers and an ever-increasing collection of hangers-on. By 1901, bankruptcy forced him to pawn his beloved Championship Belt.

On March 1, 1905, the 46-year-old even returned to the ring, recording a dramatic second-round knockout of a man nearly half his age. Unlike George Foreman, however, the knockout did not herald a return to the ring, but rather a new beginning outside of it. Perhaps because he regained a measure of self-esteem, he reached a turning point in his life. He vowed never to drink again, steered clear of the violence that had marred his career and became one of the nation's foremost temperance lecturers. The man who had visited every saloon in America even supported antisaloon legislation. He died on February 2, 1918, with much more fame than money to his name, but with a good deal more self-respect than he owned at his athletic peak.

His legacy, however, is the whole package. As an athlete, it was not only boxing that he moved out of the shadows and into the spotlight, but the business of athletics, too. As a celebrity, his feats and flaws were equally on display, and that sort of spotlight has remained undimmed through the succeeding generations—from Babe Ruth to Barry Bonds.

"Without really intending it, he had helped make boxing, and indeed American sport, both a cultural and a commercial enterprise. Unknowingly, he had become a grandfather to the modern sporting tradition in America," Isenberg explains. "He was the best in us, and the worst, too. Love him or hate him, at his apogee it was difficult to ignore him. . . ."

"I'll Fight Anyone—Except . . ."

John L. Sullivan grew up amid anti-Irish sentiment, yet he, too, became a powerful voice of prejudice. The man who challenged America to a fight later amended that by saying, "I will not fight a Negro. I never have and never shall." His personal color barrier left one of his most talented contemporaries, a black man named Peter Jackson, out of title contention. And while his racism reflected the rising intolerance of the times, it certainly fostered it, also.

Even in his retirement, Sullivan remained actively racist. He became an important voice in the search for a "Great White Hope" to dethrone America's first black heavyweight champion, Jack Johnson. He also appeared on stage in *Uncle Tom's Cabin*, as many had done before him. But in Sullivan's version, Simon Legree was the hero.

19

Amos Alonzo Stagg

Sheer longevity is not enough to crack *The Sports 100*—if it were, the likes of Bear Bryant, Don Shula, Gordie Howe and Nolan Ryan would appear on the list. But in the case of Amos Alonzo Stagg, his longevity is second to none in the world of sports.

Stagg was born during the Civil War, on August 16, 1862. He died on March 17, 1965, at the age of 102, while the United States was embroiled in Vietnam. He was born before the arrival of American football, yet he lived to see Gale Sayers run. He scored his team's only points in the first-ever public basketball game in 1892, yet he lived long enough to see Wilt Chamberlain score 100 exactly seventy years later.

In fact, Stagg has the remarkable distinction of having been a contemporary of every single person listed among *The Sports 100*. He had the honor of observing everyone from Walter Camp to Joe Namath, John L. Sullivan to Muhammad Ali, James Naismith to Bill Russell, Cap Anson to Curt Flood. When baseball's first star player, Jim Creighton (#47 on the list), died, Stagg was two months old. When Stagg died in 1965, Michael Jordan (#15) was twenty-five months old.

Only a few years earlier, Stagg had joked, "I may go on forever because statistics show that few men die after the age of 100." But his legacy guaranteed immortality anyway. Had Stagg died forty years earlier, his rank among *The Sports 100* would be unchanged, because his role as a gridiron innovator, along with his contributions as a basketball pioneer, mark him as one of the most important people in American sports history.

Stagg was born in West Orange, New Jersey, one of eight children of a cobbler, each of whom fought hard to help the family escape poverty. Stagg escaped through education, earning a scholarship to a prep school, where he pitched for the school's baseball team. At the age of twenty-two, in 1884, Stagg enrolled as a predivinity student at Yale University.

Meanwhile, Stagg became the university's top athlete. In 1889, as an end on the football team, he was named to Walter Camp's first All-America team. But "Lon" Stagg, as he was called, earned greater fame on the baseball diamond. He pitched Yale to several championships, once struck out twenty batters in a game, and then, in the spring of 1888, hurled a 2-1 exhibition victory over the National League's Boston Beaneaters. Within a week, he was offered professional contracts from six National League teams, including a $4,200 offer from the New York club. That offer caused one early sportswriter to comment, "So long as a pitcher gets $4,200 for six months and a preacher $600 for a year, so long will there be good pitching and bad preaching."

But Stagg preferred to preach. He also reportedly disliked the character of professional baseball, a contempt he would later transfer to pro football. Yet, soon after refusing the offers, Stagg came to the realization that his poor public speaking skills were unsuited to the ministry. He quit the Yale Divinity School and became a faculty member at the YMCA Training School in Springfield, Massachusetts. He agreed to coach the school's football team, reasoning that "the coaching profession is one of the noblest and farthest reaching in building manhood. No man is too good to be the athletic coach for youth." And so the gridiron became his pulpit.

It was also in Springfield that Stagg's friend and colleague, James Naismith, first devised the game of basketball. When the Springfield students took on the faculty in the game's first public appearance on March 11, 1892, the students won 5-1. Stagg scored the one point.

When Stagg's former Bible teacher at Yale became the University of Chicago's first president in 1892, he offered Stagg a hefty $2,500 salary and an associate professorship to become the institution's first athletic director. "After much thought and prayer," Stagg replied in a letter, "I have decided that my life can be used in my Master's service in the position which you have offered me."

Thus began Stagg's forty-one years at Chicago, where he coached track, baseball, basketball and football. By bringing basketball to the Midwest, Stagg was instrumental in the game's rapid growth. As the first college in the area to play the game, Chicago was forced to schedule contests against local YMCA squads. But in 1896, Stagg's team faced Iowa in the first-ever intercollegiate basketball game. In fact, though Stagg is one of only two men who have been inducted into the College Football Hall of Fame as both a player and a coach, he is also in the Basketball Hall of Fame as a contributor.

Indeed, Stagg's contributions go beyond even the football field and the basketball court. As Chicago's track coach, he was a member of six U.S. Olympic Committees, and as a baseball coach, he is believed by some to have invented the indoor batting cage and the headfirst slide. He was also instrumental in the formation of the Western Conference, which became the Big Ten Conference.

Stagg posted a 214-111-27 record as Chicago's football coach, including a national championship in 1905, when the Maroon shut out eight of its nine opponents. As the years wore on, however, and Stagg earned the reverent title

"The Grand Old Man of College Football," Chicago began to struggle as a private school competing against big state universities. By 1932, a new president had taken over, and he had visions of forsaking athletics to make Chicago an elite academic institution. The 70-year-old Stagg was asked to retire and accept an honorary position as supervisor of athletics. "I could not and would not accept a job without work," he responded. "I am fit, able and willing, and I refuse to be idle and a nuisance."

It was then that Stagg embarked on the next phase of his coaching career at the College of the Pacific in Stockton, California. "I went west when I was a young man," Stagg explained. "I'm going west again, and I'm still a young man." In 1938, Pacific closed out its season with a 38-0 pasting of Chicago, which dropped its football program the following year. Though Stagg lost more games than he won on the coast, he did lead Pacific to three conference championships in his fourteen seasons, and when his nationally ranked squad went 7-2 in 1943, the 81-year-old was named national Coach of the Year.

Three years later, he was again asked to step down from active coaching, and so he packed his bags once more. This time, it was to Susquehanna College in Pennsylvania, where he joined his son, Amos Alonzo, Jr., as an assistant coach. Though Amos Jr. later claimed they were co–head coaches, Susquehanna's 21 victories with the elder Stagg on the sidelines have not been added to his record. Still, he managed to total 314 career victories, a total bested in Division 1-A only by Bear Bryant and Pop Warner.

In 1953, with his wife ailing and in need of warm weather, Stagg finally took an advisory role as special kicking coach at Stockton (California) Junior College. He remained in the position for seven years until September 16, 1960, when Stockton's head coach received a note from Stagg. "For the past seventy years I have been a coach," it read. "At ninety-eight years of age, it seems like a good time to stop."

Thus ended the coaching career of one of the game's greatest innovators. As veteran football writer Tim Cohane has explained, ". . . any time anybody thinks he has come up with something new, he soon discovers it is merely a reclamation with modification of something first used sixty-five to seventy-five years ago, and probably by Stagg."

Among the many developments that have been credited to Stagg are the huddle, the lateral pass, the reverse, the man-in-motion, the onside kick, the quick kick, the fake placekick, the end around, the flea flicker, cross-blocking, the 7-2-2 defense, the charging sled, the tackling dummy, padded goalposts and lighted practice fields. He was also the first to award letters to varsity athletes and to write a book of football plays for teaching the game.

Pop Warner is credited with inventing and popularizing the wingback formation, but Stagg may have made use of it as early as 1890, at Springfield. Knute Rockne played a vital role in developing the forward pass as an offensive weapon, but Stagg helped push through the play's legalization in 1906, and then installed several dozen pass patterns to make use of it.

Indeed, Rockne is also credited with perfecting the shift from the T-formation, which, along with the single- and double-wing, was one of the most popular formations in the 1920s and 1930s. But Rockne learned the formation from his coach at Notre Dame, Jesse Harper, who was Stagg's quarterback at Chicago.

Or as Rockne put it, "I got it from Coach Harper, who got it from Coach Stagg, who got it from God."

THE ANTI-PRO

While few men had a greater influence on college football than Amos Alonzo Stagg, fewer still were stronger opponents of the professional version of the game. It was he who instigated a resolution, adopted by the Big Ten Conference, which called for all former college players who had turned professional to mail back their varsity letters, and on November 1, 1923, Stagg issued a plea to "all friends of the game" to unite against what was then thought to be an uncouth competitor to the college game.

"To patronize Sunday professional football games is to cooperate with forces which are destructive of the finest elements of interscholastic and intercollegiate football," he explained. "If you believe in preserving interscholastic football for the upbuilding of the present and future generations of clean, healthy, rightminded and patriotic citizens, you will not lend your appearance to any of the forces which are helping to destroy it."

Amos Alonzo Stagg is not a member of the Pro Football Hall of Fame.

20

Red Grange

Those who saw him play couldn't say enough about Red Grange's skills. Sportswriter Damon Runyon called him "three or four men and a horse rolled into one." Grange's college coach, Bob Zuppke, described him as "a football stylist, a symphony of motion" who "came nearer to being the perfect football player than anyone I have ever known."

But beyond his talent, his well-documented collegiate feats or his equally well-remembered humility, it was one fateful decision made by Grange that earned him a nod as one of history's twenty most important sports figures: Red Grange decided to play professional football.

Today, it is news if popular collegiate gridiron stars choose not to pursue pro football exclusively (i.e., Bo Jackson and Charlie Ward), but in Grange's day, professional football was less than professional. "The game was confined mainly to tank towns . . . where gatherings—you couldn't call them 'crowds'—numbered four or five hundred on a good day," *Sports Illustrated*'s John Underwood explained. "People who patronized professional football were thought to be of a caliber you now associate with Roller Derby."

But college football was king, and Grange was its most princely performer. When the lure of money prompted him to continue his athletic career, it was only a matter of time before he carried—literally—pro football into the realm of respectability.

Grange was born on June 13, 1903, in Forksville, Pennsylvania. His mother died when he was five, and his father moved the family to Wheaton, Illinois. At Wheaton High School, he scored 75 touchdowns. He was also a state track champion, captain of the basketball team and a good enough baseball player to later receive an offer from Connie Mack.

An All-American halfback at the University of Illinois from 1923–1925, Grange scored 31 touchdowns and collected 3,637 total yards. He exceeded 100 yards rushing eleven times, 200 yards three times and 300 yards twice. His familiar orange number 77 on a blue jersey became legend once sportswriter Grantland Rice christened him the "Galloping Ghost."

On October 18, 1924, Grange put on perhaps the best peformance in the history of college football. In front of a sellout crowd of nearly 67,000 at Illinois, he dominated a Michigan squad that hadn't lost in 20 games. In the first quarter alone, he ran the opening kickoff back 95 yards and then scored touchdowns on runs of 67, 56 and 45 yards. After sitting out the second quarter, he later added a fifth running TD and passed for a sixth, amassing 402 total yards in 41 minutes.

The following season, Grange and the Fighting Illini traveled to Penn, where all of the important eastern writers of the day converged to form their own impression of the midwestern star. After Illinois had upset Penn 24-2, thanks to 363 yards and three touchdowns from its star, Damon Runyon announced, "He is Jack Dempsey, Babe Ruth, Al Jolson, Paavo Nurmi and Man o' War. Put them all together, they spell Grange."

All throughout the autumn of 1925, rumors had circulated that Grange would be leaving school following the football season. Two days after his final game, Grange not only confirmed the rumors, he shocked the nation by signing a professional contract with the Chicago Bears. C. C. Pyle, a man previously known only for owning two movie theaters, had proposed a barnstorming tour in which Grange would play a series of exhibition and regular-season games with the Bears. In return, Grange would receive $100,000—about twice Babe Ruth's salary and well beyond what was believed to be the previous high football salary of $500 per game.

The announcement sparked outrage from observers all over the college ranks, who considered pro football a shady undertaking and a threat to the college game. Even Zuppke, Grange's coach, reportedly told him, "Football isn't meant to be played for money. Stay away from professionalism." Grange responded by pointing out that Zuppke was paid for coaching, so why couldn't he be paid for playing? "I think I might have been more popular if I joined the Capone mob," Grange later recalled. "But I had a chance to make a lot of money, and I had to do it while the name Red Grange still meant something. I knew that in a few years there would be other Red Granges and I'd be forgotten."

There were, indeed, other Red Granges, but the original's timing—debuting in professional football's infancy and riding the wave of sports hysteria during the Golden Age—hoisted upon him the role of pro football messiah.

Grange's first appearance in a Bears uniform came on Thanksgiving day in a game against the Chicago Cardinals at Wrigley Field. Though he rushed for 96 yards, the game ended in a 0-0 tie. Grange and the Bears then began a pair of tours that featured seventeen games in seventeen cities over sixty-six days, much of it covered by many of the nation's most prominent sportswriters. The first tour consisted of eight games in the East and Midwest in just twelve days. The most successful exhibition was at the Polo Grounds in New York City, where 65,000 fans showed up, saving football's New York Giants from financial ruin. The second tour featured nine games in the South and West over a span of six weeks, highlighted by a pro-record 75,000 spectators at the Los Angeles Coliseum.

However, a closer look at the event draws mixed reviews. Grange himself was decidedly unspectactular, and, in fact, after injuring his left arm playing against the Giants, he barely played in the next five games, sitting out the last two completely. In addition, only five of the seventeen games drew more than 10,000 spectators. After the team's appearance in Boston, the *Boston Globe* even ran a headline saying, "Professional Exhibition Convinces Boston Fans That Football Is a College and School Game."

Two researchers in particular, Dan Daly and Bob O'Donnell, authors of *The Pro Football Chronicle*, claim that the "Ten Weeks That Shook the Football World," as they describe it, hardly transformed the game. "To sum up the Grange tours in a sentence: He made a lot of money, and he went over big in New York. We all know the effect the latter can have on the writing of history," explain the authors. They also point out that the tour "wasn't about establishing the credibility of the National Football League. Any progress made along those lines was purely coincidental. This tour was about money. This tour was about squeezing every last dollar out of the Grange phenomenon. When you schedule eight games in 12 days, you're not overly concerned with the quality of play."

Many of the crowds even booed Grange, especially when his injuries forced him out of the game. This, combined with consistent criticism about his decision to turn pro, caused him to boil over at one point and wonder, "What's the disgrace of being a professional, I'd like to know? You never heard a howl about Christy Mathewson or Eddie Collins or any other college man playing professional baseball."

Yet, the fact remains that Grange's barnstorming meant that nearly 300,000 people caught a glimpse of professional football, most of them for the first time. And it wasn't Grange's game that was most important, it was his name. "As a football player heralded as the greatest of all time, Grange has proved a failure," the *Chicago Tribune* explained after the tour. "But as a gate attraction Red can be said to have been a winner."

Indeed, Grange was such an attraction that he and C. C. Pyle decided to start their own league—the American Football League—in 1926. Grange's league lasted only one year, and then his team, the New York Yankees, joined the NFL, in 1927. In the third game that season (against the Bears), Grange badly injured his knee. He was never the same. After missing all of 1928, during which he acted in a pair of silent films and ended his association with Pyle, Grange returned to the Bears in 1929. He played for six more seasons and became an integral part of the Bears' new man-in-motion T-formation, which revolutionized the game.

After retiring, Grange coached for a couple of years, sold insurance and became one of the first successful athletes-turned-announcers. He lived to be ten years older than his old jersey number, passing away peacefully on January 28, 1991. Having lived so long, Grange was able to observe the long-term impact he had on the game. "We made enough pro football converts all over the land to give the sport the shot in the arm it so badly needed," he recalled, "and, from the 1925 season on, professional football began to grow steadily in popularity."

Most observers agree. "Grange," wrote John Underwood, "single-handedly took professional football out of the dark ages." Indeed, he gave the league its most important requirement for success: attention. And in any project in its infancy, there is nothing more important than publicity—good or bad. In the end, largely due to Grange, professional football became a valid option, for both players and fans.

CASH AND CARRY

Though promoter Charles C. "Cash and Carry" Pyle's working relationship with Red Grange dissolved in 1928, his efforts to turn sport into spending money didn't end there. Aside from attempting to form a new football league in 1926, he also organized the first pro tennis tour. This time his top attraction was international amateur star Suzanne Lenglen, whom he paid $75,000. Lenglen toured the country with five other players, netting Pyle some $80,000, but the project was disbanded after a few months.

Less successful was another Pyle promotion two years later—a Transcontinental Marathon from Los Angeles to New York City, which came to be called the Bunion Derby. More than 200 participants began the race on March 4, 1928, but just a few dozen arrived in New York eighty-four days later. Only 800 people watched what was supposed to be the grand finale in Madison Square Garden, and Pyle lost an estimated $50,000 on his last major sports venture.

21

Arnold Palmer

Arnold Palmer's legacy comes in two forms: Arnie's Army and Arnie's bank account.

As a golfer-hero, Palmer arrived just as televised sports did, and he became golf's most popular figure, swelling galleries and taking the sport to unprecedented levels of awareness, interest and passion. "Basically, he took a game that was a little too prissy, a little too clubby, a little too saturated with Ivy League men trying not to soil their cardigans, and breathed sweet life into it," wrote *Sports Illustrated*'s Rick Reilly. Or, as Vin Scully explained, "In a sport that was high society, he made it High Noon."

As a golfer-businessman, Palmer's relationship with attorney Mark McCormack evolved not only into the formation of International Management Group—once described as "the House That Palmer Built" (see chapter 12)—but essentially into the creation of the sports marketing industry. Palmer, the player, was greatly responsible for golf's evolution into a major American sport; Palmer, the pitchman, contributed to sport's evolution into a major American business.

His success was a product of both style and substance—and plenty of each. It was said that it was more fun watching Palmer play a bad round than watching anyone else play well; that in victory, he seemed immortal, but in defeat, he revealed himself to be comfortably human. Indeed, Palmer's game seemed a succession of disasters followed by brilliant recovery shots, such that one writer commented that he seemed to be able to "get it up and down in two from the deck of a sinking ship."

He was known for his dramatic charges to victory, but he was nearly as adept at losing dramatically, as in the 1961 Masters, when he needed only a par on the final hole to win and recorded a double bogey, or in the 1966 U.S. Open, when he led by five strokes with four holes to play only to lose in a playoff. Of course, that was part of Palmer's charm. "Of all the greats who have come before him and after him," wrote Dan Jenkins, "there was never one in his prime who created so much suspense and drama when he addressed a shot. One way or another, you knew something was going to happen."

Palmer was no expressionless machine on the golf course like Ben Hogan before him or, to some extent, Jack Nicklaus after him. He would cringe and moan and converse and cajole. He was less a focus of the gallery's attention than an object of affection. He was, said fellow pro Mark O'Meara, "probably the greatest people-person in the history of golf."

It is likely that there has been no phenomenon in sport like Arnie's Army, a roaming tribute to one man's charisma; a swarming mass that would often conquer two holes at a time, half watching Palmer play, the other half waiting for him at the next hole. Palmer drew crowds the way Muhammad Ali did, and he played like Ali, too. Noted one observer, "Palmer usually walks to the first tee unlike any other pro. He doesn't walk on to it, as much as climb into it, almost as though it were a prize ring."

Born in Latrobe, Pennsylvania, on September 10, 1929, Arnold Daniel Palmer was introduced to golf with a sawed-off set of clubs at age three. After learning his trade as a caddie, he won state interscholastic titles in 1946 and 1947, enough to earn him admission to the National High School Sports Hall of Fame. Palmer went on to Wake Forest University, where he became a three-time Atlantic Coast Conference champion. As a senior, he quit school to join the Coast Guard during the Korean War, finding himself stationed in Cleveland, where he won two Ohio Amateur titles.

In 1954, Palmer burst onto the national scene by winning the U.S. Amateur Championship. Seven months later, he turned professional, and in 1955 he won his first PGA Tour event, the Canadian Open. Palmer won two tournaments in 1956, and four in 1957. In 1958, he began a six-year run matched by only a handful of golfers in history. In those half-dozen years, he took all seven of his major titles, winning every Grand Slam tournament except the PGA Championship, where he placed second three times. He would go on to sixty-one PGA Tour victories and several more on the Senior Tour, including two PGA Senior Championships and the 1981 U.S. Senior Open.

If any year best captures the image and impact of Palmer, however, it is 1960, a year in which he placed at least seventh in all four Grand Slam events, winning two of them, and named *Sports Illustrated*'s Sportsman of the Year. As Jenkins explained, "It wasn't until 1960 that he became Arnold Palmer, the Arnold of 'Whoo-ha, go get 'em, Arnie!'"

First came the Masters, where Palmer triumphed by recording birdies on each of the final two holes, the kind of final-round charge that Palmer seemed to invent. He had won the Masters for the first time in 1958, and would win it again in 1962, despite being three strokes back with nine holes to play, and again in 1964. In fact, Palmer never finished worse than ninth at Augusta National between 1958 and 1967. Coincidentally, the tournament was first broadcast on CBS in 1956, meaning in a national audience's first dozen glimpses of Augusta's majesty, Palmer was always king—or at least challenging for the crown.

Hitching up his pants, grimacing or grinning with every shot, Palmer was made for television in much the same manner as President John F. Kennedy. Much as it would with Michael Jordan two decades later, the merger of sport and television made Palmer a star. That was most evident in the 1960 U.S. Open, where the sport enjoyed an almost mythical meeting of the generations, in the forms of 47-year-old Ben Hogan, 20-year-old Jack Nicklaus and 30-year-old Palmer. Explains McCormack, "It was the last dying gasp of Hogan, the first glimmer of the marvelous potential of Nicklaus, and the brightest moment in the era of Palmer. He would never win another Open, but Palmer won this one like no one ever has."

After three rounds at the Cherry Hills Country Club, outside Denver, Palmer was tied for 15th place, seven strokes behind the leader. Having been given absolutely no chance of winning, he drove the green of the par-four first hole, birdied the next four holes and six of the first seven and carded a 30 on the front nine. His 65 for the round catapulted him past Hogan (who faltered only at the end and placed ninth) and Nicklaus (who finished second). With the charge of all charges, Palmer had struck a chord with the American public, and when he stepped back from his final putt, and flung his visor into the air, all of American golf rose with it.

However, Palmer's influence wasn't limited to this side of the Atlantic. In 1960, he also decided to compete in the British Open for the first time, hoping to match Hogan's feat of winning three Grand Slam titles in one year. Palmer didn't win; he placed second. But merely by bringing his popularity and reverence for history to golf's birthplace, he made a remarkable impact.

The British Open had lost its luster for Americans. Ben Hogan, for instance, competed in major championships for three decades, but only once overseas (though he won it). Sam Snead played in ninety-two major tournaments in his career, but just three British Opens (though he, too, won one). Palmer failed to win it in his first attempt, but he was so captivated by the event that he returned almost every year. Naturally, he won the event in his second and third appearances. "When Palmer went, all the other Americans went, too," said Frank Hannigan, former executive director of the U.S. Golf Association, "and the British Open was restored to its former majesty."

How popular was Palmer? When the Duke of Windsor was asked if he could be any man in the world other than himself, he announced he would like to be Arnold Palmer. When Palmer competed in a 1972 exhibition match in Stockholm, his caddie was Prince Bertil of Sweden. When Palmer's shot struck a spectator at a tournament in 1987, the woman told him, "This is such an honor to be hit by you, this is the greatest day of my life."

The politically conservative Palmer was frequently badgered to run for office, coming closest in the 1960s when Pennsylvania Governor Raymond Shafer collected more than $1 million in pledges in an attempt to make Palmer his successor.

Palmer declined, though he did say, "I thought seriously about the presidency, but I decided I couldn't afford the pay cut."

Indeed, Palmer's popularity has been parlayed quite ingeniously into profit. In 1960, Palmer asked McCormack to review an endorsement contract. The end result was the creation of International Management Group, with Palmer owning 10 percent. As Larry Guest, author of *Arnie: Inside the Legend*, explains, "It was a simple act that would change the scope of capitalism, not only in pro golf, but in myriad other sports. Arnie would become the preeminent athlete pitchman; McCormack would become the preeminent athletes' agent."

Palmer has totalled less than $3.5 million in earnings on the regular and senior PGA tours, yet he earns roughly four times that amount each year in endorsement and appearance fees, at an age when most men are collecting only social security. In 1994, at age sixty-five, having recorded his last major PGA Tour victory thirty years earlier, the "crown prince of athletic pitchmen" earned $13.5 million in endorsements, a total surpassed only by Michael Jordan, Shaquille O'Neal and Nicklaus, all of whom followed Palmer's lead.

However, even Palmer's endorsement opportunities are dwarfed by the breadth of Arnold Palmer Enterprises, which encompasses everything from apparel design, aviation firms and auto dealerships to land development, golf course design and club management. Palmer is also co-founder of The Golf Channel, a cable television venture launched in 1995 and an example of Palmer's using his influence off the course to take advantage of his impact on it.

But Palmer also planted money trees on the golf course. Just as the Big Three of the court (Magic, Bird, Jordan) took basketball to a higher plane in the '80s, the Big Three of the links (Palmer, Player, Nicklaus) did the same for golf twenty years earlier. Once a sport for those who already had money, golf became an opportunity to earn it. Of the three, however, it was Palmer whom the Associated Press tabbed as Athlete of the Decade. And it was Palmer, through his celebrity and television appeal, who played the largest role in bringing the green to the greens.

The total purse on the PGA Tour was barely $600,000 when he first turned professional. By 1966, it was $3 million; by 1972, it was up to $7 million and the number of tour events had increased by more than 50 percent. In 1980, the PGA Tour money leader award was named after Palmer, who had been the first to earn $100,000 in a season and $1 million in a career. He was both a product and a cause of the golf explosion.

So what kind of legacy did Palmer forge? Leave it to a contemporary of Palmer's, golfer Charlie Sifford, to put his impact in proper perspective. "If it wasn't for Arnold," he explained, "some of these scraggly wimps would be out pickin' cotton today. If they realized what he's meant to golf, they'd get down and kiss his feet."

STAYING POWER

The following were the top ten highest paid athletes (including salary/winnings, endorsements and appearance fees) of 1994, according to *Forbes* magazine:

1. Michael Jordan (basketball/baseball) $30.0 million
2. Shaquille O'Neal (basketball) $16.7 million
3. Jack Nicklaus (golf) $14.8 million
4. Arnold Palmer (golf) $13.6 million
5. Gerhard Berger (auto racing) $13.5 million
6. Wayne Gretzky (hockey) $13.5 million
7. Michael Moorer (boxing) $12.1 million
8. Evander Holyfield (boxing) $12.0 million
9. Andre Agassi (tennis) $11.4 million
10. Nigel Mansell (auto racing) $11.3 million

22

Jim Thorpe

Before Red Grange, there was Jim Thorpe. Before Jesse Owens, there was Jim Thorpe. Before Bo Jackson, there was Jim Thorpe. And before Michael Jordan, there was Jim Thorpe. Their various feats were, to some extent, merely imitations of his.

Certainly, nobody has been so universally touted as history's finest all-around athlete. In a 1950 Associated Press poll, Thorpe was named the greatest male athlete of the past half-century, with nearly three times as many first-place votes as runner-up Babe Ruth. This followed a similar poll ranking him just ahead of Red Grange as the top football player of the past fifty years.

Thorpe is in the National Indian Hall of Fame, the Pennsylvania Hall of Fame, the National Track and Field Hall of Fame, the College Football Hall of Fame and the Pro Football Hall of Fame. After dying of a heart attack on March 28, 1953, Thorpe was buried in Mauch Chunk, Pennsylvania, which agreed to change its name to Jim Thorpe in return for the honor. Engraved on the front of his red granite memorial are the words, "SIR, YOU ARE THE GREATEST ATHLETE IN THE WORLD," a remark bestowed upon him by royalty at the 1912 Olympic Games. Surrounding the epitaph are four etchings depicting four aspects of Thorpe's life—his Native American heritage and his careers in track and field, football and baseball.

In later years, Thorpe's family would attempt to return his body to his native Oklahoma, to be given a proper Indian burial. Thorpe, they say, had been exploited in death. With the epitaph, the four etchings and the eternal misgivings over his burial, never was a man's legacy so succinctly encapsulated.

Thorpe's remarkable impact as an American Indian cannot be overlooked. Boxer John L. Sullivan, an Irish-American, had come to prominence some two decades earlier. Jack Johnson, an African-American, gained the heavyweight championship at about the same time Thorpe arrived on the national scene. And baseball had a handful of talented Native American players, including Hall of Famer "Chief" Bender. But Sullivan was still white, Johnson was loathed by much of the American public and baseball's Native American stars weren't nearly at Thorpe's level of fame. Even as Thorpe fashioned his greatest triumph, the pentathlon and decathlon gold medals in the 1912 Olympics, American journalists were referring to him as "that child of the forest." To Thorpe, it was merely another hurdle.

Thorpe's grandfather had been a trapper of Irish descent; his grandmother a member of the Thunder Clan of Chief Black Hawk in Iowa. Their son, Thorpe's father, was the best athlete on the reservation. He moved to the Oklahoma Territory and married a full-blooded Indian, who gave birth to Thorpe in their one-room cabin on May 28, 1888. A member of the Sac and Fox tribe, the boy was called Wa-tho-huck, which meant "Bright Path."

James Frances Thorpe, as he was christened, actually had a twin brother, Charlie, who died of pneumonia at age eight. It was the first of several losses Thorpe would experience. Both of his parents were dead by the time he was seventeen, and his first son died as an infant. The tragedies made Thorpe introverted as a child, but, by 1907, he had begun to find his way, through the promise of an athletic career at the Carlisle Indian School in Pennsylvania.

The perhaps-apocryphal story concerning that spring reveals that Thorpe was headed to the football field when he stopped to watch members of the school track team practice the high jump. They kept raising the bar until none could jump over it, and then Thorpe asked to try, clearing the bar on his first attempt and breaking the school record. That performance earned him a spot on the track team, setting the stage for the second of Thorpe's four-pronged legacy.

Thorpe dominated the 1908 track season, taking first place in five events at the Pennsylvania Intercollegiate Meet. The following year, he won six gold medals and a bronze in seven events against Lafayette. These performances were par for the course for Thorpe, so much so that he found himself a member of the U.S. Olympic team at the 1912 Stockholm Games.

Thorpe conquered Sweden. First, he turned the pentathlon—a now extinct one-day competition in the broad jump, 200-meter dash, 1500-meter run, discus throw and javelin throw—into his world stage. He won every event but the javelin throw, in which he placed third, and easily ran away with the gold medal. He then participated in the three-day decathlon, his first ever, and proceeded to record 8,412 out of a possible 10,000 points, nearly 700 ahead of the silver medalist.

It was while King Gustav V of Sweden was honoring him for his victories that he told Thorpe, "Sir, you are the greatest athlete in the world." To this, Thorpe reportedly answered, "Thanks, King." The performance turned him into a national celebrity. In fact, after being honored with a ticker tape parade in New York City, Thorpe admitted, "I heard people yelling my name—and I couldn't realize how one fellow could have so many friends."

Of course, by then he should have been used to the cheering, albeit on a slightly smaller scale. With a combination of size, strength and speed seen in no other athlete of his era, he was already regarded as one of America's most talented football players. In Thorpe's four seasons at Carlisle, under coach Pop Warner, the team went 43-5-2, outscoring its opponents by more than one thousand points. After logging little playing time in 1907, Thorpe had arrived in 1908. He scored five touchdowns and passed for another in the first half of one game, kicked three field goal in another and scored his team's only touchdown in three other contests. "No college player I ever saw had the natural aptitude for football possessed by Jim Thorpe," said Warner, who coached for forty-four years.

After leaving school for two years, Thorpe was even better in 1911 and 1912. He had four field goals in one game, and an 83-yard punt in another. In 1912 alone, he scored at least three touchdowns in a game five times. And he was just as good on the other side of the ball, picking off four passes in one contest.

But Thorpe was not only a football and track star. He also excelled in basketball, baseball, lacrosse, tennis, handball, bowling, golf, swimming, billiards, gymnastics, rowing, hockey and even figure skating. Yet, on January 28, 1913, the world's greatest athlete suddenly became the world's most humiliated, as a *New York Times* headline announced, "Olympic Prizes Lost; Thorpe No Amateur." It seemed that in those two seasons Thorpe took off at Carlisle, he spent his summers playing baseball for $25 a week. Unlike most collegians who competed, Thorpe used his real name. It proved costly.

Having been asked to respond to the allegations, Thorpe wrote to amateur sports czar James Sullivan, saying, "I was not wise in the ways of the world and did not realize this was wrong, and that it would make me a professional in track sports . . . I am very sorry, Mr. Sullivan, to have it all spoiled in this way and I hope the Amateur Athletic Union and the people will not be too hard in judging me."

The people weren't, but the AAU was, replying, "The Amateur Athletic Union regrets that it permitted Thorpe to compete in amateur contests during the past several years, and will do everything in its power to secure the return of prizes and readjustment of points won by him, and will immediately eliminate his records from the books."

Many observers strongly condemned the short-sighted ruling. The *Buffalo Enquirer* added, "Jim Thorpe, amateur or no amateur, is the greatest athlete today in the world. They can take away his tin medals and his pieces of pottery and they can hold him up to the scorn of a few 'pure athletes,' but the honest world, the thinking world, the great majority of men and women will always consider him the athlete par excellence of the past fifty years in this country."

Devastated at being made a scapegoat in a misguided attempt to deter professionalism, Thorpe, nevertheless, remained one of sport's biggest names, and received several offers to appear on stage and screen. In a reflection of the hierarchy of discrimination at the time, when the nation was searching in vain for a fighter to dethrone boxer Jack Johnson, the American Indian was even touted as perhaps the best "Great White Hope" available.

But, instead, Thorpe chose to pursue the very game that had stripped him of his glory, signing with the National League's New York Giants. Manager John McGraw privately intimated that he was signed to sell tickets, and, indeed, Thorpe struggled in the big leagues, batting .252 over six seasons with the Giants,

Cincinnati Reds and Boston Braves. However, Thorpe continued to play some form of professional baseball for fifteen years.

But there was still big league football. By the time Thorpe joined the Giants, pro football was beginning to catch on, with Ohio as its stronghold. In 1915, the Canton Bulldogs pulled their biggest coup by signing Thorpe to a $250-per-game contract. He was football's greatest drawing card at a time when it needed one badly. Canton had been averaging close to 1,200 spectators per game, but the club drew 8,000 in Thorpe's first contest, a trend that would continue. Greater profits translated to the hiring of more All-Americans, and Canton dominated pro football until World War I halted the progress of the game. After the war, the forerunner to the National Football League was formed, and the league's PR-minded owners tabbed Thorpe as their figurehead president.

By 1922, Thorpe had organized his own team, the Oorang Indians, most of whom were Carlisle graduates. The team lasted two seasons, and then Thorpe became somewhat of a vagabond, playing with seven teams in the next seven years. He didn't walk away from the game for good until after he had passed his fortieth birthday.

Thorpe's life, after athletics, marked the same fall from glory found in the stories of Joe Louis and John L. Sullivan. Twice divorced and a victim of alcohol abuse, he found survival difficult during the Depression, and drifted from job to job. He occasionally worked as an extra in Hollywood films, usually as an Indian chief; joined the lecture circuit and then the Merchant Marines; and then found work as a bouncer. When the film "Jim Thorpe—All-American," starring Burt Lancaster, was released in 1951, Thorpe, who had already sold his life story for a pittance, didn't receive a dime. The world's greatest all-around athlete was living in a trailer park when he died.

Many of Thorpe's friends and family members pointed to the loss of his gold medals as the true beginning of his downfall. As Thorpe himself had once written, "Rules are like steam rollers. There is nothing they won't do to flatten the man who stands in their way." As early as 1943, attempts had been made to get him reinstated, but it wasn't until October 13, 1982, that the International Olympic Committee returned Thorpe's name to the record books. Three months later, his gold medals were returned.

Thorpe's legacy—as a Native American All-American, as football's first national drawing card, as the ultimate athlete and as a victim of the backlash against professionalism—had already been secure. But now, some three decades after his death, he could finally rest in peace.

Poll Vault

A February 1950 poll, taken by the Associated Press, tabbed Jim Thorpe as the greatest athlete of the first half of the 20th century. The following is a list of those top ten selections (with their vote totals):

1. Jim Thorpe	875
2. Babe Ruth	539
3. Jack Dempsey	246
4. Ty Cobb	148
5. Bobby Jones	88
6. Joe Louis	73
7. Red Grange	57
8. Jesse Owens	54
9. Lou Gehrig	34
10. Bronko Nagurski	26

Babe Didrikson Zaharias

Fame and athletic dominance, alone, aren't enough to merit inclusion among America's most important sports figures. They generally have to be accompanied by an impact, a profound legacy that altered the sporting scene. But Babe Didrikson's fame and dominance were her impact.

At a time when female athletes were considered freakish at best, downright unacceptable at worst, Didrikson became one of the most popular athletic figures in the nation—and, for the most part, she maintained that popularity for more than two decades. Along the way, her influence came intangibly, in the form of an increased awareness of female athletic potential, and then, quite tangibly, in the form of the Ladies' Professional Golf Association.

Didrikson was called the "Jim Thorpe of modern women athletes," but that may not do her justice. Her athletic feats over the course of twenty-five years are nothing short of astounding. Between 1930 and 1932, she set American, Olympic or world records in no less than five different track and field events. At the 1932 Amateur Athletic Union national meet, she scored enough points to win the *team* championship single-handedly. And then, at the Summer Olympics later that year, she surpassed three world records, earning two gold medals and a silver.

She was an All-American semiprofessional basketball player, often scoring more points than opposing teams. And she was an excellent baseball and softball player, even appearing in exhibitions with a handful of major league baseball clubs. She had a 170 bowling average, several tennis and diving championships and, supposedly, the ability to punt a football 75 yards. After being named Associated Press Woman Athlete of the Year in 1932, as a track and field star, Didrikson won it again thirteen years later as a golfer. She went on to earn the honors four more times in the next decade, winning eighty-two golf tournaments as an amateur and professional.

"My goal," she wrote in her autobiography, "was to be the greatest athlete that ever lived." She didn't say "female athlete," and that, alone, provides notice of her contribution to sport, as well as her near-limitless skills. And she nearly lived up to her promise. An American poll in 1950 tabbed her as the greatest female athlete of the half-century. A decade later, in international voting to determine history's greatest athlete—male or female—she finished 17th, ahead of men like Red Grange, Joe DiMaggio, Bill Russell and Ben Hogan.

Didrikson's career spanned a decidedly unsympathetic era for female athletes. Even her friend, writer Paul Gallico, fanned the flames of chauvinism, calling her one of those women "who made possible deliciously frank and biological discussions in the newspapers as to whether this or that woman athlete should be addressed as Miss, Mrs., Mr. or It."

It also has been suggested that Didrikson, herself, fanned those flames. Susan K. Cahn, author of *Coming On Strong: Gender and Sexuality in Twentieth-Century Women's Sport*, writes that her "disdain for dresses, men, and middle-class etiquette as well as her later involvement with commercial promotions made her the perfect target for horrified foes of track and field. They saw the young athlete's lean physique, short hair, ever-present sweatsuit, and plain, unadorned appearance as evidence that athletic accomplishment did indeed result from or cause masculinity."

Yet, it was just that athletic accomplishment that made her a cultural pioneer. "Had she been more sensitive to the hostility around her, to the climate of negativism toward women's sports, she might not have tried at all. But she was dealing in instinct rather than intellect, and she could only do what was natural for her," write William Oscar Johnson and Nancy P. Williamson, authors of *"Whatta-Gal": The Babe Didrikson Story*. "She was not a feminist, not a militant, not a strategist launching campaigns against sexual liberation. She was an athlete and her body was her most valuable possession."

Didrikson's father emigrated from Norway in 1905, his wife and Babe's three older siblings joining him three years later. Mildred Ella Didriksen (original spelling) was born on June 26, 1914, in Port Arthur, Texas (she didn't become "Babe" until she clouted five home runs in one baseball game). In 1915, a hurricane destroyed the family home, and they moved seventeen miles away to Beaumont. It was an impoverished, gritty existence.

She played every sport in high school, with such success that one account of her basketball prowess in the school yearbook explained, "When 'Babe' gets the ball, the scorekeeper gets his adding machine, and then he sometimes loses count." Didrikson was so talented that, in 1930, she was recruited by the Casualty Insurance Company in Dallas, which offered her $75 a month to drop out of school and become a stenographer. Though she did work full days, she was, in reality, a semiprofessional athlete for the company's athletic teams, known as the Golden Cyclones.

She had led the Cyclones to second place in the 1930 and 1931 AAU national track and field meets, also scoring more than 32 points a game to lead her team to a national basketball title. The *Dallas Morning News* already touted her as "the world's outstanding all round feminine athlete," but the publicity turned her into a self-centered prima donna, and her teammates cultivated a genuine dislike for her. Her celebrity grew even greater at an AAU meet on July 16, 1932, when she won six gold medals and broke four world records, totalling 30 points. The entire second-place team scored 22.

It was during the height of the Depression, when more than 15 million Americans were out of work, that Didrikson approached her peak. Her performance and personality captured the imagination of the public at the 1932 Olympic Games in Los Angeles. Didrikson became a sports legend due to a combination of factors—among them the need for Depression-era escapism, the hyperbolic residue from sport's Golden Age, Hollywood's preoccupation with celebrity and, most of all, the package that made up the Babe.

"I came out here to beat everything in sight, and that's just what I'm going to do," she said, exhibiting the country charm of Dizzy Dean, the brashness of Muhammad Ali and the skills of Jesse Owens. She won the 80-meter hurdles and the javelin throw, in which she shattered the world record by more than eleven feet. She then joined teammate Jean Shiley in setting a world record in the high jump, the only other event in which she was allowed to compete. But Shiley was ruled the winner, and Didrikson the silver medalist, because Babe's head cleared the bar before the rest of her body, a rule that no longer exists. After the Games, Grantland Rice was moved to describe Didrikson as "the most flawless section of muscle harmony, of complete mental and physical coordination, the world of sport has ever known."

She returned to Texas confronted by a crowd of 10,000, a dozen bands and a parade, but she soon fell victim to a lack of athletic opportunity. Didrikson was banned from amateur competition after allowing her name and likeness to be used in an automobile advertisement. She then became one of the first women to attempt to make a living as a professional athlete. As her biographers explain, she found that "to be a great woman athlete and a professional in the 1930s was like being . . . a great actress with only a traveling cornfield carnival for a stage."

She peformed on the vaudeville circuit, traveled with a basketball squad called Babe Didrikson's All-Americans and toured with the bearded House of David baseball team. All the while, she still collected a regular paycheck from Employers Casualty. Though she earned more than $40,000 in less than four years, the new Didrikson persona—humbled but still lacking humility—was scorned by many as an example of the dangers of women's athletics.

Joe Williams, of the *New York World-Telegram*, tried to shrug off her Olympic feats, writing, "By her championship accomplishments she had merely demonstrated that in athletics women didn't belong, and it would be much better if she and her ilk stayed at home, got themselves prettied up and waited for the phone to ring."

But Didrikson would return to the top in a completely different sport—and still be there two decades later. She took up golf, one of the few sports widely regarded as respectable for women. After six months of lessons in 1933, she entered her first tournament in 1934. In 1935, she entered the Texas Women's Amateur Championship, and promptly won it. But the victory was followed by a USGA ruling that due to her professional status in other sports, she must be barred from amateur golf.

Unfazed, Didrikson signed with Wilson Sporting Goods and announced that she would be "a business woman golfer," touring for two months with golf great Gene Sarazen. She soon took another major step, changing her looks and attempting to appear more feminine. In 1938, she met professional wrestler George Zaharias, known as The Weeping Greek from Cripple Creek, and by the end of the year she was Babe Didrikson Zaharias.

Yearning for more tournaments, Zaharias decided to regain her amateur status, and the USGA finally reinstated her in 1943. The 1945 season earned her AP Woman Athlete of the Year honors, and beginning in the summer of 1946, she won seventeen straight tournaments. By August 1947, she was a professional once again, and though she earned more than $100,000 commanding lucrative exhibition fees, she won only $3,400 on the tour. Along with another star golfer, Patty Berg, Zaharias decided to expand the women's tour, creating the LPGA.

She was George Halas and Red Grange rolled into one, as one of the tour's founders as well as its biggest drawing card. Her rivalry with Berg and Louise Suggs had much the same impact on the LPGA that the Magic versus Larry battles would have on the NBA. Zaharias also played to the galleries in much the same manner as Arnold Palmer a few years later. Said Berg, "Babe changed the game of golf for women—not only by bringing about the LPGA, but by her kind of golf. She came along with that great power game, and it led to lower scores and more excitement . . . And she brought all that humor and showmanship to the game. She humanized it."

But her most dramatic accomplishment was still to come. In April 1953, she was diagnosed with colon cancer and underwent a colostomy, yet fourteen weeks after surgery, she was playing in a golf tournament. In her next tournament, she finished third, and when the season ended she was sixth on the earnings list, edging out returning war hero Ted Williams for the Comeback of the Year award. The following year, she won five tournaments, including her third U.S. Open title, this one by a record twelve strokes. She had come back from radical cancer surgery to regain her position as the world's foremost female athlete.

But in 1955, the cancer returned, and the woman who had compiled a more publicized athletic career than any female in history slowly began to waste away. When she died, on September 27, 1956, her friend, President Dwight D. Eisenhower, opened a press conference by saying, "Ladies and gentleman, I should like to take one minute to pay a tribute to Mrs. Zaharias, Babe Didrikson. She was a woman who in her athletic career certainly won the admiration of every person in the United States, all sports people over the world. I think every one of us feels sad that finally she had to lose this last one of all her battles."

As a crusader for equality in the eyes of the American public, however, she had come a long way toward winning the war.

THE ORIGINS OF THE LPGA

In December 1944, a group of women, led by Betty Hicks and Hope Seignious, formed the Women's Professional Golf Association. For four years, Seignous, whose father had helped finance the tour, devoted herself to making the WPGA work. She organized countless clinics, published a women's golf magazine and put on a Women's Open Championship. But by 1948, the WPGA was in serious trouble.

Babe Didrikson Zaharias, George Zaharias, Babe's manager Larry Corcoran and Patty Berg met in Miami and decided to start a new association with the financial backing of Wilson Sporting Goods. The LPGA began with eleven charter members, playing in nine tournaments for nearly negligible prize money. Today, the LPGA Tour includes more than three dozen tournaments and more than $20 million in prize money.

24

Henry Chadwick

What are the chances of this happening today? A sportswriter has been heralded for his innovations and his lengthy tenure as a chronicler of baseball games, but he has repeatedly criticized players for their behavior, has never been shy to announce his importance to baseball, and often implies that he has meant more to the game than those who play it. Finally, at the age of eighty-three, he passes away. And here's the kicker: To honor him, the following day, flags in every big league ballpark are flown at half-mast.

Today, an unlikely scenario, but not in 1908. After all, Henry Chadwick was not your ordinary sportswriter. In fact, he is the only journalist honored with a plaque in the Baseball Hall of Fame, having been enshrined in 1938, before the likes of Eddie Collins, George Sisler and Rogers Hornsby. Only a few years before Chadwick's death, President Theodore Roosevelt himself called him the "Father of Baseball." And, while that may be a case of attributing fatherhood where none exists, Chadwick certainly was the game's guardian through adolescence.

The man most responsible for popularizing America's national game was not a native-born American. Chadwick was born in England on October 6, 1824, the son of a newspaper editor. He immigrated to Brooklyn in 1837, and lived there for the rest of his life. Chadwick played the British games of cricket and rounders, baseball's antecedents, as a youngster, and by 1856, having decided on a career in journalism, he was covering cricket for *The New York Times*.

It was in that year that Chadwick saw his first baseball game, featuring the famed New York Knickerbockers at Elysian Fields in Hoboken, New Jersey. He would later remember it as a nearly religious experience. He had found his calling. "It was not long before I was struck with the idea that base ball was just the game for a national sport for Americans," wrote Chadwick, "and, reflecting on the subject, it occurred to me, on my return home, that from this game of ball a powerful lever might be made by which our people could be lifted into a position of more devotion to physical exercise and healthful out-door recreation that they hitherto, as a people, had been noted for."

It was an idea as incongruous as it was ambitious. Said baseball historian Tom Gilbert, "If you would have said in 1856 that baseball was going to be the national sport, you would have gotten laughter in most places. In other places, they would have said, 'What's baseball?'" But Chadwick turned his vision into reality, becoming the dominant voice in turning a fringe participant sport into a game inseparable from the American experience.

Convincing his editor at the *Times* to let him cover baseball, Chadwick moved on to the *New York Clipper* two years later. He remained there for thirty-one years, simultaneously stringing for just about any publication willing to cover baseball. "He would get up at five in the morning, take a cold water plunge and then put in twelve or sixteen hours of writing," Gilbert explained. "He was like a one-man publicity machine for baseball."

As not only the nation's first baseball writer, but its first real sportswriter, Chadwick helped carve out a place for sports in American society, particularly his beloved diamond game. He did it by the sheer quantity of his work.

"People at the time thought that Chadwick's promotion and coverage of the game was actually an active reason why baseball became more popular," said Gilbert. "It added a lot of respectability, and at that time there were a lot of puritanical prejudices in America against sports in general. And Chadwick had these sort of Victorian values that he felt baseball embodied—discipline, self-control, hard work. He never talked about fun."

For years, Chadwick rallied in print against baseball's corrupting influences—from alcohol to gambling to high salaries—a moral stance that was embodied, at least in theory, in the formation of the National League in 1876. A typical Chadwick admonition saw him cautioning that "broken fingers may be easily mended, but a disfigured reputation may never be entirely repaired. Once more, abandon the bat, boys, if you cannot keep the game pure."

He took his self-imposed role as the conscience of the game quite seriously. More and more, he referred to the "good old days" of the game, while he paradoxically pointed it toward the future. But, as Harold Seymour writes in *Baseball: The Early Years*, his holier-than-thou attitude began to irritate the subjects of his diatribes. "Often . . . he saw the best in the old and the worst in the new," Seymour explains. "No matter how justified his criticism, it was not always appreciated."

Yet Chadwick's influence on baseball went deeper than simply his role as promoter and observer. He was an integral player in the codification and transformation of the rules, as well as the compilation of statistics and records. In 1858, Chadwick published the game's first printed rule book. He is also credited with developing the first scorecard, the first box score and many of the game's most fundamental statistics, while guiding the game through countless rules changes in the early years. "The game would look nothing like it looks now without him," noted Gilbert. "Without him, for instance, it would be legal to catch a fly ball on one hop. There's a whole list of silly rules he fought against and central rules he put in."

Even Chadwick admitted, rather immodestly, "Step by step, little by little, either directly or indirectly, did I succeed in assisting to change the game from the almost simple field exercise it was some twenty years ago to the manly, scientific game of ball it is now."

He was able to promote his opinions about matters on or off the field even more successfully once he delved into the publication of annual guides. Aside from editing the first weekly devoted to baseball, *Ball Players Chronicle* (1867–1869), he produced *Beadle's Dime Base Ball Guide* (1860), *Haney's Base Ball Book of Reference* (1866–1870) and *DeWitt's Base Ball Guide* (1869–1880). In 1872, Chadwick published the first listing of all professional baseball players, including all pertinent biographical information. Five years later, he compiled *Our Boys Base Ball Guide*, a guide to baseball slang that included words like "passed ball," "pop up" and "doubleplay."

Along with authoring how-to booklets on handball, cricket and even chess, Chadwick published *The Art of Batting*, *The Art of Base Running* and *The Art of Fielding*. In 1887, when the Base Ball Reporters Association of America was formed, the 63-year-old Chadwick was elected vice-president. Perhaps most important, Chadwick edited *Spalding's Official Baseball Guide*, which became the voice of the National League as well as a running history of the game, from 1881 until his death on April 20, 1908.

Just before his death, he had concluded a friendly feud with Albert Spalding about the origins of baseball. Spalding hired a commission to research the matter, which erroneously labeled an American, Abner Doubleday, as the inventor of the game. Chadwick knew better, explaining that "from this little English acorn of rounders has the giant American oak of Base Ball grown, and just as much difference exists between the British school-boy sport and our American national game, as between the seedling and the full grown king of the forest."

He didn't plant the tree, but he nurtured it.

25

Pete Rozelle

The National Football League was born in 1920, in a Hupmobile showroom in Canton, Ohio, but the modern NFL was born at the annual league meetings in late January 1960.

The owners who had gathered at Miami's Kenilworth Hotel were distraught. A rival league, the American Football League, had been formed a few months earlier. Even worse, NFL commissioner Bert Bell had died of a heart attack in October. The outlook was bleak, and most observers echoed the sentiments of Washington Redskins owner George Preston Marshall, who predicted they would "never find a commissioner as good as Bell, no matter whom they pick."

The leading candidates to replace Bell were Marshall Leahy, the NFL's legal counsel, and Austin Gunsel, the acting commissioner and league treasurer. Neither one was able to obtain the neccesary votes for election, and over ten days and twenty-three ballots, the owners were at a stalemate. It was at this moment of desperation that Los Angeles Rams owner Dan Reeves made a suggestion. What about his general manager, Pete Rozelle? To which another owner responded, "Rozelle? Who's he?" And so began the future of the NFL.

Rozelle had a reputation for genius, an amiable personality and, most important, no enemies. But his background was limited. After all, he was just thirty-three years old. "His suit had been tact, not toughness," wrote Kenneth Rudeen in *Sports Illustrated*, "and his life did not appear to have conditioned him in any specific way for the problems ahead."

Before he was Pete Rozelle, slick Park Avenue executive, he was Alvin Ray Rozelle, a grocer's son, born March 1, 1926, in South Gate, California. Rozelle was raised in nearby Lynwood, where he played high school tennis and basketball. He served in the Navy for three years after high school, returning home, in 1946, to Compton Junior College, where he worked as the school's athletic news director and as a sports stringer for local newspapers.

The Rams had arrived in Los Angeles in 1946, as well, setting up training camp at Compton. The contacts Rozelle made landed him a job as the team's public relations director six years later, after he had spent four years publicizing athletics at the University of San Francisco. In 1955, Rozelle left the NFL—he thought for good—and joined a public relations firm, his biggest account being the 1956 Melbourne Olympics. But in 1957, he was lured back as the Rams' general manager, becoming a solid but unspectacular executive.

And now, suddenly, he was being considered for one of the most powerful positions in sport. Rozelle, who had accompanied his boss to the meetings, was asked to leave the room at an evening session. In order to avoid the media waiting outside, he spent his time in the men's room, washing his hands every time a reporter entered. When he was finally retrieved, and told he was the new commissioner, he informed the gathering, "Well, I can honestly say I come to you with clean hands."

Rozelle's election was greeted with ridicule. Many sportswriters gave "the boy czar" a few months until he would be looking for new work. The *Los Angeles Herald Examiner* commented, "The enlisting of Pete Rozelle as czar of the National Football League has to be the zaniest act of the century." There seemed to be nothing all that special about the new NFL commissioner. But, as David Harris, author of *The League: The Rise and Decline of the NFL*, explains, "He was a man whose pervasive ordinariness masked what would later prove to be extraordinary talents."

When Rozelle took office in 1960, there were twelve NFL teams, there was no Super Bowl, most teams were worth about $1 million and there was a Gallup Poll out revealing that 34 percent of the nation considered baseball their favorite sport, while only 21 percent preferred football. By the time he left office, there were twenty-eight teams, the Super Bowl had become America's preeminent sporting event, the Dallas Cowboys had just been sold for $140 million and the Gallup Poll results were virtually reversed. Rozelle's tenure was nothing if not successful.

The young commissioner's first move was to transfer the league offices from Philadelphia to Manhattan. His past and the league's future revolved around marketing, he figured, and so the league would benefit by being as close to Madison Avenue—literally and figuratively—as possible. Rozelle's next order of business was to build upon Bert Bell's attempts to create harmony among league owners.

He strove to transform the league into "a single entity, like Sears or McDonald's," and his television policy was the perfect example. In 1960, CBS had contracts with nine NFL teams, each negotiated separately. The three remaining teams broadcast their games on other networks. The following year, the big-market teams, like the New York Giants and the L.A. Rams, earned around $500,000 from television revenue; the small-market teams, like the Green Bay Packers, took in about $150,000. As revenues increased, Rozelle realized the disparity would increase even more. So he proposed that television rights be sold as one package and all revenues be divided equally.

Rozelle borrowed the idea from the AFL, but the AFL had adopted it out of necessity. To make it a success in the NFL, Rozelle had to convince the owners in the league's major markets—the ultimate capitalists—that a socialistic policy was best for all concerned. Upon doing so, he then had to assure the plan's legality by obtaining a limited antitrust exemption from Congress. The result was the Sports Broadcasting Act of 1961. Writes Harris, "The bright, earnest, vanilla young commissioner had proved one of the better outside operators Capitol Hill had seen in a while."

Rozelle made a two-year deal with CBS in 1962 for $4.65 million annually. Two years later, the NFL was the beneficiary of an all-out network bidding war, leading to a $14.1 million-a-year contract. By 1967, teams like the Packers were enjoying ten times the share of broadcasting rights than they had received in 1960. Said Vince Lombardi, "What Rozelle did with television receipts probably saved football at Green Bay."

By 1966, Rozelle had extended an olive branch to the AFL, the resulting merger doubling the league's size, visibility and national impact. TV revenues, of course, continued to rise exponentially. By 1983, each of twenty-eight NFL teams was receiving some $15 million annually. The year after Rozelle retired, the league signed a contract bringing each club $32.5 million a year over four years. Under Rozelle, television and pro football had become inseparable.

But Rozelle's marketing of the NFL came not only through television images but through the image of the league itself. Soon after the championship game capping the 1962 season (in which the small-market Packers beat the big-market Giants), rumors of a betting scandal began to surface. Rozelle patiently gathered evidence for three months and then, with the league's credibility at stake, announced at a press conference that there was "no evidence that any NFL player had given less than his best in playing the game . . . ever bet against his own team . . . [or] sold information to gamblers."

He then suspended indefinitely two of the game's biggest stars, Paul Hornung of the Packers and Alex Karras of the Detroit Lions, for placing large bets on NFL games over the past few seasons. His performance under pressure, said Dallas Cowboys general manager Tex Scramm, "was the thing that made everybody accept him as commissioner and no longer as a boy playing the part."

By then, of course, Rozelle had firmly asserted his power in league circles. And when, later that year, he became the only sports executive ever to be named *Sports Illustrated*'s Sportsman of the Year, the magazine said of him, "He bucked the almost universal trend in professional sport by emerging as a strong commissioner—making vigorous decisions, not all of them popular, and proving that he could act independently of the owners who hired him."

Early on, Rozelle took on two of the league's longtime power brokers. In 1962, he forced the Redskins' George Preston Marshall to adhere to his television plan. Two years later, he disciplined George Halas after the Chicago Bears' owner-coach complained about officiating. "It's more like we work for him than he works for us," said Philadelphia Eagles owner Leonard Tose.

In fact, Rozelle became more than simply accepted, he was venerated. Jack Kent Cooke, owner of the Redskins, called him "as skillful a politician as I have met in my life"—this coming from a man based in Washington, D.C. AFL founder and Kansas City Chiefs owner Lamar Hunt, himself a monumental figure in the sport, referred to Rozelle as "the most important person in the history of professional football." Pittsburgh Steelers owner Art Rooney described him as "a gift from the hand of Providence."

Not that Rozelle didn't encounter problems. Lawsuits profilerated in the latter half of his tenure, as the growth of the '60s and the unity of the '70s turned into disharmony in the '80s. There were court battles—between owners and players, owners and owners, owners and the league. There was Al Davis's successful suit against the league, allowing him to move his Oakland Raiders to Los Angeles. There were players' strikes totalling fifty-seven days in 1982 and twenty-four days in 1987.

On the whole, however, there is no disputing that Rozelle took a still-maturing league and turned it into the model organization in professional sports. By March 1989, though, too much time in the courtroom had left Rozelle ripe for retirement, and so, four years after his Hall of Fame induction and twenty-nine years after taking office, he announced it was time for a vacation. Said New York Giants owner Wellington Mara, in a typical reaction, "I believe Pete Rozelle forevermore will be the standard by which all sports commissioners are judged."

26

David Stern

David Stern never played pro basketball. In fact, at 5-foot-9, he never even came close, his most sustained trip into organized ball being a stint in the New York Lawyers League. But few people in history have had a more profound impact on the game.

Born September 22, 1942, in New York City, Stern used to sneak out of his parents' midtown delicatessen and into Madison Square Garden to watch his beloved Knicks. This was in the 1950s, when the National Basketball Association was still a curious phenomenon, an interloper in hockey arenas, struggling to survive. That Stern would eventually lead the upstart league to a select position in American sport, alongside the NFL and Major League Baseball, seemed as improbable as a 100-point game and a $70 million contract. But stranger things have happened.

Stern would become NBA commissioner, and the NBA would be transformed, according to *Sports Illustrated*, into "an entity that is the envy of professional sports—an innovative, multifaceted, billion-dollar global marketing and entertainment company whose future literally knows no bounds." Stern would be voted sport's Executive of the Decade by the Associated Press in 1989 and the "Most Powerful Person in Sports" by *The Sporting News* twenty-five months later.

Sports Illustrated's E. M. Swift would describe Stern as "the best commissioner in sports, the best in the history of basketball and every bit the equal of the best sports commissioners of all time, such as the National Football League's Pete Rozelle and baseball's Kenesaw Mountain Landis." And thus, *The Sports 100* would rank Stern among the most important figures in American sports history, right behind Rozelle, just ahead of Landis.

Stern is a lawyer by trade, a graduate of Rutgers University in 1963 and Columbia Law School in 1966, at which time he joined a law firm that represented the NBA. He then went on to play a role in some of the league's landmark events, including an antitrust settlement in 1976 that led to free agency and the ABA-NBA merger. In 1978, then-Commissioner Larry O'Brien persuaded Stern to join the NBA full time, as its first general counsel. Two years later, O'Brien created a new position for Stern—executive vice-president, business and legal affairs. His responsibilities were primarily in the areas of marketing, public relations and broadcasting, all of which had hardly been tapped as the league entered the '80s. In fact, at the time, the NBA was on the brink of disaster.

In 1980–1981, the league drew nearly one million fewer fans than in the previous season, arenas were filled to only 58 percent capacity, and sixteen of twenty-three teams were reported to be in the red. It was assumed, by most NBA executives, that as many as one-fourth of the league's franchises would soon fold. Television showed little interest in the game (the 1980 NBA Finals were shown on tape-delay), and Madison Avenue was even less interested, believing the league had no marketing potential, lending credibility to a 1982 *Los Angeles Times* report that three out of four NBA players had drug problems.

Sports Illustrated's pro basketball preview ran under the headline "Can the NBA Save Itself?" The answer was yes, and the turnaround, beginning at about the time Stern was unanimously voted to replace the retiring O'Brien as commissioner in late 1983, has been remarkable. As the decade began, prospective buyers were reluctant to purchase the league's premier franchise, the Boston Celtics, for $18 million. Within a decade, the league's premier player, Michael Jordan, was earning twice as much as that annually in endorsements alone, and the Celtics were worth in excess of $100 million.

NBA Properties, the corporation responsible for all of the league's licensing merchandise, engaged just five employees in 1982, and was satisfied with merely breaking even. Within a decade, more than 100 employees were overseeing more than $1 billion in gross retail sales of NBA products. When Stern took over, the league's TV contract with CBS brought in just $22 million annually; in 1994, the NBA and NBC negotiated a four-year, $750 million deal. In Stern's first seven seasons as commissioner, the league set seven attendance records, reaching 90 percent capacity.

Perhaps the most important step toward the league's success was a landmark Collective Bargaining Agreement orchestrated by Stern in 1983. At the time, the NBA Players Association, led by Larry Fleisher, was contemplating a playoff strike, with the owners appearing to be equally entrenched. The Magic Johnson–Larry Bird rivalry had yet to appear in the NBA Finals, and Michael Jordan was a college sophomore. Fleisher realized that if several NBA franchises folded, several dozen players would be unemployed, and so the union agreed to a radical financial restructuring. The owners would receive an evolving salary cap for each team; the players would receive 53 percent of gross revenues. The agreement ended nearly a decade of confrontation between the owners and players, turning them into partners. It also turned the league into a model the other major professional sports hoped to follow, as the NFL instituted a salary cap nearly a decade later and similar attempts to do so in baseball and hockey led to a pair of strikes in 1994.

But while the other pro leagues were mired in lawsuits and walkouts, the NBA was able to concentrate on marketing its talent instead of mending its image. (At least until 1995.) And marketing is where Stern is at his best. Said Orlando Magic general manager Pat Williams, "David Stern can sell an anvil to a drowning man. He can sell a pogo stick to a kangaroo."

Stern's first order of business was to put the league's house in order. The NBA of the '70s and early '80s gave the impression of two dozen passengers scrambling for the last spot in a lifeboat. But Stern would accept nothing less than total harmony. Said a former employee, "All the teams were islands unto themselves. What Stern did was take the islands and turn them into a continent."

That done, Stern embarked on a mission to overhaul the NBA's image. To rid the league of its drug-infested reputation, the 1983 Collective Bargaining Agreement included a progressive yet firm drug program, designed to help players who came forward.

In 1985, Stern established the NBA draft lottery, which helped in three ways. First, it discouraged teams from playing to lose at the end of the season. Second, it increased the hype for incoming players, who quickly became touted as a "certain lottery pick." Finally, it became one of several peripheral television events, including two instituted a year earlier—the All-Star slam-dunk contest and three-point shootout.

The Legends Classic was another addition to the All-Star lineup, but it has since been replaced by an exhibition featuring the league's top rookies, an example of Stern's philosophy. No pro league has better prepared itself for the years ahead than the NBA, not only in terms of its future stars but also in its dealings with its future fan base. League-produced television shows, advertisements and highlight films have been geared to the MTV generation, and it has responded.

The NBA also has surpassed pro baseball and football in the international market. NBA games are now televised in more than 100 countries and foreign sales of NBA products have passed the $250 million mark. The 1992 Olympic "Dream Team" members were treated like international rock stars. Basketball is fast approaching soccer as the world's most popular sport—both a product and a cause of the NBA's success.

In the sound-bite, tabloid, slam-dunk world of the '90s, the NBA has dominated sport's cutting edge. Stern, with the strategy of a lawyer and the personal touch of a deli-owner, has essentially done with the NBA in the '80s and '90s what Pete Rozelle did with the NFL in the '60s and '70s. He has been so successful that the National Hockey League hired Stern's deputy, Gary Bettman, to work the same magic on the ice.

To nobody's surprise, when Rozelle stepped down as NFL commissioner in 1989, Stern was rumored to be at the top of the owners' list for prospective replacements. NBA owners responded by rewarding Stern, the ultimate free agent, with an unprecedented five-year $27.5 million contract, including a $10 million signing bonus. As one executive explained, "You have franchise players. He's a franchise commissioner."

TALENT OR TIMING?

Is David Stern's success a product of circumstance? Is the NBA's ascension due less to his leadership and more to fortuitous events like the arrival of players with star appeal and the emergence of a generation of sports fans with fast-paced sensibilities?

"Without Bird and Magic and several other players, it wouldn't have mattered if it was David Stern or David Copperfield," said Roy S. Johnson, senior editor at *Money* magazine. "You can't market what you don't have, at least not for very long. You can't market air; you can market Air Jordan."

Certainly, the league's stars played a pivotal role in the NBA's rise to prominence. But, most likely, Boston Celtics owner Alan Cohen owns the most sensible perspective on Stern's impact. "I don't buy that argument about his being in the right place at the right time," he said. "Timing is important, but with the same sequence of events, with the wrong guy in the pilot's seat, none of this happens."

27

Bobby Jones

When Bobby Jones retired from competitive golf in 1930, he did so not only at the top of his game, and not only at the top of *the* game but, quite possibly, at the top of any game at any time. Perhaps no athlete ever went out in a blaze more glorious. Jim Brown had rushed for 1,544 yards in his last season, a total since surpassed several times; Sandy Koufax's 27 wins and 317 strikeouts in his final campaign a year later also have been exceeded; Michael Jordan retired triumphantly only to return seventeen months later. But what Jones did in his farewell tour—win golf's Grand Slam—has never been matched, and what Jones did for golf in his brilliant career is just as unparalleled.

"Before Bobby Jones, the amateur golfer in America was considered an affluent fop who could not sign his name without two hyphens and an apostrophe. He was the sort of fellow who, if dissatisfied with his play, would sooner buy the course and redesign it than overhaul his game," writes Wells Twombly in *200 Years of Sport in America*.

In 1913, former caddy Francis Ouimet's U.S. Open victory had awakened Americans to the sport's potential. When Jones began assaulting the record books in earnest a decade later, the unthinkable soon happened: a golfer took his place alongside boxers and baseball players and football greats as an American sports deity. "In short," Twombly claims, "he gave golf a stature in the country that it had never had before; he made it a major sport."

Robert Tyre Jones, Jr., was born on March 17, 1902. He preferred Bob, but the world came to know him as Bobby. Jones had been born in Atlanta, but a fortuitous move to the suburb of East Lake, at the age of five, left him to grow up just off the thirteenth green at the local golf course.

In some respects, his adulthood was simply a matter of overcoming his youth. As a child, his head seemed too large for his body. Yet he grew into a very good looking man. His early golf experiences were marked by a self-destructive temper, but he grew into a model of decorum. He suffered from a digestive ailment which doctors believed would kill him before he reached maturity, yet he became a bona fide immortal.

From the beginning, however, he was a golf prodigy. At the age of nine, he won the East Lake junior club championship; at age ten, he shot a 90; at age eleven, he carded an 80; and at age twelve, he reached 70. As a 13-year-old, he became East Lake men's champion and won the prestigious Roebuck Invitational over the top amateurs in the South.

In the following year, 1916, he qualified for the U.S. Amateur Championship and made his first national headlines by leading after one round and reaching the quarterfinals of the match play tournament. It was then that famed sportswriter Grantland Rice, who would become a longtime friend and supporter, declared that Jones's name was "already written on the sporting scroll where only the select, those who combine surpassing skill with lion-hearted courage, have any reason to belong." Jones was fourteen years old.

Over the next seven years, Jones came to be regarded as somewhat of an underachiever, a victim of his fiery competitiveness. At no time was this more evident than in the 1921 British Open, when a disappointed Jones picked up his ball midway through the third round and quit on the spot. It was his first trip to St. Andrews, and he was vilified by the British press. It also may have been a turning point in his career, as he would never fail to win another British Open in which he was entered. In fact, he would come to be so beloved across the Atlantic that when he made a surprise visit to Scotland and St. Andrews, six years after retiring, he found 5,000 spectators awaiting him at the first tee. Twenty-two years later, he was made a Freeman of St. Andrews, the first American to receive such a title since Benjamin Franklin.

Jones would become equally revered in his home country. The events leading to such acclaim began in 1923, when Jones "finally" won the U.S. Open in an 18-hole playoff. The victory was perceived by many as long overdue, yet Jones was still only twenty-one years old. It was as if Ken Griffey, Jr., had been chastised for hitting "only" 87 home runs before his twenty-third birthday.

But discussion of Jones's "lean years" may be a product of hindsight, because for the next eight years he dominated golf as nobody had before and nobody has since. From 1923–1929, he entered the U.S. Open seven times, finishing first three times and second four times. Over that span, America's second most successful golfer, Walter Hagen, never even led in any single round of the Open. Even his close calls weren't close. In 1929, Jones was forced into a 36-hole playoff for the title; he won by 23 strokes.

One of those seconds in the Open would have been a first had Jones not displayed the kind of behavior that led Herbert Warren Wind of the *New Yorker* to describe him as "that rare sort of hero—in sports or any other field—a man whose actual stature exceeds that of the mythological figure he has been made into." In the 1925 U.S. Open, Jones called a one-stroke penalty on himself when the blade of his iron touched the grass as he lined up a shot, moving his ball ever so slightly. Nobody else saw it, but Jones would not ignore it. He wound up losing the tournament in a playoff, but when he was praised afterward for his sportsmanship he replied, "You might as well praise a man for not robbing a bank."

It was that kind of character that made Jones the most genuinely liked and admired golfer of his era, even while he was, according to writer Charles Price, showing an "arrogance toward par" and a "disrespect for the record books." In fact, of the twenty major championships in which Jones competed from 1923–1929, he placed first nine times and second seven times, including four U.S. Amateur titles, two British Open crowns and at least one major title every year. He consistently dominated a game in which even the best of shots can hit a pebble and roll into the rough, and even the worst golfers can play beyond their skills for a weekend.

But, in 1930, Jones outdid even himself. The term "Grand Slam" had yet to be coined, but it was widely understood that golf's four major titles at the time were the British Open, the British Amateur, the U.S. Open and the U.S. Amateur. When Jones won the first two events that year, he returned home to a ticker-tape parade in Manhattan—and this in the midst of the Depression.

Next up was the U.S. Open, and Walter Hagen, never known for his modesty, admitted, "Here is the greatest field ever assembled on any golf course. Here you have the survivors of 1,200 entries and yet it is one field against one man—Bobby Jones." Jones proved the point by using his famous putter, which he called "Calamity Jane," to roll in a 40-foot birdie attempt on the final hole for the championship. Afterward, Grantland Rice quoted a spectator as saying Jones "has caught the fancy of this country as no man, barring Lindbergh, has caught it."

By the time the U.S. Amateur rolled around ten weeks later, the press and the public had picked up on the "Grand Slam" phrase coined by writer O. B. Keeler, though one wag actually wrote that Jones was "storming the Impregnable Quadrilateral of Golf." By any name, it was an attempt at an unprecedented feat, and the pressure on Jones was enormous. According to Jones's biographer Dick Miller, the U.S. Amateur was "more than a golf tournament. It was a battleground of hope for a people experiencing the dread of the Depression. Jones held the promise of a man fulfilling his greatest potential against staggering odds."

The tournament was held at the same Merion Cricket Club, in Philadelphia, where Jones had first burst on the scene in 1916. It has been estimated that more than two million words were written about Jones over the course of the event, that 5,000 people turned out to watch him play his practice rounds and that a phalanx of fifty U.S. Marines was called upon to keep the adoring crowds from their hero. That Jones would win was never in doubt.

To that point, Jones had entered 52 golf tournament in his career; he had won 23 of them. He had recorded 13 major titles, a total surpassed only by the sport's most enduring champion, Jack Nicklaus. Only Ben Hogan's 1953 campaign, in which he entered six tournaments and won five, including three majors, even came close to matching Jones's 1930 heroics.

Jones received the first-ever Sullivan Award that year, given to the nation's outstanding amateur athlete. That, of course, may be the most amazing aspect of Jones's career—he did it all as an amateur competing primarily against professionals. In the words of one chronicler, Jones "played no more golf than the average dentist." He usually entered only four or five tournaments a year, sometimes just the U.S. Open and U.S. Amateur. He was essentially a golfer only on weekends, and selected ones at that. The rest of the time, he was an attorney in his father's firm.

Jones had received a mechanical engineering degree from Georgia Tech, and then a degree in English literature from Harvard. He then entered Emory University Law School at the height of his fame, passing the bar at about the time he was passing all others in the annals of the game. Golf may have been his passion, but it was not a priority. "First come my wife and children. Next comes my profession—the law," he once explained. "Finally, and never as a life in itself, comes golf."

Of course, regardless of his playing status, Jones's popularity raised every facet of the game. He was a lifelong amateur who still did wonders for the professional game. Said Hagen, "A first-place finish used to be worth a thousand dollars until he came along. He never won a cent in prize money, but when he left, prizes were up around five thousand dollars. That's the effect Bobby Jones had on golf."

Seven weeks after slugging golf's Grand Slam, Jones, still only twenty-eight, sent a letter to the United States Golf Association announcing his retirement. He delved into his law practice upon leaving the competitive game, but he didn't leave the game itself. In fact, he made a series of golf instructional videos and even became a vice-president of A. G. Spalding & Bros., for whom he designed the first matched set of steel-shafted clubs.

Jones could be found on the links until 1948, when he was suddenly stricken with a mysterious ailment. Later diagnosed as syringomyelia, a rare disease of the central nervous system, it slowly paralyzed him. He twice underwent spinal surgery, was forced to walk with a cane and was eventually confined to a wheelchair, his weight having dropped to 100 pounds.

Jones died on December 18, 1971, having fought off the disease for nearly a quarter of a century. "As a young man he was able to stand up to just about the best that life can offer, which is not easy," asserted Herbert Warren Wind, "and later he stood up, with equal grace, to just about the worst."

THE MASTERS

The man whose play defined golf's Grand Slam redefined it after his playing days were over. It was Jones who created Augusta National Golf Course, designing it with one of the world's leading golf architects, Dr. Alister MacKenzie.

The Georgia jewel was completed in the fall of 1932, and after Jones made an unsuccessful attempt to host the U.S. Open he decided to form his own tournament. He would hold it when the climate and the course was at its best, in early spring. Though the first tournament began on March 22, 1934, it soon came to be played in the last four days of the first full week in April. Originally called the First Annual Invitation Tournament, it was soon known as the Masters.

Jones was a playing host in the first tournament, and though he struggled to a first-round 76, his fame was still such that the next morning's *New York Times* headline read "Unsteady Putting Drops Jones to Tie for 35th, Six Shots Behind Golf Leaders." Even the final headline announced "Augusta Golf Tourney Won by Horton Smith as Jones Finishes 13th."

In the more than six decades since, Augusta National, with its magnolia trees, pine forests, dogwood and azaleas, has come to be the Churchill Downs and the Indianapolis Speedway of golf. The Masters, with its steady parade of green jackets, quickly became one of professional golf's four major championships, a modern Grand Slam event along with the U.S. and British Opens and the PGA Championship. And it has done so despite the fact that it is not actually the championship of anything; it is just a memorial to Jones, which is more than enough.

28

Knute Rockne

Was there ever a more unlikely American hero than Knute Rockne? He was born with a decidedly un-American name—Knute (pronounced Ca-nute) Rokne (originally without a "c")—and thousands of miles from American soil (in Voss, Norway). It was March 4, 1888, less than four months after a small college in Indiana, called the University of Notre Dame, had competed in its first intercollegiate football game.

Less than four decades later, Knute (which came to be pronounced Newt) Rockne (with a "c") would hold the golden keys to the Golden Dome in the Golden Age of sports. His name would be as well known as Babe Ruth, Jack Dempsey, Bobby Jones; Notre Dame's fame would be just as far-flung. And barely a decade after that, the all-too-brief life of Rockne, the Norwegian immigrant, would be celebrated in a film entitled—what else?—*Knute Rockne, All-American.*

Rockne came to the United States at the age of five, joining his parents and three sisters in Chicago. He became an outstanding amateur pole vaulter and half-miler, but he was forced to leave high school without a diploma after cutting classes to practice for a track meet. In 1910, after a short stint in the working world, he was accepted at Notre Dame, which then enrolled 400 students. He was already twenty-two years old when he arrived in South Bend, older than most of his classmates, and feeling like, in his words, "a lone Norse Protestant . . . invader of a Catholic stronghold."

Rockne took care of the religious dilemma by converting to Catholicism in 1925; he took care of the loneliness by joining the varsity football team. Despite his lack of size—he was just 5-foot-8 and 165 pounds—he was the school's starting left end from 1911–1913, during which Notre Dame didn't lose a game and outplayed its opponents by an average score of 40-3.

It was as a receiver that Rockne, along with Notre Dame quarterback Gus Dorais, would make his first monumental impact on the game. By 1913, Notre Dame had yet to become a legendary football factory, and Army already was. It was a big coup for the Irish, and an accident of scheduling for the Cadets, when Notre Dame managed to secure a match-up against Army on November 1. The Irish wanted nothing more than to make an impact on Eastern football, and so Rockne and Dorais took it upon themselves to practice a new strategy while at their summer jobs in Ohio.

The forward pass had been legalized in 1906. Still, the accompanying rules made it a less-than-desirable device. A pass had to cross the line of scrimmage within five yards to the left or right of the center and couldn't travel more than twenty yards. An incomplete pass, if touched, could be recovered by either side. The shape of the ball made it difficult for quarterbacks to throw spirals, and most pass routes called for receivers to run to a spot on the field and wait, where they would catch it much like a medicine ball. There was no such thing as pass interference, and nobody had thought of catching the ball on the run. Nobody, that is, until Rockne.

In 1912, the 5- and 20-yard rules were obliterated, and defenders were not allowed to deliberately interfere. The Irish tandem decided to make use of the new rules. Dorais learned how to throw a spiral and practiced throwing short, medium and long, as well as rolling out and fading back. Rockne learned how to catch the ball while in full stride.

When the season rolled around, Notre Dame and coach Jesse Harper used the pass play sparingly in the first three games, which the Irish won by a combined 167-7 margin. But when it came time to travel to Army, Harper unveiled his weapon. Dorais threw only four passes in the first half against Army, but one was a touchdown toss to Rockne, and Notre Dame led 14-13. Then in the second half the Irish took control of the game. Dorais completed 10 of 13 passes, including seven to Rockne, as Notre Dame trounced Army 35-13.

For the day, Dorais completed a record 14 of 17 passes for 243 yards, spurring *The New York Times* to announce: NOTRE DAME OPEN PLAY AMAZES ARMY. "The Westerners," said the article, "flashed the most sensational football ever seen in the East." The Notre Dame game turned out to be Army's only loss of the season, and Cadet coach Charley Daly—who once disdained the forward pass—immediately began to put together a passing attack. As for the Irish, Rockne wrote in his autobiography that the victory "gave the greatest impetus yet to the development of the Notre Dame spirit."

But for Rockne and Notre Dame, it was only the beginning. After four years as an assistant coach, Rockne replaced Harper as head coach in 1918. Over thirteen seasons, his teams would go 105-12-5, including four national championships. Success begat success, and by the time Rockne died, twenty-three of his former players were college head coaches, many were assistant coaches and more than 150 were coaching high school football.

Though it was enough to earn Rockne election, in 1969, as the greatest coach in football's first century, his influence is based on more than just unmatched success. His impact came as an innovator, a motivator and a promoter of the game, and in each facet he was virtually peerless.

When Rockne took over as head coach, he inferred a responsibility to the university and to the game. Notre Dame had been playing primarily in the Midwest, but Rockne scheduled games from coast to coast. His team was called "Rockne's Ramblers," and its slate, filled with many of the nation's top schools, was described as a "suicide schedule." Almost single-handedly, Rockne created the notion of intersectional rivalries, and forged the legend and national following of Notre Dame football. And since the game's beginnings at Harvard and Yale, no institution has been more important to college football. Rockne was to the Irish what Ruth was to the Yankees.

In 1920, during Rockne's second season as head coach, the Irish played in front of a total of 85,000 fans. By 1929, more than 550,000 people were watching Notre Dame football. Rockne's final season was the team's first in Notre Dame Stadium, which had more than twice the capacity of the old field and which Rockne had helped design and necessitate.

But, as a coach, Rockne revolutionized football on the playing fields, as well. He became known for the "Rockne system," which brought deception and finesse to the game. Rockne called it "smart football," but it was really the arrival of modern football, a more wide-open, marketable version.

Rockne perfected the shift from the T-formation, spawning an offensive style that came to rival the wingback formation for popularity during the era. He also essentially anticipated the modern platoon and specialization system when he introduced what he called his "shock troops," a form of platooning in which a second team started and then the regular team took over, sometimes after a full quarter had elapsed.

"Every so often," explained writer Paul Gallico, "a genuine colossus appears whose influence and teaching cannot be underestimated, and Rockne towered head and shoulders over the best of his profession." His fame grew with each season, especially when he became a syndicated writer, a renowned public speaker, a radio personality and the author of three books.

By 1930, Rockne had become a college football legend, but that year he even unwittingly gave pro football a boost. Like many other college proponents, Rockne held professional football in low regard, yet he agreed to pit an all-star squad of recent Notre Dame graduates against the NFL's New York Giants after the college season. The Irish were expected to roll to an easy victory, but the Giants viewed it as an opportunity to showcase the talent in the NFL. Before a crowd of 55,000 in the Polo Grounds, New York won 22-0 and silenced a great many detractors.

Ironically, the loss proved to be Rockne's last contest. On March 31, 1931, Rockne boarded Transcontinental-Western's Flight 599 from Kansas City to Los Angeles, where he was headed to make a football demonstration film. Shortly after takeoff, the plane flew into a storm and crashed into a wheat field near Bazaar, Kansas.

Rockne died at the age of forty-three, and an entire country mourned. There were telegrams of condolence from General Douglas MacArthur, President Herbert

Hoover, even the King of Norway; radio stations played funeral music and the Notre Dame victory march. Ten thousand people packed Chicago's Dearborn Street when his casket arrived, and 100,000 more lined his funeral route in tribute to a man who had made an impact unlike any other's on the pageantry and popularity of college football.

THE GIPPER

George Gipp had been one of college football's greatest players, gaining nearly 5,000 total yards for Rockne from 1918–1920. But on December 14, 1920, at the age of twenty-five, Gipp died of a throat infection, reportedly leaving Rockne with one last message: "Some time, Rock, when the team's up against it, when things are wrong and the breaks are beating the boys—tell them to go in there with all they've got and win just one for the Gipper."

It has been estimated that Rockne gave less than a dozen impassioned speeches during his thirteen years as head coach, and it was apparently eight years before Rockne found the right moment to make good on Gipp's request. At halftime, with the Irish locked in a 0-0 tie with Army, Rockne recounted Gipp's deathbed appeal. Ever since, historians have wondered whether Gipp actually made the request, or whether it was just another brilliant movitational ploy by Rockne. Regardless, it worked. Notre Dame won 12-6.

29

Jesse Owens

"In America," Jesse Owens once said, "anyone can become somebody." And so the grandson of an Alabama slave grew up to be a national hero, performing one of the most profoundly symbolic feats in the annals of American sport.

His four gold medals at the 1936 Berlin Olympics, under the eyes of Adolph Hitler, turned him into one of the first African-American athletic heroes in the United States, as well as a symbol of patriotism and promise in America. It is only because Owens was largely unable to turn his fame into sustained influence that he does not rank even higher in *The Sports 100*.

James Cleveland Owens was a child of poverty, born on September 12, 1913, in northern Alabama. He had nine brothers and sisters, three more who died at birth, and a father who did not have particularly high hopes for his race. "J.C., it don't do a colored man no good to get himself too high," he once told his son. "'Cause it's a helluva drop back to the bottom."

Shortly after World War I, the Owens family moved north to Cleveland, where Owens took up track. His early mentor and track coach, Charles Riley, told him to run "like the ground was a burning fire." And Owens did. By 1928, he had set world records for junior high school athletes in the high jump and long jump. By then, he was also known as "Jesse," the result of a teacher's mistaken bastardization of "J.C."

Soon, Cleveland's black press was calling him "the outstanding individual track man in northeastern Ohio." He finished first in 75 of 79 races in high school, leading his team to the National Interscholastic Championship in 1933 by winning the long jump, tying a world record in the 100-yard dash and setting a new one in the 220-yard sprint.

Owens went on to Ohio State, despite protests from the black community about the reputation for racial prejudice in Columbus. It was the first of several unpopular stands (among blacks, at least) that Owens would take. As William J. Baker explains in *Jesse Owens: An American Life*, "To demand of him 'a militant spirit' was to command the sun to stop shining. He was no political fighter. He had learned long ago to survive by turning his head, not merely the other cheek."

It was on May 25, 1935, at the Big Ten Championships, that the Jesse Owens legend began to take form. In less than an hour, Owens broke three world records (in the 220-yard sprint, long jump, and 220-yard low hurdles) and tied one more (in the 100-yard dash). Owens followed the feat by winning four events at the NCAA Championships, earning him international acclaim. He also became the first African-American to captain a Big Ten team when Ohio State tabbed him for the track honors.

Though Owens had failed to make the 1932 U.S. Olympic team, he seemed a cinch for the 1936 squad. But Nazi discrimination, particularly against Jews, drove many to consider a boycott of Berlin's Games. Some black writers supported a boycott, but most hoped for an opportunity for black athletes to shine, thus, as Baker says, "striking a blow against both German and American arrogance."

Once again, Owens's perspective was contrary to that of most blacks. "If there is discrimination against minorities in Germany," he said, "then we must withdraw from the Olympics." In the decades to come, as many blacks began to support the notion of Olympic boycotts, Owens would take an opposite stand.

The Amateur Athletic Union narrowly voted to send its athletes to Berlin, and Owens made the team as one of ten black males and two females on the track and field squad. Along with five black boxers and two black weightlifters, the nineteen black athletes were nearly five times as many as on any previous American Olympic team. The recent defeat of an emerging African-American icon (heavyweight boxer Joe Louis, at the hands of German Max Schmeling six weeks before the Games) made the Olympians all the more eager to succeed.

On July 15, 1936, Owens and the rest of the Olympic team embarked on a nine-day trip to Europe, aboard the S.S. *Manhattan*. "While I was going over on the boat," Owens recalled, "all I could think about was taking one or two of those gold medals." As it turned out, his dreams came two or three medals short of reality.

The opening ceremonies on August 1 were dominated by Nazi symbols, as Hitler fully expected his notion of Aryan supremacy to manifest itself on the athletic fields. One German official even complained that the Americans were letting "non-humans, like Owens and other Negro athletes" compete. But the 110,000 observers in Berlin's Olympic Stadium were soon captivated by Owens's feats.

On August 2, black American Cornelius Johnson had won the high jump competition, but Hitler had left the stadium just before Johnson stood for the national anthem. The timing may or may not have been purposeful, but by the time Owens won his first gold medal the following day (tying a world record in the 100-meter dash), Hitler had decided to stop congratulating the winners. He didn't congratulate Owens, but he didn't publicly receive a German gold medalist either. Nevertheless, headlines like "HITLER SNUBS JESSE" soon appeared in American newspapers, and an enduring legend was born that Owens later did little to discourage.

The following day, Owens set a new Olympic record of 26 feet, 5 1/4 inches in the long jump. Afterwards, he walked arm-in-arm off the field with German silver medalist Lutz Long. Owens later described their friendship as the product of "two uncertain men in an uncertain world." Eight years later, Long died in combat, fighting for Hitler.

Owens set another Olympic record by running the 200-meter finals in 20.7 seconds on August 5, winning his third gold medal. It was supposed to be his last event of the Olympiad, but three days later Owens found himself added to the American 4 × 400-yard relay team. In a controversial move that some saw as an appeasement to Hitler, he and black teammate Ralph Metcalfe had replaced Marty Glickman and Sam Stoller, the only two Jews on the U.S. track and field team.

Owens ran the opening leg, as the U.S. easily won the gold medal in an Olympic-record 39.8 seconds. Though the German team actually recorded more overall points at the 1936 Games, Owens's four-gold performance gave the Americans a moral victory and made him a household name around the globe. "Owens was *the* black athlete in all of America," writes Baker. "He was Mr. Olympics, even for people who knew little and cared less about the Olympic games; he was Mr. Track and Field, even for people to whom only baseball, football and boxing really mattered."

Had Owens remained a powerful symbol of racial empowerment and a voice against injustice, he would own a higher ranking among *The Sports 100*. But, in many ways, his post-Olympic experience diminished the impact of his athletic feats.

Owens's Olympic glory translated into what *The New York Times* called "a sheaf of cables from American promoters offering him fantastic prices for personal appearances." Owens then refused to continue to participate in a post-Olympic barnstorming tour of Europe, saying, "All we athletes get out of this Olympic business is a view of a train and an airplane window . . . A fellow desires something for himself."

He discontinued his studies at Ohio State, but most of the lucrative offers he expected turned out to be hoaxes. "It became increasingly apparent," Owens later recalled, "that everyone was going to slap me on the back, want to shake my hand or have me up to their suite. But no one was going to offer me a job." Owens's get-rich-quick hopes ran right into racial barriers. Claims Baker, "From Nazi Germany he returned to racist America, to be sent again to the back of the bus."

Owens soon changed his mind about turning professional, but the AAU wouldn't reinstate him as an amateur. And though he followed Joe Louis as the second black man to be named Associated Press Athlete of the Year, he didn't even earn the Sullivan Trophy as the nation's top amateur athlete.

Owens did manage to earn at least $20,000, still an impressive sum in 1936, including an estimated $10,000 for throwing his support behind Republican presidential candidate Alf Landon ("Worst race I ever ran," said Owens). How-ever, he spent his money lavishly, and by the end of the year, he found himself racing against a thoroughbred horse in Cuba for $2,000. "People said it was degrading for an Olympic champion to run against a horse, but what was I sup-posed to do?" he later explained. "I had four gold medals, but you can't eat four gold medals."

In the next few years, Owens led a 12-piece band of black musicians, man-aged a touring all-black basketball squad, organized a touring softball team, worked as a playground director in Cleveland, started the Jesse Owens Dry Cleaning Company and continued to race in all sorts of suspect exhibitions. The U.S. Gov-ernment soon charged Owens with failing to pay income tax on his 1936 earn-ings, the first of two such charges against him, and in May 1939 he filed for bankruptcy.

Though World War II revived Owens's reputation somewhat, as he once again became a patriotic symbol, he still failed to cross over into the consciousness of white America. "Since the Berlin Olympics, he had made his way on the black night club circuit, endorsed products sold only in the black press, taken govern-ment appointments that catered to blacks, dealt with Ford Motor Company's black workers, and sold his athletic skills to farcical black barnstorming teams," writes Baker. "For all his fame, ambition and personal charm, Jesse Owens seemed unable to break out of the racial ghetto in which the great majority of less success-ful blacks languished."

Unlike Jackie Robinson, Owens didn't seem to want to rock the boat. "We all know what's wrong with this world," he said. "You know it. I know it. I can't change it with wild words." Unlike Joe Louis, he didn't remain a front-page icon for fifteen years. Unlike Muhammad Ali, he was no activist. He didn't oppose the Vietnam War, and, in fact, he insisted on calling the boxer "Cassius Clay."

Indeed, Owens scarcely acknowledged the civil rights movement. His politi-cal leanings actually represented a preference for the status quo. In the radical 1960s, Owens was for the Establishment. The man who had been such a resound-ing symbol of opportunity in 1936 did not evolve into a continued symbol of change. *Sports Illustrated*'s William Oscar Johnson said of him, somewhat dispar-agingly, "Jesse Owens is what you might call a professional good example."

But Owens's reputation as a national hero did continue to grow as television increased the stature of the Olympics. Even as his records began to fall, his star began to rise. In 1976, he received the nation's highest civilian honor, the Medal of Freedom. He even began to change his political and social perspective. Whereas he had published a book called *Blackthink,* in 1972, in which he criticized "pro-Negro bigots" as "professional haters," two years later his next book was entitled *I Have Changed.*

By the time Owens died of lung cancer, on March 31, 1980, it was clear that his athletic feats, if not his activist words, had impacted American culture. Explains Baker, "Although he was never a spokesman for black rights, he repre-sented an essential ingredient of black progress."

30

Kenesaw Mountain Landis

The Landis legend goes something like this: Baseball was in trouble. When eight members of the Chicago White Sox were accused of throwing the 1919 World Series, it came as the last straw to a sporting public that had all but lost faith in the game. Baseball was on the brink of extinction—until one of the country's most respected jurists agreed to turn his attention to it. At the behest of a desperate group of well-meaning owners, Judge Kenesaw Mountain Landis took over control of the game. He ruled with an iron hand, but a fair heart. He fearlessly drove the forces of gambling from the game, restoring America's confidence in its heroes and bringing integrity to a sport that many believed would be tainted forever. Beloved by both players and owners alike, Landis saved the national pastime.

The Landis reality is something quite different. Let's take the myths one at a time.

Was baseball in trouble? No, it was simply in disarray. Though the Black Sox scandal did come as a shock to the system, it was not the first time a game-fixing scandal had come to light. It was just the most noticeable imprint gambling had left on the game after several decades of permeating the ballparks. World War I had taken a toll on box office figures, but the 1919 and 1920 seasons, before Landis arrived, marked a remarkable rebound in attendance. A young slugger named Babe Ruth seemed to be setting new home run records with each swing of the bat, and fans were responding accordingly. Indeed, the only thing on the brink of extinction when Landis took over was the spitball.

Were the owners well-meaning? Hardly. They were simply weary of the egomaniacal and arbitrary rule of the game's most powerful figure, American League president Ban Johnson. In fact, baseball owners had been looking to overhaul the game's organizational structure since making peace with the upstart Federal League (an attempt at a third major league that lasted two seasons) in 1915. After the settlement, several owners began to maneuver toward replacing the game's governing body, the three-man National Commission, which consisted of the president of each league and a commissioner chosen by both.

The Black Sox scandal simply accelerated the demise of the National Commission, convincing baseball magnates to put the Lasker Plan in action. The Lasker Plan was a blueprint for the future of the game, designed by Chicago businessman Albert D. Lasker. It called for another three-person ruling body for baseball, but comprised of men with no financial connection to the game. The trio would have "unreviewable authority" over the game.

The owners' thoughts then turned to Landis, a well-known federal judge and baseball fan. They originally had planned to hire three all-powerful executives, including a chairman (with a $25,000 salary) and two associates (paid $10,000 each). But they were so enamored at the prospect of obtaining Landis that they offered him a $50,000 salary and absolute authority. Sportswriters began calling Landis the "Czar" of baseball; he preferred "Commissioner." *The New York Times* proclaimed, "BASEBALL PEACE DECLARED; LANDIS NAMED DICTATOR."

But who was this man to whom they had chosen to give unlimited power? He was a white-haired, frail, overly serious, undereducated, vindictive, grandstanding judge who often made legal decisions based on personal predilections and who had an ego the size of the Green Monster.

Born in Millville, Ohio, on November 20, 1866, he was named after Kennesaw Mountain (minus an "n") in Georgia, where his father had been wounded while serving as a physician during the Civil War. Raised in Logansport, Indiana, Landis dropped out of high school, taught himself shorthand and found a job as a clerk in a South Bend courthouse. He finished high school at night and then obtained a law degree from Union Law School in Chicago in 1891, despite never having attended college.

Through his father's connections, Landis went to Washington two years later as a secretary to U.S. Secretary of State Walter Q. Gresham. When Gresham died in 1895, Landis returned to Chicago, where he was put in charge of the 1904 gubernatorial election campaign of Frank Lowden. When Lowden lost the election, he declined a federal judgeship offer and instead recommended Landis. President Theodore Roosevelt appointed Landis judge in the U.S. District Court for the Northern District of Illinois.

Was Landis one of the country's most respected jurists? Again, no. He was just one of its best known. One observer remarked that Landis's career "typifies the heights to which dramatic talent may carry a man in America if only he has the foresight not to go on the stage."

Landis intruded on the national consciousness in 1907, when he jumped on the Roosevelt trust-busting bandwagon and imposed a famous $29.4 million fine against Standard Oil in a freight rebate case. As happened remarkably often with Landis, the case was overturned on appeal, and the fine was never paid. Eleven years later, during World War I, Landis trampled on the Bill of Rights in his effort to punish opponents of the war, sentencing ninety-four members of the Industrial Workers of the World to prison, some for up to twenty years.

When baseball became Landis's stage, gambling became Act 1, Scene 1. Did he remove gambling's tainted fingers from the game? In an arbitrary manner, sort of. Did he restore the public's confidence in the game's integrity? Yes, if only because the public quickly became seduced by the Landis legend. "If I catch any crook in baseball, the rest of his life is going to be a hot one," he announced. He then accepted $10,000 from the owners, to be put toward investigating crookedness in the game.

The Black Sox scandal, in particular, speaks volumes about Landis, about his erratic legal mind, his righteous facade, his arbitrary nature and his tendency to prefer rhetoric over reason. The accused Black Sox players had yet to go to trial, but in a blatant disregard for due process, Landis proclaimed, "There is absolutely no chance for any of them to creep back into Organized Baseball. They will be and will remain outlaws . . . It is sure that the guilt of some of them at least will be proven."

The players were then acquitted, albeit under shadowy circumstances, yet on the following day Landis made the statement for which he is most famous. "Regardless of the verdict of the juries, no player that throws a ball game; no player that undertakes or promises to throw a ball game; no player that sits in a conference with a bunch of crooked players and gamblers where the ways and means of throwing games are planned and discussed and does not promptly tell his club about it, will ever play professional baseball."

According to baseball historian Bill James, at least thirty-eight men were involved in various scandals during the decade leading up to 1927, when Landis signed the second of four seven-year contracts (taking a $15,000 raise). Of those thirty-eight men, at least half were banned outright from baseball. By the time Landis entered his second decade as the game's czar, baseball's scandal-plagued era was at an end, due in part to a series of anti–game fixing rules Landis pushed through in 1927.

Yet the game's established stars were often allowed to escape the judge's wrath. In 1927, it came to light that two of the game's biggest names, Ty Cobb and Tris Speaker, had attempted to fix a game in 1919. Landis made a show of investigating the matter and then said, "Won't these God damn things that happened before I came into baseball ever stop coming up?" The man who announced he would clear every gambling element from the game then established a five-year statute of limitations on baseball offenses.

Landis also looked the other way when it came to integration. "Negroes are not barred from organized baseball . . . and never have been in the 21 years I have served," Landis said publicly. Yet privately he maneuvered to assure the continuation of baseball's segregationist policies. Indeed, when maverick owner Bill Veeck, Jr., informed Landis of his plan to purchase the Philadelphia Phillies and stock the club with black players in 1944, the next morning he discovered the team had been turned over to the National League. It was later sold for half the price Veeck had offered. Only after Landis's 78-year-old body gave out on November 25, 1944, was the door opened for Branch Rickey and Jackie Robinson.

And so history has not accorded Landis the kind of admiration he enjoyed during his reign as lord of the national game. *Sports Illustrated*'s Ron Fimrite, for example, stated that Landis "was granted extraordinary powers to 'safeguard the interests of the national game of baseball.' And he used that power arbitrarily, sometimes even whimsically." Historian John Thorn claimed, "There was a crisis in baseball, and they needed somebody, but I don't think Landis's vision was great. I think he was simply an autocrat. Landis was a showboat judge who finally found a jurisdiction in which he couldn't be overturned."

But Landis's influence on the game must be viewed by taking into account the reactions of contemporary observers, not just the hindsight of historians, which is why, despite his numerous faults and misguided decisions, he still ranks relatively high among *The Sports 100*.

In 1922, for instance, Landis asserted his authority by going head-to-head against the game's biggest attraction. Babe Ruth had ignored a rule against postseason barnstorming by World Series participants, and Landis called the case "a question of who is the biggest man in baseball, the commissioner or the player who makes the most home runs." He suspended Ruth for the first six weeks of the season, and one newspaper reacted by saying, "[Ruth] will not gain friends . . . by an attitude of defiance toward the commissioner, who has taken upon himself the task of ridding baseball of abuses and keeping it free from them. Baseball needs a Landis much more than it does a Ruth."

While history has disproved the latter part of that statement, at the time, it was believed to be true. And the public's faith in the game was based on their beliefs. Even disgruntled owners realized that if they didn't continue to renew his contract it would look as if they were discarding virtue for greed. And so, in the end, it may be the fact that these decisions were the sole responsibility of just one man—rather than the actual decisions themselves—that proves to be Landis's most important legacy.

FEDERAL JUDGE

One of Landis's most important contributions to baseball actually came nearly six years before he was chosen as the game's first commissioner. It concerned a challenge to Major League Baseball's monopoly in the form of the Federal League.

The Federal League had been founded as a minor league, but, in August 1913, it announced, much like the American League had a dozen years earlier, that it would pursue major league players. Its prime attraction: no reserve clause and long-term contracts. Joe Tinker, the famous shortstop of the Tinker-to-Evers-to-Chance double play combination, became the first big-name player to jump to the league, preceding more than 200 players' defections through the 1915 season.

In January 1915, the upstart league sued Major League Baseball for denying access to the players' market. The case was heard in the U.S. District Court of Northern Illinois—Landis's court. He announced that "any blows at the thing called baseball would be regarded by this court as a blow to a national institution." Taking the case under advisement, Landis proceeded to stall for a year, just enough time for the two warring leagues to organize a peace settlement, which essentially called for $600,000 in exchange for the dissolution of the Federal League.

It was largely this bit of maneuvering by Landis that led baseball's owners to tab him for the commissioner's job several years later, as they paradoxically looked for change in a man who represented to them "a friend of the established order of things in the national pastime."

31

Lester Patrick

There was something entirely appropriate about Bobby Orr walking up to the podium in the Waldorf-Astoria in 1979 and accepting the National Hockey League's Lester Patrick Award for "outstanding service to hockey in the United States." Said Orr, "This is a very special honor for me because of the name it bears. I really don't know as much as I should know about the Patricks, but I do know of the tremendous contribution they have made to hockey. As I accept this award, I humbly acknowledge that contribution."

Lester Patrick was born on New Year's Eve, in 1883, in Drummondville, Quebec. Ten days short of his second birthday, he was joined by a younger brother, Frank. Together, they would influence their chosen sport in so many ways and in so many places that hockey, without the Patricks, might not resemble modern hockey at all. In fact, to some extent, Orr's career actually symbolized the Patricks' impact on the game. It could be seen in everything, from his offensive domination to the simple act of standing side-by-side with his fellow defenseman, from his #4 jersey to his performance in the playoffs, from his roots in Canada to his feats in America.

Though a great many of the Patricks' contributions were made in tandem, only the older brother has been ranked in *The Sports 100*. It is by no means, however, a concession of convenience. According to hockey historian Stan Fischler, "No single individual contributed more to the improvement of professional hockey on every level—playing, coaching, managing, and operating—than Lester Patrick."

Lester and Frank were the oldest of Joe and Grace Patrick's eight children. Joe Patrick built a thriving lumber company from the ground up, necessitating frequent moves by the clan and assuring that his eldest sons were to hockey what Johnny Appleseed was to farming. Lester took up hockey at the age of ten, when his family moved to Montreal. It was 1893, the same year in which an amateur team from his home city became the first to receive a silver trophy named after its donor, Lord Stanley of Preston. In later years, the Stanley Cup would frequently be found in Lester's hands.

Lester's first significant impact on hockey came in 1904. Having dropped out of Montreal's McGill University after one year, he found himself playing defense for a club in Brandon, Manitoba. It was there that he ignored an unwritten rule in which defensemen only halted the opposing offense, and never handled the puck. Instead, he fashioned an end-to-end rush, scoring a dramatic goal.

"The crowd loved it and from that point on defensemen have become as much a part of an attack as the two wings and center," writes Fischler in *Those Were The Days*. "Conceivably, if Lester had not decided to make that rush in Brandon, Bobby Orr might never have been more than a defenseman who hurled the puck from one end of Boston Garden to the other." Lester would also reposition the defenseman so that instead of standing one in front of the other, they stood abreast, as they do today.

In 1906, while Frank enrolled at McGill, Lester led a new team, the Montreal Wanderers, to the Stanley Cup title, scoring the game-winning goals in a 12-10 triumph. After the team took the Cup again the following year, the Patrick family moved once more, this time to British Columbia. Lester played for the local hockey team while Frank was back East, his hat trick leading the McGill squad to a victory over Harvard University in the first-ever international collegiate hockey game.

At the time, full professionalism was beginning to appear in Canadian hockey leagues, and, by 1909, Lester had finally convinced his father of its merits. He signed with the Renfrew (Ontario) Millionaires for the remarkable sum of $3,000 (Frank signed for $2,000) in the newly formed National Hockey Association and was named team captain.

It was about then that the family lost its fortune, when a flood destroyed the Patrick Lumber Company's mill. But Joe Patrick restocked the company's resources, and, by 1911, he had sold his business for $440,000. Having returned west to help the family recoup the losses from the flood, the Patricks decided to combine fame, fortune, location and imagination to form a league of their own. The Pacific Coast Hockey Association was born, highlighted by Canada's first artificial ice rinks. Lester would operate a franchise in Victoria. Frank would run a Vancouver franchise and its 10,500-seat stadium, billed as "the globe's largest indoor sports emporium." A third franchise was to be located in nearby West Minster.

"Since then," writes Eric Whitehead, author of *The Patricks: Hockey's Royal Family*, "a lot of entrepreneurs have invested many times a half-million dollars in sports franchises and allied ventures, but there is no record of any one man or one family risking everything they owned on such a nebulous venture with such slim chance of reward."

After the three-team PCHA raided National Hockey Association rosters for twenty-three top players, the league's first season began, in January 1912. Lester was the owner, coach and star of the Victoria team. Frank, an excellent defenseman, would spend a dozen years as the league president. In tandem, they were virtual dictators of the league, powerful mavericks in professional hockey and the most visible figures in the game.

By the 1913–1914 season, the PCHA had become so strong that the rival NHA agreed to pit its top team against the Patricks' top team in a postseason battle for the coveted Stanley Cup. It was a major victory for the maverick brothers, though their league still remained on thin ice. But even their failures turned into important contributions. When the West Minster team folded, most of its players moved to a new team in Portland, Oregon, making it the first U.S.-based team in a Canadian-based major hockey league. When Victoria closed shop for a spell, the Patricks added a new club in Seattle, which, in 1917, became the first American team to win the Stanley Cup.

Along the way, the Patricks revolutionized the game on the ice, as well. Among their contributions were numbering of players' jerseys, the practice of awarding points for assists, the double-referee system and the advent of the penalty shot. The Patricks introduced the notion of making line substitutions as play continued, which dramatically changed the tempo of the game. They were the first to allow goaltenders to leave their feet to make a save and the first to install blue lines.

In 1918, they came up with the idea of a playoff between the first- and second-place teams to decide the league's Stanley Cup challenger. Writes Whitehead, "The idea was tried, and the fans liked it. They've been liking it ever since, while providing a multi-million-dollar bonanza for sport in North America." Even nearly a half-century afterward, Arthur Daley of *The New York Times* wrote, in a 1967 tribute to the Patricks, that they "should have a monument raised in their memory for that idea alone."

By 1925, professional hockey was growing and consolidating. The NHA had merged with the Canadian Hockey Association to create the National Hockey League, while the PCHA had merged with the Western Canada Hockey League. Though Lester's Victoria club won the Stanley Cup that year, eastern hockey had regained much of the sport's power base, and the NHL was beginning to thrive, moving into American cities like Boston, New York, Pittsburgh, Detroit and Chicago. In 1926, the Patrick brothers, each having retired from playing the game, made a momentous decision. They would combine their league into three strong teams, and then sell them to the NHL. The $377,000 deal has been called "the biggest mass sale of players in sports history."

It was then that Lester was handed a new role in professional hockey: as a virtual ambassador for the game, to America. In October of 1926, he was offered a job as coach of the upstart New York Rangers. The Rangers finished atop their division, which would eventually be called the Patrick Division, in their first season, and won the Stanley Cup the following year. In that 1928 series against the Montreal Maroons, Patrick's only goalie was taken away in an ambulance, and the 44-year-old coach cemented his place in hockey lore by inserting himself in goal and leading the team to an overtime victory.

Though the Rangers shared Madison Square Garden with another NHL club (the New York Americans), from the beginning, Lester Patrick's club was the toast of the town. Their coach's personality was vital in selling hockey to New York, and particularly to the city's sportswriters. He would conduct frequent seminars for the press, described by Whitehead as being "almost Shakespearian in nature, couched in a fine lyrical prose that could charm the most cynical audience." New York's scribes began to call Lester "The Silver Fox" in reference to both his appearance and his craftiness.

After coaching the Rangers to another Stanley Cup in 1933, Lester stepped down in 1939, having compiled a 312-242-115 record. He remained the team's general manager, and, in 1940, the Rangers won the Cup again (their last until 1994). Six years later, Lester decided it was time to retire from the game.

On December 3, 1947, Madison Square Garden hosted Lester Patrick Night, honoring his years of service and his induction into the Hockey Hall of Fame. Wrote New York columnist Gene Ward, "Lester Patrick, the man long known as The Silver Fox and as Mr. Hockey, was heaped with words of praise and with gifts which, when all stacked together, failed by far to measure up to what he himself has contributed to the game of hockey."

Lester, whose sons and grandson also played in the NHL, died on June 1, 1960. His brother, Frank, followed twenty-eight days later.

32

Magic Johnson

What other athlete could take the nickname "Magic" and make it so much his own that we would all but forget his real name was Earvin Johnson? Sports heroes have been known as Red and Whitey and Babe and Bear and Pop and Doc. But Magic? When he was first given the nickname, his mother worried that it would "give him a lot to live up to at some point." It did, and he did.

Who could call him Johnson? It was too plain, too common. Even *The New York Times* must have been tempted to call him Magic. And never once did the nickname appear ill fit to the man, until the day a killer virus forced him into retirement, providing a stage for his most significant performance and allowing the world to realize he was just Earvin after all.

Magic's impact as a player, as a personality, as a symbol and, ultimately, as an educator/activist is still fresh in our memories; in the case of the latter, it is ongoing. And so it is difficult to bestow upon him a legacy. It is likely, however, that his legacy will only become more significant in the future.

As a player, he was unprecedented. Less than four decades earlier, men as tall as 6-foot-9 were largely considered too clumsy for basketball. Johnson was a 6-foot-9, 225-pound point guard. He had Bill Russell's size and Bob Cousy's flash. As Jerry West, former star and current general manager of the Los Angeles Lakers, once admitted, "I thought I'd seen it all when it came to basketball—every style, every size and shape player there was . . . And then I saw Magic Johnson."

There had been other big guards in the NBA. Oscar Robertson was 6-foot-5; George Gervin was 6-foot-7. But a 6-foot-9 ballhandler? A record-setting passer in a power forward's body? His 9,921 career assists were an NBA record, until broken by John Stockton, a player almost exactly in the Cousy mold. Yet Magic broke that mold. Wrote Alexander Wolff, in *100 Years of Hoops*, "Magic, who was once the avant-guard, is a prototype." Indeed, there are several "Magic Johnson–types"—big men with small games—roaming NBA arenas in the '90s.

"Magic Johnson did no less than force everyone who watched basketball to examine the preconceptions about what constituted the prototypical NBA player," wrote *Sports Illustrated*'s Jack McCallum. Size no longer pigeonholed an athlete into a position, as Magic proved so profoundly in Game Six of the NBA Finals in his rookie season. With Kareem Abdul-Jabbar injured, Magic put on a performance which, as one writer put it, "should have ended forever any doubts about his nickname." He jumped center to open the game, played every position on the court and led L.A. to the title by collecting 42 points, fifteen rebounds, seven assists and three steals. And he was still just three years removed from high school.

Much of the eastern viewing public was forced to watch that game on tape delay, but Magic's personality and his rivalry with Larry Bird would spawn a national love affair with basketball. It began on March 26, 1979, when Magic's Michigan State team and Bird's Indiana State squad squared off in the finals of the NCAA Tournament, resulting in what still remains the largest television audience ever to watch a tournament game. Magic's side won, 75-64, but the hype surrounding the event made basketball the ultimate victor.

"That game was the turning point for what we now know as March Madness," explained Roy S. Johnson, co-author of *Magic's Touch*. "It wasn't always March Madness. It was just the NCAA Tournament. But after that, it became every little boy's dream to play in that game."

It was a seminal moment in basketball history. But for Magic and Bird, the game was also a springboard. Even more so than college football, college basketball is a virtual sporting hors d'oeuvre, an appetizer for the professional game. The public becomes attached to collegiate stars, and the best of them become standout pros. When Magic and Bird entered the NBA at the same time on different sides of the country as members of the league's two most storied franchises, it was, according to McCallum, "a fortunate accident of timing that did nothing less than rescue pro basketball."

Bird had been drafted in the first round by the Boston Celtics as a junior-eligible in 1978, but stayed on to compete as a senior. Magic, almost three years younger, decided to turn professional following his sophomore season, and was drafted #1 overall by the Lakers. And, thus, the NBA had two rookies in 1979, named Magic and Larry. Their rivalry would become the essence of the NBA in the '80s and the single most salient factor in taking the league from the precipice of disaster to the cutting edge of popularity.

"The NBA of the '70s was the enclave of the selfish and the satisfied, a place where individual talent flourished at the expense of team play," wrote McCallum. "That's the way the average fan saw it, anyway, and there was more than a little truth in that perception. More to the point, attendance was flagging, advertisers were turned off, TV viewers weren't watching, several owners were talking about selling, and a bone-deep malaise permeated the whole sport. Magic and Bird turned it all around."

Over the next twelve years, one or the other—or, most dramatically, both— would appear in eleven different installments of the NBA Finals. Magic would win five championships. But then again, he was a winner all of his life.

Born August 14, 1959, in Lansing, Michigan, Earvin Johnson, Jr., was the middle of seven children who grew up in a three-bedroom house. He was a die-hard Detroit Pistons fan, and he took his basketball everywhere. By the tenth grade, he was 6-foot-5 and known as Earvin "Magic" Johnson throughout the state. As a senior, he led Everett High School to the state championship. That, combined with Michigan State's title in 1979 and the Lakers' title in 1980, gave Magic three championships at three different levels in four years. Said one observer upon watching Magic celebrate the third, "He thinks every season ends this way."

But not every moment was magical for Johnson, who missed forty-five games with a knee injury in his second season. After the season, he signed a 25-year $25 million contract with the Lakers, then the longest and most lucrative contract in sports history. But the enormity of the contract only raised questions. Was he paid more than Kareem? Was he now part of management, a possibility that, even if untrue, represented a remarkable achievement for a 22-year-old black athlete?

The contract also made it easier for observers to call Magic a spoiled, over-paid crybaby when he was blamed for getting Lakers coach Paul Westhead fired early in the 1981–1982 season. The two had disagreed over how to run the Lak-ers' offense, and Westhead lost his job one day after Magic told reporters he hoped to be traded. Cheers quickly turned to boos around the league. Many in the media were relentless, particularly Jim Murray of the *L.A. Times*, who wrote, "Now we know why they call him Magic. He made the boss disappear."

But Magic's perpetual smile and radiant performance would win back the fans. He was not particularly fast or acrobatic on the court. In fact, in some ways, he was a throwback and a pioneer at the same time. He didn't score like Bird; he didn't soar like Michael Jordan. But one way or another, he was going to beat you. Said Julius Erving, "He's the only player who can take only three shots and still dominate a game."

Magic, along with Kareem and coach Pat Riley, would lead the Lakers to nine appearances in the NBA Finals and five titles, including triumphs over Bird and Boston in 1985 and 1987. Magic would become a three-time league MVP (1987, 1989 and 1990) and a three-time playoff MVP. He would average 19.4 points, seven rebounds and 11.4 assists per game, recording a record 136 triple doubles, a statistic that was essentially invented by his all-around game.

But nothing Magic Johnson ever did on the court shook the world like his announcement on November 7, 1991, that he had contracted the HIV virus that causes AIDS. Riley had once warned, "Magic is a stage name . . . It's fantasy. Nobody can be magic for the rest of his life." Sadly, Riley proved prophetic as Magic proved mortal.

He had discovered he was HIV-positive after failing a routine insurance physi-cal, and, after missing the first three games of the season, he stood at a podium at the Great Western Forum and told the world. He stated that he was retiring from the NBA, that his new wife was healthy and that he was determined to become a spokesperson in the fight against the disease and a proponent of safe sex.

Like only a few select athletes before him, Magic Johnson became far more than a sports figure; he became a significant cultural symbol—a lesson to some, a warning to others. While one celebrity's impact can be overstated, it is not exaggerating events to say that his announcement caused many to reexamine their attitude toward AIDS, not to mention promiscuity, and served as a wakeup call to millions.

This wasn't just a modern Lou Gehrig saying he had been given a bad break. This was a disease with as much social as medical baggage, and this was a man whom television had brought into the home, rather than just someone we read about in the sports pages. There had been high-profile victims of AIDS, but none had his charisma and universal appeal.

As Leigh Montville wrote in *Sports Illustrated*, "He has probably spent more time with us—and we have spent more time with him—than most of our blood relatives. Now he was sick? A disease that we had viewed mostly with passive dismay was suddenly immediate, real."

Many declared it a blessing in disguise for AIDS education because the disease had finally found a victim who seemed to captivate the kind of people whom educators most needed to reach. "If the people battling HIV had called central casting to summon the perfect spokesman, they could not have improved upon Magic Johnson," explained AIDS activist Randy Shilts. "No human being in the history of the AIDS epidemic is better positioned to get the battle against AIDS moving than Johnson."

The announcement also brought promiscuity among athletes out in the open, something years of paternity suits had failed to do. The subject had always been glossed over with a wink and a smirk. Now, especially coming on the heels of Wilt Chamberlain's claim that he had slept with 20,000 women, athletes' sexual peccadillos were suddenly discussed in more moralistic and political tones. Sally Jenkins of *Sports Illustrated* wrote, "Johnson has not been a hero to women. He has been a hazard."

But Magic backed up his promises. He formed the Magic Johnson Foundation to fund efforts in fighting AIDS. He helped create a half-hour television show to educate youngsters about the disease, and a book, *What You Can Do to Avoid AIDS*, with profits going to the Foundation. Soon after his press conference, he had been appointed by President Bush to the National Commission on AIDS, but, as he educated himself about the disease, he became increasingly disenchanted with the Bush administration's efforts. Less than a year later, he resigned, claiming the president had "dropped the ball."

Throughout, he remained in good health and found it difficult to stay away from the game. He would serve as a color commentator for NBC's pro basketball telecasts, return to the Lakers bench for a short stint as the team's head coach, and make a triumphant—if temporary—return to the court as MVP of the All-Star Game in February of 1992. He also would round out his résumé by winning a gold medal at the 1992 Summer Olympics, following the birth of a healthy son, thus sending a powerful message that being HIV-positive didn't mean he couldn't go on with life's activities.

So encouraged was he by his performance that he announced plans to return to the NBA for the 1992–1993 season. But the social stigma surrounding the disease, in the form of whispers among his NBA colleagues, led him to abort his comeback. It also led Dr. David E. Rogers, vice-chairman of the National Commission on AIDS and the NBA's first AIDS advisor, to point out that the "unreasonable fears . . . of his fellow players did something to him that the AIDS virus couldn't. It made him quit."

But Magic has hardly removed himself from the game or the spotlight. He has barnstormed with an all-star team against various national teams, continues to host a summer exhibition to benefit the United Negro College Fund and has purchased minority ownership in the Lakers. As he once explained, "Maybe one day I'll be able to help us get this thing under control, and then I can become an example to young people in a different way. Not as Magic Johnson dealing assists on the fast break, but as Earvin Johnson dealing with life—dealing with AIDS."

33

Larry Bird

Legendary basketball coach Pete Newell may have come up with the most appropriate analogy to the phenomenon that was the rivalry between Larry Bird and Magic Johnson. "If you were Raquel Welch and you lived across the street from Marilyn Monroe," he said, "you'd make damn sure you looked good every time you went out the front door."

The existence of Larry Bird forced Magic to constantly better himself and his game; the existence of Magic motivated Bird to do the same. Together, they lifted college basketball, and then professional basketball, to unprecedented popularity. But as much credit as each deserves for lighting a fire under basketball, it was the Bird-and-Magic tandem that captivated America. As *Sports Illustrated*'s Jack McCallum explained, "Individually they were great players, together they became an epic tale."

Both hovered around 6-foot-9 and 220 pounds. Both came from large families in modest circumstances. Both boasted all-around games envied by, perhaps, all but Oscar Robertson. Both were among the best team players in the game's history. But the essence of the rivalry was predicated not on the similarities between the two, but on so many apparent differences.

It was West Coast versus East Coast, Hollywood flash verses blue-collar Boston, Laker Showtime versus Celtic Mystique, the Magic man verses the "hick from French Lick." Magic, always smiling and outgoing, was an answer to the media's prayers; Bird, shy and private, was introverted enough to be described as "basketball's Howard Hughes." Magic won titles in 1980, 1982, 1985, 1987 and 1988; Bird won in 1981, 1984 and 1986. Bird was a three-time MVP, from 1984 through 1986; Magic was a three-time MVP, in 1987, 1989 and 1990. Magic signed with the Lakers for a record rookie salary of $500,000 in 1979; Bird signed for more a month later.

Who was better? Bird got the nod in the first half of their careers, Magic in the second half, as Bird was slowed by injuries, forcing his retirement in 1992. But the question was more important than the answer. Robertson and Jerry West had done battle; Wilt Chamberlain and Bill Russell had gone head-to-head dozens of times. But the Magic versus Bird rivalry was as much cultural as physical, and, thanks primarily to them, it was played out on a much larger scale. "You take two dynamic players like that," said former Celtics coach Bill Fitch, "and put them on stage in the NCAA Finals, then the NBA Finals so many times, it was just special. It lifted the whole league."

But as much as Bird helped save basketball, basketball might have helped save Bird. One of six children, he was born December 7, 1956, in French Lick, Indiana. His mother was a waitress, his father an alcoholic laborer who killed himself soon after his son had enrolled at Indiana University in the fall of 1974. Bird lasted just a few weeks with Bobby Knight, and, after a brief stop at a junior college, he found himself back in French Lick, working for the sanitation department. The man later renowned as one of the NBA's best at talking trash had quit school to collect it.

One year later, already having married, divorced and fathered a child, Bird returned to school. He chose to play for Indiana State, a little-known university that would fly with Bird to the nation's #1 ranking. Bird would average 30.3 points per game over three seasons, becoming one of only a handful of collegians to exceed 2,000 points and 1,000 rebounds. Indiana State went 25-3 in his first season, reached the NIT quarterfinals in his second, and coasted to the finals of the NCAA Tournament in his third and final season, taking a 33-0 record into the contest.

After Bird had recorded nine assists, 16 rebounds and 35 points on 16-of-19 shooting in a semifinal triumph over DePaul University, Michigan State coach Jud Heathcote had remarked, "That's not a Bird, that's a whole flock." But Heathcote's squad proved too much for Bird in the finals, holding him to 19 points and two assists. Of course, the 1979 NCAA Tournament final is remembered not as Bird's loss, but as basketball's gain. Said Al McGuire, who did the color commentary for NBC, "The college game may have already been on the launching pad. But if it was, it wasn't until Bird and Magic came along and pushed the button that it took off."

The Michigan State–Indiana State game spawned an explosion in televised college basketball, particularly on the fledgling ESPN network, which began to show every game it could find. In 1981, CBS paid $48 million for the rights to the NCAA Tournament. Nine years later, the same network bid $1 billion for seven years. In 1979, a Final Four appearance had brought just over $39,000 to a school; by 1989, it was worth $1.2 million.

The marquee matchup of Magic versus Bird gave birth to March Madness, but it has been suggested that the presence of Bird, in particular, was the key ingredient. As Harvey Araton and Filip Bondy, authors of *The Selling of the Green*, explain, ". . . the underlying and most powerful magnetic appeal was the emergence of a white superstar at a time when the sport had clearly given way to the dominance of blacks. With the racial sideshow, this 1979 final would fare as well in Peoria as it did in the heart of Watts."

Indeed, while Magic is ranked just ahead of Bird among *The Sports 100*, primarily because his HIV announcement transcended either of the duo's contributions on the court, Bird made a significant impact of his own simply by being a white superstar in a league that had become nearly seventy-five percent black. The United States, sadly, remains a race-conscious nation, and white would-be basketball fans, particularly in Boston, a city not known for its racial harmony, may have harbored a desire to see a little bit of themselves in their heroes. Bird fit the bill—and then some.

He became the league's biggest draw. The Philadelphia 76ers and Julius Erving didn't sell out; the L.A. Lakers and Magic Johnson didn't either. But Boston, with Bird and more white players than black players on its roster, sold out 27 of its first 41 road games. The Celtics had sold out one home game in 1978–1979; after Bird took over, Boston Garden sellouts became as common as the opening tip. "Larry Bird was the white hope. His Celtics were the white alternative," write Araton and Bondy. "Together, they sold big."

There were some whispers that the legend that began to surround Bird was a white-manufactured phenomenon. In fact, after his Detroit Pistons lost to the Celtics in the 1987 Eastern Conference Finals, Isiah Thomas echoed teammate Dennis Rodman's statement that if Bird were black "he'd be just another good guy."

But, as far as Bird's abilities were concerned, racial bias was a two-way street. As Magic explains in his autobiography, "At first, many black fans didn't think he was all that good. It was hard for them to accept that this guy could really play . . . Sooner or later, the black fans came around. They might not have liked Larry Bird, but they had to respect him."

Even Red Auerbach had his doubts, or at least he claimed to while negotiating Bird's rookie salary. "A cornerman can't dominate the game," he said. "A big man, occasionally even a guard. But one man playing a corner can't turn a franchise around." He was wrong, of course. Bird essentially became a point forward, joining Magic in restoring the art of passing to the NBA and turning the Celtics from a 29-53 team in 1978–1979 to a 61-21 team the following year. Until Bird won his first MVP trophy in 1984, centers had won eighteen of the previous 19 MVP awards. No center won another one until 1994. Magic and Bird had altered the focus of the game.

Bird would average 24.3 points, 10 rebounds and 6.3 assists over the course of his career. He would be described by Lakers general manager Jerry West as being "as nearly perfect as you can get in every phase." And he would become known for sinking shots nobody else would be allowed to take, explaining, "I'm like a gymnast. I'm into degree of difficulty."

Perhaps most amazing, Bird's accomplishments came despite obvious physical limitations. "My own physical gifts are limited," claims Magic, "but compared to this guy I'm one of the Flying Wallenda Brothers. White men can't jump? He was living proof." Yet he was also a living legend who joined his great rival and, eventually, good friend in carrying collegiate and professional basketball higher than anyone ever imagined it would go.

MAGIC VERSUS LARRY

Between 1979 and 1991, Magic Johnson and Larry Bird faced each other 38 times on the basketball court—once in college and 37 times in the NBA. Over the long haul, Magic's teams outperformed Bird's. He won their one collegiate battle, and his Lakers beat Bird's Celtics in 22 of 37 games and two out of three NBA Finals. Individually, the rivalry was more even:

	Larry Bird (Pts-reb-assists)	Magic Johnson (Pts-reb-assists)
1979 NCAA title game	19—13—2	24—7—5
18 NBA in-season games	21.7—10.3—6.2	19.4—7.0—11.5
19 playoff games	25.2—11.1—4.6	20.7—7.5—13.5
Total (Bird versus Johnson)	23.4—10.8—5.3	20.2—7.3—12.3

34

Ban Johnson

"Some people believe that the man makes history. Others argue that history makes the man," historian Harold Seymour writes in *Baseball: The Early Years*. "More likely, history is to be made when the times are ripe and the right man is on hand to seize the opportunity."

As professional baseball stumbled toward the close of the nineteenth century, the National League's monopoly at the major league level sustained repeated challenges. There was the American Association, which successfully kept pace with the more established league from 1882 to 1891. There was the Union Association in 1884, and the Players' League in 1890. But it took one man's efforts and one man's vision, combined with some fortuitous timing, to achieve a lasting victory. Ban Johnson became the right man for the job.

Johnson's legacy is the American League and, by extension, its impact on the game—from the World Series to the Yankee dynasty to the designated hitter. Had he realized the significance of his role in shaping the game, instead of later despairing about his diminished role in ruling it, he might have died a happier man.

The genius behind baseball's junior circuit was the son of a college professor, born Byron Bancroft Johnson on January 5, 1864, in Norwalk, Ohio. He played baseball at Marietta College and in the semi-professional ranks, and then began covering the game as a sportswriter for the *Cincinnati Commercial-Gazette*. He struck up a friendship with Reds manager Charles Comiskey, who would spearhead both his arrival and his demise.

In 1894, prodded by Comiskey, Johnson took over as president of the Western League, a minor league which had been reorganized a number of times over the preceding seasons. At the time, the circuit consisted of teams in Milwaukee, Minneapolis, Detroit, Grand Rapids, Toledo, Indianapolis, Kansas City and Sioux City. After a year, Sioux City was replaced by a St. Paul franchise, and within two years the Western League already was being touted as perhaps the "strongest minor ever."

Johnson declared that his league could survive on its own, and soon a series of events provided him an opportunity to prove it. The National League was at its nadir. It had moved from an eight-team league to a 12 team circuit by merging with the American Association in 1892, but mismanagement and factionalism in the ensuing years had weakened it considerably. After the 1899 season, the National League was pared back down to eight teams.

Sensing an opportunity, Johnson renamed his circuit the American League and expanded into Chicago and Detroit. Though the American League was a step down from the National League in talent, its absence of rowdyism made it a virtual equal when it came time to count the gate receipts. In the autumn of 1900, Johnson continued his bold assault on the National League. He decided to move East into Washington, Baltimore and Philadelphia, the first two being National League outcasts but the latter being a National League stronghold. He then refused to renew his application to the National League for protection under the National Agreement, a peace pact regulating competition among leagues for players and territories, and announced that the National League could no longer draft his players. He then revealed plans to form a team in Boston, as well.

"The National League has taken for granted that no one had a right to expand without first getting its permission. We did not think that this was necessary and have expanded without even asking permission," Johnson explained in February 1901. "If we had waited for the National League to do something for us, we would have remained a minor league forever."

He concluded with a typically confident flourish. "The American League will be the principal organization in the country within a very short time," he said. "Mark my prediction."

Baseball became involved in a trade war, with both leagues bidding for players' services and salaries rising accordingly. Dozens of players jumped at the new league's salary offers. In fact, seventy-four National League veterans went over to the American League in the next two years, including Cy Young, Willie Keeler and Nap Lajoie. In 1902, the American League outdrew the National League by more than 500,000 fans.

Before the 1902 season, Johnson had dropped Milwaukee for a franchise in St. Louis, and after the season he made his final change, replacing Baltimore with a team in New York. The eight-team circuit—made up of clubs in New York, Boston, Philadelphia, Washington, Detroit, Cleveland, Chicago and St. Louis—would remain stable for more than fifty years.

The National League knew it had been beaten and offered that the two leagues consolidate into one 12-team circuit, but Johnson, once again, declined, and the old league was forced to accept the new. On January 9, 1903, representatives of both leagues met and ironed out a peace pact. Playing rules and schedules would be planned cooperatively, and a new National Agreement to govern organized baseball was created, including a three-man National Commission to govern the game. The president of each league would be on the commission, while the third member, chosen by them, would act as chairman. Johnson had won the war, and, as it turned out, his victory was a boon to baseball.

Having made the most successful power play in baseball since William Hulbert founded the National League a generation earlier, Johnson aimed to maintain control of the game. He became the most powerful force on the National Commission, partly because of his personality and partly because the National League went through several presidents. The American League continued to outdraw the senior circuit each year, even before the emergence of Babe Ruth, but Johnson's leadership made the entire game prosper.

Yet, time erodes gratitude, and power corrupts. The American League president's imposing personality and his heavy-handed decisions eventually brought about his downfall. "Johnson could be vindictive and even petty, and at times he seemed overly impressed with himself," Seymour explains. "Particularly in the later years of his presidency, he overstepped his prerogative and in the end had to face a revolt by his own club owners."

Ironically, it was Charles Comiskey who led the revolt. Once Johnson's closest ally, the two began to feud in 1905, when Johnson upheld the suspension of one of Comiskey's Chicago players. The ensuing years brought more disagreement, and the owners became bitterly divided between Johnson's supporters and detractors. Eventually, the anti-Johnson forces won out, and, by 1920, a two-man board of review in the American League had usurped Johnson's powers, making him a virtual figurehead. When the full force of the Black Sox scandal hit later that year, baseball's sixteen club owners unanimously voted to replace the three-man National Commission with a single all-powerful executive, electing the first commissioner of baseball, Judge Kenesaw Mountain Landis.

The owners who had protested Johnson's "czarism" had cultivated just that in Landis, which left Johnson increasingly bitter. In fact, he is reported to have complained, "I'm about as important around here as the office boy." He was finally forced out of office in 1927.

On March 28, 1931, some six years before he was voted into the Baseball Hall of Fame, Johnson died, a man unhappy with the course his life had taken, but, perhaps, unaware of his lasting legacy.

35

Lamar Hunt

When chroniclers explain that Lamar Hunt was born into money, they mean lots of it. His father was, after all, ultraconservative billionaire oil tycoon H. L. Hunt, a man who—when his youngest son was born on August 2, 1932, in El Dorado, Arkansas—could have purchased the whole state as a birthday gift. Lamar Hunt had money, and he used it to make more. But he also used it to become one of the most influential figures in American sport. In fact, he can lay claim to being arguably one of the ten most important figures in each of three different sports. How many people can say that?

Hunt founded the American Football League, and was a key player in orchestrating its eventual merger with the NFL, doubling the scope of professional football. He was the primary financial force behind the North American Soccer League, the organization that brought Pelé to the States and lifted soccer into the American consciousness. He formed World Championship Tennis, the circuit that helped launch the tennis world's acceptance of open competition and professionalism. The arbiters of each sport have elected Hunt to their Hall of Fame.

From the beginning, Hunt preferred to combine sport and business, perusing box scores for attendance figures while others scanned RBI totals. Of course, money is what makes sport a business (and business a sport), and Hunt's money was the key to the North American Soccer League. The 17-team NASL had been formed in 1967, but it was down to five teams by the end of the following year. One of those teams, however, was the Dallas Tornado, owned by Hunt, whose reputation and deep pockets were significant factors in the league's survival.

Hunt convinced his colleagues to hire Phil Woosnam as league commissioner, and Woosnam promptly hired former London sportswriter Clive Toye as his assistant. Toye eventually took over the New York Cosmos and lured the great

Pelé to the United States in 1975. Pelé fueled a boom in the league, which contributed to a boom in the game. The soccer great returned to his native Brazil following the 1977 season, and the NASL was dead by 1985, but it had made its mark.

Another Hunt investment that didn't last the long haul, but had an important short-term influence, was World Championship Tennis (WCT), which Hunt created in 1967 with New Orleans promoter Dave Dixon. "Professional tennis is going to be big, very big," Hunt said at the time. He had made the same declaration about American professional soccer, but this time he proved more prescient.

At the same time, another professional circuit, the National Tennis League (NTL), emerged, and, together, the leagues signed most of the world's top players to pro contracts. Hunt eventually bought out Dixon's share, and his organization soon absorbed the NTL. World Championship Tennis challenged the virtual monopoly of the International Lawn Tennis Federation and revealed the potential of a grandiose professional tour.

In 1971, Hunt staged a $1 million World Championship of Tennis tournament, featuring thirty-two players and a $50,000 first-place prize, the largest in tennis up to that time. But, like the NASL, the WCT eventually faded from the picture. The Association of Tennis Professionals was created in 1972, and the ATP Tour soon took over control of the tennis circuit. Once again, however, Hunt's millions had made their mark.

Before Hunt had ever seen a soccer game and before he became an avid tennis player, he played football. At Southern Methodist University, he was a third-string end, and a teammate of Raymond Berry and Forrest Gregg, two men who would follow him into the Pro Football Hall of Fame. Hunt's fond memories, as well as his love of Dallas, drove him into the game in which he made his most profound impact—professional football.

In 1959, Hunt decided to make a bid for the NFL's frailest franchise, the Chicago Cardinals. He would buy the struggling team and move it to his hometown, one of many prospective owners interested in doing the same. He was rebuffed in his attempt and returned home, but along the way he encountered, as he put it, "the proverbial light bulb in your head." If all these people were interested in obtaining a professional football franchise for their city, why not gather them together into a new league?

But, as football historian Bob Carroll writes in *When the Grass Was Real*, "the relatively short history of pro football had a lesson for brave new entrepreneurs who dared consider starting up a football organization to oppose the entrenched National Football League. The lesson was simple: DON'T."

Three competing leagues, each named the American Football League, had attempted to challenge the NFL—in 1926, 1936–1937, and 1940–1941—and each had failed. Only the All-American Football Conference had been moderately successful, surviving for four years (1946–1949) before merging three teams in 1950. But Hunt was undeterred by history. He first approached Bud Adams, a Houston oil baron who, likewise, had been frustrated in his attempts to join the NFL ranks. The duo found four other charter members in Denver, Minneapolis and the all-important markets of Los Angeles and New York City, a group that would come to be known as "The Foolish Club."

The league was officially formed on August 14, 1959, at about the same time that a new baseball organization, the Continental League, announced its intentions to become a third major league. The Continental League forces were led by baseball legend Branch Rickey; the AFL was led by a pair of oilmen. The press and public believed, erroneously as it turns out, that the baseball league would be the one to succeed.

The cynics gained ammunition at the press conference announcing the formation of the AFL when Hunt revealed why he would never be known for putting his mouth where his money was. One reporter remembered Hunt speaking "almost in a whisper, without any force or authority," after which another in attendance is said to have remarked, "Wait till George Halas gets ahold of this punk."

But appearances can be deceiving, and the AFL plodded on. The six teams became eight with the addition of clubs in Boston and Buffalo, and the league held its first draft in November, signing Heisman Trophy winner Billy Cannon to play with Houston and hiring former South Dakota governor Joe Foss as commissioner.

Amid all the preparations, Hunt and Bud Adams had been offered NFL expansion franchises but had remained loyal to their cause. However, the AFL's Minneapolis club chucked loyalty for stability, accepting an expansion offer with the established league early in 1960, and shaking the faith of more than a few AFL owners. A few months later, however, the new league received a major boost when Foss announced a five-year television contract with ABC. This guaranteed the league national exposure and some financial stability for even its weakest teams, as the league had adopted the novel concept (soon copied by the NFL) of sharing television revenues equally.

Like most upstart leagues, the AFL benefitted by being more fan-conscious, permitting names on the back of uniforms, using the two-point conversion and, unlike the NFL, allowing TV coverage of anything that happened on the field, including fights. The league also made an important decision not to raid NFL rosters, only signing players when their contracts ran out. Still, Hunt's creation struggled to survive.

The Denver franchise nearly went bust before being bought by a syndicate in 1961; the Boston Patriots and Oakland Raiders were vagabond outfits without stable stadiums; the L.A. Chargers had to move to San Diego to stay alive, costing the league an important market; and the New York Titans were badly managed. Even Hunt found it necessary to move his team from his beloved Dallas to Kansas City, following the club's championship season in 1962, though he had to be persuaded to drop the name "Texans."

"We were faced with the task of getting our income up where it exceeded our expenses," Hunt explained, "and it was really a race against time because we couldn't go on losing a lot of money. We had to begin to show some success."

Somehow, the league made it through its first few seasons, and soon things began to look up. In 1963, the AFL signed eight #1 draft choices, and Al Davis became head coach and general manager of the Raiders, turning the league's most dismal franchise into a winner. The following year, Sonny Werblin, president of the Music Corporation of America, purchased the hapless New York Titans. Werblin changed the team's name to the Jets and signed quarterback Joe Namath, turning the team into the league's most profitable and important franchise. The AFL had turned the corner toward prosperity.

After Foss signed a five-year, $36 million TV contract with NBC, the league announced intentions to expand. Naturally, this triggered an NFL response, resulting in the Atlanta Falcons joining the NFL and the Miami Dolphins joining the AFL. In 1966, the league wars began in earnest. The NFL signed three rookies to contracts even more lucrative than Namath's, and the two leagues spent an estimated $25 million to sign their draft choices. On April 8, Al Davis, a hawk in the war, took over for Foss as commissioner. About five weeks later, all-pro kicker Pete Gogolak defected from the AFL's Bills to the NFL's New York Giants, instigating an all-out bidding war, leading Davis and AFL owners to open negotiations with dozens of NFL stars, particularly big-name quarterbacks.

Relations between the two leagues seemed strained at best, but behind the scenes, Hunt was working toward a compromise. Four days before Davis was named commissioner, Hunt, representing the AFL, held a secret rendezvous with Cowboys president Tex Schramm, representing the NFL, in the parking lot of Love Field airport in Dallas. The meeting may rank in significance only behind the 1920 gathering that spawned the NFL because this one set the stage for a merger between the two leagues, which was officially announced on June 8.

The provisions of the agreement called for all existing franchises to be maintained, a championship game between the two leagues to be held following the 1966 season, and a common draft to begin in 1967. The two leagues would play separate schedules until 1970, at which time inter-*conference* play would begin. In just one decade, thanks in large part to Hunt, the NFL had grown from twelve teams to twenty-six.

The NFL's Green Bay Packers won the first two championship games (it would soon be called the Super Bowl) handily, but Namath's Jets fashioned an improbable upset in the third encounter, putting to rest any whispers that the AFL played an inferior brand of football.

Super Bowl IV in 1970 was technically the last contest between teams from the NFL and the AFL. It pitted the Minnesota Vikings, a club which symbolized the NFL's attempt to squash the new league a decade earlier, against Hunt's Chiefs, the team that started it all. Just as the AFL had been, the Chiefs were an overwhelming underdog; and, once again, Hunt's side won.

THE SUPER BOWL

How did the Super Bowl become the Super Bowl? Shortly after the AFL-NFL merger in 1966, a committee—consisting of three AFL representatives (including Lamar

Hunt), three NFL owners and Pete Rozelle—was formed to iron out the details of the agreement. According to Hunt, in one of those meetings, an owner began to discuss the particulars of the "championship game" and another owner replied, "Which championship game?" Hunt piped in, "You know, the last game, the final game, the Super Bowl."

"Everybody kind of looked at me funny, but this committee began referring to this new game that was being created as the Super Bowl," Hunt recalled. "The league itself took a different stance. The league called it the AFL-NFL World Championship Game, and that's what was printed on the trophy. Pete Rozelle thought that was a lot more dignified. I think everybody thought it was more dignified. But the press seized on the idea of Super Sunday, and that's where the name came from."

36

Arthur Ashe

Arthur Ashe once said that if he were remembered only as a tennis player, he would consider himself a failure. Ironically, had Ashe's life consisted only of his tennis career, he still would have transcended the white lines in the manner that became his barometer for success.

As the first African-American Davis Cup participant and the first black male to win the U.S. Open and Wimbledon, Ashe was a stark and stoic symbol of the penetration of a lily-white sport. Ashe left his mark on the game viscerally, through his pioneering success, but also financially and philosophically, through his actions as a leader in the formation of the Association of Tennis Professionals (ATP). Had he done nothing more, he would own a spot among the 100 most important people in American sports history, but as it turned out, his accomplishments on the court paled beside his efforts to defeat social, political and medical injustice.

His sporting legacy is as broad in scope as his convictions were deep. He was a racial symbol, inspiring a generation of blacks to take up a previously uninviting sport. He was a publicist of sorts, joining with the likes of Billie Jean King, Chris Evert and Jimmy Connors to fuel the tennis boom of the 1970s. He was an author, his history of the black athlete, *A Hard Road to Glory*, and his fifteen years of opinions in *The Washington Post* exhibiting a brilliant intellect. He was a practical and productive activist. He was a so-called crossover sports hero.

Perhaps most important, Ashe was a reminder of priorities. "From what we get, we can make a living; what we give, however, makes a life," he wrote in his memoirs, *Days of Grace*. With sports serving as a background, Ashe gave us the gift of reflection. He made us think—and think hard—about racism, about health, about education, about charity. When he announced, in 1992, that he was infected with the AIDS virus, he made us think more—about life and death and privacy.

His life was cut tragically short, yet perhaps no athlete has ever fashioned a more useful existence. Other athletes have left the playing fields for greater accomplishment, leaving their outstanding athletic careers as distant memories. Byron White became a Supreme Court justice; Bill Bradley a senator; Paul Robeson an activist and, eventually, a martyr. But, for them, their sports persona was all but incidental in the long run. For Ashe, it remained a vital part of his character, his appeal and his efforts.

In the end, he was simply a tennis player—in the sense that Frederick Douglas was a writer, Abraham Lincoln was a politician, and Martin Luther King, Jr., was a reverend—but he was a man who redefined the notion of the athlete as statesman. He was a child of segregation, a product of the worst in America, and yet he was a symbol of the very best.

The world that Arthur Robert Ashe, Jr., entered on July 10, 1943, was full of contradiction to—and contempt for—black Americans. A war was being fought against intolerance abroad, but it was flourishing at home. Segregation was the rule in Richmond, Virginia, where he was born, and monuments proudly lionized Confederate generals. Fifty years later, upon his death, Ashe would become the first person to lie in state in the Virginia Governor's Mansion since General Stonewall Jackson.

Ashe's mother died when he was six, a tragedy to which he attributed what many perceived as his icy emotional reserve later in life. His father was the caretaker of the largest playground for blacks in Richmond. His house was next to the playground, and four tennis courts were next to the house. Thus tennis came to Ashe through the realities of segregation, yet it also provided him a means to escape it. His career began at the age of seven, when Richmond's most accomplished black player—a man named, appropriately, Ron Charity—stopped his practice, walked over to Ashe and asked, "Would you like to learn how to play?"

Ashe was barred from playing on most public courts and in most local tournaments involving whites, yet he still managed to earn a tennis scholarship to UCLA, where he then earned a business degree. In 1963, as a 20-year-old, he was asked to become the first African-American on the U.S. Davis Cup team. Over the next fifteen years, he won 28 of 34 Cup matches.

In 1968, Ashe lifted his tennis game to a new level, leading the U.S. to its first Davis Cup win in five years, winning the national amateur title and becoming the first U.S. Open champion in the open era. Ashe turned professional in 1970, won the Australian Open, and then, two years later, became the first American tennis player to exceed $100,000 in annual earnings. Also in 1972, he became a leader of the fledgling ATP, the players' union that further transformed the game into its modern professional form by wresting control from the International Lawn Tennis Federation and the governing bodies of the four Grand Slam tournaments. In 1974–1975, he served as the organization's president.

Ashe's greatest tennis triumph came in 1975, when he used a cerebral approach to defeat the game's most dominant player, Jimmy Connors, in the Wimbledon finals. Said Roy S. Johnson, senior editor at *Money* magazine, "Seeing a black man playing tennis was weird in itself, but seeing him win the most prestigious tournament in the world by himself in a manner that belied everything Americans seemed to hold true about black Americans was something that was pretty indescribable."

Ashe's tennis career ended abruptly when he suffered a heart attack in July 1979, and then underwent a quadruple coronary bypass operation six months later. He officially retired from tennis in 1980, at the age of thirty-seven, telling the press, "The doctors say I will live to be 100, but they won't put it in writing."

His body may have been telling him to simply rest on his laurels, and his accomplishments—thirty-three tournament victories and thirteen straight years ranked among the top five players in the world—were such that to do so would have brought no shame, yet Ashe was still haunted by a gnawing dissatisfaction. "I don't think I wanted to be immortal, not in any literal sense . . . But I did want to achieve something more than I had accomplished on the tennis court," he explained.

One of Ashe's favorite prayers, articulated by W. E. B. DuBois, asked the Lord to "make us not great but busy." In the years following his retirement from tennis, Ashe was both. Along with being an outspoken opponent of South African apartheid and remaining a key figure in professional tennis by acting as the non-playing captain of the U.S. Davis Cup team from 1980–1985, he formed the African American Athletic Association, the Ashe-Bollettieri Cities (ABC) tennis program, Athletes Career Connection, the Safe Passage Foundation, the Arthur Ashe Institute for Urban Health, and the Arthur Ashe Foundation for the Defeat of AIDS.

Ashe responded to what Kenny Moore called "a series of summonses from causes close to his heart, one being that heart itself." And, thus, he also devoted his efforts to the American Heart Association, the United Negro College Fund and a U.S. foreign policy think tank, TransAfrica. He taught a college course on "The Black Athlete in Contemporary Society" and then spent nearly $300,000 to hire a team of researchers to help him compile his definitive three-volume history of the African-American athlete.

Passionate yet practical, cool under fire yet full of smoldering convictions, Ashe had forged a legacy of good works and lasting images of transcendence. Said his friend Bryant Gumbel in an HBO special, *Arthur Ashe: Citizen of the World,* "He was an ambassador of what was right. He was an ambassador of dignity. He was an ambassador of class."

Even his death was translated into an opportunity for more good works by him and a lesson to be learned by us. In the last thirteen years of his life, Ashe had become, in his words, "a professional patient." Following his heart attack and quadruple bypass in 1979, he had required another bypass in 1983, after which he had received a blood tranfusion. Five years later, he entered New York Hospital for brain surgery and discovered he had acquired the AIDS virus, almost definitely as a result of the blood tranfusion, which had occurred two years before mandatory testing for the HIV virus was required in donated blood.

Believing a public announcement would infringe on his family's right to privacy, particularly that of his young daughter, Camera, he revealed his illness only to his closest friends. But in April 1992, Ashe discovered that *USA Today* was preparing to follow up rumors that he was HIV-positive. The newspaper's editors disagreed with Ashe's insistence that he was not a public figure and told him that if he would not confirm the rumors, they would attempt to find someone who would.

"Match point had come, and I had lost it," Ashe explained. "All I could do now was try to control the announcement itself, to have it heard directly from me." Just a few months after Magic Johnson's shocking announcement that he was HIV-positive, Ashe told the world that he was already stricken with full-blown AIDS. The fact that Ashe was one of the disease's so-called "innocent" victims put a different twist on the announcement, as did the realization that he had been forced into going public with his private turmoil. Like so many other issues Ashe had taken up, his announcement made people think—about the rights of the press and the rights to privacy.

Ashe was angry that "this newspaper, any newspaper or any part of the media, could think it had a right to tell the world I had AIDS." *USA Today*, alone, received more than 700 letters, the great majority of them agreeing with Ashe, but an editorial in the national newspaper suggested a "conspiracy of silence has not served the public. Ashe is not a public official, but for many people, young and old, he's probably as influential as any president."

The entire event had hit Ashe hard because, as he put it, "If one's reputation is a possession, then of all my possessions, my reputation means most to me." Yet, to no one's surprise, he turned the stigma of AIDS and the desperate need for research funding into a motivational tool for educating the public and for raising money to combat the disease throughout the world.

"I do not like being the personification of a problem, much less a problem involving a killer disease, but I know I must seize these opportunities to spread the word," Ashe wrote in *Days of Grace*. He created the Arthur Ashe Foundation for the Defeat of AIDS, received the first Annual AIDS Leadership Award from the Harvard AIDS Institute, and addressed the United Nations on World AIDS Day. Despite his personal trauma, however, he still campaigned for the rights of others, and even in his last days, he was arrested, as planned, at a demonstration in Washington, D.C., to protest inhuman treatment of Haitian refugees. Ashe had another heart attack following the event, but it was his inability to fight off pneumonia that finally took his life on February 6, 1993.

More than 5,000 people filed by his casket in the Virginia Governor's Mansion, mourning the loss of a child from the segregated South who had become a gift to the world, a victim of years of illness who had fought to erase decades of injustice, a man who, says Roy S. Johnson, "had the frailest of bodies but moved mountains."

Ashe and Apartheid

Memories of a childhood in segregated Virginia had spurred Ashe to fight against South African apartheid as early as 1969. After being denied permission to play there in 1970, he took his fight to the World Tennis Union and the United Nations. In 1973, he competed in South Africa for the first time, requesting and receiving integrated seating at his matches.

He visited three more times over the next four years, changing the life of at least one young black South African who saw in him the possibility for escape and emergence and told Ashe, "You are the first truly free black man I have ever seen." Ashe favored international sanctions against South Africa, played a major role in having the country banned from Davis Cup play, became a founding member of Artists and Athletes Against Apartheid, and was even arrested outside the South African embassy in 1985.

Still, Ashe retained a modest perspective of his efforts, even in the face of the martyrdom illness had cast upon him, claiming, "Compared to [Nelson] Mandela's sacrifice, my own life . . . has been one of almost self-indulgence. When I think of him, my own political efforts seem puny." Yet when Mandela first encountered Ashe in person, after obtaining his freedom, it was he who held Ashe in a warm embrace.

37

Walter Byers

The backbone of college athletics, the National Collegiate Athletic Association, has been around since 1906. However, in at least its first four decades of existence, the NCAA was basically, as one writer described it, "a loosely knit debating society."

But the NCAA evolved dramatically—from a group formed by a handful of institutions hoping to solve the problem of violence in football into a monolithic organization generating billions of dollars in revenue and having turned college athletics into one of sport's most marketable entities. The man most responsible for that evolution is Walter Byers, the association's first executive director. Even Donna Lopiano, executive director of the Women's Sports Foundation, and certainly no admirer of the NCAA's longtime chief, was forced to admit, "The NCAA was nothing without Walter Byers."

For more than forty years, the NCAA had relied on volunteer support. It was essentially a part-time preoccupation. But in 1949, Kenneth L. "Tug" Wilson, commissioner of the Big Ten Conference and secretary-treasurer of the NCAA, suggested to the association's Executive Committee the need for a full-time executive. Plans were made for the creation of a central office, which at the time was located in the Big Ten offices, and two years later 29-year-old Walter Byers, who had been an assistant under Wilson for four years, was tabbed for the job.

The following July, Byers moved the show to Kansas to assure a central location for the offices and to reflect the NCAA's broadening base. But Kansas City also happened to be where Byers was born (March 13, 1922) and raised, on his father's prosperous farm and cattle ranch. After starring as a 5-foot-9, 170-pound all-city football center in high school, Byers attempted to walk onto the Rice University team, where his coach told him he was too small to be of any use. When a bum ankle added injury to insult, he quit the team and, after one year, switched to the University of Iowa and to baseball.

Byers was only nine hours short of a journalism degree in 1943 when he quit again, this time to enlist in the Army. Again, he was derailed by physical limitations, eventually being handed a medical discharge due to eye problems. Byers then decided to forego the remainder of his education for a chance to join the work force, an act he would frown upon in NCAA athletes decades later. After working for United Press in several cities, primarily covering sports, Byers found himself back in Chicago working as Tug Wilson's assistant, soon to be handed the NCAA's top job. Who could have known that a failed collegiate athlete without an undergraduate diploma would become the most powerful man in college sports?

Not only was Byers the association's first executive director (in fact, its first full-time administrative officer)—until his retirement in 1988, he was the only executive director the NCAA had ever had. His staying power gave him tremendous influence, particularly within the organizational structure of the NCAA. The executive director is the association's most powerful full-time employee, providing day-to-day guidance and year-to-year philosophical continuity. And by overseeing its growth for thirty-seven years, Byers made the NCAA largely a product of his sensibilities.

In the beginning, however, he had a rather ambiguous job description. "When my contract was first drawn up, there was talk of setting down my duties. But there was no precedent," Byers explained in an interview during his first decade at the helm. "Finally it was decided just to say I was hired as executive director and see where that took us."

Where it took the NCAA depends on one's perspective. It certainly took the association to unimagined heights. When Byers first took over, his one full-time employee was his secretary. Today, some 150 staff members are employed at NCAA headquarters, now located in Mission, Kansas. In Byers's first five years as executive director, NCAA membership nearly doubled; by the time he retired, membership had more than quadrupled.

Former Big Ten Commissioner Wayne Duke, a longtime assistant under Byers, believes his former boss was the key to the explosion in college athletics since World War II. "The NCAA prospered, in my opinion, because of three factors— enforcement, football on television and the basketball tournament," he told McCallum. "And Walter was the architect of all three."

The pre-Byers NCAA was long on rules but short on ways to enforce them. A three-member Compliance Committee had been established in 1948, but an ineffectual enforcement procedure resulted in the committee's quick demise. In Byers's second year, the Compliance Committee was replaced by a Membership Committee and its investigative arm, a Subcommittee on Infractions. The following year, the NCAA Council was granted the power to impose penalties of various levels, which enhanced the system's credibility.

Rules regarding recruiting and eligibility have since proliferated, but the NCAA's manner of investigation and enforcement has come under frequent attack. One district court judge in *The NCAA v. Tarkanian* (1988), even went so far as to say, "These NCAA practices might be considered 'efficient,' but so was Adolph Eichmann and so is the Ayatollah." Byers himself has been called "the Simon Legree of American athletics."

Byers's second year was also the first in which the NCAA negotiated a television contact, a $1.14 million deal with NBC. By 1960, the NCAA had signed a two-year, $6.25 million contract with CBS; six years later, ABC bid $32.2 million for a four-year deal; and by the end of the decade, the television pact had expanded to include championship events in five other sports. By 1984, the NCAA's TV football revenues exceeded $60 million.

As for the basketball tournament, it was a 24-team afterthought when Byers took over. By 1960, Byers had pushed through the notion of automatic conference qualifiers and the suggestion that any schools chosen to compete in the tournament owed their first allegiance to the NCAA, and not to the older (and more prestigious) National Invitation Tournament. Early on, Byers realized the benefit of extracting a revenue base from the postseason playoffs, and the Final Four was on its way to merging with television and becoming the NCAA's most lucrative annual bonanza.

"In the same way that shoe companies have made pro basketball superstars, Walter Byers made college basketball and the Final Four," explained Donna Lopiano. "He positioned it as an NCAA property and sold it for all its worth to make it the Super Bowl of college sports."

The NCAA also finally included women's sports under its umbrella late in Byers's reign, though that happened despite his leadership. In fact, Byers opposed gender equity legislation, claiming it would mean the "possible doom of intercollegiate sports." But once it appeared obvious that the federal government intended to enforce such laws, the NCAA succeeded in assuming leadership of women's intercollegiate athletics.

In the process, Byers had not endeared himself to the leaders of the women's sports revolution. Indeed, if nothing else, Byers served as a lightning rod for criticism in his thirty-seven years at the helm. "The NCAA consists of so many people, it's hard to find any one person to attack in it," he once explained. "I seem to be the logical choice."

And the criticism continues even several years after Byers's retirement. In 1992, for instance, three economists published a study entitled *The National Collegiate Athletic Association: A Study in Cartel Behavior,* which claims that the NCAA evolved under Byers "from a problem-solving association into a rent-producing cartel." The authors add that "college sports have grown from a small cottage industry into a business grossing over $1 billion in revenues per year," but "schools and coaches have prospered; athletes have not."

In early 1995, Byers shocked observers by announcing a change of heart, suggesting that college players deserved to be paid what the market will bear. To many, however, this was analogous to Wilt Chamberlain preaching abstinence.

That Byers left a legacy of college athletics as big business is unquestionable, but at what price? "When you look at the origin of rules enforcement and its political nature; when you look at the decision to make intercollegiate athletics an entertainment entity, saleable not only to the press but to TV, that was Walter Byers," Lopiano declared. "And when you look at this huge establishment that got turned upside down in terms of whether it was an educational thing or not—the tail wagging the dog—give the credit to Walter."

REIGN MAN

Walter Byers's reign as NCAA executive director lasted longer (thirty-seven years) than that of any other U.S. sports czar. The following are the closest contenders:

• Clarence Campbell (NHL president), 31 years (1946–1977)

• Pete Rozelle (NFL commissioner), 29 years (1960–1989)

• Frank Calder (NHL president), 26 years (1917–1943)

• Kenesaw Mountain Landis (baseball commissioner), 24 years (1920–1944)

• Avery Brundage (U.S. Olympic Committee president), 24 years (1929–1953)

38

Wayne Gretzky

What Babe Ruth was to baseball in the '20s, and what Wilt Chamberlain was to basketball in the '60s, Wayne Gretzky has been to hockey in the '80s and '90s—at least in the sense that his statistics have taken him so far beyond even the accepted measure of excellence that they have obliterated old standards.

Through 1994–1995, Gretzky had accrued 60 NHL scoring records. He had the most goals (92), assists (163) and points (215) in a season; he had the most goals (814), assists (1,692) and points (2,506) in a career. He had ten scoring titles, the first six of them won by an average of 73 points, a total which would have led the league in Gordie Howe's rookie year. He had nine Most Valuable Player awards, three more than any other player in any team sport ever.

But dominance can lead to different things. Chamberlain scored points as no basketball player ever had, but his influence on the game was minor in comparison, largely because pioneers like George Mikan and Bill Russell had come before him. However, Ruth not only took offense to uncharted territories, he took his sport there, too. Of the two, Grezky's influence is most similar to Ruth's.

"Hockey needed a shot in the arm when he came along," Bobby Hull would later explain. "It needed a champion." Hockey received just that, as Gretzky became the face of the NHL. In the process, he destroyed its lingering stereotype as a collection of gap-toothed goons. He brought a Hollywood aspect to a sport that needed it badly, and then—when he moved to the Los Angeles Kings—he brought the sport to Hollywood.

He was born in Brantford, Ontario, on January 26, 1961. By 1963, he could skate, and by the time he was six, Gretzky was competing against 10-year-olds in the Brantford Atom League. He scored one goal that year, then 27 the following year, then 104, then 196. At the age of ten, he recorded 378 goals in 69 games, winning the league scoring title by a mere 238 goals. At the age of fourteen, he left home to play junior hockey, scoring two goals in his first game. At the age of fifteen, he was the subject of a 30-minute television show.

Gretzky went on to play Junior A hockey in Sault Ste. Marie, collecting three goals and three assists in his first appearance, and receiving aftershave lotion as the 16-year-old Player of the Game. He went on to break the all-time single-season scoring record at that level with 182 points.

Because Gretzky was underage, he opted to play in the World Hockey Association, the upstart rival to the NHL, then in its seventh and final season. He played eight games with the Indianapolis Racers, before being traded to the team with which he would become synonymous, the Edmonton Oilers. On his eighteenth birthday, he signed a 10-year, $3 million contract. Naturally, he scored 43 goals and 104 points in 1978–1979 to earn Rookie of the Year honors.

Edmonton was one of four WHA teams to merge with the NHL the following year, a season in which the 19-year-old Gretzky became the youngest player to exceed 50 goals in a season, tying Marcel Dionne for the scoring title with 137 points and earning the Hart Trophy as league MVP. From then on, every season seemed to bring a new assault on the record books.

In 1980–1981, Gretzky broke Bobby Orr's single-season assists mark and Phil Esposito's record for single-season points, finishing with 109 assists and 164 points. In 1981–1982, he became the first man ever to score his first 50 goals in fewer than 50 games. He did it in his 39th. Gretzky went on to total 92 goals, 16 more than Esposito's previous record. He added 120 assists, surpassing his own mark, and finished with an unheard-of 212 points, 60 more than anyone else had ever recorded. It was as if someone had suddenly come along and hit 85 home runs or struck out 535 batters. He had played in just three NHL seasons, but already he owned twice as many league records as anyone who had ever played the game.

Gretzky began the following season with a record 30-game scoring streak. He would go on to score four goals in the third period of the All-Star Game, break his own assists record with 125 and finish with 196 points. His fourth straight MVP award marked the first time that had ever been done, yet he wasn't even halfway toward filling his trophy case. For an encore in 1983–1984, Gretzky broke his own consecutive-game streak by scoring in 51 straight games, a total equivalent to a 102-game hitting streak in baseball. He finished with 87 goals, adding 13 in the playoffs for exactly 100 total. Only two decades earlier, 50 goals had been a nearly unattainable mark.

By then, Gretzky had established himself as hockey's Great One, but he had also been saddled with the reputation that he sparkled during the regular season but disappeared in the playoffs. He exorcised those demons when Edmonton destroyed the four-time defending champion New York Islanders in the 1984 Stanley Cup finals and began a dynasty of its own. The Oilers would win four Stanley Cups over the next five years.

Gretzky set a new assists mark in 1984–1985, and then shattered it a year later when he collected 163 assists and a record 215 points. Not only was he breaking every record, he had reached the point where he was rebreaking them. And he was doing so with a style that altered the way the game was played and perceived. Gretzky was a relatively scrawny hockey player, a shade under six feet and 170 pounds. As a result, he has recorded more goals in a game than fights in his entire career. He also has been an outspoken critic of violence in the game, and certainly a factor in the league's attempt to curb fighting.

Hockey in the '70s had been symbolized by the Philadelphia Flyers' style, and kids growing up used to emulate the Broad Street Bullies. Now they mimic Gretzky's artistry. "People are again relating to hockey as a game of skill, because that's the way Wayne plays," Bobby Hull told *Sports Illustrated*. "We were getting away from that. Scouts had been forgetting about the goals-assists-points column and, because of the success of the Flyers, going right to the columns that told about penalty minutes and size . . . But now they're looking for goals and assists again."

But even more important than Gretzky's impact on the ice has been his influence off of it, his role as the most marketable and marketed hockey player in history, the most visible symbol of a game desperate to reach into mainstream America. Bobby Orr declared, "Hockey can't afford to lose its Gretzkys . . . if Wayne is influencing the hundreds of thousands, the millions of kids that I think he is—well, put it this way: Thank God he's around."

To many Americans, Gretzky *is* hockey. Both he and the game have profited from the association. In 1994, *Forbes* ranked him as the world's sixth highest paid athlete at an estimated $13.5 million annually, about one-third of it in endorsements. Over the years, Gretzky would host "Saturday Night Live," hit all the major talk shows, grace the cover of *Time* magazine, dine with the Prime Minister of Canada and the President of the United States, and pose for both LeRoy Neiman and Andy Warhol.

Gretzky was once asked to autograph a sleeping baby; he once received mail addressed only "Wayne Gretzky, Kanada." He would guest star on "The Young and the Restless" and be a celebrity judge on "Dance Fever." The latter occurred in 1981, and marked the first time he saw Janet Jones. She would become a movie actress; he would marry her in 1988, an event newspapers touted as "Canada's Royal Wedding," featuring 200 credentialed media, 700 guests, and 10,000 well-wishers waiting outside the Edmonton church. It was hockey's version of Joe DiMaggio and Marilyn Monroe.

By the time of the wedding, Gretzky's relationship with Edmonton coach and general manager Glen Sather and owner Peter Pocklington had soured considerably. And Pocklington shocked the sports world in August 1988 by trading hockey's biggest star and two teammates to the L.A. Kings for two players, three first-round draft choices and $15 million.

Gretzky broke down at the press conference announcing the move, and the entire event, surrounded by finger-pointing and innuendo, was just about the biggest news in Canada since the British Parliament granted its independence. The *Edmonton Sun*, for instance, carried a front-page story about the trade, followed by a box reading: "MORE STORIES INSIDE PAGES 2, 3, 4, 5, 6, 10, 11, 18, 19, 23, 30, 36, 37, 38, 39, 40, 41, 43, 46 AND 47."

Gretzky felt a sense of urgency to "keep from being the biggest flop in Hollywood since 'Heaven's Gate.'" As it turned out, it was the best move that he or the NHL could have hoped for. In Gretzky's first few years in Edmonton, he had turned hockey's worst road draw into its best. If he could do that in hockey-saturated Canada, what could he do in the United States? The Kings had lost $5 million the previous year, yet while ticket prices doubled with Gretzky's arrival, season ticket sales more than tripled. The Great Western Forum, long a chic place for celebrities to be seen on basketball nights, became a hockey happening.

On Gretzky's first shot as a King, he scored a goal. He would finish with 168 points, winning MVP honors for the ninth time. Gretzky, who earned All-Star MVP honors in a dramatic return to Edmonton midway through the season, led his new team against his old in the first round of the playoffs. L.A. won in seven.

Gretzky would lead the Kings to the Stanley Cup finals four years later, by which time hockey had expanded or announced plans to expand into Anaheim, San Jose, Miami and Tampa Bay. He had assured the league success in the Sun Belt. But it was back in Gretzky's second season in L.A. that he enjoyed perhaps his greatest moment. It happened on October 15, 1989, back in Edmonton.

"When I was a kid, I wanted to play, talk, shoot, walk, eat, laugh, look and be like Gordie Howe," Gretzky, who donned #99 in honor of Howe's #9, liked to explain. He had always felt a bond with Howe. In fact, the two first met in 1972, when Howe presented the 11-year-old Gretzky with an award at a banquet and gave him a piece of advice. "Kid, keep practicing that backhand," he said. "Someday, it's going to be an important shot."

On that October night, with Howe in attendance, a last-minute game-tying backhander gave Gretzky his 1,851st career point, breaking his idol's record. Naturally, he went on to score the game-winning goal in overtime—on another backhander. He would go on to break Howe's NHL goal-scoring record in 1994, having finally conquered all of hockey's hallowed numbers long after he had conquered hockey.

A Higher Plane

The following chart compares the peformances of Babe Ruth, Wilt Chamberlain and Wayne Gretzky in their first ten full seasons. The year listed for Chamberlain and Gretzky represents the year in which the season ended; Gretzky's WHA season is not included.

Ruth (home runs) previous record: 24	Chamberlain (scoring) previous record: 29.2	Gretzky (points) previous record: 152
1920: 54*	1960: 37.6*	1980: 137*
1921: 59*	1961: 38.4*	1981: 164*

1922: 35	1962: 50.4*	1982: 212*
1923: 41*	1963: 44.8*	1983: 196*
1924: 46*	1964: 36.9*	1984: 205*
1925: 25	1965: 34.7*	1985: 208*
1926: 47*	1966: 33.5*	1986: 215*
1927: 60*	1967: 24.1	1987: 183*
1928: 54*	1968: 24.3	1988: 149
1929: 46*	1969: 20.5	1989: 168

(* denotes led league)

39

Curt Flood

"I am pleased that God made my skin black," Curt Flood remarked in 1972, "but I wish He had made it thicker."

Flood had been a minor league baseball player in the 1950s, not long after Jackie Robinson broke the color barrier, and he was one of dozens of African-American players who integrated southern playing fields. He was also one of many with bitter memories of the experience. "My teammates despised and rejected me as subhuman," he said, recalling his days in the Carolina League. "I would gladly have sent them all to hell."

When the civil rights movement gained momentum in the 1960s, Flood found himself increasingly more sensitive to injustice of every kind. And, in 1969, he began a fight for justice that would prove to have a dramatic effect on professional athletics in America. It was a fight Flood technically lost, but two decades of hindsight have labeled it an undeniable moral victory. And more than any other athlete, Curt Flood can be credited with ushering in the big-money era of sports.

Born on January 18, 1938, in Houston, Flood first signed with the Cincinnati Reds in 1956. He was traded to the St. Louis Cardinals late in 1957 and for a dozen years he was one of their best players, batting .293 and winning seven Gold Gloves in center field. By 1969, he was earning $90,000 per year, one of the game's top salaries, but he received a jolt following the season, when he discovered he had been traded.

After twelve seasons with the Cardinals, Flood found out about the trade when a newspaper reporter called him for his reaction. Not only that, he had been traded from one of the game's most successful franchises to the Philadelphia Phillies, a club Flood believed to be the least desirable for black athletes. He had friends, family and business interests in St. Louis, and he didn't want to leave. Only thirty-one years old, he considered retiring—and then he changed his mind.

Having fought so hard to overcome the lingering effects of slavery in the United States as a black man, Flood decided to attack what he considered Major League Baseball's enslavement of its players. He would challenge the game's reserve clause, which he described as "baseball's right to treat human beings like used cars."

The reserve clause was an agreement binding a player to his current employer, who could reserve his services for the following season. Unless a player was traded, released or sold, he was bound for life to the team that originally signed him. The reserve system was first instituted in 1879. At first, only five players per team were reserved, but that number gradually increased until the early 1890s, when all player contracts included the reserve clause.

The system—and indeed Major League Baseball's unlimited power to conduct its business—had received a series of challenges, the first coming in 1890, when a majority of players formed the Players' League, substituting three-year contracts for the reserve clause. But the league only lasted one season; the reserve clause lasted another eighty-five years.

Twenty-five years after the Players' League folded, another major league challenger, the Federal League, did the same. One of its clubs, the Baltimore Terrapins, was unhappy with the settlement of the inter-league dispute and filed an antitrust suit against baseball that found its way to the U.S. Supreme Court in 1922. Justice Oliver Wendell Holmes, Jr., writing for a unanimous court, contended that baseball was not subject to the Sherman Antitrust Act, which outlaws monopolies from operating in interstate commerce. Holmes ruled that the game was not "trade or commerce in the commonly-accepted use of those words." In addition, he stated that the movement of teams across state lines was merely "incidental" to business.

Though Holmes did not claim, as many believe he did, that baseball was a sport and not a business, the famous "antitrust exemption" has been interpreted as such over the years. The Supreme Court has proved reluctant to overturn the 1922 ruling, while Congress has generally considered it a matter for the courts to decide. And for more than half a century, the exemption gave baseball executives legal ammunition in support of the reserve clause.

In 1948, a 27-year-old outfielder named Danny Gardella sued Major League Baseball for $300,000 after being blacklisted because he jumped to the Mexican League. The Second Court of Appeals ruled in his favor, saying the "involuntary servitude" of the reserve clause violates the Thirteenth Amendment. The 1922 ruling had essentially been reversed, but after Major League Baseball appealed, Gardella settled out of court for $60,000.

Five years later, the case of *George Toolson v. New York Yankees, Inc.* reached the Supreme Court. After refusing to report to the Yankees' farm team in Binghamton, New York, Toolson had been placed on a list of ineligible players and blacklisted. He sued on the grounds that the reserve clause constrained trade, in violation of antitrust laws, and he lost by a 7-2 vote.

It was this kind of history that Curt Flood was up against. Though he had the backing of the Major League Baseball Players Association, MLBPA executive director Marvin Miller still cautioned him that it was an uphill battle which would endanger his playing career. Flood stood by his convictions, which led Miller to say that "his decision to challenge the reserve clause took at least as much courage as Jackie Robinson needed in his rookie season."

On Christmas Eve, 1969, Flood wrote a letter to baseball commissioner Bowie Kuhn explaining that he was not a piece of property and that he believed he had the right to consider any and all offers. Kuhn responded, "I certainly agree with you that you, as a human being, are not a piece of property to be bought and sold. This is fundamental in our society and I think obvious. However, I cannot see its applicability to the situation at hand . . . " The fight was on.

"This case would be of great importance, not only to Curt Flood, but to all the players, including thousands who might still be in Little League," stated Miller, who chose former U.S. Supreme Court Justice Arthur Goldberg to represent the center fielder. Flood sued Kuhn, the presidents of both leagues and the twenty-four team owners for $3 million, triple damages and free agency. The trial began in May 1970, and three months later, the federal district court ruled against Flood.

Though a handful of high-profile witnesses had spoken out against the reserve clause in court (notably Jackie Robinson, Hank Greenberg and Bill Veeck), Flood's major league colleagues failed to go to bat for him. Not one active player had appeared in court. Flood was left to say, "If I had six hundred players behind me, there would be no reserve clause."

Flood and Miller appealed the decision, but in January of 1971, the Second Circuit Court of Appeals upheld the lower court's ruling. *Flood v. Kuhn* would have ended there, had the U.S. Supreme Court not surprised legal observers by agreeing to hear another appeal. But on June 6, 1972, Flood lost once again, by a 5-3 score, his battle an apparent failure.

Yet, Flood's fight had put the reality of the reserve clause up to public scrutiny, and many didn't like what they saw. The *Washington Post* called the court's decision a triumph of tradition over logic. Even six of the eight ruling justices had admitted that baseball was, indeed, interstate commerce, leading Miller to say, "I don't think I've ever read such criticism of a majority decision of the court by the very justices who formed the majority."

As for Flood, he became a bit of a martyr for the cause. He had actually returned to baseball in 1971, after being "traded" from the Phillies to the Washington Senators, but after batting .200 in thirteen games, he quit. At age thirty-three, his year away from the game had eroded his skills. He had lost another battle—against time.

But in the long run, Flood's cause won the war. "The arguments against the reserve clause had never before been made so lucidly or so forcefully," Miller explains in his memoirs. "Much more important—what *Flood v. Kuhn* really accomplished—was, in the much-used phrase of the 1960s, raising the consciousness of everyone involved with baseball: the writers, the fans, the players—and perhaps even some of the owners."

The Players Association soon changed tactics. Instead of going to court, players were encouraged to play out their contracts and their one option year. Then, they filed a grievance to claim free agency. This time, they won. After nearly 100 years, the players had finally gained their freedom, in part because Curt Flood had opened the floodgates.

EMANCIPATION PROCLAMATION

Dec. 24, 1969:

Dear Mr. Kuhn,

After 12 years in the major leagues, I do not feel that I am a piece of property to be bought and sold irrespective of my wishes. I believe that any system that produces that result violates my basic rights as a citizen and is inconsistent with the laws of the United States and the several states.

It is my desire to play baseball in 1970 and I am capable of playing. I have received a contract from the Philadelphia club, but I believe I have the right to consider offers from other clubs before making any decisions. I, therefore, request that you make known to all the major league clubs my feelings in this matter and advise them of my availability for the 1970 season.

Curt Flood

40

Joe Namath

The image and story are among the most enduring in the annals of sport. It is 1969, and Joe Namath is the brash young quarterback of the New York Jets, who are the top dogs of the American Football League, which is widely recognized as the second-rate, younger brother of the NFL.

His Jets have earned the dubious right to take on the powerful Baltimore Colts in Super Bowl III. The Colts are led by Johnny Unitas, Namath's boyhood idol. As the game approaches, the Colts take on the appearance of prohibitive favorites, the point spread fluctuating between 17 and 19 points. In the first two Super Bowls, the NFL's Green Bay Packers had won by an average of 22 points, and observers are expecting more of the same.

Then, Namath, a drink in his hand, addresses a gathering at a Miami Touchdown Club banquet three days before the game. "We're going to win Sunday," he says. "I'll guarantee you."

The aura surrounding Namath's personality, along with some early evidence of what would become the media's Super Bowl frenzy, turn the statement into bold headlines: "NAMATH 'GUARANTEES' JET VICTORY." Suddenly, not only the quarterback's reputation is on the line, but that of the upstart AFL, as well. The Orange Bowl, on January 12, 1969, has become a stage for an inter-league morality play. But Namath's confidence is contagious, and while the injured Unitas can only play part of the game, Namath leads the Jets to a 16-7 victory. He runs off the field, one finger held high in the air.

Yet, that was all after the fact. Super Bowl III may have been Namath's crowning moment, but it wasn't necessarily his most important. His biggest impact probably came three years earlier, when he signed the most lucrative contract in pro football history, and immediately put the AFL on the map.

When Jets owners Sonny Werblin signed Namath to a three-year, $427,000 contract the day after Namath nearly led Alabama to a brilliant comeback victory in the 1965 Orange Bowl, the quarterback immediately became the AFL's most famous player. Werblin also signed Heisman Trophy–winning quarterback John Huarte to a $200,000 deal, but it was Namath who received all the press attention and who emerged as a sports icon, legitimizing the AFL with his mouth, his right arm and his pocketbook.

A league bordering on minor league status, in the eyes of many, became a threat to the NFL's Sunday monopoly, and it happened largely because in Namath, the AFL had perhaps the game's top drawing card, as well as its top player. "Namath may be Johnny Unitas and Paul Hornung rolled into one," Dan Jenkins wrote in *Sports Illustrated* in 1966. "He may, in fact, be pro football's very own Beatle."

Nothing boosts a struggling league like publicity, and nothing feeds publicity like an athlete who takes over New York City. Werblin was paying Namath handsomely, but the attention that the contract brought was priceless. As the authors of the *Pro Football Encyclopedia* explain, "Some people talked about the two fine young quarterbacks Werblin had signed, some talked about the misplaced values of a society that rewarded football players with small fortunes while grossly underpaying schoolteachers, but the important thing was that they talked."

After Namath's first season, the AFL, which had worried about franchises folding only a few years earlier, was voting to expand the league. By the end of his second season, the leagues had voted to merge. The Super Bowl triumph only showed that the victory was complete.

Namath's path to fame was as unlikely as his guaranteed victory. The man who took over the Manhattan social scene as Broadway Joe, and who came to embody the anti-Establishment sixties and the sexual revolution, was the product of a steel-mill town in Pennsylvania and a football factory in Alabama.

"I arrived in Beaver Falls for the first time, May 31, 1943," Namath wrote in his autobiography. ". . . I wore my hair short then." Beaver Falls, Pennsylvania, is where they manufacture football players and steel; Namath wanted to be the former so he could escape the latter. But his size kept him from making the cut the first time he tried out for his high school football team. Only after growing three inches and gaining twenty-five pounds during each of his last two years did he become a 6-foot, 185-pound All-State quarterback and baseball star.

Namath had planned on joining the Air Force after high school, but he found himself choosing between baseball and football. He received bonus offers as high as $25,000 from big league scouts and football scholarship offers from more than fifty universities. After choosing the University of Maryland, Namath failed the entrance exam. Still hoping to escape the Pennsylvania winters, he opted for the University of Alabama and coach Bear Bryant.

Namath started for Bryant as a sophomore, and Alabama went 10-1. The following year, the Crimson Tide went 9-2, though Namath was suspended from the final regular season game and an appearance in the Sugar Bowl for breaking team rules (i.e., drinking). A knee injury, the first of many, kept Namath on the sidelines for much of his senior season, but he limped into a game against Georgia Tech and led Alabama to the national title.

The NFL's St. Louis Cardinals and the AFL's Jets had been involved in a bidding war for Namath's services throughout his senior year, but the Jets won the battle by offering football's most lucrative contract. The Jets went 5-8-1 in 1965, as Namath fought to overcome his teammate's resentment of his sudden wealth and fame to earn Rookie of the Year honors. New York went 6-6-2 the following season while the crosstown Giants won only one game. The Jets were the talk of the town, an unthinkable prospect only a few years earlier. In 1967, the Jets improved to 8-5-1, and Namath became football's first 4,000-yard passer. The following season, of course, was capped by Super Bowl III, as the Jets, once doormats in a second-rate league, became professional football's world champs.

Bear Bryant had called Namath "the greatest athlete I've ever coached." Boston Patriot owner Billy Sullivan declared him "the biggest thing in New York since Babe Ruth." Al Davis simply said, "He tilts the field." But Namath became just as famous for his off-the-field exploits. The marriage of person, place and time—Namath, New York and the nation's budding social revolution—produced a celebrity the likes of which sports had never seen. The nation's quarterback was also the Great American Bachelor; he was an excellent passer, an even better swinger. Stories about Namath concerned themselves as much with his lifestyle as his right arm and his bad knees. In the '90s, Namath's excess and eccentricities are all but commonplace among athletic superstars; in the '60s he was a happening.

Namath became a marketing sensation, the first great modern commercial property out of professional football. He mixed Madison Avenue finesse with tie-dyed inclinations, sexual innuendo with blue-collar appeal. He hit all the major talk shows, presented at the Emmy Awards, starred in a panty hose commercial, and even shaved his beard in a Schick commercial for $10,000. "He poses a question for us all," Jenkins wrote. "Would you rather be young, single, rich, famous, talented and happy—or president?"

Following the Super Bowl victory, Namath came out with an autobiography entitled *I Can't Wait Until Tomorrow . . . 'Cause I Get Better Looking Every Day.* It wasn't a book about X's and O's or even really about football. It was, as co-author Dick Schaap explained, about "broads, booze and betting." What other athlete, at the age of twenty-five, could pull off a book with chapter titles like "I Like My Girls Blond and My Johnnie Walker Red"?

A quarter-century later, Namath's autobiography reveals a man at the peak of celebrity and the height of youthful arrogance. Joe Namath, on lying: "I don't ever lie. Well, I hardly ever lie. At least, I don't lie to guys" . . . Namath on Johnny Unitas: "I used to think Johnny was the best quarterback of all time. I still rate him one of the top two" . . . And Namath on sex: "If a doctor told me I had to give up women, I'm sure I'd give up doctors."

Prior to the 1969 season, NFL commissioner Pete Rozelle censured Namath for associating with known gamblers at the Manhattan nightclub he owned, Bachelors III. Namath chose to retire from the game in a tearful press conference, instead of acquiescing to Rozelle's demand to sell the restaurant. By the time the season began, however, Namath had agreed to a compromise. He would sell his ownership in the restaurant but retain the right to invest in other Bachelors III restaurants around the country. He played in the NFL for another nine seasons.

Namath had peaked with Super Bowl III. He would total five knee surgeries in thirteen seasons, standing on the sidelines in 42 of his final 108 games and finishing his career with the Los Angeles Rams in 1977. In the long run, he was more a media darling than a great quarterback. In his career, he threw 173 touchdown passes and 202 interceptions, including 16 games with three pickoffs, seven games with four, five games with five and three games with six. In his thirteen pro seasons, he played on only four winning teams.

But, as his agent, Jimmy Walsh, said, toward the end of Namath's career, "Eventually, Joe Namath the football player will not be as significant as the *idea* of him." He was right.

41

Bill France, Sr.

There are some who claim being America's most important auto racing figure is akin to being the world's loudest mute. Most likely, they live in northern climes, where stick-and-ball games dominate the sports pages and only racing's foremost events earn headlines. However, in the South—where speedways dot the landscape from Rockingham, North Carolina, to Hampton, Georgia, to Bristol, Tennessee—racing is a religion.

And missionaries like Richard Petty and A. J. Foyt and Mario Andretti and Al Unser and Dale Earnhardt have spread the religion to all parts of the country, such that, according to a 1990 survey conducted by the Goodyear Tire and Rubber Company, 26 percent of Americans are race fans, including some 14 million women. Auto racing has become more than just a regional passion; it is a large part of America's sporting culture.

Racing's most popular attraction is the circuit conducted by the National Association for Stock Car Auto Racing—NASCAR. It is the creation of one man—Bill France, Sr., a man whom *The New York Times* called "as close to being a racing institution as any man can be."

In the beginning, however, he was simply a banker's son, born on September 26, 1909, in Washington, D.C., and given the name William Henry Getty France. But he preferred Bill, and he was more mechanic than money manager, though he would prove to be very much of both. France grew up working in garages and service stations, occasionally sneaking the family Model T out to a nearby speedway for some laps. "My dad never could figure out why his tires were wearing out so quickly," he recalled.

He built his own racing car and competed in a handful of dirt-track races, where he learned that one needed a well-built car to win and that even winning didn't guarantee that one would receive prize money promised by unscrupulous promoters. In 1934, France decided to pack up his wife and infant son and head south to Miami. He made it as far as Daytona Beach, where he took a job as a mechanic at a local auto agency.

The sands of Daytona Beach just happened to be the site of numerous speed runs, including a 276-mile-per-hour performance by Sir Malcolm Campbell and his bullet-shaped Bluebird in 1935. But the beaches of Daytona became treacherous at those speeds, and by 1936, when Campbell broke his own mark by 25 miles per hour, he did so in the new land-speed Mecca, the Bonneville Salt Flats in Utah.

Daytona Beach had enjoyed its run as a racing center, and so it scrambled to maintain its reputation. By 1938, the city was in search of a racing savior. France answered the call, along with a local restauranteur named Charlie Reese, and within months, they had realized a profit in excess of $4,000 on stock car races. World War II interrupted their plans, particularly those of Reese, who was killed during the fighting. Afterwards, France returned to promoting stock car racing, which was, at the time, essentially a competition between bootleggers. These were men whose cars were built faster and better equipped so they could illegally transport moonshine around the South, one step ahead of the law. It was literally an outlaw sport.

France saw a need to regulate promoters and assure collection of prize money, to form a standard set of rules and specifications for all drivers and automobiles, to inaugurate a national championship through a point system, to provide insurance for the drivers, and to create a central headquarters. And so he did. As *Sports Illustrated*'s Brock Yates explained, France "manhandled a boisterous backwoods pastime into a multi-million-dollar business" turning "claques of contentious, jealous, suspicious, greedy, shortsighted, hayseed dirt-track jalopy jockeys and promoters [into] the most tight-knit, prosperous racing organization in the world."

Having succeeded in Daytona Beach, he promoted additional races elsewhere, occasionally making money only by winning the races himself. But France was thinking in much bigger terms. "Drivers, companies, track owners, pit crews . . . everybody could join under one umbrella," he recalled. "And that was the time that I saw what an advantage it would be to move from leadership *on* the track to leadership *of* the track."

On December 12, 1947, France met with other Southeastern race promoters and formed NASCAR. The key to its success was its reliance on stock car racing instead of modified racing. Not only did spectators appreciate watching extraordinary feats in virtually the same car they drove to work, but car manufacturers were soon eager to promote their products through NASCAR competition, spending millions of dollars in the process.

To France, "stock" cars also meant equal competition and strict regulations to assure that no automobile would have an unfair advantage over another. His resolve was tested in NASCAR's first Grand National championship, in Charlotte, North Carolina on June 19, 1949. When Glenn Dunnaway, the apparent winner, was found to have used an illegal piece of equipment, the kind usually used by bootleggers, France disqualified him. The owner of Dunnaway's car took NASCAR to court, and France emerged with his first victory, but not his last.

"The era during which most of the cars were owned by bootleggers had come to an end," writes Peter Golenbock, author of *American Zoom,* a history of NASCAR. "A new age, that of the superspeedway, was about to begin."

As Daytona Beach became more attractive to both racing fans and northerners searching for sun, France realized a need for better facilities. By 1959, a swampy thicket at Daytona's western edge had become Daytona International Speedway. Whereas tracks had traditionally been dusty ovals of less than a mile long, Daytona was a sparkling two-and-a-half-mile "tri-oval" with a straightaway along the backstretch and thousands of unobstructed seats along the straightaway. It was like building the Astrodome amid a row of shanties.

"One can read that the track is two and a half miles around, and intellectually one knows that is a long distance," Golenbock explains, "but even if you've been to the Rose Bowl or to the Kentucky Derby, the first vision of Daytona brings a whistle or some sort of exclamation, much like when you look across the Grand Canyon or Niagara Falls for the first time."

It was an unconventional track, built for speed, excitement and spectator convenience. Shaped essentially like a giant "D," it was steep (banked at 31 degrees at each of two big turns) and wide enough to allow passing in the turns. The resulting high speeds and high drama would transform the sport.

The first Daytona 500 took place on February 22, 1959. After a dead heat, it took three days to determine the winner of the first race, Lee Petty, who said, "We knew stock car racing was never going to be the same again." Lee's son, Richard, would go on to win the Daytona 500 seven times, while the success of the superspeedway would usher in the construction of several more. Included among these was another Bill France creation, the Talladega Speedway in Alabama, longer and steeper than Daytona.

The unveiling of the world's largest and fastest motorsports oval, combined with a recent rash of deaths on the track, led to a showdown between France and the newly formed Professional Drivers Association, in 1969, just before Talladega's first event. Concerned about safety, the PDA voted to boycott the upcoming race. By then, France was accustomed to confrontation.

In 1961, he had thwarted driver Curtis Turner's attempt to organize his colleagues into joining the Teamsters Union, in part because he believed teamster boss Jimmy Hoffa was eager to bring pari-mutuel betting to NASCAR. Throughout the decade, he had resisted attempts by Ford, Chrysler, Firestone and Goodyear to dominate NASCAR, by repeatedly creating restrictions to equalize competition.

When France's drivers walked out in 1969, he simply gathered a collection of replacements and staged a successful race without them. Before doing so, the 60-year-old climbed into a stock car to demonstrate the track's safety, reaching 176 miles per hour. "By managing to put on his race before a modest but enthusiastic crowd," wrote Yates, "France had maintained control of his organization and had proved that he and his network of speedways were the critical element in successful racing, as opposed to the transient stardom of a few drivers or the presence of ultrafast racing cars."

NASCAR's Grand National circuit, stock car racing's major league, was eventually renamed the Winston Cup Series after R. J. Reynolds Tobacco Company began sponsorship in 1971. The company's sponsorship also led NASCAR to drop its shorter races and dirt-track races, reducing the schedule but raising the stakes. In 1972, France turned the day-to-day operations of NASCAR over to his son, Bill France, Jr., but the elder France still remained a prominent voice when it came time to make the big decisions.

France died on June 7, 1992, by which time the organization he had created had grown to enormous proportions. NASCAR membership has reached nearly 45,000. The Winston Cup Series, consisting of thirty-one stops in nineteen different sites from Florida to Michigan to California, awards more than $25 million in prize money. Dale Earnhardt, the top money-earner in 1994, took home $3.3 million, including a $1.25 million bonus as Winston Cup champion. More than four million fans attend Winston Cup events each year, and television coverage reaches some 200 million.

France had turned a bootleggers' diversion into a major sport, an American passion. But even as he saw it happening, he harbored no fear, even if it would all come crumbling down. "After all," he said, "I can always go back to pumping gas."

42

Tex Rickard

Hype is the lifeblood of boxing, and George Lewis "Tex" Rickard was the pioneer of boxing hype. He was the man most responsible for taking the fight game from the outback to the arena; the promoter who not only made boxing big business, but also turned it into an increasingly respectable one. "He commercialized boxing," wrote Nat Loubet in *The Ring* magazine, "and it has been a commercialized sport ever since."

Prizefighting, illegal in most states when Rickard first found his way into the sport, was churning out million-dollar gates by the time he was through with it. Along the way, he built—or at least rebuilt—a sports palace called Madison Square Garden; placed his own pro hockey team there at a time when the Canadian game was just feeling its way into America; made and lost and made again more money than most people saw in a lifetime; and became one of American sport's most fascinating figures.

And all that came after Rickard had squeezed a half-dozen lifetimes into his first thirty-four years. Born on January 2, 1870, in a cabin in Kansas City, Missouri, Rickard became, according to historian Eric Whitehead, a "brash adventurer and soldier-of-fortune who . . . dug for gold in the Yukon, ran gambling saloons in the Klondike, hired out as an armed mercenary in South Africa and a cattleman in Paraguay."

The Yukon gold rush of 1895 netted Rickard $60,000. He used it to build a gambling hall, which promptly went under. Near-broke, Rickard simply constructed another saloon and casino, made half a million dollars in four years, and then lost most of it again. In 1903, he followed the gold rush to Goldfield, Nevada, where he built another saloon and where he found himself drawn into a line of work different from gambling and prospecting, yet very much the same.

Rickard wanted to draw attention to Goldfield, and by 1906 much of the country's attention was focused on prizefighting, in particular a lightweight title match between the champion, Battling Nelson, and a black former champion, Joe Gans. In order to promote Goldfield, Rickard decided to promote the fight. At the time, it was customary for promoters to offer the boxers a share of the gate receipts—and to take their sweet time in actually parting with the money. Rickard created the exception that became the norm by guaranteeing a $30,000 purse for the fight. He also agreed to pay the fighters then and there.

It was enough to draw the bout, as well as 7,500 spectators from all over the country, to Goldfield on September 3, 1906, putting the mining town's name on the lips of interested observers from coast to coast. That, in turn, was enough to leave Rickard a profit in excess of what the fighters received. "I never knew what the fight game offered until then," Rickard later explained, "I wasn't a boxing expert, but what happened in the Gans-Nelson show made me think—how long has this been going on? My mind was now made up . . . from then on, whether I knew it or not, I was in the fight business."

Four years later, Rickard was the force behind one of the most anticipated and significant events in sports history: the heavyweight title fight, on July 4, 1910, between black champion Jack Johnson and white former champion Jim Jeffries. It was Rickard who lured Jeffries out of retirement by offering an unheard-of guaranteed purse of $101,000—sixty percent to the winner—and who fueled the notion that Jeffries was the "Great White Hope," transforming a simple prizefight into an epic racial confrontation. Rickard had turned fighters into symbols, a trick-of-the-trade that continued, whether the fighter was Joe Louis or Gerry Cooney or George Foreman.

"If a prizefight could draw so many people to a desert from all parts of the world," Rickard explained in his frontier drawl, "I figured, then nothing could stop me from drawing 'em with other big name fights, especially if I could stage them in localities where train service could bring 'em in comfortably and where there were thousands of fans whom I could entice from places close to the arena."

And so, six years later, in 1916, he leased Madison Square Garden, which was then actually located in Manhattan's Madison Square, and matched newly crowned heavyweight champion Jess Willard against Frank Moran, attracting a gate in excess of $150,000. According to Joseph Durso, author of *Madison Square Garden: 100 Years of History*, the arena possessed "a memorable past and a memorable debt," but the Willard-Moran fight "helped to revive the spirits and the bank account of the threadbare building on Madison Square." Before long, Rickard would do much more than just that.

In 1919, however, Rickard took big-time boxing to Toledo, Ohio, of all places, constructing a 90,000-seat stadium and promising Willard a $100,000 guarantee in a title bout against an up-and-coming heavyweight named Jack Dempsey. The fight drew a gate of more than $450,000, of which Rickard took nearly one-fifth. But more important, the fight revealed the potential appeal of the Manassa Mauler. Dempsey, like Rickard, had been a product of the nomadic West, a roamer, a dreamer. "They were, in fact, like two answers looking for a question," Durso writes. "And they found it together in the East."

Whether Rickard made Dempsey or Dempsey made Rickard is debatable. But the promoter is ranked ahead of the fighter for two reasons. First, Rickard came first. Before Dempsey had even escaped his teens, Rickard had turned Gans versus Nelson and Johnson versus Jeffries into financial bonanzas. Second, while several fighters had approximated Dempsey's fame, beginning with John L. Sullivan, forty years earlier, and others had approached Dempsey's skills, notably Jack Johnson, no promoter had yet come close to Rickard's talent for the boxing business.

Described as "part [carnival] barker, part adventurer, part hustler, but all promoter," Rickard was a showman in his ever-present straw hat and bow tie and his beloved cigars. In the Roaring '20s, Rickard was a man for his time, but behind the scenes he was ahead of his time. "He was a hayseed, a rube," *Los Angeles Times* columnist Jim Murray wrote, some sixty-five years later, "but he beat New York at its own game."

When Dempsey, who had not fought in World War I, took on French light-heavyweight champion George Carpentier, a war hero, in 1921, Rickard billed it as the soldier versus the draft dodger. The fight attracted 80,000 fans to Jersey City, New Jersey, and yielded boxing's first million-dollar gate. Two years later 90,000 spectators at the Polo Grounds watched Dempsey knock out Luis Firpo of Argentina, and three years after that some 120,000 people jammed Philadelphia's Sesquicentennial Stadium and paid nearly $1.9 million, as Dempsey lost his title to Gene Tunney. The rematch, at Chicago's Soldier Field in 1927—the legendary "Battle of the Long Count"—netted the sport's first $2 million gate.

Rickard's impact on boxing, however, was just as profound indoors, specifically, in Madison Square Garden. In 1920, with prizefighting finally officially legalized in New York, Rickard had signed a 10-year lease for $200,000 a year with the New York Life Insurance Company, which controlled the Garden by then. Within a few years, boxing alone had produced a total gate of some $5 million at the Garden. But it wasn't enough for New York Life, which announced plans to demolish the sporting shrine in 1924.

"I am sorry to say good-bye to the old place. It has been good to me, and I have had a lot of fun in it," said Rickard. "I am also rather proud of the fact that I am the only man who made it pay." He then rounded up a syndicate, raised more than $5 million and constructed a new arena at Eighth Avenue and 50th Street. The "House That Tex Built" was far from Madison Square, but he was savvy enough to christen it Madison Square Garden II. In fact, it was actually Madison Square Garden III, the first arena by that name having been raised in 1874 and razed in 1889, and it would become the center of sports and entertainment in New York and thus the nation.

Rickard would install an ice rink, as well as his own hockey team, which he called Tex's Rangers, a key ingredient in the survival of pro hockey in America. The Garden would later have much the same effect on college basketball, with the institution of intersectional doubleheaders and the National Invitation Tournament, and on pro basketball, with the formation of the New York Knicks.

Of course, it also would be home to rodeos, ice shows, dog shows, benefits, political rallies and, of course, prizefights. Rickard built it with boxing in mind, and Friday night fights became an institution. For several years after, whoever controlled the Garden essentially controlled boxing.

The arena would last until the late '60s, when Madison Square Garden IV was built above Penn Station. But Rickard wasn't as fortunate. He died after an appendicitis attack in Miami Beach on January 6, 1929, four days after his fifty-ninth birthday. His body was flown back to New York, where thousands of mourners filed past his 2,200-pound, $15,000 bronze casket in the Garden. It was, notes Durso, "a parting salute that rivaled most of the events he had staged."

43

Bill Russell

At just under 6-foot-10, Bill Russell was called the "world's largest eraser," but his mark as a basketball player is permanent.

There has likely never been a winner like Russell. He led the University of San Francisco to the NCAA title in 1955, added another title and an Olympic gold medal in 1956, and then moved on to the Boston Celtics at the hub of the greatest dynasty in the history of professional sports. Boston won the NBA title in Russell's first pro season and then ten more over the next twelve years, the streak ending only when Russell retired.

That's two collegiate championships, a gold medal and eleven NBA titles in fifteen years. Nobody else has even come close. Russell averaged only 15.1 points per game in his career, and never more than 18.9 in any season. Yet he earned five Most Valuable Player awards, and, in 1980, the Professional Basketball Writers' Association of America voted him the greatest player in the history of the NBA. What did he do to deserve such praise? Said Russell, "I like to think I originated a whole new style of play."

He did it by unveiling the most potent weapon in any team's arsenal—defense—and by dominating the game in the process. The Celtics had won five straight scoring titles when Russell arrived, but never a championship. With Russell they would earn as many league titles in thirteen seasons as any other franchise has won in the history of the NBA. Along the way, the team's makeup and style would become a blueprint for success in the league, starting with a man in the middle who could rebound and block shots, which Russell did better than any man who ever lived.

Russell had been a late bloomer as a basketball talent, his scholarship to San Francisco being his only offer and USF being a school with little sports history to speak of, and no basketball gym at all. But it was there that he developed a love affair with the rebound, an ability to soar above the rim, and an affinity for responding to opponents' shots with a disdainful swat.

He was such a voracious rebounder that the NCAA elected to widen the foul lane from six to twelve feet in 1955—the so-called "Russell rule." In the NBA, he went on to average 22.5 rebounds per game. Of the four highest single-game rebound totals, Russell produced three.

Blocked shots didn't become an official statistic until after Russell retired. Had it existed in the '60s, he would have dominated the record books. In *Elevating The Game*, author Nelson George explains, "In the mid-fifties, a time when the jump shot was still disdained by classroom-ball coaches, the idea of leaving your feet to attempt a block was equally heretical." Today, it is as integral to the game as the dribble and the fast break.

Russell's innovative defense would take the NBA to a new dimension. "Before Russell came along, no one had ever blocked shots in the pros or forced teams out of their offensive patterns," said his coach for a decade, Red Auerbach. "He put a whole new sound in the game, the sound of his footsteps. A guy would be going in all alone for a layup, and he'd hear the sound of those footsteps behind him. After this happened a few times, guys started hearing Russell's footsteps even when he wasn't there."

Had Russell done nothing else but redirect the flight of the ball—in a game based almost entirely on the flight of the ball—he would still own an impressive spot among *The Sports 100*. But he also happened to be the first African-American head coach of a major league team in the modern era.

Another black man, John McLendon of the short-lived American Basketball League, had coached the ABL's Cleveland Pipers in 1961, but the league was hardly major in status. However, when Auerbach stepped down as Boston coach five years later, he handed the reins over to Russell. Under pressure to continue the success, Russell's Celtics won two titles in three years before he, too, stepped down. He would later become coach and general manager of the Seattle SuperSonics and then the Sacramento Kings.

But before joining a different club, Russell provided commentary for ABC's Sunday afternoon "NBA Game of the Week," becoming the first regular African-American sports announcer on national television. He also was instrumental in convincing the NBA to hire a friend of his, Ken Hudson, as the league's first black referee. The events are significant because, to Russell, his color was of the utmost significance. He was always a black man first, an athlete second.

"It may not be that the revolt of the black athlete began with Bill Russell," writes Wells Twombly, in *200 Years of Sport in America*, "but he certainly gave it impetus. It disturbed white America when Jackie Robinson turned out to be a man of temper and independence, not at all the imperturbable character that Branch Rickey had created. Bill Russell . . . proved almost as disconcerting."

Just as Russell's game was marked by rejection of opposing attempts, his character was marked by dignified refusal. In his first autobiography, *Go Up for Glory*, published in 1966, he refused to dwell on the good fortune of the athlete, instead reminding all of the burden of the black athlete. Domination of pro basketball was not the realization of a dream to Russell, it was merely a stop along a road to some higher calling. For that, he was called an ingrate.

Russell refused to ignore what he perceived as a quota system in the NBA, announcing that the practice was to "put two black athletes in the basketball game at home, put three in on the road, and put five in when you get behind." He refused to stand by quietly when white players received opportunities he felt should have gone to black ones, and when reporters spoke of white players' minds and black players' talents. When Abe Saperstein offered him a lucrative salary to join his Harlem Globetrotters after college but treated him like an intellectual inferior, Russell refused to play for the man. When a coffee shop in New York City refused him service, Russell refused to play in that night's exhibition game, essentially boycotting a city.

Leigh Montville of *Sports Illustrated* called Russell "one of the most cantankerous figures ever to have walked across the American sports page. Few other athletes spoke their minds more often on more controversial subjects. No other athlete did less to curry favor with the fan." Indeed, Russell refused autograph requests, just like he refused to show for his induction to the Hall of Fame.

"You owe the public the same thing it owes you. Nothing," he told the *Saturday Evening Post,* in 1964. "I refuse to misrepresent myself . . . I don't think it is incumbent upon me to set a good example for anybody's kids but my own." Charles Barkley would later echo some of Russell's sentiments. In the '90s, they struck a chord. In the '60s, they struck a nerve.

Like his younger contemporary, Muhammad Ali, Russell refused to be what everybody wanted him to be. He was who he was. "I can honestly say that I have never worked to be liked. I have worked to be respected," Russell wrote in his autobiography. "If I am liked, then that is an extra bonus of the world we inhabit. If I am disliked, it is the privilege of those who wish to dislike me—as long as it is not based on prejudice."

Wearing a goatee at a time when it somehow hinted at subversion, and speaking out at a time when most athletes were expected to stick to the script, William Felton Russell was considered so militant by some members of the media that they dubbed him "Felton X." But he was more than outspoken; he was a man of action.

As famed civil rights lawyer William M. Kunstler would later recall, "Russell was the only professional athlete who demonstrated enough interest in the deep South civil rights struggles of the early Sixties to come take a look at what was happening in that arena. Of course, at nearly 6-foot-10, he was also no small target, but he later claimed his Celtics teammates comforted him before his trip by telling him, "You'll be fine down there, Russ. Just make sure you stay *inconspicuous.*"

Russell had been born in Monroe, Louisiana (February 12, 1934), and raised in the Jim Crow South. When he was nine, the Russell clan was one of thousands of black families that migrated to California, eventually settling in Oakland. By the time he returned to the South, in the '60s, he had risen from his segregated youth to become the soul of an integrated national champion unit, but he returned, not out of pride in his social standing, but out of social conscience.

"It is not that all professional athletes lack the necessary courage or compassion to become part of ongoing social conflicts. Yet they have so often kept their toes out of churning waters," wrote Kunstler. "Russell was a most happy exception."

His influence off the court, then, was much like his impact on it—startling, powerful, reverberating.

WHAT ABOUT WILT?

When Wilt Chamberlain was offered a $100,000 salary one season, Bill Russell was promptly offered $100,001. Such was the nature of their rivalry, one of the most compelling in sports history.

Chamberlain was probably a better basketball player than Bill Russell. By the time he retired he had recorded game, season and career records for points and rebounds. In 147 head-to-head battles between the two giants, Russell averaged 14.5 points and 23.7 rebounds. Chamberlain averaged 28.7 points and 28.7 rebounds.

Russell, however, was still more important—on and off the court. Russell was an activist; Chamberlain criticized militant blacks. Russell was the backbone of a team that formed the backbone of the NBA; Chamberlain was a wanderer, competing for three different franchises. Russell was a defensive pioneer; Chamberlain was an offensive anomaly. Even in 1962, when Chamberlain averaged more than 50 points per game, NBA players voted Russell the league MVP. Obviously, they thought he was more important, too.

Jack Kramer

Jack Kramer essentially created modern tennis in all its forms. "Big Jake" had an enormous impact on the game as a player, a professional, a promoter and a powerbroker. His post-playing career was much like his court persona—aggressive and innovative, precise yet dramatic. On the court, this became known as the "power" and "percentage" game. Off the court, it was much the same thing.

As a player, Kramer revolutionized court sense and strategy. As a professional, and then a promoter, he set the game on its modern course by showing the financial promise of professionalism and the inadequacies inherent in the amateur version. And as a powerbroker, he pushed for the advent of "open" tennis and presided over the infancy of the Association of Tennis Professionals.

Nobody in the history of American tennis did more things, in more ways, over a longer period of time than Jack Kramer. Indeed, only the transcendant accomplishments of Billie Jean King and Arthur Ashe prevent Kramer from being the highest-ranked tennis figure among *The Sports 100*.

Kramer's amateur career was cursed with ill-timed injuries, but his promotional career transformed the relationship between tennis and money. So it is quite appropriate that the man whose career was defined by luck and money hails from Las Vegas, born there on August 1, 1921. The son of a railroad engineer, John Albert Kramer dreamed of playing professional baseball and loved to play football, but after his family moved to San Bernardino, California, he soon became one of the many tennis prodigies to emerge from the West Coast.

In 1936, he won the national boys' singles title, and three years later he became America's youngest Davis Cup participant. He teamed up with his close friend Ted Schroeder to win the national doubles championship in 1940 and 1941, adding a mixed doubles title in the latter year, as well. Kramer lost in the finals of the U.S. Nationals in 1943 and then enlisted in the U.S. Coast Guard.

The war took a large chunk out of what might have been Kramer's peak years, and freak injuries and illness, such as appendicitis, food poisoning and a badly blistered hand, kept him from winning more Grand Slam titles. Yet he returned to win the U.S. title in 1946, and repeat as champion again in 1947, when he also earned a Wimbledon crown for good measure. But, as Will Grimsley writes, in *Tennis: Its History, People and Events,* "By this time, Kramer's ears had become sensitive to the pleasant clang of cash registers." Those sensitive ears spurred tennis toward its modern form, eventually leading to the arrival of open tennis in 1968. Until then, the game had been a divided affair.

"There were amateurs and there were professionals and heaven forbid that they should ever meet," explains Richard Evans, author of *Open Tennis.* "All those terrific human traits such as snobbism, power complexes and pure selfishness had ensured that any player who signed a professional contract was automatically banned from competing at Wimbledon or any of the other great championships run under the auspices of the International Lawn Tennis Federation . . . Those who stayed with the so-called amateur game were forced to put bread on their table by receiving money under it."

Kramer had been scratching out a living as an amateur, with a $60-a-week side job at a meat-packing company, so he jumped at the opportunity to turn professional in 1948, when promoter Jack Harris guaranteed him $50,000. Kramer's opponent in an 89-match cross-country exhibition tour was the ever-boastful Bobby Riggs. Kramer won 69 of the 89 matches.

In 1949, with Riggs now acting as promoter, Kramer took on his successor as national amateur champion, Pancho Gonzales, in 123 matches. Again, Kramer dominated, winning 96 of them. Two years later, his touring opponent was Pancho Seguera; Kramer outplayed him 64-28. In 1952, after a contract dispute with Riggs, Kramer became a promoter himself, embarking on a long and influential career as a power player of a different sort.

Soon after turning professional, Kramer had admitted in a magazine article that he—like many others—had been a "paid amateur" who often padded expense accounts and accepted unpublicized appearance fees from promoters. But as a promoter he made no attempts to hide the fact that the game had become captivated by the almighty dollar, and he lured a steady parade of high-profile amateurs with high-priced contracts. Over the next half-dozen years, Kramer promoted tours involving some of the biggest names in the sport—Frank Sedgman, Tony Trabert, Ken Rosewall, Gonzales. In 1957, he signed Australian Lew Hoad, winner of the previous two Wimbledon titles, to a $125,000 professional contract.

In the process, Kramer contributed to a decline in popularity of amateur tennis. "Personalities were being pirated before they could make a name for themselves," Grimsley explains. "Tennis was degenerating into a secondary sport, greeted with a polite yawn by the news media and obscured by booms in big time pro golf, football and basketball."

Having become nearly as controversial as he was influential, Kramer relinquished his role as promoter in 1960, instead overseeing the formation of the International Tennis Players Association, and essentially turning the tour over to the players. "I felt that my presence in the movement might be detrimental to the pro game," Kramer explained. "It was necessary that the pros work in harmony with the amateur associations. I didn't want to be a stumbling block."

Though Kramer's first attempt at such an organization wouldn't endure, a dozen years later, he would preside over one that would. The Association of Tennis Professionals (ATP), with Kramer as its first executive director in 1972, heralded the arrival of modern tennis. It was essentially a product of the revolution which Kramer had helped spawn and which came to a head in the late sixties.

The forces leading to the advent of open tennis and the creation of the ATP were much like the atmosphere that led to the acceptance of professional baseball exactly a century earlier. It was, in many ways, simply a reaction against the hypocrisy of "shamateurism" and the deleterious effects it was having on the popularity of the game. Also, like baseball, tennis evolved toward its modern form with a big push from opportunistic entrepreneurs, like Lamar Hunt and his professional World Championship Tennis circuit.

The maturity of professional tennis, with its modern origins in the Kramer Tour, was drawing the balance of power away from the game's snobbish and stodgy amateur officials, and open tennis was more or less the compromised result. Having had its fill of fake amateurism and having recognized the growing attraction of professionalism, the British Lawn Tennis Association pushed to replace amateurs-only championships with tournaments open to both amateurs and professionals.

In March 1968, the International Lawn Tennis Federation bowed to the pressure and voted to sanction a limited number of open tournaments. In June, the first-ever open Wimbledon championships were held, with Rod Laver, a professional, taking the title.

Hunt's organization and the ILTF made peace in 1972, but shortly thereafter the players formed the ATP to watch over their own welfare, which nobody had seemed to care much about during the game's power struggles. The man the players chose as their organization's first executive director was Jack Kramer. "As soon as the ATP was formed, the cliché became reality. The game would never be the same again," writes Evans. "No one could have been better suited to the task than Kramer, a former outlaw who was now prepared to ride with the sheriff's posse."

Yet Kramer soon rekindled the outlaw image by leading, along with players like ATP president Cliff Drysdale and Arthur Ashe, a boycott of Wimbledon in 1973. All but a handful of the ATP members withdrew their names from the tournament, sending a message that tennis would no longer be controlled by dictatorial amateur officials, but by a democracy that included the players themselves.

The battle eventually led to the realization of the players' vision—with the athletes having an equal voice in what became the Men's International

Professional Tennis Council. And so, as he had fathered modern tennis technique three decades earlier, Kramer had now helped father the game's modern organizational form.

THE BIG GAME

They called Jack Kramer's version of tennis the "Big Game" or the "Power Game," but essentially what Kramer popularized and perfected became the basis of the modern game. He transformed tennis style into an exciting blend of science and skill, a mix of aggression and automatic response. Kramer is often erroneously credited with introducing the big serve and volley to the game, but he did create the combination of the two as a constant source of pressure.

Kramer consistently attacked from the net after putting his opponent on the defensive with a powerful serve or approach shot. Kramer's success was largely a result of combining this aggressive style with "percentage tennis," which made a science out of sport. Kramer would hit the ball in certain spots in certain situations, incorporate theories of angles, and place his serve according to the score of the game. By blending pressure and precision to near perfection, according to Julius Heldman, in *Styles of the Greats*, "the Kramer theory of modern tennis completely changed the complexion of the game."

45

Avery Brundage

Avery Brundage is perhaps the most enigmatic personality in *The Sports 100*. For nearly half a century, he was the single most important American figure in amateur sports, serving as president of the Amateur Athletic Union for seven years, president of the U.S. Olympic Committee for a quarter-century and president of the International Olympic Committee for two decades. But in many ways, Brundage's impact was as muddled as his character. He was a hypocrite, an autocrat, a narrow-minded idealist, a man who spoke of the future but worshipped the past, and who preached Olympic brotherhood, but failed to practice the same.

"He was usually seen by those Americans who were aware of him at all as a crusty octogenarian bureaucrat given to sour statements about amateurism and its corruption. A spoilsport. An anchronism," writes Allen Guttmann, author of *The Games Must Go On*.

Brundage was accused, at one time or another, of being anti-Semitic, a Nazi, a Communist, racist and, perhaps most often, dictatorial. "He strode the earth as if he were a crowned monarch," William Oscar Johnson wrote in *Sports Illustrated*, "and he ruled the Olympic movement as if it were his fiefdom." Added John Powers in *Sport* magazine, "The Games were his religion—for better, for worse, and for 60 years of his life—and Brundage ran them with a papal infallibility." Indeed, for half of his eighty-seven years, Brundage considered himself the conscience of amateur sport.

Born in Detroit, on September 28, 1887, Brundage's family was deserted by his father when he was six. Raised by his mother in Chicago, he graduated from the University of Illinois, where he starred in track and field. In 1912, he competed in the Olympic Games in Stockholm, Sweden.

French educator Pierre de Coubertin had created the International Olympic Committee in 1894, which staged the first modern Games two years later in Athens, Greece. The first Olympics attracted twelve nations, including thirteen American Olympians, and little interest. But, by the time Brundage competed in the fifth Olympiad, the Games had become a relatively smooth-running affair.

He finished an impressive sixth in the pentathlon, but dropped out of the decathlon after realizing he was too many points behind, an act for which he never fully forgave himself. Jim Thorpe won both events handily.

He returned home and found work as a superintendent of a construction firm, starting his own company three years later. He was extremely successful, and by 1927, his net worth was estimated at $1 million. When the Crash of 1929 left him virtually bankrupt, he simply amassed an even greater fortune in construction and real estate.

Brundage had continued his athletic participation after returning home from the Olympics, winning national track and field "all-around" competitions in 1914, 1916 and 1918. However, while one newspaper praised his performance after the second all-around title, it reminded its readers that he was "not a Jim Thorpe." Thorpe, of course, had been stripped of his gold medals after it was discovered he had been paid to play baseball one summer, a decision Brundage never reversed.

Brundage began his career in amateur sports administration by becoming a member of the board of directors of the Chicago Athletic Association. He then moved to the Central Amateur Athletic Association, and finally, in 1928, he was elected president of the national Amateur Athletic Union. During his seven-year reign, he forged temporary peace for the first time between the AAU and the younger NCAA. In 1929, he was named president of what would become the U.S. Olympic Committee (succeeding General Douglas MacArthur). He would soon become involved in a war of his own.

In 1931, when the International Olympic Committee chose Berlin as an Olympic site, Adolph Hitler was not in power. A few years later, as the 1936 Berlin Olympics approached, and Hitler's anti-Semitism became apparent, an intensive boycott campaign emerged across America. But as he would for years, Brundage preached the separation of politics and sports. He condemned the notion that the American athlete should be "a martyr to a cause not his own," and the "Jewish propaganda" that aroused criticism of his actions. "Radicals and Communists," he said, "must keep their hands off American sport."

Brundage's primary concern was simply over the issue of whether qualified German Jews were being barred from Olympic competitition, but he put his trust in Nazi propaganda, and American Olympic officials put their trust in him. A Gallup poll revealed that 43 percent of the population favored a boycott, yet Brundage's influence was enough that in the summer of 1936 he could be found leading U.S. Olympians into Berlin's Olympic Stadium.

During the battle over the boycott, Brundage's own anti-Semitic views came to the fore. According to Guttmann, he seemed to have "gone beyond the honorable defense of German culture and to have become a shameless apologist for the Nazis." Indeed, he would later collect anti-Semitic literature and blame the Jews for pushing the U.S. into World War II. And during the Games, Marty Glickman, one of the two Jewish athletes removed from the 1936 400-meter relay team, accused Brundage of wanting "to save Hitler . . . the embarassment of having Jews on that winning podium."

Jesse Owens used the opportunity to become a worldwide hero, but there were still many who claimed Brundage had helped manufacture a victory for Nazi propaganda. Explains Guttmann, "To the degree that Owens made a mockery of the Nazi myth of 'Nordic' superiority, the games were not a propaganda coup, but the overall impression of the games must have added to Hitler's prestige."

The event also added to Brundage's prestige. He was named one of three U.S. representatives on the International Olympic Committee that same summer, became a member of the IOC Executive Board in 1937, and was named an IOC vice-president in 1946.

To nobody's surprise, Brundage was an outspoken isolationist during World War II, becoming increasingly political and vocal against the war even as he denounced the politicization of sport. When the war caused the cancellation of the 1940 summer and winter games, Brundage responded by creating the Pan-American Games, though America's entrance into the war delayed their start until 1951.

Brundage's tireless efforts to keep alive the Olympic movement during and after the war led to his election as IOC president in 1952. The first and only American to hold the most powerful position in international sports, he remained in office until 1972. "He was the Olympic high priest, guardian of the flame, and for twenty years the Games were whatever Avery Brundage said they were. He decided where they were to be held, who was allowed in and who was tossed out," wrote Powers. "He was 'Slavery Avery' to many, and his Olympian commandments were timeless and inflexible—no professionals, no politics, no exceptions."

The "Apostle of Amateurism," as Brundage has been called, interpreted the Olympic code as defining an amateur as anyone whose income is not derived from sport—any sport. Thus, a professional baseball player, like Jim Thorpe, could not compete for his country as a decathlete. "Sport is recreation," said Brundage, "it is a pastime or a diversion, it is play, it is action for amusement, it is free, spontaneous and joyous—it is the opposite of work."

In his bid for purity over professionalization, Brundage also campaigned against commercialization of the Olympics in all its forms. Athletes couldn't publish their memoirs until they retired; they couldn't publish articles about their experiences in sport; and they certainly couldn't use their Olympic fame to boost a business venture, even their own business. Brundage even advocated the removal of team sports and the elimination of the Winter Games because they were more susceptible to commercialization.

His struggle to keep the Games apolitical was equally intense, with the result that he constantly found himself surrounded by political controversy. Brundage attempted to reduce nationalism in the Games, suggesting, and almost achieving, replacement of national anthems with an Olympic anthem.

Brundage was so enamored with the Olympic ideal that the once-fervent anti-Communist even pushed the IOC to allow the Soviet Union to return to the Olympic fold during the Cold War's infancy in 1952. He did the same with the People's Republic of China, but when he also recognized Nationalist China, the exiled government in Taiwan, as an official entry, the PRC balked. Brundage's attempts to appease the PRC were interpreted by the American press as a blatantly political move. Suddenly, the man who had condemned a Communist conspiracy in the 1930s was being accused of those leanings himself. Still, the PRC boycotted the Games until 1980.

Brundage continued to preach against using the Olympics as a political statement, though that didn't stop dozens of nations from doing so. In 1968, he became the center of a social and political maelstrom in his own backyard when sociologist Harry Edwards led a boycott movement among African-Americans, partly in response to the IOC's decision to readmit South Africa—despite its continuing policy of apartheid—to the Games.

Edwards and his colleagues presented a list of six demands, the second being: "Removal of the anti-Semitic and anti-black personality Avery Brundage from his post as Chairman of the International Olympic Committee." When several African nations also threatened to boycott, the South Africa decision was quickly reversed, but the anti-Brundage rhetoric continued. Said sprinter Tommie Smith, "I don't want Brundage presenting me any medals."

Brundage's alleged racism may have stemmed largely from his obsession with the separation of sports and politics. He seems to have been satisfied if an athlete could compete on a racially integrated team, ignoring the fact that the same athlete might have to return home in the back of the bus. And so, when Smith and teammate John Carlos used their moment atop the medal stand to display a clenched-fist protest, the IOC immediately banished them from the Games. He then called for the "black power" salute to be removed from the official Olympic video, even though he had seen no problem with the Nazi salutes in 1936.

Whispers began, even among IOC members, that Brundage had stayed on too long, and in 1972 he stepped down as president. But, before doing so, he presided over his final Olympic Games—in Munich. As had happened thirty-six years earlier in Germany, Brundage emerged somewhat triumphant amid tragic circumstances. Before dawn on September 5, Palestinian terrorists took eleven Israeli athletes and coaches as hostages, demanding the release of 236 prisoners in return. German officials responded with an ill-fated attack that resulted in the death of every hostage. Brundage and the IOC were faced with a difficult decision regarding the continuation of the Games.

In front of thousands of mourners and millions of television viewers, Brundage summed up his long-held views by announcing, "Sadly, in this imperfect world, the greater and the more important the Olympic Games become, the more they are open to commercial, political and now criminal pressure . . . The Games must go on and we must continue our efforts to keep them clean, pure and honest."

It was to be Brundage's final moment in the Olympic spotlight. He died on May 8, 1975, having said, "When I'm gone, there's nobody rich enough, thick-skinned enough and smart enough to take my place, and the Games will be in tremendous trouble." What the Games have become, to some extent, is every thing Brundage feared. Commercialization has turned the games into marketing bonanzas; professional athletes have appeared in everything from tennis to basketball; large-scale boycotts, one led by the U.S. itself, have affirmed the position of the Olympics as a political tool.

Though, in the long run, Brundage seems to have lost his battles, the most powerful American in Olympic history left an undeniable imprint on American amateur athletics and on the world stage. "Whether we think of him as idealistically inspired or as quixotically unrealistic, he was one with his vision," writes Guttmann. "Thanks largely to him, for better or for worse, the games have gone on."

46

George Mikan

He was nearsighted, clumsy, benign. Growing up on a farm near Joliet, Illinois, his biggest athletic accomplishment was winning the county marbles championship. He was cut from his first basketball team and told he wasn't good enough for the University of Notre Dame's squad. But George Mikan grew to be 6-foot-10 and 245 pounds, and he proved to be the big man who opened doors for all other big men in basketball—a monumental impact from any perspective.

Mikan was born on June 18, 1924, and raised in Chicago's suburbs. After failing to make his high school team, in large part because of his coach's contention that "you can't play with glasses on," he transferred to a prep seminary, essentially foregoing basketball to study for the priesthood. For a time, it appeared that Mikan would be closer to God than the basket, but he eventually gravitated back to the game. By the time he graduated high school, he was nearly 6-foot-8 and a competent enough player to earn an invitation to play at Chicago's DePaul University.

At about the same time, Mikan earned the opportunity to show Notre Dame coach George Keogan what he could do. Keogan realized it wasn't much, and told Mikan to stick with a smaller school where the coach could spend more time on him. "It was," claimed one writer, "like the Boston Red Sox telling Babe Ruth they needed money to finance a Broadway play when they traded him to the New York Yankees."

Mikan's first year on the DePaul varsity team, 1942, coincided with Ray Meyer's first season as head coach. Both would grow into basketball legends, a process that began when Meyer realized Mikan was not only quite a project, but quite a quick learner. That Meyer even realized the potential was a tribute to them both, because in those days big men were only a small part of the game.

According to Robert W. Peterson, author of *Cages to Jump Shots*, the average basketball player in the first half of the century was probably under six feet tall. Peterson points out that "conventional wisdom was that large men were too clumsy and uncoordinated to play basketball. Better a six-footer who was fairly fast, quick and graceful than a really large man who stumbled over his own feet. No doubt many big men accepted that judgment and never seriously tried to learn the game, or, if they did try, faced ridicule for their initial efforts and dropped out."

The first inordinately tall player to gain fame was 6-foot-7 Stretch Meehan, who starred at Seton Hall and in the professional Eastern League in the 1920s. His slightly younger contemporary, 6-foot-5 Joe Lapchick, played for the Original Celtics, the most famous team in the game's early years. He was considered basketball's top center; he was also considered a giant.

But the game soon began to grow taller. By the end of the 1930s, most good teams included two or three players at least 6-foot-4, and some taller players even earned All-America status. As basketball evolved into a more offensive affair, more shot attempts meant more rebound attempts, giving the big man a new, more athletic role. Yet the big men still received little respect. It seems they weren't quite good enough to dominate, so they weren't quite good for the game.

Then, along came George Mikan. "No matter where a tall guy went in those days," Mikan explained, "there was always someone to tell him he couldn't do something." But not Ray Meyer. He just made Mikan work harder than everyone else. From the first day, Meyer had preached to his team, "Big men go to the basket; little guys go away." But then he took the concept to an extreme. "I dismissed the other players from spring practice and kept George there alone for about six weeks," said Meyer. "I felt sorry for him."

Soon Meyer's sympathy was geared more toward his opponents. Mikan scored 10 points in his first varsity game, and hovered around that average all season. He led DePaul to a 19-5 mark and to the NCAA Tournament. The following year, DePaul went 22-4, and won two games in the more prestigious (at the time) National Invitational Tournament. Mikan, wearing his famous #99, was an All-American.

In response, the NCAA Rules Committee enacted the modern goaltending rule, making it illegal to bat the ball on the way down. So in 1944–1945, Mikan simply turned his offensive performance up a notch, leading the nation in scoring with 20.9 points per game. In a 97-53 victory over Rhode Island State in the semifinals of the NIT, he scored as many points as the entire opposing team. DePaul went on to win the championship, as Mikan was named the tournament's MVP.

Mikan averaged more than 23 points per game during the 1945–1946 season, earning his third straight All-America selection. It was then that his fortunes and those of professional basketball collided. Just as his college career was coming to a close, the pro game was elevating itself toward its modern form. "Mikan's arrival came at the right time for profesional basketball," writes Peterson. "He was the game's first true superstar, and when he appeared on the scene, the pro game was poised to begin its bid for recognition as a major part of the national sports scene."

Mikan signed a five-year, $60,000 contract with the Chicago American Gears of the National Basketball League (NBL), giving the then nine-year-old league an unprecedented amount of attention. Like Red Grange signing with the Chicago Bears and Joe Namath joining the New York Jets, Mikan's arrival helped legitimize a struggling organization.

In his first paid competition, #99 scored 100 points in five games to earn the MVP trophy of the 1946 world pro tournament. In Mikan's second season, the owner of the American Gears attempted to start his own league with Mikan and his teammates as the focus. When the plan collapsed, the Chicago players were distributed throughout the NBL, and Mikan ended up a member of the first-year Minneapolis Lakers. Led by Mikan, the Lakers promptly won the league title.

The following year, Minneapolis and three other teams withdrew from the NBL and joined the three-year-old Basketball Association of America, the presence of Mikan and others immediately making the BAA the nation's premier pro basketball league. Finally, in 1949, the NBL and the BAA merged to form the NBA.

As he had been in the NBL and the BAA, Mikan was the first great drawing card of the NBA. In fact, one Madison Square Garden marquee read simply: "TONIGHT: GEO MIKAN VS. KNICKS." From 1948–1951, he averaged 28 points per game, earning him the honor of being named the greatest basketball player of the first half of the twentieth century in an Associated Press poll. In his first nine pro seasons, Mikan led the Lakers to six league titles, averaging more than 23 points per game. "He's six feet, ten inches," commented one reporter, "and he couldn't be greater if he were ten feet, six inches."

By 1954, however, Mikan decided his oft-injured body had suffered enough. The advent of the 24-second clock that year and the excitement it generated meant the NBA could survive the loss of its most popular player. It also meant Mikan's game would suffer amid the league's growing running style. So Mikan retired, making an aborted comeback attempt one year later before concentrating on a law practice in Minneapolis. He later watched his son, Larry, play his way into the NBA that his father helped create.

So what, then, is Mikan's legacy? It essentially comes in three forms. First, his success turned the very notion of height and hoops on its head. "Normally, big men started to play after they got their size," Meyer explained. "It was after George Mikan that players came along and grew as they played." In other words, Mikan showed big kids that they could play, too, and they grew into dominant big men.

Certainly, he wasn't the first tall basketball star, but he was the best of the first batch of big men. And certainly the trend toward taller players was already in evidence, but Mikan provided a dramatic example of its possibilities. As Wells Twombly writes in *200 Years of Sport in America*, "He began the process of reshaping it from a game of workmanlike earnestness to a captivating spectacle of leaping, soaring giants."

But Mikan's success also changed the rules of the game. Along with Oklahoma A&M's 7-foot center Bob Kurland (whom he met in two memorable postseason games), Mikan's defensive prowess spurred the college game's adoption of the goaltending rule in 1945. And then, six years later, his offensive abilities led to the NBA's decision to widen the lane from six to twelve feet. For the first time, teams began to double-team the post on defense and focus their offense around the man in the middle. As former Laker teammate Jim Pollard declared, "In my lifetime, I've only seen two centers who could just take charge of a game, who could put so much fear in other players that they stayed away from the middle. One was Bill Russell. The other, and he was even more dominant, was George Mikan."

Finally, Mikan provided publicity for professional basketball when it was fighting for survival. It was the same type of name-recognition boost that he would later give (on a smaller scale) to the ABA as the upstart league's first commissioner from 1967–1969.

The absence of television, of course, made Mikan's impact in this regard far less salient than that of Michael Jordan, Magic Johnson, and Larry Bird. Indeed, despite Mikan's fame, the NBA's slow-paced game still needed to be saved by the 24-second clock, and, thus, he ranks below that trio. But Mikan still can boast the honor of being professional basketball's first franchise player, the franchise being the league itself.

47

Jim Creighton

More so than any other team sport, baseball is a game of individuals. And no position in sports—not football's quarterback, not basketball's point guard, not even hockey's goaltender—has more influence on the outcome of a game than baseball's pitcher. Indeed, over the years the evolution of baseball has essentially been tied to the evolution of the pitcher.

When the Knickerbocker Base Ball Club drafted the first codified rules of the game in 1845, only one rule pertained to pitching: "The ball must be pitched, not thrown, for the bat." In the days when baseball was only beginning to distinguish itself from its ancestral games, the pitch was yet to evolve.

"Pitched, not thrown" meant that the ball was lofted underhand, stiff-armed, stiff-wristed, closer to the method preferred in cricket and even bowling than the overhand, arm-snapping, ninety mile-per-hour versions of today. And it was pitched "for the bat," not "against the bat." The pitcher, then standing behind a line just forty-five feet from the batter, wanted the ball to be put in play, so that his fielders—gloveless though they may have been—could provide the defensive heroics. In fact, the batter could even request a high pitch or a low pitch, and the pitcher was forced to comply.

Strikes and balls weren't even part of the game until 1858 and 1863, respectively. They didn't have to be. Pitchers weren't there to challenge hitters; they were there to provide for them. Granted, the pitcher did have the benefit of some of the earlier days' quirkier rules, such as one-bounce catches counting as outs and nine balls being required for a walk, but his role was far from the dominant position it has become. "Of all the positions in the game's original 1845 design," write authors John Thorn and John Holway in *The Pitcher,* "only right field was less demanding and less prestigious than pitcher."

So how did we get here from there? How did a transformation in technique and philosophy turn a virtually punchless position into an assortment of split-fingers and spitballs, changeups and chin music, brushbacks and breaking pitches, relief specialists and rotator cuffs? It was a 17-year-old pitcher, in 1858, who got the ball rolling.

Jim Creighton was born on April 15, 1841, in New York City. While still a teenager, he became renowned as an excellent cricket and baseball player. Soon, he became baseball's first true star. In an era when Brooklyn and New York constituted the center of the baseball world, Creighton was Brooklyn's hero. After starting his pitching career with the Niagaras of Brooklyn, he was lured to the Star Club of Brooklyn and, in 1860, to the Excelsiors of Brooklyn.

Publicly, the Excelsiors professed strict amateurism in the days where the "evils" of professionalism were thought by many to be a threat to the game. But that didn't stop them from raiding their rivals to obtain Creighton and paying him under the table, thus making him the first known professional player.

Creighton thrived, throwing baseball's first recorded shutout on November 8, and the team became an influential force in the development of the game. The Excelsiors barnstormed through the East, defeating fifteen straight local all-star teams in contests that often drew thousands. Baseball's first great tour aroused unprecedented enthusiasm for the game and inspired the organization of baseball clubs in the areas visited.

Creighton's success fostered a growing transition in baseball, essentially transforming it from a participatory game to a spectator sport. As late as the mid-1850s, the concept of a baseball fan was all but nonexistent. But soon players became so talented that they were no longer regarded as just athletic colleagues but athletic heroes. By 1860, thousands of fans were flocking to watch Creighton pitch.

But even more than Creighton's skills, it was his style that revolutionized baseball. He was widely considered a faster pitcher than had ever been seen before, and his pitches tended to tail and dip, making him likely the first hurler to have "good stuff." One contemporary called Creighton's pitches "fairly unhittable." Another considered them "swift as they could be sent from a cannon."

Creighton's secret to success? He violated the rules. Though he was an underhand pitcher (overhand was not allowed until 1884), he used a barely perceptible snap of his wrist and bend of his arm, allowing him to be the first to put spin on the ball. By changing the pitcher's style, he changed the pitcher's role. "Until Creighton, the idea of the pitcher was just lobbing the ball up to the batter," Thorn explained. "He established the position as a direct opponent of the batter, rather than an ally of the batter."

Soon, as others began to imitate his delivery, umpires chose not to penalize him for his innovative circumvention of the rules. As pitching improved, games became lower scoring and more appealing. In 1872, baseball's foremost authority, journalist Henry Chadwick, proposed the legalization of the wrist snap. In

Creighton's heyday, typical games featured dozens of runs per contest, but by 1875, baseball had experienced its first 1-0 game and its first no-hitter.

Creighton soon discovered he could not survive on speed alone, so he developed one of the game's first changeups, but it was his original wrist snap that set the stage for baseball's subsequent pitching revolutions. Thorn and Holway explain that "once Creighton snapped his wrist, it was only a matter of time before other spinning pitches—notably the curve, but also the drop (sinker), the rise, the in-shoot (screwball) and spitter—were invented."

Baseball's evolution has been a constant parade of pitching revolutions. Until Babe Ruth's home runs altered the balance of the game—perhaps the only on-field impact more significant than Creighton's—pitchers tended to pace themselves. After all, they were almost always guaranteed that the ball would stay in the park.

Over the years, various rules changes—from the ban against spitballs to the raising and lowering of the strike zone and the mound—have served to stifle and strengthen the pitcher's impact. And the advent of relief pitching, with its first cautious origins coming under manager John McGraw at the turn of the century, has had a remarkable impact on the game. Yet, Jim Creighton's wrist snap remains the basis of all other pitching innovations.

Creighton's tragic death was perhaps befitting baseball's first hero. On October 14, 1862, during a game against the Unions of Morrisania, the 21-year-old clouted a home run. It proved to be the last swing of his life, as he sustained a ruptured bladder in the process. Four days later, he was dead.

Creighton's grief-stricken friends buried him in Brooklyn's Greenwood Cemetery under a marble pillar. Carved upon the pillar were a scorebook, a cap, a base and a pair of bats. Creighton must have been holding the ball.

48

Bill Tilden

Until O. J. Simpson, Bill Tilden probably had them all beat. Few, if any, athletes ever forged such domination or received such acclaim in their chosen sport; few, if any, ever fell so far. At his peak as one of the golden boys of sport's Golden Age, Tilden was not only the world's best tennis player, he was perhaps its most unsurpassable athlete.

"Playing for himself, for his country, for posterity, he was invincible. No man ever bestrode his sport as Tilden did for those years," explains Frank Deford in his biography, *Big Bill Tilden*. "Babe Ruth, Jack Dempsey, Red Grange and the other fabled American sweat lords of the times stood at the head of more popular games, but Tilden simply was tennis in the public mind: *Tilden and tennis*, it was said, in that order."

As the 1920s brought baseball, football, boxing and golf to unprecedented levels of popularity, so they did the same for tennis. And the decade, or at least the bulk of it, belonged to Tilden, and nobody else. Tilden was known for his obsessive honesty on the court, to the point where, if he believed an incorrect call went his way, he would purposely lose a point with a dramatic flourish. Yet the honest sportsman held a painful secret.

As it turns out, his sexual interests revolved only around young boys, and in the end his personal demons caught up to him, leaving perhaps sport's most arrogant champion a broken man with a broken legacy. He ranks among the most important figures in American sports history for both the heights he reached—for willing American tennis into maturity—and the depths to which he plummeted, the lesson that forgiveness is far more elusive than fame.

In many ways, Tilden early experiences set him up as much for his rise to glory as for his fall from it. His parents had watched their first three children die from diptheria in a span of three weeks in 1884, none older than the age of three.

Tilden's older brother, Herbert, was born soon after, and "Big Bill" came along several years later. His parents had wanted a girl.

He was born William Tatem Tilden, Jr., on February 10, 1893, in Philadelphia. He grew up spoiled, in a mansion where presidents made occasional visits and the "help" referred to him as "Master Junior." Yet Tilden's father was distant to him, his mother overprotective. He was saddled with a reputation for being a sickly child, and kept out of school for private tutoring, a practice more common then with girls. His mother, tragedy having turned her into a health fanatic, also instilled within him a fear of contracting venereal disease from women.

Tilden's mother died during his freshman year at the University of Pennsylvania; his father died four years later; his brother less than two months after that. Bill, the only one left, left Penn and immersed himself in tennis. He had been unsuccessful in his first attempt to make the varsity team at Penn and, by 1915, at the age of twenty-two, he was still just the 70th-ranked player in the country. But, as he would later do so often on the court, he turned early defeat into brilliance. "Big Bill was never the best anywhere in his life," states Deford, "until suddenly he was the best in the world."

He won his first U.S. singles title in July 1918, the clay court championship, and soon surpassed Bill Johnston as America's top player. In fact, he surpassed everyone in the world by a remarkably large margin, despite the fact that he didn't emerge until he was twenty-seven. Tilden won six straight U.S. championships from 1920–1925, during which he went 66-0 in major international singles matches, and added a seventh national title in 1929. All told, he played 80 matches in the U.S. championships and won 73 of them.

In 1922, a staph infection caused him to have half of the middle finger on his right hand removed, and most observers (including Tilden) believed he would never reach the same level of proficiency. Yet he continued to dominate. In 1923, he lost only one match all year. In 1924, he never lost a match, and during the following year he produced a DiMaggio-like streak of 57 consecutive winning games.

The first American to win a Wimbledon title (in 1920), he had repeated the feat in 1921. He then stayed away for several years because he said he had nothing left to prove, but in 1930, at the age of thirty-seven, he became the oldest Wimbledon champion in history. He also won seven U.S. clay court titles, led the U.S. to seven straight Davis Cup championships, won five U.S. doubles titles and took four national indoor doubles crowns. Tilden's domination of the game finally came to an end later in the decade, but by the time he retired from amateur competition he had recorded at least 130 singles and 85 doubles tournament victories.

Like another star athlete of the time, Babe Ruth, it was not only the sheer statistical supremacy that was so captivating, it was the style. When Tilden was at his best, Franklin P. Adams wrote, he was "more of an artist than nine-tenths of the artists I know. It is the beauty of the game that Tilden loves; it is the chase always, rather than the quarry."

Tilden would toy with opponents he knew he could beat easily, even to the point of giving them a head start. Tilden explained, "The player owes the gallery as much as an actor owes the audience." Indeed, he loved the stage perhaps even more than the game, and he repeatedly tried his hand as an actor and playwright, receiving remarkably consistent critical disapproval.

Tilden also fancied himself a writer, and at his peak he was earning as much as $25,000 a year writing special newspaper columns, one of the few athletic stars who didn't require a ghost writer. He also penned several short stories, a novel and three autobiographies, none of which showed talent even close to that which he displayed on the court. His most successful forays into writing came in the form of instructional tennis articles and books. The first player to make a science of the game, he was also ahead of his time in calling for changes in tennis organization, all of which later came to pass. Among these were the advent of open tennis, team tennis, the dissolution of Wimbledon's Challenge Rounds and a change in the Davis Cup format.

Tilden's role as tennis player, innovator, theorist and ambassador turned him into an embodiment of the game. In fact, Deford claims that even if Tilden had not been the most charismatic, publicized and exciting player in tennis history, "he would still be regarded as a paramount figure in the game, because it was his genius and that application which took the whole sport . . . from one level of sophistication way up to another."

Though professionals were barred from the major tournaments, Tilden had long claimed he would never stoop to turning pro. But at the end of 1930, he did just that, becoming, according to Deford, "the Pied Piper of Professionalism." The Tilden Tennis Tour throughout 1931 was a bit like Red Grange's football tour six years earlier, only Tilden had more athletic success than Grange, beating the recognized pro champion, Karel Kozeluh of Czechoslovakia, in 63 of 76 matches. Over the next few years, his tour continued to grow in stature and he continued to beat most of his opponents, who remained the undercard to his headline act.

It was estimated that Tilden earned close to $500,000 in his six years as a pro from 1931–1937, but like John L. Sullivan before him, and Joe Louis after him, he spent most of it quickly. Like both men, his reputation also began to suffer considerably, but in his case, it was due to the growing rumors about his proclivity for young boys. When tennis began to become less of a focus, he became more overt about his sexual preferences. He had often travelled with hand-picked ball boys, even recruiting them from high schools, sometimes for companionship, other times for intimacy.

Tilden went off to California in 1939, where he could play tennis year-round and enjoy the company of the movie stars he had befriended and idolized. By then he had been blacklisted by most tennis and country clubs, but he still found opportunities to coach, frequented the stage and formed a touring tennis troup during World War II.

When the war ended, he was at the forefront of the creation of the Professional Tennis Players Association, and, though age fifty-three, he still regularly reached the quarterfinals of professional tournaments. But just as he was basking in his reentry into the thick of the tennis world, on November 23, 1946, his world came crumbling down.

Tilden was arrested for fondling a 14-year-old boy while letting him drive his car. Though he had gotten out of similar scrapes before, this time the matter would not be brushed aside. Still honest and egotistical, he pleaded guilty against his lawyer's wishes. The judge, considering him a threat to society, sentenced him to one year in prison, and "Big Bill" Tilden became prisoner number 9413.

Tilden obtained an early release after less than eight months, but he still had to undertake psychiatric treatment and stay away from juveniles. Yet, seventeen months later he was arrested once again, this time for picking up a 16-year-old male hitchhiker and making advances. And so, on his fifty-sixth birthday, Tilden was sentenced to another year in prison and ostracized by the tennis world, by his hometown, by his alma mater, and by many of his old friends. By June 5, 1953, he was dead. According to the coroner, he was "just a case of a chap sixty years old who outlived his heart."

Only three years earlier, a few days after he had been released from prison into a world that wished it had never adored him, Tilden had received word that an Associated Press poll had named him the greatest tennis player in history. He had received ten times more votes than the runnerup, yet virtually the only remaining evidence that he had ever played the game was the realization that he had transformed it.

49

Roy Hofheinz

Roy Hofheinz was always ahead of his time. He was a high school graduate by age fifteen, a practicing lawyer at eighteen, a state legislator at twenty-two, America's youngest county judge at twenty-four, a millionaire by the time he was thirty-five, and mayor of Houston at forty. Even his birth, on April 10, 1912, in Beaumont, Texas, was probably premature. Only his death, on November 22, 1982, came later than expected in view of the extravagant and caution-be-damned life that was Roy Hofheinz's.

But it was his grand design for a new baseball stadium, unveiled in 1965, that will forever mark Hofheinz as a visionary, not to mention an eccentric. Hofheinz, after all, was the man most responsible for the creation of the Houston Astrodome, the ballpark that changed the way the games were played and, as one writer insisted, "changed the very way Americans attend their games."

Hofheinz has been described as a "gaudy archetype of the Southwestern millionaire go-getter" . . . "the most inventive, imaginative and successful entrepreneur in the world" . . . "a tornado in human form" . . . a man who "could sell nasal spray to the noseless." He became judge of Houston's Harris County in 1936 and was known as the Judge thereafter. It was a sign of respect, an understanding of power, though certainly not a term of endearment. Hofheinz stepped down from the bench in 1944, vowing not to return to politics until he had made his first million. "At the time," writer Tex Maule explained twenty-five years later, "he had far more enemies than dollars, and that situation has changed only because he now has $20 million."

After making a fortune in radio stations, law and real estate, Hofheinz returned to politics as Houston's mayor, in 1952. Almost immediately, he alienated most of the city council and, though he was reelected in 1954, the resulting political gridlock led to his ouster in a special election in 1955. It was then that Hofheinz turned his attention from political games to the more sporting variety. He had struck up a relationship with Houston oilman R. E. (Bob) Smith, one of the richest men in the state. Smith brought Hofheinz into the Houston Sports Association, which was created to attract Major League Baseball to the city, and Hofheinz quickly became the movement's major player.

"I decided that the only way to sell Houston as a major league city was to come up with a stadium that would lure the baseball people," Hofheinz explained. And so, through Hofheinz's imagination and tenacity, the kind of arena that had been considered in one form or another and in one city or another for years—the world's first multi-purpose domed stadium—became reality on some 260 acres of Texas swampland.

The Houston Colt '45s joined the National League in 1962, but it wasn't until 1965 that the stadium that had given birth to the team was completed. In the meantime, the expansion club played its home games in Colt Stadium, a $2 million outdoor arena. But the Judge had already begun to make an impact on the game. As one New York television executive put it, "This guy Hofheinz is the most refreshing mind to come into baseball in years. You watch him. He'll out-O'Malley O'Malley and out-Veeck Veeck. I just hope he doesn't decide to change the rules of the game."

Instead, Hofheinz decided to change the very structure of the game. "Got to impress those fat cats from New York who come down here and expect Texans to act like Texans," Hofheinz declared. And so, with $31.6 million of public credit, Hofheinz created the Harris County Domed Stadium. Soon, with a nod to America's heroes of the 1960s, and with a wink toward the future, Hofheinz named his team the Astros, and his creation the Astrodome.

Everything about the Astrodome was grandiose. It reached 208 feet at its highest point. Its dugouts were 120 feet long, reflecting typical Hofheinzian logic that more people would be able to claim seats behind the dugout. There were even living quarters for Hofheinz himself that would have made Elvis blush, including a bowling alley, a miniature golf course, a shooting range, a barbershop and a tavern with stools that could be raised or lowered by remote control.

Besides the Astros and the Astrodome, Hofheinz's Astrodomain soon included the 474-foot-long Astrolite scoreboard, the Astrotots puppet theater, the 12-acre Astrohall exhibition arena, the 57-acre AstroWorld amusement park and an AstroWorld hotel-motel complex. It was, as *Sports Illustrated*'s Steve Rushin, explained, "enough to make you AstroSick."

The Astrodome would host some of sport's most seminal moments over the next decade, including the 1968 college basketball drama pitting UCLA and Lew Alcindor against Houston and Elvin Hayes, as well as the 1973 Battle of the Sexes between Billie Jean King and Bobby Riggs. Everyone from the circus to the Boy Scouts to the Houston Oilers would find their way to Hofheinz's big top, which Reverend Billy Graham reportedly christened "the Eighth Wonder of the World." To this, Oilers owner Bud Adams responded, "If the Astrodome is the Eighth Wonder of the World, the Judge's price for a lease is the ninth."

When Astros pitcher Larry Dierker first set foot in the Astrodome in April 1965, and stared at the translucent dome above him and the splash of color around him, he said it was "like walking into the next century." President Lyndon Johnson, a longtime friend of Hofheinz, attended the first game, an exhibition contest against the Yankees, and Mickey Mantle recorded the baseball palace's first hit and first home run.

It quickly became apparent, though, that Hofheinz's wonder had become a rather embarrassing blunder. Not only did players lose track of the ball amid the optical illusion of the Astrodome ceiling's maze of panels and girders, but on sunny days, the glare from the roof was blinding. Hofheinz and the Astros tried to solve the problem any number of ways, from colored baseballs to dozens of different kinds of sunglasses. Finally they decided to paint over the roof panels, which meant that the specially developed grass created by scientists to thrive in the dome's refracted light would receive no light at all.

As the grass died during the 1965 season, Hofheinz simply painted over it, but in 1966 he started an indoor revolution, taking an artificial surface originally developed for children's playgrounds in the inner-city and applying about 14,000 square yards of it to the ultimate adult playground. Hofheinz contacted the Chemstrand Company, a division of the Monsanto Company, which installed a surface it called ChemGrass. On March 19, 1966, the Astros and Dodgers first tested out the field's artificial infield. By July 9, the entire field was carpeted. Ballgames would never be the same again.

Joe Morgan, who was then the Astros' second baseman, later admitted, "I thought it was something that would be unique to the Astrodome because the grass wouldn't grow there. I couldn't imagine anyone using it outside. I couldn't see that it would change the game completely."

But it has. ChemGrass quickly became known as AstroTurf, which soon evolved into a lucrative industry. Within seven years, five more baseball stadiums would have synthetic surfaces, their owners preferring the large initial investment over the high cost of maintenance. Today, hundreds of high schools and colleges and more than two dozen pro baseball and football teams compete on artificial turf, a trend that is only beginning to reverse itself in the 1990s.

Artificial turf has dramatically changed the way the games, especially baseball, play themselves out. Baseball, on the fake stuff, has largely become a collection of ground-rule doubles, high-chop singles, one-bouncers from the shortstop deep in the hole and cautious steps from turf-conscious outfielders. As *Sports Illustrated*'s Ron Fimrite wrote in a 1985 special report on artifical surfaces, "Charge a ball on turf, and you risk never seeing it again."

Another result of the turf revolution is the increased emphasis on speed, which has become to football and baseball scouts what strength and a smooth swing used to be. And in football, smooth surfaces—along with the absence of wind in domed stadiums—make for a placekicker's dream conditions. In fact, such conditions are largely responsible for the NFL's decision to institute rules, in 1994, to curtail the impact of the kicking game.

Artificial turf has also combined with bigger, stronger and faster athletes to become a stage for unprecedented injuries. *Sports Illustrated*'s special report called for the replacement of synthetic surfaces, asking, "Are the rugs that cover sporting

America more trouble than they're worth?" Eight years later, the same magazine detailed yet another rash of turf-related injuries in the NFL.

Of nearly 1,000 NFL players surveyed in 1995, more than 900 said they believed playing on turf would shorten their careers. Over the years, the criticisms have come in various forms. Gene Upshaw, executive director of the NFL Players Association, said, "We believe, as we always have, that players are hurt by the turf." NFL cornerback Eric Allen added, "It's bad just to walk on the stuff, never mind try to play football on it." And baseball's George Brett insisted, "Playing on grass is like a paid vacation."

While building the Astrodome, Hofheinz had boasted, "When I'm through, no man will be able to copy what I've built." Yet Hofheinz set off an imitative wave that changed the games—and, more important, our perception of them. "Indeed, the ultimate damage the turf movement has done is to the very look of baseball," wrote Fimrite. "That pool-table image doesn't work with a game that should have the look and feel and smell of a summer outing."

Hofheinz may have stumbled across artificial turf by accident, but it was he who introduced it to the world of sports. With more than half of the pro football season and one-third of the baseball season currently being played on bogus turf, that is quite an impact.

But Hofheinz introduced more than just fake grass to the sporting world. Domed stadiums have proliferated—from the Syracuse Carrier Dome to the Louisiana Superdome to Toronto's SkyDome, a '90s version of the Astrodome that has been called "a retractable-roofed restaurant, ballpark, bar, hotel, health club, cinema, self-contained city and sold-out curiosity shop."

And even though baseball seems to be returning to its roots with more traditional parks like Camden Yards in Baltimore and The Ballpark at Arlington, new stadiums are still primarily constructed around another Hofheinz innovation: luxury skyboxes. Hofheinz built fifty-three luxury boxes with $2 million from his own pocket, claiming that he got the idea from a visit to the Colosseum in Rome, where he mistakenly believed the emperor used to sit at the top of the stadium.

Hofheinz, along with maverick owners like Bill Veeck and Charlie Finley, helped to spawn sport's transformation from an escape catering only to sports enthusiasts to a scene catering to all walks of life; from a competitive diversion into casual entertainment. Particularly in the rarified air of the skyboxes, a high-class trip to the games has come to represent a social and business status symbol, a means to both gloat and schmooze. Hofheinz led the way into what has become a gold mine for the sporting industry.

Funny, isn't it? Hofheinz merely thought he was creating a peek into the future when he built the Astrodome. Had he known it would lead to an alteration of the tactics, the fabric and the perception of the games, he might have named it after himself.

CREATING A MONSTER

Roy Hofheinz is the man who made artificial turf famous, but he wasn't the man who made it in the first place. It all started with studies conducted during the Korean War which revealed that city boys were in worse physical shape than country boys. The Ford Foundation reacted by creating a nonprofit company called the Educational Facilities Labratory (EFL) to research the matter. Its first president was Dr. Harold Gores.

Gores examined the problem and concluded that the city was less conducive to physical improvement because it simply had fewer open spaces. He then reasoned that the creation of an inexpensive soft surface could translate to more safe urban playgrounds and asked the Monsanto Company, a chemical manufacturer, to look into the matter. In 1964, the EFL paid $200,000 to install the nation's first carpeted playground, though instead of going to the city it went to a private boys' school in Rhode Island.

As it turned out, however, artificial turf has proved to be too expensive for its original intentions, and by the time Gores died in 1993, playgrounds were still made of asphalt. But the more serious playing fields had become increasingly artificial.

50

Satchel Paige

In the years leading up to Jackie Robinson's first appearance in the major leagues, in 1947, baseball executives offered any number of convenient rationalizations as to why there were no black players in the big leagues. One of the most common refrains was the contention that they just weren't talented enough for the big show.

But even the most ardent opponents of integration were unable to mute the success of one particular pitcher, a lanky whip of a man who had attracted the attention of baseball fans around the country in the preceding two decades. As Cleveland Indians owner Alva Bradley later admitted, "In 1945 there was only one Negro player mentioned as being of major league caliber. That was Satchel Paige."

There were any number of cultural influences that helped bring about the demise of baseball's unwritten ban against black players—the continued efforts of black journalists and white supporters, the sustained excellence and acceptance of Joe Louis in boxing, the hypocrisy evident in America's fight against foreign injustice in World War II, even the fact that the black population in the northern states increased by 50 percent during the 1940s. But perhaps the most significant weapon in the fight against baseball's color barrier was Satchel Paige's right arm.

Leroy Robert Paige was born on July 7, 1906, in Mobile, Alabama, the seventh of eleven children. Some say he got his nickname working as a porter at the Mobile train station; others claim it was a shortened version of "Satchelfoot," a reference to his size 12 feet. The truth can be found buried somewhere under a slew of myths and tales that would eventually surround Paige, the number rivalling those about another American baseball legend, Babe Ruth.

One writer called Paige "a Paul Bunyan in technicolor," and indeed, Ruth's legend had nothing on Ol' Satch. As with Ruth, there was even some mystery surrounding Paige's actual age. Most sources put his year of birth as 1906, but there were rumors that he was actually born in 1904 or even in 1899. Former

Negro League star Ted Radcliffe always claimed he was younger than Paige, and Radcliffe was born in 1902.

Like Ruth, Paige was sent to a reform school at a young age (twelve), and like Ruth, it was there that he learned how to pitch. After being released from the school, he joined the semipro Mobile Tigers, in 1924, where he would earn a dollar a game if the game receipts were good, a keg of lemonade if they weren't. It was the first of what would be more than forty years in baseball for Paige, most of them in the Negro Leagues.

Paige's start came just after the start of the leagues themselves. Rube Foster, one of the early twentieth century's greatest pitchers, had assembled the all-black Chicago American Giants in 1911. Nine years later, he combined several midwestern barnstorming teams into the Negro National League, and assorted other leagues soon formed. The original organizations fell victim to the Depression, but a second Negro National League and a Negro American League quickly emerged.

Paige played for the Chattanooga Black Lookouts from 1926–1928 and then the Birmingham Black Barons from 1928–1930, where his fame grew immensely. "Everybody in the South knew about Satchel Paige, even then," recalled a former teammate. "We'd have 8,000 people out—sometimes more—when he was pitching, which was something in Birmingham."

Paige was a dominant force on the mound, but his fame was as much a result of his persona as his pitching. He was 6-foot-3 and only 140 pounds when he began his career, and though he would gain another forty pounds over time, he always appeared to be a skinny collection of whip-like arms and oversized feet. "I was a serious pitcher," Paige explained, in his 1961 autobiography, *Maybe I'll Pitch Forever*. "But when you're tall and skinny as I am and when you got feet that are feet, maybe you look a little funny."

As Paige's legend grew, his showmanship did as well. He would call in his outfielders to sit behind the pitcher's mound or announce that he would strike out the first six batters he faced. Paige even had various names for his fastball— a jump ball, a trouble ball and a bee ball ("because it hums").

He was also playfully quotable, in the mold of Dizzy Dean, Casey Stengel and Yogi Berra. Paige once said James "Cool Papa" Bell was so fast he could turn off the bedroom lights and be in bed before the room got dark. When an observer at his very first tryout asked if he threw that fast consistently, he replied, "No, sir. I do it all the time."

Paige's popularity, and, thus, his gradual assault on the color barrier, took an even bigger leap forward in the 1930s when a man named Gus Greenlee decided to turn his semipro Pittsburgh Crawfords into the greatest team in black baseball—perhaps the greatest anywhere, anytime. In 1932, he purchased Paige's contract and then added four more future Hall of Famers—Josh Gibson, Oscar Charleston, Judy Johnson and "Cool Papa" Bell.

Paige was dominant. According to one source, he went 23-7 in 1932, as the Crawfords won 99 of 135 games, and then he won 31 of 35 decisions in 1933, including 21 straight wins and 62 straight scoreless innings. The Crawfords' most profound impact came on the barnstorming trail, which was always the foundation of the Negro Leagues. By the mid-1930s, exhibition matches pitting Paige against major league all-stars or the game's top pitchers were among the most popular attractions in the game.

With the nation wondering how a black ballplayer would fare against the game's biggest stars, Paige was generally at his best. Once he struck out 22 major leaguers in a game. In 1934 and 1935, he took on baseball's best pitcher, Dizzy Dean, in six exhibition contests. Paige won four of them, causing the usually immodest Dean to remark, "My fastball looks like a change of pace alongside that pistol bullet old Satch shoots up to the plate."

The Crawfords disbanded in 1937, but Paige was bigger than any one team. In fact, he became such a desired commodity that he earned as much as $40,000 annually, while most black players were taking home between $125 and $300 each month. Of course, Paige earned it by competing year-round, playing both summer and winter ball for thirty years. In fact, he once estimated that he had pitched in more than 2,500 games, winning about 2,000 of them. All those innings took a temporary toll on his arm, and, in 1939, he appeared to have lost his fastball. But he developed an array of offspeed pitches, and when his arm recovered in the 1940s he pitched better than ever.

In the process, Paige's pitching became a pitch for integration. He repeatedly proved the quality of black ballplayers in front of packed houses all over the country. By doing so, he set the stage for his former Negro League teammate, Jackie Robinson, to sign a professional contract in 1945. But while Paige publicly supported Robinson, he was privately disappointed that Branch Rickey hadn't selected him. He later wrote in his autobiography, "Signing Jackie like they did hurt me deep down. I'd been the guy who started all that big talk about letting us in the big time . . . I'd been the one the white boys wanted to barnstorm against. I'd been the one everybody said should be in the majors . . . It was still me that ought to have been first."

Ironically, although Paige was instrumental in the dissolution of baseball's color line, it seems his fame actually held him back awhile. Baseball's other master showman, Cleveland Indians owner Bill Veeck, later claimed he didn't want to sign Paige as the first black American Leaguer because he might be accused of bringing him in as a promotional gimmick. So it was only after making Larry Doby the first black player in the American League that Veeck signed Paige as the first black pitcher.

Veeck had enough showman left in him to announce the signing on Paige's forty-second birthday. *The Sporting News* bristled at the notion of signing the oldest rookie in major league history, declaring that "to bring in a pitching rookie of Paige's age is to demean the standards of baseball. Were Satchel white, he would not have drawn a second thought from Veeck."

Veeck responded by saying, "If Satch were white, of course, he would have been in the majors twenty-five years earlier, and the question would not have been before the house." As for Paige, he admitted, "I ain't as fast as I used to be. I used to overpower 'em; now I outcute 'em." But in 1948, Cleveland was in a pennant race, and Veeck thought Paige could help.

In his first two appearances, both in relief, he recorded a save and a win, pitching five scoreless innings. On August 3, in the first start of his big league career he picked up the victory. Ten days later, he shut out the White Sox on only five hits. One week after that, in front of the largest crowd ever to attend a night game (78,382 in Cleveland), he shut out Chicago again, this time on three hits. Fans were flocking to see if the legend were true, and the ageless Paige didn't let them down. Though he faded slightly down the stretch, he finished with a 6-1 mark and a 2.48 ERA, and the Indians won the World Series.

After a 4-7 season in 1949, Paige was released, but then Veeck purchased the St. Louis Browns in 1951, and, again, signed the famous pitcher. Paige's best big league season came in 1952 at the age of forty-six. He went 12-10 with a 3.07 ERA, 10 saves and a league-best eight relief victories, becoming the Browns' only all-star representative. But the following year his record dipped to 3-9, and he was once again released. Three shutout innings at age fifty-nine in 1965, and a stint as Atlanta's pitching coach in 1968 (to qualify for a pension), were all that remained of Paige's major league career.

Satchel Paige died on July 8, 1982, finally succumbing to age. His lifetime big league record of 28 wins and 31 losses reflects little about his talent and lots about the barrier he helped destroy. His 1971 induction as the first Negro League star in the Hall of Fame speaks volumes about his impact.

51

Paul Brown

With all that Paul Brown contributed to football, particularly the professional game, the last thing he needed was some sort of material reminder of his influence. And yet there may be no more appropriate tribute than that given him in 1946. For the man who brought professionalism to professional football, who conquered the gridiron at every level, and who was to Ohio football what Casey Stengel was to New York baseball, the residents of Cleveland voted to name their new ballclub the Cleveland Browns. Even Chicago's NFL team isn't called the Halases, yet Brown's impact as a coach and executive was second in pro football only to that of Papa Bear himself.

Brown was born twelve years before the NFL, on September 7, 1908, in Norwalk, Ohio, just east of Cleveland. His father, a railroad dispatcher, was transferred when Brown was nine, and the family moved to Massillon, south of Cleveland and just outside of Canton, where Brown would be immortalized exactly a half-century later. He competed in several sports at Massillon's Washington High School, including quarterbacking the football team, but when he matriculated at Ohio State University he discovered he was too small for big-time college football. He transferred to Miami (Ohio) University and became the school's starting quarterback.

His parents had hoped he would become a lawyer or a musician, and they were a bit disappointed when Brown accepted a teaching and coaching position at a prep school upon graduating. Two years later, he returned to Massillon, where he took over the football team and embarked on a career in which he found more success at more levels and in more leagues than perhaps any coach in history.

The Massillon program Brown took over in 1932 had won one game the previous season, was $37,000 in debt, and had difficulty filling its 3,000-seat stadium. He turned it into one of the nation's most successful football powerhouses, winning eighty games in nine seasons and drawing so many fans that a new 21,000-seat stadium was constructed five years later and eventually renamed Paul Brown Tiger Stadium. The Tigers of Massillon drew an average of 18,200 people per home game—from a town of just 26,000—and generated more than $100,000 in revenue.

The success landed Brown what had been his dream job—head coach at Ohio State. At thirty-three, he was the youngest head coach in Big Ten history, but, again, he was taking over a struggling program. OSU had suffered through a 40-0 shutout by Michigan in the final game of the 1940 season, but under Brown in 1941, the Buckeyes lost only one game and capped the season with a 20-20 tie against the Wolverines. The following year, the Buckeyes went 9-1 and won the national championship.

In 1943, World War II meant Brown's team could only feature players who were either too young or physically ineligible for military duty, and his "Baby Bucks" struggled to a 3-6 mark. Brown himself served a dual role the following two years as a battalion commander and head football coach at the Great Lakes Naval Training Center before turning to the professional ranks, or at least what many considered the pseudo-professional ranks, in 1946.

Arch Ward, sports editor of the *Chicago Tribune* and a promotional genius whose creations included baseball's All-Star Game, football's College All-Star Game and boxing's Golden Gloves tournament, had formed the All-America Football Conference (AAFC) in the mid-'40s. He convinced more than 100 NFL players to switch leagues, and placed a team in Cleveland, which had given so little support to its previous franchise that the NFL's Cleveland Rams moved to Los Angeles.

Brown received a $25,000 salary, five percent ownership of the team and, in a tribute to his already immense popularity in the region, the honor of calling his club the Cleveland Browns. His team won its first regular season game 44-0 and went on to produce a 52-4-3 record from 1946–1949. The Browns dominated the AAFC to such an extent that it led to disinterest about the league and, thus, a desire for peace in its war for survival against the NFL.

Despite Cleveland's four straight league titles, NFL supporters consistently disparaged the Browns by suggesting their worst teams could beat the AAFC's best. When Cleveland and two other AAFC clubs—the San Francisco 49ers and Baltimore Colts—merged with the NFL following the 1949 season, Brown had his chance to show just what a powerhouse he had created. Cleveland beat the defending NFL-champion Philadelphia Eagles in the first game of the 1950 season, on their way to the NFL title.

In fact, over the next half-dozen years, Cleveland played in six title games, winning two more championships (in 1954 and 1955). All in all, in Brown's first twelve seasons as head coach of the team that bore his name, the Browns played their way to the league championship game eleven times. Brown had conquered pro football, just as he had the high school and college game.

Of course, there have been other football coaches with impressive records, but it was Brown's innovative genius that set him apart from the others. "Where

George Halas fathered the NFL," Kevin Lamb wrote in *Sport* magazine, "it was Brown who gave birth to coaching as we know it."

It was Brown who first began to grade game films, who introduced advanced playbooks at every level he coached, who designed the draw play after watching a broken play turn into a successful gain, and who spearheaded the addition of face masks on football helmets. He was the first to use "messenger guards" to allow him to call every play from the sidelines, the first to utilize psychological and IQ testing of players, and the first to introduce the reserve "taxi squad," which originally consisted of players who were actually given jobs driving taxicabs.

"He brought a system into pro football," said Sid Gillman, himself a coaching genius. "He brought a practice routine. He broke down practice into individual areas. He had position coaches . . . He's an organizational genius. I always felt that before Paul Brown, coaches just rolled the ball out on the practice field."

Brown made use of his players' talents to revolutionize various aspects of the game—Otto Graham and passing, Lou Groza and kicking, Marion Motley and Jim Brown and the running game. Said one of his former players, Willie Davis, "Paul Brown probably was copied in the 1960s and 1970s and even today more than any other coach in the game. And for good reasons. This guy had the game down to a science." His protégés alone, including Don Shula, Chuck Noll and Bill Walsh, count nearly a dozen Super Bowl trophies among them.

Throughout Brown's reign, however, his cerebral approach to the game left him with a cold-hearted reputation. And indeed, it was interpersonal miscommunication that led to the shocking events of January 9, 1963, when a feud with new owner Art Modell (and five straight seasons without a division title) led to the end of the Paul Brown era in Cleveland.

All but exiled, Brown admitted in his autobiography, "I felt like Napoleon on the isle of Elba." But, like Napoleon, Brown returned triumphantly. Though he still had a hefty contract with Cleveland and the title of vice-president, Brown's name seemed to be associated with every coaching vacancy in the league. But, as Bob Carroll explains in *When the Grass Was Real*, when he returned he would be the man in charge, "answering only to himself and to God—so long as God didn't call the plays."

The right opporunity arose in 1967, the year Brown was inducted into the Pro Football Hall of Fame, when the AFL awarded an expansion franchise to Cincinnati. In one of sport's great ironies, Paul Brown returned to football by creating perhaps the greatest rival of the team named after him. At the age of sixty in 1968, he returned to the sidelines amid speculation that the game had passed him by.

The Bengals won three games in their first season, the most ever by a first-year expansion team in the NFL, and then won a division title just two years later. Though Cincinnati went 55-56-1 in Brown's eight seasons as head coach, the team was 11-3 in 1975, after which Brown stepped down as head coach but stayed on as part owner and general manager.

By then, Brown, who died on August 5, 1991, had grown disenchanted with the attitudes of the modern players, and it is quite possible that much of his philosophy—he reportedly advised his players to abstain from sex after Tuesdays to prepare for Sunday's game—was better suited to a different era. But since he was in many ways ahead of his time, anyway, football was only catching up.

REBREAKING THE BARRIER

Depending on how you look at it, either Paul Brown of the AAFC's Cleveland Browns or Dan Reeves of the NFL's Los Angeles Rams is the Branch Rickey of professional football.

In either case, it was clearly a matter of rebreaking the color barrier. Thirteen black players appeared in the first fourteen years of the NFL, but from 1933–1945 there were no African-Americans in pro football. However, in 1946, after Rickey had signed Robinson to a pro baseball contract, Brown and Reeves each added a pair of black players to their teams.

The Rams signed Kenny Washington, a standout halfback and Jackie Robinson's old roommate at UCLA, and another former Bruins star named Woody Strode. But Washington was already twenty-eight by then, had weak knees and played for only three seasons. Strode was three years older and caught only four passes in his NFL career. Reeves had not necessarily chosen the best players available.

Paul Brown, on the other hand, chose to sign fullback Marion Motley, who had played for Brown at Great Lakes, and guard Bill Willis, who had played for him at Ohio State. Both earned all-league honors in 1946, and both are now enshrined in the Hall of Fame.

52

Jim Brown

Jim Brown was certainly one of the finest athletes in the history of American sports, and he may rank as football's greatest star, but there were some things that he definitely was not. He was not the first African-American to dominate team sports, having followed the likes of Roy Campanella and Willie Mays. Nor was he even professional football's first black star running back; Marion Motley and Joe Perry preceded him.

Brown was not the first athlete to make the jump from the playing fields to the silver screen (see Sonja Henie); he was not the first icon to frequent the police blotter (see Bill Tilden); and he is not the most conspicuous example of good works following a great athletic career (see Arthur Ashe). Nor was Brown the most prominent athletic voice during the fight for civil rights, not as relentless or resounding as, for instance, Bill Russell and Muhammad Ali.

But Jim Brown was, to some extent, a little bit of all of these things. If not the most influential person in any one particular endeavor, he was a prominent figure in many, which is why he has earned a spot among *The Sports 100*.

As a football player, Brown was unparalleled. In his nine NFL seasons with the Cleveland Browns, he earned eight rushing titles, leaving the game with records for career rushing yards (12,312), single-season rushing yards (1,863), single-game rushing yards (237), average yards per game (104.3), yards per carry (5.22), 100-yard games (58), 1,000-yard seasons (7) and touchdowns (126). He was an eight-time unanimous all-NFL choice, a Rookie of the Year and a two-time Most Valuable Player.

By then, observers had run out of superlatives to describe Brown. "The man belonged to a higher species," wrote *Sports Illustrated*'s Steve Rushin years later.

"He was simply that rarest kind of competitor, who made men and women gape, whose performances each Sunday displayed the pure athlete in his prime. Jim Brown is why we love sports in the first place."

Brown was an all-around athlete in the class of Jim Thorpe and Jackie Robinson. He won 13 varsity letters in five sports at Manhasset High School on Long Island, averaging nearly 15 yards per carry in football, scoring more than 38 points per game in basketball, and winning a state high jump title. At Syracuse University, he went from fifth-string backup to All-American on the gridiron, earning the same honors in lacrosse, where many claim he was the finest player they have ever seen. His baseball skills earned him some interest from the New York Yankees, while his basketball talents led the NBA's Syracuse Nationals to draft him. As a college sophomore, he also placed fifth in the national decathlon championships.

Choosing football, Brown simply channelled his talents into the relentless pursuit of yardage. Hall of Fame linebacker Sam Huff described tackling him by saying, "All you can do is grab hold, hang on and wait for help." As the first back to consistently carry the ball thirty times a game, and the first big back to combine unprecedented size and quickness, he was instrumental in the development of the modern running back. Sportswriter Red Smith, an equally incomparable talent, explained simply, "For mercurial speed, airy nimbleness, and explosive violence in one package of undistilled evil, there is no other like Mr. Brown."

Yet, there was none other like Brown away from the field as well. Just as he was a combination of disparate talents on the gridiron, he seemed to face life with a similarly enigmatic mix of traits and tendencies. He was, likely, a product of his youth, which presented him with a broad range of environmental messages. At one time or another, he was surrounded by poverty and love, affluence and altruism, discrimination and respect. Traveling a path from the South to suburbia to the college campus to fame and fortune in the big city, Brown came away from it with a unique combination of anger and understanding, of selfishness, selflessness and self-worth.

James Nathaniel Brown was born on St. Simons Island off the southern coast of Georgia on February 17, 1936. He was abandoned at birth by his father, and his mother left when he was two to take a job as a domestic in New York. Raised by his great-grandmother, he went to school in a segregated two-room shack. From there, however, he moved to what must have seemed like the other side of the world—Long Island—joining his mother at the age of seven after she began doing housework for a family in Manhasset.

Gang activities became a dominant force in his life, but they were soon replaced by athletic pursuits, which led to more than forty college scholarship offers. A Manhasset lawyer named Ken Molloy, who had played lacrosse at Syracuse and had taken an interest in Brown's welfare, wanted Brown to attend his alma mater. Yet, Syracuse wasn't interested, and only when Molloy and other local citizens agreed to pay Brown's tuition and expenses during his freshman year did the university reluctantly agree to give Brown a chance.

As a non-scholarship athlete his first year, and the only black freshman on the football team, Brown was miserable. Syracuse University in 1953 was, as Brown later recalled, at a "crossroads of segregation," and Brown was placed, according to Molloy, "in the mouth of a cannon." He didn't live in the players' dorm, he didn't eat with the team, and he was all but ignored by the coaches, receiving so little playing time that he considered transferring. It was undoubtedly a defining moment in his life, but one which he survived with characteristic aplomb. By the time he graduated, Syracuse's apathy toward black athletes had turned to eagerness, and a succession of African-American football stars like Ernie Davis and Floyd Little followed, each wearing Brown's collegiate number 44.

However, the experience likely colored Brown's perspective of his role as an athlete and a public figure. He and Cleveland coach Paul Brown had repeated run-ins over the big running back's priorities and over what he perceived as racial slights that he refused to ignore. Cleveland had won seven league titles in eleven seasons before Jim Brown became the dominant force on the team; they won only one NFL championship (in 1964) in his nine seasons. In fact, his coach admitted that before the 1962 season, he seriously considered trading his star running back "because his outlooks and attitudes had had such an undesirable effect on our team." Instead, it was Paul Brown who was fired in January 1963.

At about the same time, the public began to recognize that Jim Brown was more than just a brilliant football player. "During his first couple years in the league, most fans thought of Brown as a running machine. He had a certain brooding presence, but his fiercely independent personality lay hidden for the most part by carefully bland PR," writes Bob Carroll in *When the Grass Was Real*. "Only when his autobiography, *Off of My Chest*, was published did fans learn that Jim Brown was an outspoken black man with definite ideas on improving the Browns, the NFL and the United States. If that cost him the adulation of some white fans who preferred their black athletes strong and silent, well, to hell with them."

Said Brown, "I was very conscious of the civil rights movement and very active in what I call the movement for dignity, equality and justice. In fact, it superseded my interest in sports. Sports gave me an opportunity to help the cause. And so I did that." But Brown always felt he had a calling beyond the athletic fields, and so in 1966, while filming *The Dirty Dozen* in London, he announced his retirement from football. He had gained 1,544 yards the previous year, capping the season with the NFL Player of the Year award and three touchdowns in the Pro Bowl. He was walking away from the game while still at his peak.

"All through my career I was always looking to not stay too long," Brown later explained. "For all the guys who stayed too long—Joe Louis, Muhammad Ali—I thought it was embarrassing. People had sympathy for them, and you should never have sympathy for a champion." Instead, much of that sympathy was directed toward his movie career, with Lee Marvin describing Brown's acting talents by calling him only "a better actor than Olivier would have been a fullback."

By the time Brown was inducted into the Pro Football Hall of Fame in 1971, his silver screen career had all but come to a close, but he remained an activist on behalf of the African-American community, in both words and deeds. In the 1960s, he helped form the Black Economic Union to assist black-owned businesses. Nearly a quarter-century later, he created the Amer-I-Can program, an effort to turn gang members from destructive to productive members of society. "I have never done anything more important," he admitted, "than working for social change."

In the process, he has become an outspoken critic of modern athletes, though sometimes his words seem to be those of a social activist searching for a solution and other times they seem to represent the bitterness of a former athlete. He has criticized Michael Jordan and Magic Johnson for what he perceives as their lack of involvement in the black community, and has claimed that he could create a nationwide gang truce if he had the participation of America's top twenty athletes. But he also chose to disparage Franco Harris's talents as he neared his rushing record in the early 1980s, and labeled O. J. Simpson a cocaine-abuser shortly after he was arrested and charged with the murder of his ex-wife and her friend.

The public perception of Brown continues to drift somewhere between that of a former star devoting himself to improving urban America and an angry-at-the-world, holier-than-thou figure. He explains himself by saying, "If I became a pawn of society and said the things I was supposed to say as most of your superstars do today, I would be rich and I would be given false popularity. But when history comes down, that ain't nothing. I am a free man within society. I love that."

But for all Brown's good works, repeated events have surrounded him with a bad-ass image. As Diane K. Shah explained in *Sport* magazine, "If this is Brown's failing—an honorable, honest man making his way in a dishonest world, as he would seem to have you believe—it is offset by an even greater failing: his history of lashing out at victims who have done him wrong." Brown has repeatedly been accused of violent tendencies, primarily toward women, and though he has dodged the charges as he did linebackers, they have cast him with a hypocritical reputation as someone working to control violence in urban America, but unable to control it in himself.

In 1965, he was accused by an 18-year-old of forcing her to have sex, but was later found innocent. Three years later, he was accused of throwing his girlfriend from a balcony. In 1969, he was acquitted of assaulting a man following a traffic accident. Later, he spent a day in jail after beating up a golf partner. In 1984, he was charged with rape, sexual battery and assault, and though his victim had clearly been beaten, the charges were dropped when she gave inconsistent testimony. And then, two years later, Brown was arrested for beating his fiancée after accusing her of flirting. He spent three hours in jail, but three days later she decided not to press charges.

Brown has not apologized for any of the events, and indeed barely even acknowledges them. Instead, he seems to shrug off his alleged injustice toward others by pointing to grander inequities. Whether he is an innocent man burdened with the guilt of suspicion, a good man who suffers occasional bad moments, or a bitter person searching for his own goodness, Jim Brown is certainly one of American sport's most complex and compelling figures. For a man described as having nearly superhuman athletic qualities, he has proved, as well, to possess a healthy dose of both humanity and human imperfection.

53

Jack Dempsey

As the story goes, it was the summer of 1895, and a woman named Celia Dempsey was preparing to give birth to her ninth child in a two-room cabin near Manassa, Colorado. As she awaited delivery of the child, she read a book over and over again to pass the time. It was an autobiography of John L. Sullivan, whose brilliant boxing career had ended only a few years earlier. By the time William Harrison Dempsey was born, on June 24, she was sure of one thing. This child was going to be just like the great John L.

Manassa had been only one of many stops for the Dempsey family, descendants of West Virginia's Hatfield clan of Hatfield-McCoy fame, but the birth of the young boy became the best thing that ever happened to the town, as he grew up to be the Manassa Mauler, one of the most acclaimed athletes in the most glorious era of American sports.

As baseball exploded in the 1920s with Babe Ruth's mighty swings, football expanded around Knute Rockne and Red Grange, tennis matured with the performance of Bill Tilden, and golf rode the coattails of Bobby Jones and Walter Hagen, so did boxing enjoy a boom in popularity, much of it due to the power and personality of the man later voted the greatest boxer in the first half of the twentieth century.

His family was a mix of ancestry—Scottish, Irish, Native American, Jewish—and impoverished, requiring Harry Dempsey, as he was called, to work in the mines of Colorado and Utah as an adolescent. He left home at age sixteen, riding freight trains from town to town in search of prizefights, and boxing under pseudonyms like "Kid Blackie" and, eventually, "Jack" Dempsey. Like John L. Sullivan, Dempsey attempted to support himself by entering a saloon, declaring he could beat anyone in the place and then leaving with a fistful of money.

In 1916, Dempsey moved to New York City in a search for publicity, and there was thrown into the ring, ironically, with a boxer named John L. It was only John Lester Johnson, but he was still a top heavyweight, and Dempsey left the ring with three broken ribs. In 1917, however, he was taken over by a fast-talking, sharp-dressing manager named Jack "Doc" Kearns, who was described by Red Smith as "a creative artist who seldom let truth spoil a good story" and who gave Dempsey a fighting chance to become a fighting legend.

Within two years, Dempsey had earned an opportunity to take on heavyweight champion Jess Willard. By then, Dempsey had nearly 50 victories to his credit, including 21 first-round knockouts; Willard had defended his title but once in four years. On July 4, 1919, Dempsey destroyed Willard in three rounds to become the new heavyweight champion.

Dempsey had knocked Willard down seven times in the first round alone, an unprecedented all-out attack. "Never in the history of the ring, dating back to days beyond all memory, has any champion ever received the murderous punishment which 245-pound Jess Willard soaked up in that first round and the two rounds that followed," wrote Grantland Rice. Heavyweight title fights usually went at least 10 rounds, and Willard had won his in the 26th round. This battle, over in less than nine minutes, had been, according to Rice biographer Charles Fountain, "the dawn of a new age—the age of a champion who hit so hard that he changed the very nature of his sport."

Dempsey seemed on the verge of unprecedented acclaim, yet it was muted by accusations that he had been a draft dodger during World War I. Dempsey's estranged first wife, Maxine (he would be married four times), added fuel to the fire by announcing that he had falsified his draft papers, which led to a federal grand jury indictment of draft evasion and placed Dempsey at the nadir of his popularity. But it was soon discovered that he had actually spent the war years supporting his family by boxing, working in the shipyards and raising money for relief organizations with exhibitions. When Maxine Dempsey admitted on the witness stand that she had been lying in an attempt to extort money, Dempsey was publicly exonerated, though whispers that he had been a "slacker" continued for some time.

Over the next seven years, however, Dempsey would become one of the most popular people on the planet. He would fight to defend his title only six times, but several of the bouts would rank among the most lucrative and legendary in boxing history. Dempsey's aura, along with the promotional wizardry of boxing's first big-time promoter, Tex Rickard, turned pugilism into profiteering.

No fight had ever drawn a gate of more than $1 million before Dempsey arrived on the scene, yet he was involved in five such bouts totalling nearly $9 million, beginning with a title fight against French light-heavyweight champion George Carpentier in 1921. A crowd of over 80,000 in New Jersey watched Dempsey knock Carpentier out in the fourth round.

Dempsey's next title defense came two years later, a 15-round win over a veteran fighter named Tommy Gibbons in which the town that hosted the event—Shelby, Montana—paid Dempsey $300,000, and nearly went bankrupt. Soon after, Dempsey took on Argentinian Luis Firpo in front of 90,000 spectators at the Polo Grounds in what has been described as "the most sensational four minutes in boxing history." After being floored twice (once almost entirely out of the ring) and knocking Firpo down seven times in the first round, Dempsey knocked the challenger out 57 seconds into the second round.

It proved to be Dempsey's last successful title defense. In 1926, he lost a 10-round decision to ex-Marine Gene Tunney. More than 120,000 people had crowded Philadelphia's Sesquicentennial Stadium in a rainstorm, paying nearly $1.9 million to watch Dempsey lose his championship. Dempsey and Tunney faced off again a year later, after Dempsey had knocked out Jack Sharkey, a future heavyweight champion, to earn the rematch. Some 150,000 spectators filled Chicago's Soldier Field, creating boxing's first $2 million gate, and another 50 million more listened on the radio to what became the famous "Battle of the Long Count."

After Dempsey sent Tunney to the canvas in the 7th round, he ignored the referee's orders to go to a neutral corner, a new rule implemented after Dempsey had hovered over the fallen Firpo four years earlier. After five seconds had elapsed Dempsey finally obeyed the referee, who only then began counting Tunney out. Tunney rose to his feet nine seconds into the count but fourteen seconds after being floored. He went on to win by decision, later claiming that he had deliberately waited until the count of nine before rising.

Dempsey's manager filed an unsuccessful appeal with the state athletic commission, but Dempsey later called it "the luckiest thing that ever happened to me." As a gallant loser, he became more popular than ever. In fact, he became the most beloved ex-champion the sport had seen. By the time he died, on May 31, 1983, his name had been synonymous with boxing for more than six decades, the old Colorado miner having helped turn the sport into a gold mine.

54

Wilma Rudolph

When a four-pound baby girl was born in St. Bethlehem, Tennessee, on June 23, 1940, the path ahead of her lay strewn with imposing hurdles. Poverty, prejudice and illness loomed like insurmountable obstacles to any form of achievement.

She was the twentieth of twenty-two children produced by her railroad-porter father in two marriages. She was black at a time and place in which that meant separate and unequal, an environment in which the prospects of worldwide acclaim seemed as remote as voluntary desegregation. And she was in the poorest of health.

Rudolph, who was lucky to survive her first few months at all, contracted scarlet fever and double pneumonia at age four and was diagnosed with polio soon after, leaving her with minimal use of her left leg. Her mother drove her to a free hospital clinic for therapy once a week, and her family took turns massaging her leg amid hope that she would regain its use. And at age eight she was fitted with an orthopedic shoe to help her walk, and the chances of her someday becoming an Olympic sprinter were less than nil.

Indeed, there had been a time when that was true for all women. Female athletes were not included in Olympic competition until 1928, and though Babe Didrikson's performance at the 1932 Games, and her subsequent popularity, gave notice of female athletic potential, women still struggled against male chauvinism and the notion that femininity and athleticism were mutually exclusive. African-American women, in particular, suffered from the dual disadvantage of race discrimination in obtaining publicity and sex discrimination in obtaining opportunities.

"The most striking feature of the historical record on black women athletes is neglect," writes Susan K. Cahn in her book *Coming On Strong: Gender and Sexuality in Twentieth-Century Women's Sports*. "With the exception of Josephine

Baker or Lena Horne, African-American women were not generally subjects of white popular interest or adoration."

And yet, black women began to dominate American track and field. By 1948, nine of the eleven spaces on the U.S. track team were held by African-American women, and high jumper Alice Coachman became the first black woman in history to earn an Olympic gold medal.

In 1952, three black women anchored the American gold medal–winning 400-meter relay team, but only when Althea Gibson charged through the lily-white world of tennis and won the 1957 and 1958 U.S. and Wimbledon titles did the African-American female athlete begin to receive a measure of national exposure. It was in this setting that Wilma Rudolph broke barriers by breaking records.

By age twelve, Rudolph had shed her leg brace and her orthopedic shoes, but her climb toward athletic acceptance began with her peers. "I remember the kids always saying, 'I don't want to play with her. We don't want her on our team,'" she recalled. "I never forgot all those years when I was a little girl and not able to be involved." Gradually, however, Rudolph gained more than acceptance, as she began a sensational, if miraculous, athletic career.

At segregated Burt High School in Clarksville, Tennessee, she was a four-time all-state basketball player, setting a single-season scoring record with 803 points (more than 32 per game) as a sophomore. On the track, she took state titles in the 50-, 75- and 100-yard dashes, and at age sixteen she became a member of the U.S. Olympic track squad. In the 1956 Games in Melbourne, Rudolph shared a bronze medal in the 400-meter relay after being eliminated in a preliminary heat in the 200-meter run.

She had already completed the bulk of her fairy tale route, but as she came closer to the ultimate happy ending, she was confronted by still more challenges. Rudolph became pregnant during her senior year in high school, but, after placing the child with her family, she still managed to earn a track scholarship to Tennessee State University. Then injury and illness forced her out of much of the 1958 season, a pulled hamstring forced another layoff in 1959, and a tonsillectomy slowed her early in 1960.

But Rudolph was motivated by words of encouragement she had received from none other than Jackie Robinson. No matter what, he told her, "don't let anything, or anybody, keep you from running." In July, she set a world record in the 200-meters (22.9 seconds), and then, along with six of her Tennessee State teammates, headed to Rome for the 1960 Olympic Games.

Not surprisingly, Rudolph sprained an ankle the day before her first race, yet she still won the 100-meter final by nearly three meters. Then, naturally, it rained during the 200-meter final, but Rudolph won again. By the time she anchored the 400-meter relay team, chasing down and passing her German opponents, she had become the first American woman to win three track and field gold medals.

Along with decathlete Rafer Johnson and a young boxer named Cassius Clay, Rudolph emerged from the 1960 Olympics—the first Games televised throughout

Europe—as an international star. The awards that followed—Associated Press Female Athlete of the Year (1960, 1961), the Sullivan Award as the nation's top amateur athlete (1961), induction into the National Track and Field Hall of Fame (1974), the International Women's Sports Hall of Fame (1980) and the U.S. Olympic Hall of Fame (1983)—were one thing, but the adulation was quite another.

Anita DeFrantz was a bronze medalist in rowing at the 1976 Olympics, and became the only African-American woman ever to hold a spot on the International Olympic Committee. As an eight-year-old child in 1960, she idolized Rudolph. "There she was, with the whole world focused on her," said DeFrantz. "And wasn't it wonderful. Here was someone who looked like me, and she'd done something that everybody celebrated."

As a black woman achieving in a world dominated by white men, Rudolph's acclaim was still tinged with some racism and sexism. The press dubbed her the "black gazelle," and *Time* magazine wrote, "In a field of female endeavor in which the greatest stars have often been characterized by overdeveloped muscles and underdeveloped glands, Wilma (Skeeter) Rudolph has long, lissome legs and a pert charm."

The rather backhanded compliments gave evidence of the cultural biases Rudolph had overcome. Hers was a story of courage that superseded color and of elegance in a sport so long regarded as antithetical to femininity. Said Nell Jackson, coach of the U.S. track team, "Wilma's accomplishments opened up the real door for women in track because of her grace and beauty. People saw her as beauty in motion."

Perhaps more than any other athlete in American sports history, Rudolph symbolized perseverance, a lesson she later directed to underprivileged children through the Wilma Rudolph Foundation. In fact, the only fight she seems to have lost was her battle with brain cancer, which took her on November 12, 1994, at the age of fifty-four.

Thus, Rudolph joined other black sports pioneers like Robinson and Ashe in the ranks of people who lived life to its fullest nobility before leaving it all too soon. But, as with the others, the image will always remain. "She is immortal," said DeFrantz. "We'll know about Wilma Rudolph forever."

55

Jack Nicklaus

Golf, perhaps more than any other major sport, seems to be consistently represented by a handful of personalities. The game is played by millions; the professional game is played by hundreds. But golf, at its highest level, has been played by a select group of people who carry the sport on their shoulders—Bobby Jones and Walter Hagen, Gene Sarazen and Byron Nelson, Sam Snead and Ben Hogan.

Baseball had Joe DiMaggio, but it also boasted Ted Williams and Stan Musial and Bob Feller. Willie Mays stood out, but so did Henry Aaron and Mickey Mantle and Roberto Clemente. Johnny Unitas was football's glamour star in the '50s and '60s, but so were Jim Brown, Paul Hornung, even Vince Lombardi. Perhaps only professional basketball comes closest to golf in tying its popularity to its top talent, as the modern NBA has come to rely on a handful of young stars every year to bring attention to the game.

But for more than two decades, while basketball evolved from the Russell-Chamberlain era to the Bird-Johnson era, golf was ruled by one man. There was Nicklaus and Palmer, Nicklaus and Player, Nicklaus and Trevino, Nicklaus and Miller, Nicklaus and Watson, Nicklaus and Ballesteros. But always there was Jack Nicklaus. In a sport perhaps most in need of a dominant figure at the top, Nicklaus was that person for nearly a quarter of a century. As Thomas Boswell has written, "He not only carried his sport, to most people he actually *was* his sport."

In naming Nicklaus *Sports Illustrated*'s Sportsman of the Year for 1978, Frank Deford considered the "mystic oneness that he has had with the game of golf itself during that long span and with the courses on which it is played." He wondered, "How many other champions have become so identified with their sport, with every aspect of it, with the very essence of it, that it is impossible to think of one without the other? Babe Ruth, for sure; Bobby Jones himself; Muhammad Ali.

But they are few, very few; in his remarkable career, Nicklaus has achieved that preeminence as much as anyone."

How dominant was Nicklaus? The question can be answered in words or numbers. First, the words. Gene Sarazen: "I never thought anyone would ever put [Ben] Hogan in the shadows, but he did." Boswell: "Few careers in any walk of life have started so spectacularly, then continued steadily upward, almost without interruption, for so long." And golf historian Herbert Warren Wind: "One wonders if there has ever been an athlete who has accomplished more in any sport." Or, as *Sports Illustrated*'s Rick Reilly put it, if there ever was a better golfer than Nicklaus "then Woody Allen can dunk."

The numbers are even more revealing. Nicklaus won his first major professional event, the U.S. Open, in 1962, at the age of twenty-two; he won his last, the Masters, in 1986, at the age of forty-six. From 1962–1978, he won at least one tournament every year. In all, Nicklaus has totalled nearly 100 victories in national and international events, including 71 PGA Tour triumphs and several more on the Senior Tour, including three majors. He was PGA Player of the Year five times; he was the tour's leading money winner eight times; he recorded one of the top two scoring averages 14 times.

So impressive has been Nicklaus's performance in the major tournaments that Boswell has wondered if Nicklaus must ask himself, "Let's see, is that five Masters and six PGAs that I've won or six Masters and five PGAs?" It is six Masters and five PGAs and four U.S. Opens and three British Opens. Along with two U.S. Amateur titles, that makes 20 major championships, seven more than any other male golfer and more than the combined total of Ben Hogan and Arnold Palmer. No other golfer has won every major pro event twice; Nicklaus, whom *Sports Illustrated* named Athlete of the Decade for the 1970s, has won each three times.

But all along, Nicklaus was as much a family man as a sports icon, as much a golf architect and businessman as a golfer. He had already begun cutting down his tournament appearances at an age when most pros were just getting started, leading one colleague to call him "a legend in his spare time." In that sense, he was much like the man he idolized—Bobby Jones.

Like Jones, Nicklaus was also a golf prodigy. Born January 21, 1940, in Columbus, Ohio, he grew up in the suburb of Upper Arlington, where he was an all-league basketball player but an all-world golfer. At age ten, he shot 51 over the first nine holes he ever played; at age twelve, he won the Ohio State Junior Championship; at age thirteen, he broke 70 by recording an eagle on the 18th hole. At age fifteen, he qualified for the U.S. Amateur Championship; at age seventeen, he birdied the first hole of his first U.S. Open.

Nicklaus competed in his first tour event, the Rubber City Open, in 1958, finishing twelfth. He won the U.S. Amateur the following year, and then placed second to Arnold Palmer in the U.S. Open. After another U.S. Amateur victory in 1961, as well as an NCAA individual title as a member of the Ohio State team, Nicklaus turned pro. His first tour victory, in 1962, was also his first U.S. Open triumph. He beat Palmer in an 18-hole playoff.

It was an unfortunate coincidence of time and place for Nicklaus—the fact that he burst onto the scene just in time to challenge golf's most beloved performer at his peak. He was "Fat Jack," the overweight, underappreciated interloper with the crewcut, the cartoon voice and a game as boringly consistent as Palmer's was excitingly unpredictable.

Throughout the 1960s, Palmer was golf's champion; Nicklaus was golf's challenger. "Miss it, Jack!" was nearly as frequently heard as "Go get 'em, Arnie!" But as the '70s arrived, Nicklaus lost weight, grew his hair long and began to become a crowd favorite, remaining the "Golden Bear" in intensity but no longer in appearance. "He was not homespun like Sam Snead, not funny like Trevino. His pants didn't need hitching like Palmer's," wrote Rick Reilly. "Instead, he won over America with pure, unbleached excellence."

In the process, he piled one heroic moment upon another. There was that 1962 U.S. Open and the 1965 Masters, during which he shot a 271, three strokes better than Hogan's old record, leading Bobby Jones himself to say that Nicklaus played "a game with which I am not familiar." Nicklaus had what one writer described as an "uncanny ability to produce the vital shot at the vital moment." In the 1975 Masters, for instance, he sank a 40-foot putt on the sixteenth hole on the final day to beat Johnny Miller and Tom Weiskopf. In the Doral Open that same year, he holed a 76-yard shot for an eagle on the tenth hole and then a 77-yard shot for an eagle on the twelfth.

His career was so long, he actually made two dramatic comebacks. After his first winless season on the tour in 1979, the 40-year-old Nicklaus shot a 272 at the 1980 U.S. Open, a new record. Then, after going winless in majors for six years, Nicklaus arrived at the 1986 Masters amid whispers that it was time to retire. With his adult son as his caddie, the 46-year-old shot a 65 in the final round and a 30 on the back nine to pass eight of the game's best golfers en route to his sixth green jacket.

Nicklaus's accomplishments, however, have not been limited to the fairways. He had followed Palmer's lead by signing up with International Management Group in the early '60s, but in 1968, he set off on his own, eventually forming his own company, Golden Bear International. In 1994, *Forbes* magazine estimated that Nicklaus's business enterprises—from ventures in apparel, golf equipment, television, client management, endorsements and golf course design—had given him a net worth in excess of $300 million. In 1994, he earned an estimated $14.5 million in endorsements alone, more than anyone not named Michael Jordan.

Nicklaus and golf course architect Pete Dye have been described as the "two men most responsible for changing course design to the style called 'modern.'" In fact, Nicklaus essentially apprenticed under Dye, but he himself has become so sought after as an architect that by 1990 he was charging $1.5 million for his services, $2 million in Japan. He has designed more than 100 courses in all, including twelve of *Golf Digest*'s "Top 100" courses.

And so Nicklaus and Dye have carved out an immense influence in golf course architecture, just as Nicklaus and Palmer did so in fashioning unprecedented financial empires, and just as Nicklaus and Bobby Jones grew to symbolize golf by dominating it. Nicklaus's success—his ability to design, profit from, and conquer the golf course—has resulted in an impact on golf behind only that of Palmer and Jones. And so, among male golf figures, Nicklaus trails only his boyhood idol and greatest rival in *The Sports 100*.

CHAMPION OF CHAMPIONS

The following twelve men have won the most majors (U.S. Open, British Open, Masters, PGA Championship, U.S. Amateur and British Amateur) in golf:

1. Jack Nicklaus	20	7. Arnold Palmer	8
2. Bobby Jones	13	8. Tom Watson	8
3. Walter Hagen	11	9. Harold Hilton	7
4. John Ball	9	10. Gene Sarazen	7
5. Ben Hogan	9	11. Sam Snead	7
6. Gary Player	9	12. Harry Vardon	7

56

Andre Laguerre

There is always the danger of overstating the importance of the people who cover the news, rather than those who make it. But there is also something to the notion that those in the media not only relate the news, but define it. The movement can be obvious, as in the tireless efforts of several African-American sportswriters to dissolve baseball's color barrier. Or it can be gradual and pervasive, as in the impact made by the most significant media outlet in sports over the past half-century—*Sports Illustrated*.

Touting itself as "the conscience of sport," the nation's only weekly sports newsmagazine has been at the forefront of the transformation in coverage of the games and in the games themselves over the past forty years. As writer Michael MacCambridge explained in a three-part series on *Sports Illustrated* in the *Austin American-Statesman*, it has become "an institution of American popular culture as well as the most respected sports publication in the world."

Every week, an estimated 24 million adults read *Sports Illustrated*, including more than five million women and nearly 18 million men, which represents almost 20 percent of the adult male population in the United States.

Those numbers have turned *Sports Illustrated* into a powerful starmaking vehicle. But *Sports Illustrated* also has evolved into the role of newsbreaker, as well as starmaker, occasionally producing investigative pieces—on boxing scandals, Pete Rose's troubles, drugs, academic abuses—that have shaken the sports world, or at least aroused discussion. Over the years, the magazine led a transformation in sports journalism by injecting wry wit and intelligence into its coverage of sport. Indeed, the very evolution of the subjects *Sports Illustrated* deemed worthy of coverage was both a reaction to a changing sports scene and an impetus toward that change.

The first issue of *Sports Illustrated*, dated August 16, 1954, was a sellout, but it hardly looked like today's version. It did have Milwaukee Braves star Eddie Mathews on the cover, but there were also stories about Prince Philip, puppies, boomerangs and baseball cards. Indeed, the magazine was originally marketed not to the sports fan but to the sportsman, not to the fan of the baseball club but to the member of the country club.

The format wasn't working. *Sports Illustrated*, having lost $6 million in its first year of publication and $20 million in its first six years, was losing its battle for survival—which brings us to Andre Laguerre, the man most responsible for creating America's most successful sports publication.

The son of a French diplomat, Laguerre was born in London on February 21, 1915. Though he grew up in San Francisco, he was drafted into the French army during World War II and found himself acting as a sentry outside of General Charles de Gaulle's Free French headquarters. Laguerre sent de Gaulle a note suggesting his press relations were lacking and by the end of the war he was his press attaché.

Laguerre was hired by founder and editor-in-chief Henry Lucs, Time Inc. in 1946, as a correspondent in Paris, and by 1948 he was heading the Paris bureau. By 1956, Laguerre was the company's London bureau chief and senior European correspondent. Luce phoned him and asked him to become an assistant managing editor at *Sports Illustrated* under managing editor Sidney James. Four years later, Laguerre replaced James.

Almost immediately, he redesigned much of the magazine—in style, content and philosophy. He instituted the magazine's system of using departmental editors, each overseeing a particular sport, a concept borrowed from *Time*. He also recruited some of the nation's most talented writers, both from outside and from other Time Inc. publications.

It was also Laguerre who conceived the basic structure of the magazine, which remains much the same today. He created a notebook section called "Scorecard" and followed that with a few hard news stories about the week's events, some profiles and previews, and then a lengthy "bonus piece" to close out the magazine. He injected more color into the magazine, both literally and figuratively. Said former *Sports Illustrated* senior writer Robert Boyle, "He used to say he thought a story was great if people would punch each other in a bar over it."

Indeed, Laguerre understood what sells. And so he designated one issue each February the "sunshine" issue, which has become the swimsuit edition, the most popular and publicized annual special issue of any magazine in America. Now a multimedia event, and always a feminist target, it is responsible for a large percentage of *Sports Illustrated*'s annual profit margin.

Under Laguerre, *Sports Illustrated* came to maturity, and, in the process, it benefitted from—and fed—sport's evolution into a national phenomenon. "Sports used to be the province of the local newspaper. And I think *Sports Illustrated* contributed to it becoming a national obsession," said longtime *Sports Illustrated* contributor Jeremiah Tax. "Not because we were good, necessarily, but because we did it."

Several factors contributed to *Sports Illustrated*'s remarkable growth, including the explosion of sports television and the advent of jet air travel, which expanded the magazine's audience. In addition, as ad sales rose, the magazine drifted away from the country-club sensibilities that had been driven by advertising fears. But Laguerre deserves the lion's share of the credit for *Sports Illustrated*'s emergence. *Sports Illustrated* earned a profit for the first time in 1964, and during Laguerre's fourteen years at the helm, the magazine's advertising base grew from $11 million to more than $72 million, its circulation from 900,000 to 2.25 million.

But when Henry Luce died, in 1967, it meant the beginning of the end for Laguerre. His greatest ally had been replaced by less admiring executives. In 1974, he was replaced as managing editor and offered only a research trip to study the feasibility of a European edition of the magazine. It was a rather inglorious end to his reign. One year later, he helped found *Classic—the Magazine About Horses & Sport*, and was its editor and publisher until retiring in December 1978. On January 18, 1979, he died of a heart attack.

Meanwhile, *Sports Illustrated* continued to grow. Under a succession of managing editors, it became the nation's third largest newsmagazine, behind only *Time* and *Newsweek*, and the first national magazine to use full-color photographs throughout. In recent years, *Sports Illustrated* has expanded its reach, publishing special issues for cities boasting championship teams and "classic" issues dedicated to sports history. Its video division is the nation's largest sports video marketer, and the magazine spawned award-winning *Sports Illustrated For Kids* in 1989 and Sports Illustrated Television in 1994.

A magazine about boomerangs and baseball cards has evolved into one of the most pervasive and persuasive voices in American sports, and it essentially began with Andre Laguerre. Wrote MacCambridge, "*Sports Illustrated* is still organized from his blueprint. It is still a product of his vision. And it is still judged today against what he did then."

57

Bill Rasmussen

As the man who founded the ESPN cable network, Bill Rasmussen gave sports junkies and couch potatoes a haven in which to indulge their obsessions. His creation fed the public's growing appetite for sports. It legitimized the all-sports concept as a recipe for success in various markets and mediums, and it turned into a broadcasting giant, powerful enough to transform sports television, creatively and financially. Yet it all began with two words: You're fired.

Rasmussen was born October 15, 1932, in Oak Lawn, Illinois, and attended high school in Chicago. He graduated from DePauw University in Indiana, spent two years in the Air Force, and then started an advertising service business in New Jersey. On his thirtieth birthday, he sold his business and went into radio broadcasting at WTTT in Amherst, Massachusetts. From there, he moved to an ABC affiliate in Springfield, Massachusetts, and then to an NBC station in the same city, where he served as sports director and then evening news anchor. In 1974, when the World Hockey Association's New England Whalers moved to Hartford, Connecticut, Rasmussen began a tenure as the team's communications director.

In Hartford, Rasmussen hit upon the idea of syndicating the Whalers games and University of Connecticut basketball on the state's cable systems. But just after Memorial Day, in 1978, he was suddenly fired. It was the very beginning of the cable revolution, and now Rasmussen not only had the dreams, he had the time to turn them into reality.

Rasmussen and his son, Scott, met with an RCA salesman selling channel space on a communications satellite, and learned that it was no more expensive for him to broadcast nationwide and 24 hours a day than locally and five hours a day. He opted for the 24-hour channel. "Luckily," wrote Jim Shea, in a four-part series on ESPN, published in the *Hartford Courant*, "RCA never does a credit check, never questions how the Rasmussens are going to pay. If they do, the dream dies instantly of acute asset deficiency."

Because the Rasmussens weren't required to put any money down, their biggest worry wasn't about payment, it was about programming. How would they find enough sporting events to fill 24 hours a day, seven days a week? The answer reportedly came one morning in August, while Rasmussen and son were stuck in traffic. As the story goes, they were trying to figure out how to fill the station's air time, when a frustrated Scott Rasmussen snapped, "Play football all day long for all I care."

Eureka! The moment evolved into the realization that college football games could be replayed, that there were literally thousands of collegiate events not broadcast on television, that the format would require a nightly sports show and a nationally known announcer. The creative side of the plan was rolling, but Rasmussen knew he needed financial backing.

When the *Wall Street Journal* ran a front-page story about the impending cable boom, Rasmussen realized he had stumbled upon a technological gold mine just days before the rest of the nation. On Valentine's Day, 1979, the Getty Oil Company offered to finance the network. Soon after, Rasmussen received a commitment from the NCAA to televise a package of games and a $1.4 million advertising deal with Anheuser-Busch. "We all had a sense that it could be pretty big," he recalled. "Would I have guessed that it would be in more than 60 million households? I don't think anybody guessed cable television would be in 60 million households."

Originally called Entertainment Sports Programming Network (E.S.P. Network), it was decided to change the name to ESPN-TV. When a printing error returned a logo reading simply ESPN, it was left at that. No one could have known that ESPN would become, as Shea put it, "as recognizable a monogram as CBS, ABC, perhaps even the U.S.A."

The network was formally launched on September 7, 1979, and announcer Lee Leonard inaugurated the first edition of "SportsCenter" by saying, "If you love sports, if you really love sports, you'll think you've died and gone to sports heaven . . ."

But nobody was quite sure of what to make of the network. *Sports Illustrated* called it "certainly one of the strangest creations in the history of mass communications . . . Nonstop sports around the clock, 24 hours a day, 8,760 hours a year." The first live event to air was the Professional Softball World Series. ESPN was a haphazard collection of full-contact karate, Australian rules football, tractor pulls and other less-than-minor sports. Broadcasting a few hours each weekday and all weekend, the station lost millions of dollars.

"Is ESPN really the network of the future? Can a sports network flourish indefinitely on a full-time menu of offbeat and minor league events?" asked *Sports Illustrated*. "It appears likely that ESPN will remain an upstart unless it can obtain the rights to more major events."

And that it did, along with luring Chet Simmons from NBC Sports as the new president and announcer Jim Simpson, also from NBC, as the early face of ESPN. Soon, the network found a handful of anchors and analysts—Chris Berman, Tom Mees, Bob Ley, Dick Vitale—who would prove to be mainstays in the operation. Magic Johnson and Larry Bird also played a role in ESPN's eventual success. Their 1979 dual in the NCAA Finals had carried college basketball to new heights, but the early rounds of the 1980 NCAA Tournament still had no national TV coverage. So ESPN stepped in with live and tape-delay coverage, which proved to be a boon to both parties involved.

But as ESPN's following grew, a corporate mentality grew with it. Seeing his decision-making role greatly reduced, Rasmussen decided to leave the network late in 1980. He stayed on as a member of the board of directors through 1981, and eventually cashed out for some $25 million.

By 1983, Simmons was gone, replaced by executive vice president Bill Grimes, who made the fateful decision to turn the tables on the cable companies who carry the network. Instead of paying them five cents per subscriber, ESPN asked them to pay for the right. The plan worked, and within a few years the network was making a profit. In 1985, ESPN began broadcasting NHL games. In 1987, NFL Sunday night football began, marking the cable network's arrival as a significant player in sports programming. Two years later, ESPN signed a $400 million deal with Major League Baseball.

Today, ESPN is America's largest cable network, reaching more than 63 million homes, broadcasting more than 4,500 live or original hours of sports programming each year and covering more than sixty-five sports. A big financial loser at the start, ESPN is now worth in excess of $1 billion, and it continues to grow. ESPN Sports Radio was launched in 1992, ESPN2 was unveiled in 1993, and ESPN Enterprises, Inc., has expanded the company's interests into ancillary businesses, such as pay-per-view series and video games.

As the most significant force in modern sports television, ESPN is a player—directly or indirectly—in virtually every decision regarding TV sports packages. The 24-hour all sports notion has been imitated on television and radio in dozens of cities across the country, so much so that words like "saturation" and "overexposure" have crept into sports media analyses.

As for the network's founder, he remains ESPN's biggest fan. "It's probably like raising kids and watching them grow up to be successful lawyers and doctors," said Rasmussen. "I guess, as you're growing up, you always dream about doing something worthwhile that people will remember you for. Well, they won't remember me particularly, but ESPN is certainly going to be around for a while."

58

Ned Irish

Ned Irish was not the most beloved figure in the annals of basketball, but he is certainly one of the most important. Through a little foresight and a lot of business sense, he took a regional game and transformed it into a national phenomenon.

Edward Simmons Irish was born on May 6, 1905, in Lake George, New York, and grew up in Brooklyn. He attended the University of Pennsylvania, where he was a correspondent for newspapers in New York and Philadelphia. Upon graduating, he took a job at the *New York World-Telegram*. An adequate journalist in a town full of brilliant ones, Irish soon found his calling in promotion and in the growing popularity of college basketball.

Until the 1930s, few profits could be found in either college or professional basketball. College games were crowded into campus gyms, and pro contests were relegated to dance halls or armories. Irish believed the game could only grow as large as its surroundings, a realization he supposedly came to while ripping his pants crawling through a window into a packed college gymnasium.

But basketball began its escape from its confined quarters on January 21, 1931, when New York mayor Jimmy Walker's Committee for the Relief of the Unemployed and Needy staged a college basketball tripleheader at Madison Square Garden. The gate receipts from the games were to benefit the city's unemployed, but the event itself would greatly benefit the game. Capacity crowds attended the three games, won by Columbia, Manhattan and St. John's, and two years later, 20,000 spectators took in a seven-game, full-day extravaganza. The events had been promoted by a committee of New York sportswriters, Irish being one of them.

Irish then took the concept further, believing that the arena provided opportunities to attract teams from all over the country for doubleheaders. Irish asked Garden officials to guarantee him six dates during the 1934–1935 season, guaranteeing the arena at least $4,000 per event, which was the cost of renting the arena for one night.

Irish's first doubleheader involved, appropriately, the Fighting Irish, as he figured if the biggest name in college sports couldn't draw at the Garden, nobody could. On December 29, 1934, Notre Dame took on NYU and St. John's faced Westminster of Pennsylvania. As the game approached, Everett Morris of the *New York Herald-Tribune* wrote, "Metropolitan college basketball will step out of its cramped gymnasiums and gloomy armories tonight and into the bright lights and spaciousness of Madison Square Garden for the first of a series of six doubleheaders arranged in the hope of proving this winter that the sport deserves and will thrive in a major league setting."

More than 16,000 fans filled the Garden that night, providing a gate of approximately $20,000, and the remaining doubleheaders were equally successful. Irish quit his newspaper job and became basketball director at the Garden. Over the next decade-and-a-half, top college teams from all over the country trekked to the arena, drawing as many as half a million fans in one basketball season. Throughout it all, Irish was the man with the power.

"Any athletically ambitious college—which is to say, most major colleges in the U.S.—that wanted the attention of a Garden showing had to play for Irish on Irish's terms and on the date he assigned," wrote Roger Kahn in *Sports Illustrated*. "Irish was Congress, court and executive of big-time basketball."

Two-game slates soon became successful attractions in other cities, including Chicago, Philadelphia, Boston and Buffalo, but Irish didn't stop at doubleheaders. In 1938, he and the Metropolitan Basketball Writers Association of New York organized the first national postseason tournament, to be played at Madison Square Garden. The inaugural National Invitation Tournament in 1938 featured six teams from all over the country—NYU, Colorado, Long Island University, Temple, Bradley and Oklahoma A&M. Temple took the title, and the NIT was a resounding success.

As Bill Gutman explains in *The Pictorial History of College Basketball*, it was the first time that "north could meet south and east could meet west on neutral courts, and basketball fans could not only follow their favorite teams, but could also compare the styles of basketball played nationwide and the great players who were now coming out of every section of the country."

Irish's doubleheaders and postseason playoffs, like the Cincinnati Red Stockings baseball tour of 1869 and Red Grange's football tours of 1925 and 1926, gave basketball a national audience. In fact, the NIT worked so well that the NCAA took it upon itself to plan its own tournament, which, of course, has become college basketball's showcase event.

As for Irish's doubleheader parade, it came to an abrupt halt with college basketball's point-fixing scandals of 1951, which involved many New York players and teams that had played at the Garden. New York District Attorney Frank Hogan's formal report on the scandal declared, "Underlying the scandal was the blatant commercialism which had permeated college basketball. What once had been a minor sport had been hippodromed into a big business."

It was both a testament to and indictment of Irish, who refused to accept responsibility, and whose reaction was, as Kahn put it, "alternately naive and hysterical." But soon, only sparse crowds were watching local college teams in the Garden. By then, however, Irish had turned much of his attention to the professional game.

On June 6, 1946, the second anniversary of D-Day, a group of large arena owners, led by Walter Brown of the Boston Garden and Al Sutphin of the Cleveland Arena, gathered together to form the Basketball Association of America. The league, at its inception, consisted of a group of men with successful arenas and ties to hockey teams. Irish, by then vice-president of the Garden. He became president of the New York Knicks.

In 1949, the BAA merged with the older National Basketball League to form the NBA. Irish remained one of the league's most powerful figures until, with his retirement in 1974, he became the last of the original club owners to leave the scene. It was Irish who led the battle to move NBA franchises into major cities, which took the league from its roots in Rock Island and Davenport to places like Los Angeles and Washington. And it was Irish who pressured the league into allowing him to sign the league's first black player, Nat "Sweetwater" Clifton, away from the Harlem Globetrotters in 1950.

Irish was elected to the Basketball Hall of Fame in 1964 for his role in turning college basketball, and then the pro game, into a nationwide spectacle. Though he was by no means fully responsible for the concept of college basketball in the Garden, the NIT or the BAA, he was, to a great extent, the power and the prophet who made it all work. He died on January 21, 1982, having made few friends but countless new basketball fans along the way.

59

Hank Luisetti

Of the five charter members of the San Francisco Bay Area Sports Hall of Fame, four of them—Ernie Nevers, Joe DiMaggio, Willie Mays and Bill Russell—are immediately recognized as sporting giants. Memories of the fifth inductee have faded over the years, yet he was essentially a combination of the other four. He drew popularity to his game as Nevers did for football, displayed the deceptive effortlessness of DiMaggio, possessed the all-around skills of Mays, and transformed basketball in much the manner Russell did.

Born June 16, 1916, in San Francisco, this person wore painful leg braces to correct his bowed legs. He wasn't as tall as most of the other kids he met on the basketball court; he never played in a postseason tournament or in a pro game. Yet Angelo "Hank" Luisetti single-handedly changed basketball—literally.

Until Luisetti arrived, basketball featured two basic shots—the driving layup and the two-handed set shot. The set shot had the effect of slowing the game down, both physically and aesthetically. But in Luisetti's case, necessity (the need to loft the ball over his taller playmates) led to invention (using one hand to loft the ball and the other to guide it). "When I shot with two hands, I couldn't score as well," said Luisetti. "So I just went to the one hand."

By the time Luisetti began his playing career at Stanford University, experience and a growth spurt had added accuracy and height (nearly 6-foot-3) to complement the strength of the shot. But while innovation stems from necessity, it impacts through publicity, and that meant a trip to New York City. On December 30, 1936, Stanford travelled to Madison Square Garden for a confrontation against Long Island University and its 43-game winning streak.

More than 17,000 spectators watched Luisetti lead Stanford to a 45-31 victory, scoring 15 points, an impressive amount in those days. But it was the quality of Luisetti's shots that stunned the crowd, not the quantity. It was his style that captivated. Luisetti walked off the floor to a standing ovation, and the end of LIU's streak had marked the beginning of a new era.

The New York Times's account of the event stated, "The Coast sensation surpassed everything that had been said about him . . . It seemed Luisetti could do nothing wrong. Some of his shots would have been deemed foolhardy if attempted by any other player, but with Luisetti doing the heaving, these were accepted by the crowd as a matter of course."

Luisetti brought more to the game than simply the notion of a novel shooting technique: He brought a fluidity to the competition, turning a sport of stops and starts into a frenetic, kinetic experience. And he did it on college basketball's biggest stage.

"It was a pivotal game in the sport's history, introducing the nation to modern basketball," Ron Fimrite wrote in *Sports Illustrated*. "What astonished Garden fans was not so much that Luisetti shot, rebounded, dribbled, passed and played defense better than any on the court, but that he performed almost all of these things in unorthodox ways. He dribbled and passed behind his back, and he appeared to shoot without glancing at the basket."

As Robert W. Peterson points out in *Cages to Jump Shots*, his study of basketball's early years, Luisetti's performance "did not immediately set kids in school gyms, playgrounds and barnyards to shooting one-handers." Basketball had yet to merge with television to provide an arena for instant cultural impact. "But," Peterson adds, "his example opened up new possibilities for coaches and players whose mind-set had long been conditioned by the received wisdom about shooting methods."

One year after Luisetti's first Garden performance, college basketball struck down a rule calling for a center jump after each basket. The two alterations in style (a more fluid game and a more fluid shot) complemented each other and greatly enhanced the game's offensive potential, not to mention its entertainment value.

Luisetti's was not a jump shot, as he would generally rise only a few inches above the floor, but it was its precursor. He opened a door that collegians like Kenny Sailors and pros like Joe Fulks and Paul Arizin jumped through. His style also allowed the opportunity for creativity, in all its wondrous forms, by Bob Cousy, Elgin Baylor, Julius Erving, Michael Jordan and the rest of the game's figures who turned instinct into an art form. Even more than forty years before Magic Johnson put on a one-man show in the 1980 NBA Finals, Luisetti was switching positions according to changing game situations. Against LIU, he played guard, forward and center.

But Luisetti's success couldn't be ignored. Stanford went 68-12 over Luisetti's three varsity seasons, including three Pacific Coast championships and the 1937 national title. Luisetti was a three-time All-American and two-time College Player of the Year. When he graduated in 1938, he held college basketball records for career points (1,596) and points in a game (50).

Through his scoring and playmaking, Luisetti became somewhat of a phe-nomenon, the subject of feature articles in *Life* and *Time* and even the star of a 1938 basketball movie called *Campus Confessions*, in which he performed the behind-the-back dribble shown in slow motion. Luisetti received $10,000 for the part, but he also received a one-year suspension from the Amateur Athletic Union for playing for profit.

After he was reinstated, he competed for some AAU teams and then for a service team during World War II. But he contracted spinal meningitis in 1944, and at the age of twenty-eight he was told his basketball career was over. Luisetti turned to a career in the travel-promotions business, retiring in the early 1980s. It was an ironically appropriate career choice for a man best remembered for travelling to Madison Square Garden and promoting a revolutionary form of basketball.

THE JUMP SHOT

Nowhere is basketball's transformation from a grounded game to a battle for air supremacy more evident than in the evolution of the shot. Hank Luisetti's one-handed method was merely one in a series of alterations to the concept of tossing a ball toward a basket, albeit the most important.

Luisetti's arrival didn't immediately mean the extinction of the two-handed set shot, but it did provide the impetus for creativity, and Kenny Sailors took up the gauntlet. As a means of lofting his shots over his taller brother as a youngster, Sailors had learned to jump before shooting. Luisetti had risen a few inches off the ground, but Sailors is credited with using college basketball's first jump shot. In 1943, he led the University of Wyoming to the NCAA title.

Luisetti's shots had taken him slightly up and forward; Sailors went straight up. But it was Hall of Famer "Jumpin'" Joe Fulks who pioneered the notion of hang time, out-hanging defenders to the tune of 26 points per game in his best season, with the Philadelphia Warriors in 1948–1949. Fulks's younger teammate, Paul Arizin, then combined the innovations of all three—Luisetti's one-handed style, Sailors's leaping and Fulks's hang time—for 22.8 points per game in a 10-year NBA career.

60

Howie Morenz

In 1923, when Babe Ruth batted .393 and Bobby Jones won his first major golf championship, when Jack Dempsey defended his heavyweight boxing title and Bill Tilden won his fourth straight U.S. Open and Red Grange began his football career at the University of Illinois, professional hockey found its own hero for sport's Golden Age.

Howie Morenz went by many names. The press liked to call him "The Stratford Streak," in reference to the town in Ontario he had last called home before settling in as the star of the Forum, home of the Montreal Canadiens. When it was discovered that Morenz actually moved to Stratford when he was fourteen, having been born in a nearby town called Mitchell (on September 21, 1902), the press, never at a loss for colorful monikers, simply dubbed him "The Mitchell Meteor."

Had his mother had her way, Morenz would have become perhaps the antithesis of a professional hockey player: a concert pianist. But he had to cross the frozen Thames River and its frequent hockey games on each trip to his piano lessons, and he could never quite get himself to finish the journey. Morenz grew up using old magazines tucked into his stockings as pads, using a lump of coal as a puck and controlling it with a sawed-off broomstick. But by 1922, he was good enough to score nine goals against an amateur team from Montreal, and by 1923 he was wearing #7 for the Montreal Canadiens.

The would-be concert pianist was left to play his ukelele on train rides between games, but he was a maestro on the ice. "It is possible that he was the greatest goal-scorer major league hockey has known. Or, the most exciting skater in NHL history. Or, the fastest man to lace on a pair of skates," writes Stan Fischler in *Those Were the Days*. "Perhaps he was all of these things, but we'll never know for sure." One reason we'll never know is because his career—indeed, his life—was tragically cut short in 1937. But from 1923–1937, during the infancy of the NHL, he was hockey's greatest and most marketable star.

Of his dazzling quickness, Ott Heller of the New York Rangers remarked, "When Howie skates full speed, everyone else on the ice seems to be skating backward." Added Roy Worters of the New York Americans, "Morenz is not number seven to me. He's number 77777—just a blur."

Though he never weighed more than 165 pounds, Morenz was also known for his fierce bodychecking and his willingness to substitute guts for guile, skating at opponents—and then over them. Eddie Shore, the Bobby Orr of the era, called him "the hardest player in the league to stop." Roger Kahn, writing in *Esquire*, stated simply, "Other hockey players score goals and slam through defensemen, but the furious charge down center ice belonged to Morenz alone. Like a Babe Ruth home run or a Roger Bannister mile, a Morenz charge was, in a sense, the original."

Morenz finished second in the league in scoring in his second season, leading the Canadiens to a championship. He won the NHL scoring title and the Hart Trophy as the league's most valuable player in 1928, scored 40 goals in just 44 games during the 1929–1930 season, grabbed another scoring title and Hart Trophy in 1931, and repeated as league MVP in 1932. An original inductee into the Hockey Hall of Fame and the Associated Press Player of the Half-Century, Morenz recorded 270 goals and 197 assists in his career.

Morenz was considered the "Babe Ruth of hockey," but he was Ruthian in more than just his skills; he was hockey's ambassador in spirit, as well. He was colorful, glamorous, well-liked. He was the face of pro hockey, and it was an appealing countenance. Said Fischler, "When American investors looked at hockey and saw him, they said this game can sell here."

In Morenz's first season, the NHL consisted only of the Canadiens, Toronto St. Pats, Quebec Bulldogs and Ottawa Senators. By Morenz's third season, the league included the Boston Bruins, New York Americans (now defunct), Pittsburgh Pirates (also defunct), Chicago Black Hawks (now Blackhawks), Detroit Cougars (now Red Wings) and New York Rangers. Morenz played no small role in the game's southern shift. In fact, it is believed that famed boxing promoter Tex Rickard only agreed to place an ice rink in Madison Square Garden after watching Morenz play and being assured that the Canadiens' center would appear in the opening game.

Montreal, however, remained the backbone of the league, and Howie Morenz was Montreal hockey. As Ruth did with the Yankees, Morenz was largely responsible for setting the foundation for his league's winningest franchise. The Yankees won four World Series titles with Ruth and have won 18 more after him. The Canadiens won three Stanley Cup championships during Morenz's career (1924, 1930, 1931) and 22 since.

Also like Ruth, Morenz began his career in one city but was dramatically traded to another, before closing out his career where he was originally worshipped.

But the circumstances were a bit different from Ruth's move from the Boston Red Sox to the Yankees, and back to the Boston Braves. By Morenz's tenth season, he had slowed considerably. He scored 14 goals in 1932–1933, just eight in 1933–1934, and was even beginning to hear boos from the Forum faithful. Following the season, he was traded to Chicago, part of a six-player deal.

He was a shadow of his former self with Chicago, and much the same with the New York Rangers, one year later. He appeared to be at the end of the road. But in 1936, his old coach at Montreal, Cecil Hart, was rehired and immediately found a way to get his old star back in a Canadiens uniform. Morenz was rejuvenated, and by late January of 1937, he had helped lead Montreal back into its traditional position—first place.

But on January 28, tragedy stuck. When a Chicago defender checked him into the boards, Morenz's skate became imbedded in the wood. When another Chicago defender came hurtling at him at full speed, Morenz's left leg was broken in four places.

Always known to brood after a loss, Morenz grew despondent, suffering a nervous breakdown in February. By March, however, he seemed to be on his way to recovery, and on March 8, his doctors announced that he was in good condition. A few hours later, Morenz was dead. At the age of thirty-four, his heart had stopped.

Three days later, his coffin was placed at center ice in the Forum. An estimated 10,000 in attendance stood silent, their heads bowed. Approximately 15,000 more braved the cold outside. The shock felt in Canada over Morenz's death was akin, perhaps, to that felt in America at Knute Rockne's untimely demise six years earlier. It was an ironic removal of a symbol of athletic durability much like the demise of Lou Gehrig four years later.

But Andy O'Brien, editor of *Weekend Magazine*, took the analogy even further. "The impact on the Canadian metropolis was matched in my experience only with the flash about President John Kennedy's assassination," he wrote. "Both Morenz and Kennedy had carried such a popular image of vigor and vibrant life that death seemed just too shockingly unthinkable."

But while Kennedy's death changed the course of history, Morenz had already altered the future of professional hockey.

61

Grantland Rice

When Henry Grantland Rice was born in Murfreesboro, Tennessee, on November 1, 1880, American sport was in its infancy. Baseball was only beginning to feel its way toward maturity, football was still metamorphosing from its origins in soccer and rugby, boxing was still limited to backrooms and barges, and basketball and golf had yet to be introduced. But by the time "Granny" Rice died some seventy-three years later, sport had become an inescapable component of American culture. This was not completely a coincidence of timing.

It can be argued that the 1920s and 1930s were the most significant era in the history of American sports. The 1870s and 1880s saw sport's arrival—through newspaper coverage and the contributions of men like Al Spalding, Walter Camp and John L. Sullivan. The 1960s and 1970s brought sport's transcendence—through the power of television and the personalities of the likes of Arnold Palmer, Muhammad Ali and Billie Jean King. But the Golden Age of Sports, the years dominated by Red Grange, Knute Rockne, Babe Ruth, Bobby Jones, Bill Tilden, Jack Dempsey and Howie Morenz, was the vital time of sport's emergence.

It is no accident that several athletes listed among *The Sports 100* peaked in the years between the World Wars. It is also no accident that the Golden Age also saw the maturation of newspaper sports coverage and the emergence of writers who called on all their hyperbolic talents to immortalize the heroes of the day and bestow upon them mythic names like Sultan of Swat and Manassa Mauler.

And the most well-known practioner of it, the most influential voice in the days when sportswriters were the most influential of voices, was Grantland Rice. As Charles Fountain explains in his biography of Rice, *Sportswriter*, "The twenties are the 'Golden Age' of sport because Rice saw them as golden."

Rice's writing career actually stretched from the days before Ty Cobb to Willie Mays's prime, and throughout nearly all of it, Rice was the nation's most important, most acclaimed and most prolific chronicler of the games. During his 53-year career he published more than 67 million words, his columns appearing six days a week in more than 100 newspapers. He was, according to Fountain, "a man who influenced mightily the ebb and flow of sportswriting, and colored and shaped our perceptions of an entire era of American history as well."

Rice first gained notoriety as an athlete at Vanderbilt University. Upon graduating, he obtained a job at the *Nashville News*, where he covered everything from Southern League baseball to the state capitol. Over the next decade, Rice's reputation grew as he climbed his way up the journalistic ladder and plied his trade at the *Atlanta Journal*, the *Cleveland News*, the *Nashville Tennessean,* and then the *New York Evening Mail*, where his column and his contributions to national publications like *Collier's*, *Sporting Life* and *American Magazine* made his the country's most recognized sports byline.

In 1915, Rice switched to the *New York Tribune*, where his column, "Sportlight," was syndicated around the country to more than 10 million readers, bringing him the kind of celebrity not seen again in sports journalism until Howard Cosell, a man opposite Rice in every way, emerged in the 1970s.

"For Americans of his generation he *was* the game—his story became the event, much like the telecast has so often become the event in the eighties and nineties," Fountain explains. "At some point during the twenties . . . [Rice] passed from being merely a sportswriter to a combination media conglomerate and public figure the equal of Dempsey or Ruth or Grange or any of the men he covered."

His influence extended beyond just the realm of print journalism. In 1922, Rice was the play-by-play announcer for the first World Series game ever broadcast live, and, over the next thirty years, his radio voice would become nearly as well-known as his printed word. Rice also began to produce a monthly "Sportlight" newsreel for Paramount Pictures, eventually earning two Academy Awards for best short subject. In fact, by the time the Depression arrived, Rice's various ventures were netting him close to $100,000 a year.

From the beginning, Rice had separated himself from the rest of the sportswriting fraternity—a pantheon of journalistic giants that included Ring Lardner, Damon Runyan, Paul Gallico, Heywood Broun, Fred Lieb and Westbrook Pegler—with a style consisting of verse, flowery prose and, often, unabashed adulation.

Rice's writing style and perspective came to be known as the "Gee Whiz!" school of sportswriting, while Rice's good friend Lardner and others were practioners of "Aw Nuts!" journalism. For the most part, "Gee Whiz!" died when Rice died, while the cynical, irreverent "Aw Nuts!" attitude is now sportswriting's dominant style. But it was Rice's assessment of the events that became the public's perception of its heroes and happenings during the bulk of his career, thereby coloring the age golden.

To be sure, much of Rice's work now appears over-written and overwrought, and the consensus seems to rank Pulitzer prize–winner Red Smith as history's greatest sportswriter. But even Smith himself called Rice "the greatest man I have known, the greatest talent, the greatest gentleman" and said of him, "Wherever Grantland Rice sits, that's the head of the table."

When Rice chose to, he would remove his rose-colored glasses, such as when he criticized Jack Dempsey for avoiding combat during World War I or when he called members of the 1919 Black Sox "the ultimate scum of the universe." He could also be eerily prescient, like the time he wrote that if baseball's reserve clause was abolished "there would simply be a private agreement among club owners not to raise the ante. The smaller towns must be protected, the average ball player must be protected, for the general good of the game." Thus, in two lines, Rice had predicted free agency in the 1970s, collusion in the 1980s, and the fears leading up to the baseball strike of the 1990s. And he wrote it in 1911.

Rice brought imagination, as well as dignity, to a craft that sorely needed it. He combined a classical education with a pure love of sport to create pages full of infectious enthusiasm and vivid drama. At a time when few American sports fans actually had the opportunity to watch their beloved athletes perform, they relied almost entirely on newspaper accounts, and they relied on Rice most of all. And so Rice gave them their heroes.

Like Ty Cobb. When Rice was first starting out in Nashville in 1904, he received an unsigned telegram before spring training telling him to keep an eye on a young talent named Cobb. When Rice continued to receive such letters all through the summer, he began to tell his readers to keep an eye on him, too. Cobb made it to the big leagues the following year, and only after World War II did he admit to Rice that it was he who had sent the cards.

Or Babe Ruth, who eventually became Rice's frequent golf companion. Rice was wary of Ruth's talents at first, contending it was too early to call him the greatest lefthanded pitcher the game had seen. But when Ruth started to hit, Rice left all caution behind, writing in verse: "I've seen a few I thought could hit, / Who fed the crowd on four-base rations / But you, Babe, are the Only It / The rest are merely imitations."

Or Red Grange, who may have been immortalized the minute Rice christened him the "Galloping Ghost." Grange was an All-American by any account, but he also earned that distinction because Rice said he should. In 1925, Grange's senior season, Rice took over Walter Camp's role selecting the All-America team for *Collier's*. Twenty-two years later, he was persuaded to move the team to *Look* magazine, where the Grantland Rice All-America team was selected by the Football Writers Association. Today, Rice's gray fedora and typewriter are displayed at the College Football Hall of Fame.

Rice had perhaps his greatest influence, however, on golf. He himself had become a scratch golfer and could be found on the links with everyone from Ruth to President Warren G. Harding. It was still a largely unknown sport, one in dire need of publicity, and Rice became the ultimate publicist. To some extent, he did for golf awareness what Henry Chadwick had done for baseball fifty years earlier. He had his own Sunday golf column, "Tales of a Wayside Tee," published two books on the game, and edited *The American Golfer* for ten years. During the 1920s, Rice wrote about golf nearly as much as he wrote about baseball, college football and boxing.

In fact, he greatly influenced the career's of two of golf's most important figures. In 1916, 14-year-old Bobby Jones, whom Rice had known since he was three, advanced to the quarterfinals of the U.S. Amateur championship. Rice began fashioning the legend of the man who would become his lifelong friend, calling him "the most remarkable kid prodigy we have ever seen—and here and there in sport we have looked upon one or two." It took about seven years, but Jones eventually matched his hype.

Sixteen years later, Rice did much the same for Babe Didrikson. It was Rice who first convinced Didrikson, then a track and field phenomenon, to take up golf at the 1932 Olympics in Los Angeles, playing a round with the two-time gold medal winner and comparing her favorably with the two top female golfers of the day. Eventually, Didrikson became the most important figure in women's golf.

As much influence and insight as Rice had, however, he was far from perfect. While his coverage of women athletes was generally free from stereotype, his writings on black athletes were not. The great-grandson of a slave-owner and grandson of a Confederate soldier, Rice would call Jack Johnson "The Chocolate Champ," say Joe Louis had "the speed of the jungle," and comment that Jesse Owens ran "like a wild Zulu." Among his twenty-eight All-America football teams, there were only five black players.

By the time Louis and Owens had arrived, Rice was no longer writing for the Tribune Syndicate. In 1930, he had switched to the North American Newspaper Alliance, meaning he would now be writing for the *New York Sun*. His influence diminished somewhat, but the rest of the country still got their Rice fix every day—indeed, for the next twenty-four years, until he died of a stroke on July 13, 1954.

His obituary was front-page news in New York, and he was even eulogized on the floor of the House of Representatives. Among the mourners at his funeral were Jack Dempsey, Gene Tunney, Bobby Jones, Carl Hubbell and Bill Dickey. Less than three months later, some 250 people—ranging from Eddie Arcaro and Johnny Weissmuller to Ed Sullivan and Jackie Gleason—gathered to honor Rice on what would have been his seventy-fourth birthday and to celebrate the impending release of his autobiography.

Rice's words would live on, as would his influence. Even Jimmy Cannon, who represented the new wave of sports journalism that had largely supplanted Rice, wrote, "All of us in this generation of sports writers are improved because we borrowed some of his techniques. Few handle the language with as much grace. Many of us croak because we can't sing."

GOLDEN WORDS

Perhaps the best example of Grantland Rice's lasting impact is a simple bit of verse he wrote in the spring of 1908 that has evolved into perhaps the most repeated and revered definition of competitive spirit in America. Wrote Rice, "When the One Great Scorer comes to write against your name . . . he marks—not that you won or lost—but how you played the game."

Along with creating perhaps sport's most famous saying, however, Rice is also responsible for sportswriting's most famous lead paragraph, compiled after Knute Rockne's Notre Dame backfield led the Irish to a 13-7 victory over Army on October 18, 1924. He wrote, "Outlined against a blue-grey October sky, the Four Horsemen rode again. In dramatic lore they are known as Famine, Pestilence, Destruction and Death. These are only aliases. Their real names are Stuhdreher, Miller, Crowley and Layden."

The paragraph—followed by a publicity photograph taken the following day of the backfield on horseback—was so powerful that, instead of certain anonymity, Stuhdreher, Miller, Crowley and Layden became forever known as the Four Horsemen and were even inducted into the College Football Hall of Fame as a unit.

62

Phil Knight

With one large "swoosh," Phil Knight, the founder and chairman of Nike, Inc., has transformed the games. Through product innovation, he helped change the way athletes perform and helped spur a nationwide jogging and fitness boom. More importantly, Knight and Nike have not only led the way in marketing athletes over the past decade but in making them as well.

Much like Grantland Rice was a star-maker in the 1920s, Knight has been at the forefront of a transformation in sports marketing. The relationship between athletes and endorsements used to be a one-way street when it came to creating an image, but now the businesses define the athletes as much as the athletes promote the businesses. Whether the athlete is Michael Jordan or Charles Barkley or Andre Agassi, their performance largely tells the public what they can do, but Nike tells the public who they are.

Knight himself is equal parts sports fan, businessman and philosopher—and his company is a product of all three. He was born in Portland, Oregon, on February 24, 1938, and he was talented enough as a middle-distance runner in high school to be recruited by legendary track coach Bill Bowerman at the University of Oregon, where he became the coach's guinea pig, often testing out his new homemade track shoes.

That experience turned Knight on to footwear innovation, but the topic of a 1962 term paper, written while studying for his MBA at Stanford Business School, spawned Knight's interest in the business side of sneakers. The assignment: a paper on the subject of starting up a new small business; the mission, according to his professor, "Write about something you know. And something you like." Knight knew running shoes.

In the term paper, which writer Frank Deford has described as a "$3.7 billion blueprint," Knight contended that if high-quality shoes were manufactured in Asia, where labor was inexpensive, then they could be sold in the Unites States for lower prices. He then turned the concept into reality, starting Blue Ribbon Sports, a firm distributing shoes for a Japanese company.

Knight and Bowerman each invested $500 in the company, which sold about $20,000 in shoes in 1964, and netted just over $3,000. Knight worked as an accountant, and then as an assistant professor at Portland State University, selling shoes on the side out of the trunk of his car. Knight's father had told him, "You can't make money selling track shoes," but by 1971, BRS sales had topped $1 million and Knight was devoting himself full-time to his company. Bowerman relinquished his half-partnership in the company soon after, though he remained a consultant to Knight, and his creation of a waffle-soled shoe was vital to the company's success.

The 1970s also brought a new name and a logo to Knight's company, both being virtual afterthoughts. The "swoosh" was designed by Carolyn Davidson, a graphics student at Portland State. For $35, she presented Knight with a dozen proposals, and Knight and his friends picked the one they disliked the least. It was described as "a fat check mark." The Nike name arrived soon after, when Jeff Johnson, Knight's first full-time employee, suggested—to muted approval—naming the company after the Greek goddess of victory.

Within a decade, Knight's company would be the number-one sneaker company in the U.S. Within two decades, the *Harvard Business Review* would comment that the Nike brand name was "as well-known around the world as IBM and Coke."

In between, however, Nike reached a low point in the mid-1980s, when it lost the top spot to Reebok, which had come to dominate the aerobic shoe market. After more than a decade during which profits seemed to double every year, Nike found itself in the red. It was then that Knight made a decision that would turn his company's fortunes around.

Nike's strategy had been to offer endorsement contracts to athletes who represented the sort of anti-Establishment posture Knight and Co. had cultivated, anti-heroes like John McEnroe. "The trick," Knight explained, "is to get athletes who not only can win but can stir up emotion. We want someone the public is going to love or hate, not just the leading scorer."

But after the Reebok scare of the mid-1980s, Knight understood that it would take more than just signing prominent athletes to move to the next level. Knight's first remark to his new ad agency had been, "Hi, I'm Phil Knight, and I don't believe in advertising." But it would be advertising that would turn Nike into more than just a sneaker company, and it would be a leading scorer who would pave the way.

According to Donald Katz, author of *Just Do It*, the Nike story, Knight came to believe that "if the general public could be helped to imagine the great athletes as he imagined them—as having implications of the very best that the human spirit had to offer—then those athletes would become heroes like the heroes of old . . . like heroes in books. And the people would come to these heroes and listen to what they had to say . . ."

The first such hero was Michael Jordan, whom Knight had signed in 1984. The merger's first offspring was the Air Jordan, a revolutionary air-cushioned basketball shoe so colorful that the NBA banned it—which was just the kind of publicity Nike welcomed. Television became Nike's most visible marketing tool, beginning with a 1985 commercial called "Jordan Flight" which began Jordan's rise toward his status as an American icon.

It was a defining moment for Nike and for Jordan, two giants whose fortunes became remarkably intertwined. The company was back atop the sneaker world by 1989, and Nike's advertising budget rose from under $20 million to over $150 million. During the six years before Jordan's short-lived retirement, Nike's annual sales rose from $1 billion to almost $4 billion, and profits rose by more than 900 percent. Knight's company is now responsible for close to one in three pairs of athletic shoes sold in the U.S.; it peddles its products in at least 100 countries, sells about 100 million pairs of shoes each year, and employs more than 6,500 people. One competitor in the market even revealed that his company was able to make $300 to $400 million in sales "from the crumbs that fall off Nike's plate."

Deford has compared Knight's impact as a sports manufacturer to that of Albert G. Spalding nearly a century earlier, saying Knight "has made the greatest fortune ever from athletics." But Knight holds a place among *The Sports 100* not necessarily for making Nike the king of athletic shoes, a rather tenuous hold if history is any indication, but for making Nike, as *Sports Illustrated* put it, "clearly the most efficient and powerful organization in sports."

How powerful and pervasive is Nike? More than 80 percent of NBA players wear Nikes, about one-fourth of them by contract, as do some sixty big-time college basketball programs and nearly 600 NFL and major league baseball players. The company that once turned down a contract with a young Jimmy Connors because his $1,500 asking price was too hefty pays Jordan upwards of $20 million each year.

Nike even created its own "marketing only" sports management program, with clients like Bo Jackson, Jerry Rice and Scottie Pippen. There is also a career management program that includes the NBA's Alonzo Mourning and NFL quarterback Rick Mirer. Several universities, including Miami, Michigan and USC, have signed multi-million dollar "total university relationship" contracts with the company.

"Knight is clearly in a position," wrote Deford in a *Vanity Fair* profile, "to derive more power from a product than any man ever in sport." He has overseen a metamorphosis in the relationship between business and sports, an evolution so profound that many have questioned whether the very fabric of the games has been threatened. Indeed, to many detractors Knight has become, according to Katz, "a dark plunderer who . . . invaded and sullied sport in the name of profit."

At the 1992 Summer Olympics in Barcelona, Jordan and other members of basketball's Dream Team refused to show the official Olympic sponsor's Reebok logo on their warmups, essentially pitting Nike against the U.S. Olympic Committee. Nike won, leading Deford to claim, "At the Olympics, there used to be three institutions that, in addition to the I.O.C., fought for power: the U.S. Olympic Committee, the world media, and the Communist Consortium. In 1992 at Barcelona, there were still three: the U.S. Olympic Committee, the world media and Nike." Not long after the Games, after holding out for his first contract with the Charlotte Hornets, Alonzo Mourning announced, "I work for Nike."

Nike's marketing strategy has been so successful that it has penetrated beyond sneaker sales, beyond even the perception of sports, transforming colorful sneakers—and all the psycho-social baggage that advertising has attached to them—into a sort of status symbol of the 1990s. In fact, Nike has come under further criticism since it became clear that inner-city youths were willing to commit violence in order to obtain the kind of status the sneakers brought—status that used to manifest itself in jewelry or cars.

The American public also craves its sneakers because it craves heroes, and Nike has responded by creating a link between the two. Indeed, the company has become so powerful that the Nike image has come to define the athlete at least as much as his or her actual athleticism or personality. Jordan admitted, "Nike has done such a good job of promoting me that I've turned into a dream. In some ways, it's taken me away from the game and turned me into an entertainer. To a lot of people, I'm just a person who stars in commercials."

Did Jordan make Nike, or did Nike make Jordan? The answer is not necessarily as important as the realization that it is not such a ridiculous question. Phil Knight created a force so powerful that it is able to place the cart before the horse, and the sporting public might not know the difference.

63

Althea Gibson

"Shaking hands with the Queen of England," Althea Gibson once explained, "was a long way from being forced to sit in the colored section of the bus going into downtown Wilmington, North Carolina." But it was during that long trip—from the segregated South and the streets of Harlem to Center Court at Wimbledon—that Gibson left her indelible imprint on American sport, raising consciousness as much as she raised eyebrows.

Hers was a path somewhat similar to that taken by Joe Louis and Jesse Owens in that her father was a sharecropper, her family migrated north when she was a child, and her athletic career consisted of a tireless battle against institutionalized racism. Gibson had the triple athletic and societal challenge of being black, female and a participant in what had always been primarily an upperclass, country-club sport.

That she succeeded at all was a remarkable accomplishment, but Gibson left no doubt about the magnitude of her legacy by reaching the pinnacle of athletic achievement. Her success as a tennis champion, and later as a golf pioneer, combined with the gold medals and grace of Wilma Rudolph, served as a symbol of social mobility to African-American sportswomen.

Gibson was born on August 25, 1927, in a small cabin on a cotton farm in Silver, South Carolina. In 1930, her family moved to Harlem, where Gibson became known as much for delving into mischief as for sports such as stickball, basketball and boxing. But it was in the summer of 1941 that a man named Buddy Walker started her on the road to immortality by teaching her to hit tennis balls against a handball wall.

Immediately successful, Gibson was soon invited to join New York's interracial Cosmopolitan Club, thanks to financial aid from some of its members, and she competed in tournaments sponsored by the all-black American Tennis Association (ATA), an organization spawned by the segregationist policies of the United States Lawn Tennis Association (USLTA). Gibson won two national ATA girls' titles before moving up to the women's division.

Two ATA officials in particular, Dr. Hubert Eaton and Dr. Robert W. Johnson, were instrumental in her rise to prominence. Gibson had dropped out of high school, but she returned to school when she returned to the South. She moved in with the Eaton family in Wilmington, North Carolina, while attending school and practicing on Dr. Eaton's private court. During the summer, she traveled to Lynchburg, Virginia, where she came under the tutelage of Johnson, who would also serve as Arthur Ashe's mentor only a few years later. Johnson accompanied her on the ATA tour in 1947, where she won every tournament she entered, including the first of ten ATA women's titles.

Gibson had never considered herself a crusader, saying, "I don't consciously beat the drums for any cause, even the cause of the Negro in the United States." But, as with Satchel Paige's earlier domination of baseball's Negro Leagues, she was so good the USLTA was soon unable to ignore her.

In 1949, three years after Jackie Robinson had first entered organized baseball, Gibson competed in her first USLTA-sponsored event, the Eastern Indoor Championships, and reached the quarterfinals. The following year, she won the event, but although she was now playing on the Florida A&M University team, she was still limited to only a handful of USLTA opportunities. It took an unlikely proponent of her cause, four-time U.S. champion Alice Marble, to pressure the game's governing body into further action.

"If tennis is a game for ladies and gentlemen, it's also time we acted a little more like gentlepeople and less like sanctimonious hypocrites," Marble wrote in the July 1950 issue of *American Lawn Tennis*. "If Althea Gibson represents a challenge to the present crop of women players, it's only fair that they should meet that challenge on the courts, where tennis is played."

Doors suddenly opened for Althea Gibson. In August, she was invited to play in the national championships at Forest Hills. The following year, she became the first black player to compete at Wimbledon, losing in the quarterfinals. By 1952, she was the ninth-ranked player in the USLTA standings, but when she was still playing at the same level three years later, she considered quitting the game.

Two events in 1955 turned Gibson's career around. First, she met a Harlem taxi driver and part-time tennis pro named Sydney Llewellyn, who improved her game and her mindset. Then she was chosen as one of four U.S. tennis players to embark on a State Department exhibition tour of Asia. Only a half-dozen years earlier, Gibson's skills had made her an unwanted intruder into the the stuffy, segregated world of American tennis; now she was being paraded as a representative of her country and her game.

Gibson's accomplishments over the next three years would catapult her even more profoundly onto the world tennis stage. After winning the 1956 French championships, becoming the first African-American to win a Grand Slam event, she reached her peak in 1957, winning the Australian doubles title and then the singles and doubles championships at Wimbledon. She met the Queen and returned home to a ticker-tape parade, but she admitted her biggest thrill came when she visited Harlem and saw "all those people come out of their tired old apartment houses to tell me how glad they were that one of the neighbors' children had gone out into the world and done something big."

Gibson followed her Wimbledon triumph with a title at the National Clay Court Championships and finally a victory at the U.S. Nationals at Forest Hills, where she had broken the tournament's color barrier seven years earlier. As the world's number-one-ranked player, she was named the 1957 Associated Press Female Athlete of the Year.

She became somewhat of a celebrity off the court as well. Gibson recorded an album entitled *Althea Gibson Sings*, sang on "The Ed Sullivan Show," appeared in a handful of movies, and penned an autobiography, *I Always Wanted To Be Somebody*. But after repeating as champion at Wimbledon and Forest Hills in 1958, she retired from amateur tennis and turned professional, giving clinics and playing in exhibition matches.

Soon she turned her attention to another color barrier—in professional golf. After becoming the first black woman to earn her LPGA player's card in 1964, Gibson spent seven years on the tour, recording more moral than actual victories. Once again, however, she had willed herself into acceptance and transformed a game that, until Althea Gibson arrived, had been reserved primarily for the white and the wealthy.

CHARLIE SIFFORD

The same year in which Althea Gibson won the Wimbledon and U.S. championships, another African-American was making similar strides in golf. Charlie Sifford became the first black to beat white professonals in a PGA-sanctioned event when he won the 1957 Los Angeles Open.

In 1959, Sifford was rated an "approved player" by the PGA, a category traditionally reserved for foreign competitors, and it wasn't until November 1961 that the organization officially allowed membership by those who weren't "professional golfers of the Caucasian race." Sifford became the first black to win a regular PGA Tour event in 1967, and though he won only $350,000 on the regular tour, he went on to earn more than $1 million on the senior circuit.

64

Bert Bell

When you're born with a silver spoon in your mouth and a name as seemingly ostentatious as "DeBenneville," you either live up to the hype or discard it entirely, blazing your own trail. DeBenneville "Bert" Bell chose to rid himself of the gaudy name, devoting himself instead to a struggling game. "Born to wealth and social position," wrote Red Smith, "he scoffed at the latter and blew most of the former in football, to which he dedicated his life."

As a coach, owner and then the second commissioner of the National Football League, Bell represented a transition from professional football's small-town, fringe-of-respectability origins to its big-time emergence under his successor, Pete Rozelle. The evolution from leather helmets to helmet cams would have been nearly impossible without Bell's influence and innovations, which, along with some postwar prosperity, catapulted the NFL into the modern age.

He was born February 25, 1895, into a wealthy Philadelphia family, his father eventually becoming Attorney General of Pennsylvania and his brother joining the state Supreme Court. After captaining the football, baseball and basketball teams at prep school, Bell was faced with a college choice. His father, a trustee at the University of Pennsylvania, chose for him. "Bert will go to Penn," he said, "or he'll go to Hell."

Bell, like his father and brother before him, did just that. He became Penn's quarterback, leading the team to the 1917 Rose Bowl, but it was upon leaving school that he diverged from the path to social status that had been forged by his father and brother. "I was born with the name of DeBenneville and I licked that," said Bell, playing down his social background. "I'll lick anything else that comes along."

He served as an assistant football coach at Penn and then a head coach at Temple before turning his attention to professional football, which was to snobbish sports enthusiasts what a nose ring and a tattoo are to a debutante ball. In 1933, Bell led a six-person syndicate that bought the NFL's Frankford Yellowjackets, moved the team to Philadelphia, and named it the Eagles. Philadelphia promptly lost its first game 56-0, a harbinger of things to come.

Bell bought the Eagles outright for $4,500 in 1936, and coached the team for the next five seasons, producing a dismal record (10-44-2) that was better only than the club's financial records. Following the 1940 season, Bell sold the Eagles and obtained a half-interest in the Pittsburgh Steelers with Art Rooney. Six years later, he divested himself of the team when he was tabbed to replace Elmer Layden as league commissioner. As with Rozelle after him, the choice of Bell appeared to be a questionable one at the time but proved to be a brilliant one over time.

"He fenced expertly with anti-trust suiters, shouted down owners, mothered players in trouble, stamped on gamblers and charmed Congressmen and judges," wrote John Dell in the *Philadelphia Inquirer*. "He ran a big industry with the cracker-barrel approach of a country grocer."

Indeed, while the other commissioners and presidents of the nation's major professional sports leagues during Bell's era—Ford Frick in baseball, Maurice Podoloff in basketball and Clarence Campbell in hockey—were essentially pawns of the league owners, Bell was his own man. Said Al Hirshberg of *The New York Times*, "While his brother commissioners carefully fit their behavior to the rules, Bell fits the rules to his behavior.

In fact, pro football's second commissioner was often compared with pro baseball's first commissioner, with one important exception. "Kenesaw Mountain Landis . . . ruled with an iron fist, and the owners feared him," *New York Times* columnist Arthur Daley explained. "Bert Bell kept a kid glove on his iron fist, and the owners loved him."

Only Bell's death, in 1959, ended his reign, and by then average game attendance had nearly doubled, the two-platoon system had generated unprecedented excitement, some 30 million fans were regularly watching the NFL on television, and professional football was on the brink of challenging baseball as America's favorite pastime.

Four qualities in particular marked Bell's tenure at the helm—equality, equanimity, exposure and expeditiousness. Equality was Bell's first major contribution to the league, and it actually came nine years before he was elected commissioner. In pro football's infancy, four teams—the Chicago Bears, Green Bay Packers, New York Giants and Washington Redskins—dominated the others to such an extent that it fostered disinterest in the league's other towns and cities. But as the owner of the Eagles, Bell pushed through a novel concept in 1935—a draft of college players, with the last-place team picking first, a solution to stop the rich from getting richer.

The first draft took place a year later, ushering in a new age of parity and prosperity for the game. Not only did more level competition increase the game's appeal, but the draft also eliminated the costly process that saw teams bidding for the services of All-Americans. After World War II, the system was adopted by the NBA, NHL and Major League Baseball, becoming a staple of professional sports.

Upon being elected commissioner, Bell first impressed observers with his expeditious handling of gambling threats. As Landis's regime had done for baseball a quarter-century earlier, Bell's reign marked the arrival of stringent anti-gambling codes in the league. He dealt quickly with a game-fixing scandal (an attempt to fix the championship game) in 1946, paid careful attention to any fluctuations in the betting line, and even hired former FBI agents to deal with threats to the game's integrity in every NFL city.

Equanimity was evident in Bell's handling of the first upstart league to challenge the NFL's supremacy, the All-America Football Conference (AAFC), which began competition at the same time Bell began his tenure. Instead of panicking, Bell worked behind the scenes to assure a peaceful end to a costly battle for attention. In late 1949, the two leagues merged—or, more accurately, the AAFC surrendered, three of its teams being absorbed by the NFL.

Finally, Bell got the ball rolling in the medium that is now inseparable from the NFL, obtaining as much TV exposure as possible—except in cities where there were home games that Sunday. He fought in court for the right to black out home games, saying, "You can't give fans a free game on TV and expect them to pay for the same game at the ballpark." Thus, the NFL was able to realize a remarkable attendance increase throughout the 1950s while still realizing the tremendous financial returns from television.

Bell's death was an enormous blow to the league, but ironic in circumstance. On October 11, 1959, while watching a professional football game between his two old teams, Philadelphia and Pittsburgh, in his old stadium, Penn's Franklin Field, he died of a heart attack. Wrote Red Smith, "It was almost as though he were allowed to choose the time and place."

65

Theodore Roosevelt

Theodore Roosevelt, the twenty-sixth President of the United States, would not be worthy of inclusion on the Mount Rushmore of American sports. But if the sports version allowed 100 faces, his would be one of them. Roosevelt is arguably the only U.S. President whose contributions to sport can place him among the most important figures in American athletics.

Albert Spalding himself called Roosevelt "our first Athletic President," saying he inspired the nation's youth through his "sportsmanlike qualities, energy and 'square deal' brand of integrity." But Roosevelt's athleticism was largely a response to a distinct lack of the same as a child. Born October 27, 1858, in New York City, he was a scrawny and sickly youth, nearsighted and severely asthmatic. As he entered adolescence, he was told that he would need a strong body to bolster his strong mind, and he began to work out so often, particularly after being tormented by a pair of bullies, that his father installed a gymnasium in the family home.

For the rest of his days, Roosevelt practiced what he called the "strenuous life," and, indeed, he crammed more adventure into one lifetime than most any person in any field. He was a cattle rancher in the Dakota Territories, a buffalo hunter in the Plains, a big game hunter in Africa, an explorer in Brazil and a Rough Rider in Cuba. Roosevelt was a state legislator, head of the Civil Service Commission, New York City Police Commissioner, Assistant Secretary of the Navy, Governor of New York, and Vice-President of the United States.

When President William McKinley was assassinated in 1901, Roosevelt, six weeks shy of his forty-third birthday, became the youngest-ever U.S. President. He fashioned a "Square Deal" at home and carried a "big stick" abroad; he was a trust buster; he was a conservationist; and he was overwhelmingly elected to a second term in 1904. It was as his second term was getting underway that Roosevelt made his most significant impact on American sports, but to explain we have to turn back the clock two decades, returning to when Roosevelt was just entering adulthood and football was still in its infancy.

Football was still in the process of evolving from its roots in soccer and rugby. More accurately, it was degenerating—into a brutal, violent diversion in which mass-momentum plays turned the playing fields into something resembling battle-fields. There was, for example, the "V-trick," invented at Princeton in 1884, consisting of a human wedge formed around the ball carrier. One of the most popular defenses against it: slug the point man in the jaw. At the turn of the century, the "hurdle play" arrived, featuring a small ball carrier who was literally tossed by his larger teammates over the defensive line. Naturally, defenses began to counter the play by flinging one of their own, hoping for a midair collision. It was that kind of a game.

A large percentage of the press and the public became increasingly disenchanted with the sport, as did many university officials. After a particularly violent game in 1894, Army and Navy decided to call off their series. In that same year, Harvard temporarily discontinued athetic relations with Yale after six players were carried off the field in what was described by the *Boston Post* as "a most atrociously brutal game." By now, even Walter Camp, widely known as the "Father of American Football," had seen enough. He declared, "Unless steps are taken to reform the sport we shall discover that our precious football is being relegated to the ash heap of history."

There were twelve deaths on the collegiate fields in 1902, and the following year several state legislatures came close to abolishing the game. Football was scorned as "a boy-killing, education-prostituting, gladiatorial sport" by Shailer Mathews, dean of the Chicago Divinity School, who added, "It teaches virility and courage, but so does war."

A 1905 *Chicago Tribune* article reported nine deaths at the semiprofessional level, forty-six deaths at the high school level and eighteen deaths in collegiate football. Columbia University responded by abandoning football, its president describing it as "madness and slaughter," and a majority of college presidents and medical doctors who were surveyed agreed with Columbia's stand. Henry MacCracken, chancellor of New York University, stated, "The game has no social significance, except to give ruffians on our campuses an opportunity to express themselves. There seems to be a well nigh universal consent that the present game is intolerable."

It was Judgment Day for football, but the game had a powerful ally. In fact, it had the most powerful ally—Roosevelt, who had turned himself into quite a sportsman. He loved hiking and horseback riding, wrestling and judo, swimming across the half-frozen Potomac River. A finalist in the lightweight boxing championship as a student at Harvard, he installed a boxing ring in the basement of the White House.

And he was a football fan, the father of a future Harvard player, and one of 45,000 fans in attendance when the Crimson took on Yale in 1905. Roosevelt had attended the game against the wishes of many who considered it beneath the presidency, and the game seemed to bear that out when fistfights broke out (on the field *and* in the stands) while a Harvard player was carried off on a stretcher. But Roosevelt had a favorite saying: "Don't flinch, don't foul and hit the line hard." And so he did.

"Having received the Nobel Prize for helping to end the Russo-Japanese War," writes Wells Twombly in *200 Years of Sport in America*, "he considered it well within his prowess to bring peace to the football fields of America." Midway through the 1905 season, he called several football leaders to the White House and presented them with a choice—reform the game or abandon it. He made it clear that he strongly favored the former alternative.

At first, the football rulesmakers seemed to disregard Roosevelt's power play, taking no action in their meeting the following December. Meanwhile, North-western joined Columbia in cancelling the sport, and even Harvard threatened to do the same. Cal and Stanford replaced it with rugby, a statement about just how violent the game had become. It looked as if football would continue along its path toward self-destruction.

However, NYU's Henry MacCracken took Roosevelt's admonitions to heart, gathering thirteen Eastern colleges in a special meeting on December 9. Sixty-two schools sent representatives to their next meeting, nineteen days later, and Captain Palmer Pierce, of West Point, took charge.

The gathering was originally an attempt to save football, but it became a foundation for one of the most important organizations in American sports. The representatives formed the Intercollegiate Athletic Association of the United States (IAAUS), which then formed its own rules committee, inviting the old American Football Committee, led by Walter Camp, to join forces with them in reforming football.

Representatives from the two committees met on January 12, 1906, during which Harvard's Bill Reid was elected to replace Camp as secretary, and immediately began refining the rules of the game. The new American Intercollegiate Football Rules Committee approved the forward pass, established a one-yard neutral zone between the offensive and defense line, and disallowed kicking of loose balls. Perhaps most important, by requiring at least six men on the offensive line, mass-momentum plays were eliminated.

The game was on its way to respectability, as was the IAAUS. "I firmly believe the IAAUS will finally dominate the college athletic world. It stands for purity, for rational control, for fair play," said Palmer Pierce, who served as the organization's president from 1906–1913 and 1917–1929. "As its aims and methods become better understood, its strength will grow until its influence will become truly national." Pierce was right. In 1910, the IAAUS changed its name to the National Collegiate Athletic Association. By 1995, it boasted more than 900 member institutions.

So why not credit MacCracken or Pierce or Reid with saving football and spawning the NCAA? Why Roosevelt? Because it was his voice, more than any other, that had the power to determine the fate of football. He chose reform over abolition, and he made it so. By the time he died, on January 6, 1919, college football was challenging pro baseball as an American passion.

Roosevelt made a tangible contribution to the future of the sport, but his intangible influence may have been just as significant. As the "Athletic President" he did more than just tolerate sports like football and boxing which were fighting for acceptance; he supported them by his words and his actions.

Certainly, Roosevelt was the right man in the right position at the right time. In fact, had Richard Nixon been born about a half-century earlier, he might have snared a spot among *The Sports 100*. As it was, the American sporting scene was already firmly entrenched when he came to power, so he was left to design a handful of plays for the Washington Redskins. But Roosevelt essentially came into power during the same period as did American sport, and he was as important to sport as it was to him.

THE THEODORE ROOSEVELT AWARD

The Theodore Roosevelt Award, the highest honor the NCAA confers, is presented annually to "a distinguished citizen of national reputation and outstanding accomplishment who, having earned a varsity athletic award in college, has by his continuing interest and concern for physical fitness and competitive sport and by the example of his own life exemplified most clearly and forcefully the ideals and purposes to which college athletic programs and amateur sports are dedicated." The awards recipients have ranged from Dwight D. Eisenhower and Byron "Whizzer" White to Jesse Owens and Althea Gibson.

66

Walter O'Malley

To many baseball fans, and particularly to the residents of Brooklyn in the 1950s, there has never been a villain like Walter O'Malley. He spurned passion for profit, say his chorus of critics. He heralded the end of innocence.

But ask their Californian contemporaries, and they are bound to interpret O'Malley's relocation of the Dodgers from Brooklyn to Los Angeles in a different light. To them, The Man Who Stole the Dodgers from Brooklyn is The Man Who Brought Major League Baseball to California.

And if you then turn to neutral observers for an opinion, they may waver on the character of the man, but they cannot deny his impact. "Brooklyn fans view O'Malley as third in line to Stalin and Hitler," said baseball historian John Thorn. "But historians like myself might say that he is the Johnny Appleseed of baseball. Baseball was definitely going to move west, but nobody had the nerve to do it until O'Malley did."

Baseball dominated the sporting landscape in the 1950s, as it had for nearly a century, but there were signs of decay. Partly due to the emergence of television and partly due to a mass migration to the suburbs, attendance was down in both leagues. American League attendance reached 11 million in 1948, but it was down below 7 million just five years later. National League attendance also dropped, peaking at 10.4 million in 1947.

For half a century, sixteen major league teams had been located in ten Eastern and Midwestern cities. All but Detroit, Cleveland, Washington, D.C., Cincinnati and Pittsburgh were two-team communities, and by the 1950s, support in the two-team communities had primarily become imbalanced toward one franchise or the other.

The first club to respond to such troubles, the Boston Braves, moved to Milwaukee in March 1953. It was the first franchise shift since the old Baltimore

Orioles moved to New York in 1903, and success came immediately. The Braves drew more fans in their first nine games in Milwaukee than they had in seventy-seven games in Boston, in 1952. Braves owner Lou Perini realized a 1953 profit of a half million dollars, and by 1956, his franchise had become the first National League team to draw two million fans.

By 1954, the St. Louis Browns had become the new Baltimore Orioles. One year later, the Philadelphia Athletics moved to Kansas City. Baseball had embarked upon an era of rejuvenation through relocation, but the game at the major league level still could be found no farther west than Missouri.

It was in this environment that Walter O'Malley began to maneuver in Brooklyn, a community with what many perceived as an incomparable passion for its big league ballclub. Brooklyn had been consolidated within New York City back in 1897. It was, technically, no longer a big league city, but it still had a big league team. Brooklyn's club was more than just a sports entity; it was a means of clinging to community pride.

Brooklyn had boasted a major league team since 1884, and Ebbets Field had hosted baseball since 1913. The stadium had been built at a cost of $750,000 in a part of the borough known as Pigtown. At the time, it was a spacious 25,000-seat palace surrounded by open fields. By the 1950s, its evolved surroundings had rendered it cramped and increasingly obsolete. The once-fashionable area had become run down, the open fields had become crowded city streets and the ballpark was difficult to reach. Walter O'Malley began to look for a way out.

O'Malley had always been considered an outsider by Dodger loyalists, even though he was a native of New York City. Born on October 9, 1903, O'Malley obtained an engineering degree while finishing first in his class at Penn, earned a law degree from Fordham, and then started a law practice in Manhattan. In 1941, he became the Dodgers' attorney. By 1944, O'Malley had purchased twenty-five percent of the club. By 1950, after purchasing Branch Rickey's share of the team for $1 million, he was the team's president.

O'Malley was renowned for his dispassionate reliance on the bottom line. "It has always been recognized that baseball was a business, but if you enjoyed the game you could also tell yourself that it was also a sport," wrote Red Smith. "O'Malley was the first to say out loud that it was all business—a business that he owned and could operate as he chose."

In the mid-1950s, O'Malley campaigned for a new stadium, asking for the assistance of New York City officials in acquiring land for a new site. He would then finance the stadium through private capital. But New York power brokers dragged their feet, even when O'Malley began to make noise about leaving Brooklyn altogether. Said Branch Rickey, "It would be a crime against a community of three million people to move the Dodgers."

To many observers, baseball's other franchise shifts had been justified. The Braves, for instance, had lost more than $1 million in their last two seasons in Boston. But the Dodgers were the only National League team to earn a profit every year from 1952–1956. Why move a successful franchise?

However, much of the profit was due to television revenue and not gate receipts. In fact, despite recollections to the contrary, Dodger fans were not selling out Ebbets Field. Even in the team's world championship season of 1955, Brooklyn averaged just over 14,000 spectators per game.

"Other considerations influenced O'Malley's decision to move the Dodgers: his ability to persuade the New York Giants' owner, Horace Stoneham, to transfer his team to San Francisco; the advent of jet airline service, which removed the impediment of extended travel for other National League teams; and the migration of the middle class to the suburbs, which made fans reluctant to attend night games in the inner city," Paul Sullivan explains in *The Dodgers Move West*. "Yet of all the factors contributing to the Dodgers' decision, the political choices of the two cities were ultimately decisive. In the end it was more important to Los Angeles politicians to attract the Dodgers than it was for New York politicians to keep the team."

California had been home to organized baseball since the mid-1800s, as well as some terrific Pacific Coast League teams since the late nineteenth century. It had also spawned some of baseball's best players, including Ted Williams, Joe DiMaggio and Tris Speaker, yet it had not attracted Major League Baseball. The St. Louis Browns had considered moving there in 1941, only to have their plans derailed by World War II. The Pacific Coast League had then made an unsuccessful bid to raise itself to major league status.

In 1947, National League clubs unanimously approved a plan to expand into four California cities, only to have the proposal voted down by the American League. Los Angeles officials had come tantalizingly close to major league acceptance several times, and they jumped at the chance to get the Dodgers. L.A. officials, Sullivan writes, "apparently offered the Dodger president everything but a tollbooth on the Harbor Freeway."

In New York, meanwhile, a succession of proposed plans fell through, including a multipurpose sports center and a proposed 50,000-seat dome in Queens. Even the failed Queens proposal—the city's last gasp—meant the Dodgers would definitely be leaving Brooklyn. In the end, they moved about 3,000 miles farther. On September 24, 1957, the Dodgers played their final game at Ebbets Field. Brooklyn lost the game, and then lost the Dodgers.

Politics aside, most observers of the Brooklyn tragedy agreed with the assessment of Arthur Daley of *The New York Times*, who wrote, "Other teams were forced to move by apathy, or incompetence. The only word that fits the Dodgers is greed." Even on the occasion of O'Malley's death, some two decades later on August 9, 1979, hundreds of thousands of former Brooklyn Dodger fans would have been more than willing to engrave those words upon his tombstone. They would have had to travel to California to do so.

But, just as observers in the 1950s had divergent views of the man, historians in the 1990s can take two distinct perspectives of his legacy. On the one hand, he destroyed New York City baseball, which had been the heart of Major League Baseball for half a century. O'Malley sucked the soul out of a community that had lionized Babe Ruth, Lou Gehrig, Joe DiMaggio, Jackie Robinson, John McGraw, Mel Ott, Bobby Thomson, Yogi and Campy, Reese and Rizzuto. The Willie versus Mickey versus the Duke argument was still raging full force in 1958 when O'Malley made his momentous decision.

On the other hand, his move revitalized the Dodgers, and transformed the game. The Los Angeles Dodgers won the 1959 World Series, and, in 1962 Dodger Stadium opened in L.A.'s Chavez Ravine. Since then, the Dodgers have won eight pennants and four world championships. Seasonal attendance figures of three million have been commonplace. In fact, in 1985, an economist hired by the Major League Players Association referred to the Dodgers as "probably the most successful sports franchise that has ever been fielded."

O'Malley's impact, however, is not merely evident in the Dodgers' success; it can be found in the Dodgers' imitators. Brooklyn was the first community to cry foul after losing a baseball team, but several soon followed. Remember the Milwaukee Braves? The Seattle Pilots? The Washington Senators? Though the Senators' move to Texas in 1972 represents baseball's last franchise shift, the Dodgers' move also indirectly led to baseball's expansion. When the Giants and Dodgers left New York, plans for a new Continental League were hatched, primarily in an attempt to find a replacement franchise in the Big Apple. This led to baseball's first expansion since 1903, with the addition of teams in New York, Houston, Los Angeles and Minnesota.

O'Malley's pioneering move also heralded a dramatic shift in the focus of every professional sport. Before 1958, baseball's outer limits were Kansas City to the west and Washington, D.C., to the south. Today, there are five teams in California, two in Canada and Texas, and one each in Washington state, Colorado, Georgia and Florida. Every other major sport has expanded in a similar manner.

It took dozens of years, but professional sports finally evolved from an Eastern creation into a national concept. And Walter O'Malley took the first big leap by donning a black hat and riding West.

67

Abe Saperstein

No team in history has done more for their sport," *Los Angeles Times* columnist Jim Murray wrote about the Harlem Globetrotters. "Not the '27 Yankees, the Four Horsemen of Notre Dame, the Dream Team or the Lombardi Packers."

Indeed, the Globetrotters may rank as the most famous and beloved team in American sports history. They have played before an estimated 100 million spectators in more than 100 countries; they have their own star on Hollywood's Walk of Fame; and they are listed in the *Guinness Book of World Records* for drawing 75,000 fans to a game at Berlin's Olympic Stadium in 1951. They haven't lost a game since January 5, 1971.

But the Globetrotters represent more than just America's "Ambassadors of Goodwill," draped in red-white-and-blue affection. As one of the few outlets for pre–World War II African-American athletic participation, as world-famous representatives of the game in the years when it was still struggling for widespread acceptance, and as a collection of talent and innovation that heralded and helped spawn the modern court game, the Globetrotters also rank as one of the most important creations in American sport. And, thus, the team's founder, Abe Saperstein, owns a place among *The Sports 100.*

From the beginning, Saperstein's life was a cultural stew. He was a Jewish kid born in London, England (July 4, 1903), who grew up in a tough Irish neighborhood in Chicago. After graduating from high school, he drifted into semipro baseball and basketball before embarking on a business career.

At the same time, Chicago was also home to the Savoy Big Five, an all-black basketball team run by a black man named Dick Hudson. The team played on Sundays at Chicago's Savoy Ballroom. Saperstein entered the picture late in 1926, when both he and Hudson realized it would be easier for a white man to book the team outside of Chicago. The following year marked the beginning of the Harlem Globetrotters.

Saperstein's team didn't actually play its first official game in Harlem until 1968, but Saperstein saw the marketing potential in the name and realized there was room for another all-black squad to compete with what was perhaps the nation's most talented team, the Harlem Rens. Saperstein then piled his team into his Model T, and, on January 7, 1927, 300 spectators in Hinckley, Illinois, watched the beginning of what would become sport's most enduring barnstorming tour.

The Globetrotters went 361-32 over their first three seasons. By 1940, the team had surpassed the Rens, taking the professional basketball world title. Over the next decade, the Globetrotters were good enough to outplay a series of college All-Star teams and even defeat the NBA-champion Minneapolis Lakers. In fact, when the league was struggling, the Globetrotters were often there to keep it afloat. In double-bill events, the NBA games would be the opening act for the headline act, the Globetrotters. Yet, it was the growth of the NBA, and the influx of black players into the league, that eventually caused a decrease in the team's stature.

Just as Satchel Paige had opened eyes to the talent and potential drawing power in baseball's Negro Leagues, the skill displayed by and affection given to the Globetrotters made the integration of professional basketball possible. It is no accident that the the NBA's first black impact player, Nat "Sweetwater" Clifton, was a former Globetrotter. Yet, integration meant Saperstein would no longer get his pick of all the African-American players in the nation.

The NBA didn't want Saperstein's team, just his players. When Saperstein later failed in his attempts to obtain NBA franchises in San Francisco and Los Angeles, he formed his own league, the American Basketball League, in 1961. He owned the ABL's Chicago franchise and served as league commissioner. The ABL was the first league to adopt the three-point field goal, but it folded midway through its second season.

By then the 5-foot-3 Saperstein was, according to Murray, "so round that, when someone dubbed him 'Mr. Basketball,' they didn't know whether that was a nickname or a description." But speculation surrounding the integration of the NBA raises questions about his motivation. Many observers believe that Saperstein, fearful of the impact an integrated professional league would have on the Globetrotters, attempted to prevent it. Ironically, his failure in that attempt was largely a result of his team's enduring success.

Humor became integral to the Globetrotters' persona once Saperstein realized the team would no longer showcase the world's top talent. However, the team's transition from serious competition to clowning entertainment began as early as 1929, when center Inman Jackson joined the squad. His form of entertainment would later be refined by the likes of Reece "Goose" Tatum and Meadowlark Lemon.

Yet the team's court gestures also played a large role in taking basketball skill to a higher plane. The fast break, the slam dunk, the behind-the-back pass, the between-the-legs dribble, the weave . . . all may have originated with Saperstein's travelling team. Marques Haynes, who joined the Globetrotters in 1946, elevated the art of dribbling and became an inspiration to subsequent players, including Magic Johnson.

But while some describe the team's combination of style and stitches as a product of the genius of Saperstein and his players, others deride it as an enduring case of racial stereotyping. In *Elevating the Game*, author Nelson George claims the organization under Saperstein was "a definitive example of white paternalism and Black male submission." *Sports Illustrated* agreed in 1968, calling the Globetrotters "the white man's encapsulated view of the whole Negro race set to the rhythms of *Sweet Georgia Brown*."

But the fact remains that the racial climate of the times, the struggle for survival and the integration of baseball had much the same effect on the black-owned Negro Leagues. And whatever Saperstein's motivations, his legacy still remains that of a man who created opportunities for African-Americans at a time when few existed. Subsequently, some of the proudest and most insightful black men in sports, including Bob Gibson and Wilt Chamberlain, wore the red-white-and-blue.

In any case, the modern Harlem Globetrotters are being transformed into a symbol of African-American self-determination and success. Saperstein died on March 15, 1966, and the team was purchased by a series of outside investors. But in 1993, Mannie Jackson, a senior vice-president at Honeywell, Inc., and a former Globetrotter, became the organization's first black owner. He has already made moves to restore the team's luster since the basketball explosion of the 1980s diminished the star of the sport's pioneering franchise.

The Globetrotters are no longer in a position to change the face of basketball, but they still lead the league in smiling faces.

68

Vince Lombardi

By the time Baltimore Colts running back Alan Ameche plunged into the end zone from one yard out, observers were already calling it "the greatest game ever played." More accurately, it might be described as the most important. The 1958 NFL championship game between the New York Giants and the Baltimore Colts was a landmark event in football. It was the first-ever nationally televised title game, and some 11 million American homes had remained on the edge of their seats throughout. Ameche's game-winning touchdown had been made necessary when Baltimore tied the game at 17-17 with seven seconds remaining in regulation time, resulting in the first sudden death overtime period in football history. It had been the right game at the right time for the NFL, and it is widely considered the moment that set pro football on its way to conquering autumn.

But somewhat overlooked is the fact that one member of the Giants was appearing in his last game as an assistant coach. He would become an NFL head coach a few months later and he, more than any other figure, would embody the emergence of professional football. His name became a symbol for his profession; his game became the standard.

Lombardi was this popular: In September 1968, CBS preempted "The Ed Sullivan Show" to broadcast an hour-long special titled *Lombardi*. Can you picture NBC abandoning "Seinfeld" for a special called "Seifert"? That television should honor Lombardi was appropriate because the Packers and TV arrived at nearly the same time. Commissioners Bert Bell and Pete Rozelle were the architects of the NFL's emergence, but Lombardi became the image of the NFL when image really was everything.

Lombardi was a product of Brooklyn, born on June 11, 1913, the oldest son of a disciplinarian father. Football would become his religion, but he started out with the real thing, spending three years in a preseminary high school before transferring to Brooklyn's St. Francis Prep. He became an all-city guard and halfback, earning a scholarship to Fordham Univeristy.

Lombardi's coach at Fordham, Jim Crowley, had been coached in high school by Curly Lambeau, who founded the Green Bay Packers and coached the team for three decades. Crowley had gone on to Notre Dame, where he became one of the famed "Four Horseman" under Knute Rockne, who also had coached Lambeau. So Lombardi's ties to the patriarch of the Packers and the king of coaches began even before he picked up his first playbook.

The assistant coach to whom Lombardi became closest at Fordham was Frank Leahy, who went on to coach the Fighting Irish to four national titles. Indeed, this particular family of coaches—Rockne and Leahy, primarily at Notre Dame, and Lambeau and Lombardi, mostly at Green Bay—produced a combined coaching record of 546-194-43, including 18 championships.

Lombardi was a 170-pound guard in the mid-1930s, a member of Fordham's line called "The Seven Blocks of Granite." Upon graduation and after a stint as a semiprofessional player and a semester at Fordham Law School, he took a job as teacher and assistant football coach at St. Cecilia High School in Englewood, New Jersey, in 1939. There he was known for the qualities that would come to define him—preparedness, impatience, avolcanic temper, near-unreasonable expectations, outsized emotions, a penchant for motivation, relentless domination and fierce loyalty. Said one observer at the time, "He had the will of a perfectionist, the mind of a fundamentalist, and the heart of a father."

After taking over as head coach in 1942, Lombardi lost his first game and then embarked on a 32-game non-losing streak, including 25 straight wins. Before one game against arch-rival Brooklyn Prep, one of his players received a postcard from his upcoming opponent ridiculing him and his teammates. Properly motivated, St. Cecilia won handily. The postcard, of course, had been written by Lombardi.

Lombardi moved to the college ranks in 1947, becoming an assistant coach at his alma mater. He coached under Red Blaik at Army from 1949–1953 and then accepted a job with the New York Giants. Under ineffectual head coach Jim Lee Howell, he essentially became co–head coach in charge of the team's offense while another assistant, Tom Landry, coached the defense. Landry, of course, would go on to enormous success with the Dallas Cowboys. But Lombardi would dominate the '60s to such an extent that Landry's success in the '70s seemed a bit like Wings following the Beatles.

Lombardi's troops were among the first to study photos of an opponent's defense during the game, though at the time the equipment consisted of Polaroids lowered from the scout's box to the bench inside an old sock. It was primitive but productive. The Giants won the NFL title in 1956, Lombardi's offense scoring 47 points in the title game.

In 1958, the Philadephia Eagles offered him a head coaching position, but he was talked out of it by the Giants, who went on to play the Baltimore Colts in that memorable championship game. Football was on its way, and not coincidentally, so was Lombardi. When Blaik retired at West Point following the season, and Lombardi was passed over for the position, he resorted to his second choice: the Green Bay Packers. He was named coach and general manager on February 4, 1959.

The Packers' board of directors had been looking for someone to take control of a rudderless organization that hadn't had a winning season in a dozen years. The same Colts team that the Giants had taken into overtime had beaten the Packers 56-0 in 1958, a year in which Green Bay went 1-10-1, the worst record in the history of pro football's oldest franchise. "I need to win only two games next season," Lombardi joked, "and Green Bay will have improved 100 percent."

The Packers had some talent—Bart Starr, Paul Hornung, Jim Taylor, Ray Nitschke, Forest Gregg—but as football historian Bob Carroll explains, "Michelangelo could carve the *Pieta*; most of us couldn't get a decent doorstop out of the same chunk of marble."

In Lombardi's first three months on the job, he reportedly watched 20,000 feet of film on the Packers. In his first training camp, he gave notice of training camps to come. Several players lost as many as twenty pounds. Said one of them, "We thought we were in Alcatraz." Added a sportswriter, "Compared to Vince, Simon Legree was a humanitarian."

The Packers opened the 1959 season with a win, after which the players carried Lombardi off the field. Green Bay won its first three games, lost the next five and then won the last four to finish with a winning record. Some 7,500 fans welcomed them home following their seventh and final victory; Lombardi received a $10,000 bonus and Coach of the Year honors. One group also voted him "Italian of the Year," leading Lombardi to wonder, "Where does that leave Pope John?" The legend had begun.

After a 6-0 pre-season in 1960, the Packers won the Western Conference title, losing to Philadelphia in the championship game. Another undefeated exhibition season followed in 1961, as well as another conference crown. This time, Green Bay won the NFL title—by thrashing Lombardi's old Giants team 37-0. Afterward, even West Point approached Lombardi about coming back, the intitial offer made by President John F. Kennedy himself.

Lombardi won with motivation. Said one observer, "Until I saw the Packers under Lombardi, I seriously doubted a pro team could match a college team in unadultered spirit." He won with strategy. His "big back" offense would become the most imitated in the NFL, and his signature play, the "power sweep," would become the most intimidating. And he won with understanding. Just like the era's other two mythical coaches, Red Auerbach and John Wooden, Lombardi appeared color blind. At a time when several NFL teams were racked with racial dissension, the Packers were a model of harmony.

Green Bay lost only one game in 1962, outscoring opponents 415-148, and again beating New York in the title game. During the season, CBS broadcast a prime-time half-hour special on the team, and articles on Lombardi or the Packers appeared in every national magazine. An underappreciated sport only a few years earlier, pro football had become fashionable, and Lombardi's team embodied the game.

Green Bay fell to second place in each of the next two seasons, but before the 1965 season—and four years before Joe Namath's famous Super Bowl guarantee—Lombardi stated simply, "We'll win it." And they did. In fact, they began a string of three straight championships, including the first two Super Bowls in January of 1967 and 1968, becoming the first and only team to perform the three-peat since the advent of the playoff system. The winning Super Bowl team now receives the Vince Lombardi Trophy.

Lombardi emerged as a living legend. "He is respected, admired, looked on with awe as if he were some great natural phenomenon like the Grand Canyon or the Rocky Mountains," wrote a *Green Bay Press-Gazette* columnist in 1968. But many in the press, while acknowledging his success, were just as eager to criticize his style. *The New York Times* claimed he had a "soul of solid rocks," and critics condemned him as a poster boy for tyranny, a destructive influence on youth coaches across the country who had latched on to his dictatorial manner.

Certainly, Lombardi perfected the my-way-or-the-highway approach. Though he inspired as much devotion and passion in his players as fear and loathing, the media seized on references to his authoritarian bearing, like those of defensive tackle Henry Jordan, who said, "He treats us all the same—like dogs."

Two weeks after the Packers' victory in Super Bowl II, at a press conference attended by 120 reporters, Lombardi announced that, while he would remain Green Bay's general manager, he was retiring as head coach. In nine seasons, he had won 98 games, six Western Conference titles and five NFL championships. A team that hadn't had a winning season in twelve years never had a losing season under Lombardi. In the first year without Lombardi at the helm, however, Green Bay finished 6-7-1.

Lombardi fully expected never to return to the sidelines. Meanwhile, he was actually considered as a possible vice-presidential nominee by both political parties in 1968, as well as a candidate for baseball commissioner. Instead, the world got Spiro Agnew and Bowie Kuhn. It quickly became clear, however, that Lombardi missed coaching. Out of respect for his longtime assistant, Phil Bengtson, who had replaced him, he was reluctant to return with the Packers. He would also only consider offers that included equity in the team, which he found when the Washington Redskins offered him five percent ownership. Lombardi asked out of his five-year contract with Green Bay, and the would-be politician headed for Washington.

In a town used to celebrity, Lombardi turned heads. He also became increasingly political, a conservative critic of the anti-Establishment '60s. In football, he and Joe Namath were the game's biggest drawing cards, but in spirit Lombardi was the anti-Namath.

Like the Packers before Lombardi, the Redskins hadn't had a winning season in years—since 1955. And like Green Bay, Washington, under Lombardi, recorded seven wins and five losses. But just as Lombardi seemed poised to create another dynasty, it all came to a tragic end. He entered Georgetown University hospital in the summer of 1970 with abdominal pains and was diagnosed with colon cancer. It was one battle he couldn't have prepared for, and by September 3 he was dead.

Lombardi had been a pro football coach for only ten seasons, but then again, he had *been* pro football. His 105-35-6 overall record, a .740 winning percentage, remains the best in history, earning him entrance to the Hall of Fame on the very next ballot. Canton is no Alcatraz, but you have to wonder if somewhere out there he doesn't have Jim Thorpe and Red Grange and Bronko Nagurski running windsprints.

THE ONLY THING

Vince Lombardi's famous line—"Winning isn't everything. It's the only thing"—is perhaps the most repeated in sports history. But even from Lombardi's mouth, the line wasn't original. It was first uttered by Vanderbilt football coach Red Sanders in the 1940s, and later by John Wayne in a 1953 film, *Trouble Along the Way*, the story of a small-town football coach. As it was, Lombardi always claimed his words had been misunderstood.

69

Bill Veeck

"Nobody ever paid to see an owner yet," Milwaukee Brewers owner Bud Selig once claimed, "and nobody ever will." As acting commissioner of Major League Baseball and one of the precipators of the 1994–1995 power struggle between players and owners, Selig would probably prefer that his proclamation of old remain under wraps (lest it be pointed out that his words have essentially become the Players' Association's party line). But Selig can rest easy. He wasn't disparaging all owners—just Bill Veeck.

Then again, if Veeck were still around, it seems certain he would have wanted no part of the baseball strike. He was, according to *Chicago Tribune* columnist Bob Verdi, "a man unalterably opposed to joylessness," and to pull the plug on the national pastime would have been unthinkable to him—much more of a blight on the game than some fireworks . . . or midgets . . . or Bermuda shorts . . . or Disco Demolition Night.

The bulk of the sports magnates included in *The Sports 100* embody power and influence, money and respect. Bill Veeck was all about perspective, on and off the field. "Bill brought baseball into the twentieth century," said his longtime friend, legendary slugger Hank Greenberg. "Before Bill, baseball was just win or lose. But he made it fun to be at the ball park."

Veeck ranks among the least popular and most popular franchise owners in big league history. Described by Greenberg as "the only owner I ever knew who gave a damn about his players," Veeck was generally waved off by his fellow owners with a shrug or a sneer. Yet he inspired as much devotion among fans as he did distaste among his colleagues. "To walk through the streets of Chicago with Bill Veeck," wrote Ed Linn in *The New York Times*, "was to encounter a movie gallery of faces lighting up at the sight of him."

Veeck began and concluded his life in Chicago, primarily at Wrigley Field, though the Cubs were not among the three major league and two minor league franchises he owned in six different stints. His early experience with the Cubs was his schooling in the business of the game almost from the day William Louis Veeck, Jr., was born on February 9, 1914, in the Chicago suburb of Hinsdale, Illinois.

His father, William Louis Veeck, Sr., took over as president of the Cubs in 1919, holding the position until his death in 1933. Bill Jr. played football at Kenyon College in Ohio, but when his father died he left school for a career in baseball. He joined the Cubs front office, learning every aspect of operating the franchise and eventually assuming the position of club treasurer, all the while attending night school to study accounting and business law. In 1941, he struck out on his own, purchasing the minor league Milwaukee Brewers with longtime Cubs first baseman Charlie Grimm and embarking on a career in which he would transform baseball philosophically and financially.

"You can't win every game but you can make every game entertaining," Veeck explained. Promotion, for Veeck, was as much a statement as a financial tool. Games are fun; fun draws fans; fans bring money. Tongue in cheek, money in hand, Veeck set about reinterpreting the notion of fun at the old ballpark.

In Milwaukee, Veeck's giveaways ranged from a 200-pound block of ice to two dozen live lobsters; his stunts included an outfield fence that moved in when the home team was hitting. His team, on the verge of bankruptcy and having drawn only 75,000 fans two years earlier, drew almost 275,000 in 1942. Veeck was named Minor League Executive of the Year by *The Sporting News*.

Upon joining the Marines in 1944, Veeck was sent to the South Pacific, where an anti-aircraft artillery piece crushed his lower right leg, which was amputated when he returned home. It was one of dozens of serious ailments Veeck suffered through for the next forty years, as he spent nearly as much time in the hospital as at the ballpark, surviving some thirty-four different operations and returning each time with a wider smile.

If a man can be defined by an image, Veeck could be summed up by the way he spent his final years, roaming the Wrigley Field bleachers, shirtless, chatting with fans, waving to the cameras, stubbing his cigarette out in the ashtray he built into his peg leg. This was a man who always answered his own phone, who watched his team not from an owner's box but alongside his paying customers, who never wore a tie, and who seemed to live on beer and cigarettes. It was this common touch that he brought to the most uncommon of businesses.

In 1945, after the Brewers had won three straight American Association pennants, Veeck sold the team and came away with, as one writer described it, "$250,000 in cash . . . and a yen for a big league club." That club proved to be another team in financial straits, the Cleveland Indians, which a Veeck-led syndicate purchased for $2.2 million. The team doubled its attendance in Veeck's first year, and, in 1948, Cleveland won the World Series and set an American League attendance record.

Veeck found a unique way to show gratitude to his fans during the championship season. Joe Early, a night watchman at a local auto plant, had complained to the *Cleveland Press* that the average fan deserved a night in his honor instead of the players. Veeck, always a good listener, came up with "Good Old Joe Early Night," during which the fans received giveaways and Early received thousands of dollars in gifts, from an outhouse and a cow to a refrigerator and a new Ford convertible. Following the season, Veeck was once again named Executive of the Year, this time in the major leagues.

After selling his interest in Cleveland for a $600,000 profit in 1949, Veeck purchased yet another perennial doormat, the St. Louis Browns, in 1951. It was there that Veeck unveiled some of his most outrageous promotions, including *the* most outrageous on August 19, 1951. With no advance billing, a crowd of 18,000 on hand for a doubleheader watched a midget named Eddie Gaedel jump out of a cake at home plate in between games in honor of the American League's fiftieth anniversary. What nobody knew was that Gaedel had been signed to a legitimate $100 contract. When the Browns came to bat in the bottom of the first inning, he strolled up to the plate, wearing number $1/8$ and pinch-hitting for the starting center fielder.

Gaedel was quickly followed by St. Louis manager Zack Taylor carrying a sheaf of papers proving the legitimacy of the prank, which was in turn followed by a 15-minute debate ending in the Browns' favor. Gaedel walked on four pitches, partly because the pitcher was laughing so hard, and was replaced by a pinch-runner. The stunt, like the moving fences of a decade earlier, led to a rapid closing of a loophole in the rules. Gaedel was banned from baseball, and all subsequent player contracts would have to be approved by the league president.

Veeck's promotions were often ridiculed by colleagues like former Minnesota Twins owner Calvin Griffith, who claimed he would "spend two dollars and one cent to get two dollars in the till." But Veeck understood the value of publicity, good or bad. As he wrote, in the first of his four autobiographical works, *Veeck—As in Wreck*, "It's fine to be appreciated for a day . . . It's better for the box office, though, to be attacked for a full week." Old-guard stuffed-shirts were venemous in their attacks following the Gaedel stunt, but before the week was out Veeck had come up with another.

In a home game featuring the last-place Browns (who would go on to lose 102 times and finish 46 games behind the Yankees) against the seventh-place Philadelphia Athletics, Veeck put the fate of his club in the hands of the "Grandstand Managers Club," composed of 1,115 fans sitting behind the home dugout with large white signs reading "YES" or "NO." The fans responded to questions posed by St. Louis coaches, while Zack Taylor, the real manager, sat in a rocking chair smoking a pipe and wearing bedroom slippers. A's manager Jimmy Dykes blasted Veeck for making "a travesty of the game," but that may have been because the fans made all the right moves in several critical situations and the Browns won.

The Browns didn't win enough, however, to save the franchise, and with the team continuing to fail artistically and financially, Veeck asked the other owners to permit a move to Baltimore. They wouldn't allow it—until after Veeck had sold the club. The owners also prevented Veeck from purchasing the Athletics in 1954 and the Detroit Tigers in 1956, but he returned two years later after acquiring a controlling interest in the White Sox.

Chicago won its first pennant in four decades in 1959, and set a team attendance record the following year, while Veeck introduced the exploding scoreboard and players' names on the backs of uniforms. He also had a group of midgets dressed as Martians land on the field in a helicopter and "kidnap" Chicago's diminutive doubleplay tandem of Nellie Fox and Luis Aparacio, at which point the leader of the Martians, Eddie Gaedel himself, said, "I don't want to be taken to your leader. I've already met him."

But it was also during Veeck's first tour with the White Sox that he put his accounting and law background to use, altering the business of baseball through some creative accounting. According to Andrew Zimbalist, author of *Baseball and Billions*, Veeck "reasoned that players were an asset to a baseball team just as machinery was an asset to a manufacturing concern and, like machinery, players had a fixed useful life. By assigning a high share of the purchase price of a baseball franchise to the value of its players (in those days it was typical to assign 90 percent or more), an owner could then depreciate (or deduct from taxable income) a certain share of the purchase price each year."

The tax loophole was more beneficial to ownership groups with baseball profits exceeding the tax write-off or with income from other businesses. Thus Veeck's boondoggle made baseball ownership more attractive to wealthier individuals or groups and, since the value of the club fell as the players were fully depreciated, it made these owners more willing to sell out after only a few years. So, to some extent, the man who was so devoted to baseball's fans and to the interpersonal aspects of the game fostered a trend toward corporate ownership and money-first loyalties.

Ill health forced Veeck to leave baseball in 1961, and it was another fourteen years before he returned to the game, rounding up enough investors to repurchase the White Sox for $10 million, saving the team from being moved to Seattle. Immediately, he reverted to his maverick ways, becoming the only owner to vote against a lockout in response to the advent of free agency. "Of course, nobody agreed with me, which made it just like the old days," Veeck recalled.

He earned Executive of the Year honors once again in 1977 when he rebuilt Chicago into a pennant contender, but the demands of free agency soon forced him out of the game for good. Veeck died of a heart attack on January 2, 1986, at the age of seventy-one. Five years later baseball's maverick joined baseball's immortals in Cooperstown. "There is no way anyone can fit his story on some bronze plaque," wrote Bob Verdi, "but at least they've added a lot of life to that venerable museum."

LARRY DOBY

Had Branch Rickey not been the baseball executive who broke the major league color barrier, Bill Veeck surely would have. As early as 1943, Veeck attempted to purchase the Philadelphia Phillies and stock the club with black talent, only to have Commissioner Kenesaw Mountain Landis maneuver behind his back to void the deal. Once Jackie Robinson emerged as a Dodger, in 1947, observers knew it was only a matter of time before Veeck signed the game's first black American Leaguer to play for his Cleveland Indians.

But unlike Rickey, Veeck didn't feel the need to place an additional burden on his player by making him play his way through the minor league system. "One afternoon when the team trots out on the field," he told one writer that April, "a Negro player will be out there with them." And that's what happened. Veeck signed Larry Doby on July 5, and he was playing against the White Sox just a few hours later.

70

Pop Warner

The first football game Pop Warner ever saw was the one in which he first stepped into a football uniform. His last game, some sixty years later, was a decidedly different form of football, and he had much to do with it.

Warner ranks as one of the most enduring, successful and innovative football coaches in the annals of the game. He coached in 457 contests with six teams over 44 seasons, posting a 319-106-32 mark, churning out 44 All-Americans along the way. Among the innovations credited to Warner are the three-point stance, the screen pass, the spiral punt, the wingback formation, the unbalanced line, the shifting defense, the rolling body block, the blocking dummy, numbering players' jerseys, and the use of thigh and shoulder pads. Even his name is now synonymous with youth football, yet as a youth all Warner wanted to be was a baseball player.

Born April 5, 1871, in Springville, New York, Glenn Scobey Warner dreamed of being a major league pitcher. But by the time he enrolled in Cornell University's College of Law, a two-year undergraduate program, Warner was tipping the scales at over 200 pounds—this during a time when even football players rarely did. A gridiron career was almost inevitable, but a meeting on a train ride was a product of fate.

Carl Johanson, captain of the Cornell football team, met Warner on a train heading toward the school and sensed a recruiting opportunity. "I met a young fellow about six feet two or three," Johanson later recalled, "and I thought to myself, 'That boy would fill a big hole in my line.'"

But Warner had other ideas. "Up to that time," he later remembered, "I had not only never seen the game of football but had not thought of ever trying to play it." Nevertheless, Johanson placed Warner at left guard, and Warner experienced his first game, a 58-0 wipeout of Syracuse, from the middle of the trenches. "I was feeling pretty good about my playing," said Warner, "until I shook hands with my opponent and told him it was my first game and was informed it was his first game also."

Warner was older than most of his teammates. At age twenty-two, the distinction earned him the nickname "Pop," and it stuck. He graduated in 1894, after becoming one of Cornell's best players, and hoped to begin a law career. But he soon found himself unemployed. He was convinced by Cornell's football manager to return to the university and take graduate courses while playing football (in those days, a graduate student could play on the team). Warner was captain of the 1894 Cornell squad.

Following the season, both Iowa State and Georgia contacted him about coaching their fledgling teams, and he took both jobs. In August and September, he would train the Iowa State squad, then he would spend the season coaching Georgia. Warner then coached at Cornell for two seasons before packing up his bags and moving to the Carlisle Indian School in Pennsylvania. He coached there for five seasons, went back to Cornell for three more, and then returned to Carlisle in 1907. Warner's return coincided with the arrival of Jim Thorpe, and the two would go on to make Carlisle famous.

Warner moved on to the University of Pittsburgh in 1914, where his teams won 33 straight games and two national championships. Then it was Stanford, where Warner won 71 of 96 contests and made three Rose Bowl appearances. He closed out his half-a-century of football by coaching at Temple University from 1933–1938, where he had only one losing season.

Through it all, Warner kept tinkering with the game in an attempt to give his teams a distinct advantage. As another Hall of Fame coach, Andy Kerr, explained, "I consider Warner to be the greatest creative genius in American football. Most of us coaches are imitators, but Pop was an inventor."

One of the inventions was the wingback formation, in which the halfback (in the single-wing) or halfbacks (in the double-wing) lined up just behind and outside the ends. The formation became a staple of the 1930s before it was supplanted by the modern T-formation.

But for the most part, Warner was more of a maverick innovator. As fellow coaching legend Amos Alonzo Stagg explained, "Glenn was never very active on the rules committee. But we'd make up a rule and Glenn would think up a way to get around it within the rules, and we'd have to meet his challenge. He kept us on our toes, I can tell you." It was, for instance, as a result of an unstoppable Warner formation featuring six players in the backfield that a rule was instituted requiring seven men on the line of scrimmage.

In fact, much of Warner's tinkering revolved around his eternal search for a loophole in the rules, like the time he had straps sewn on either side of the halfback's uniform. When the ball was snapped to the halfback, a player on each side would grab a strap and throw him through the line. The play was ruled illegal the following year. And there was also the time he had oval-shaped leather patches sewed onto his players' uniforms. He called them chest protectors, but they just happened to look like footballs. To opposing defenses, it looked like a half-dozen players were carrying the ball.

Perhaps Warner's most famous gambit occurred in 1903, when Carlisle visited mighty Harvard. With Carlisle leading 5-0, Harvard's kickoff was taken at the five-yard line, and the ballcarrier was quickly surrounded by his teammates. He then slid the ball under the back of teammate Charlie Dillon's jersey, where a rubber band had been sewn to hold it in place. When the players scattered, the chaos began. "The stands were in an uproar, for everybody had seen the big lump on Dillon's back," Warner later recalled, "but the Harvard players were still scurrying wildly around when Charlie crossed the goal line."

As Warner grew older, however, he began to express distaste about where college football was headed. In a *Saturday Evening Post* column he wrote in 1934, Warner claimed, "The time has come to deflate football down to normal. Football is just a game, and the object of it is to bring two teams together in friendly rivalry and see which one can win by fair play and clever strategy . . . Those purposes can be served without ballyhooing athletic teams into great money-making machines."

It is appropriate, then, that Pop Warner's name today is most readily associated with football at its purest. Toward the end of his career, a man named Joseph Pomlin formed a 16-team youth football league in Philadelphia and named it after Warner, who was then coaching at Temple. The Pop Warner Conference eventually grew into the Pop Warner Foundation, which now sponsors more than 4,000 youth football teams across the country.

Confident that his name would live on, Warner died on September 7, 1954, at the age of eighty-three, remembered by sportswriter Red Smith as "one of the truly original minds in football." As a seminal figure in the development of the game he ranks below men like Walter Camp and Knute Rockne, and as a source of fundamental innovations he is not at the level of Amos Alonzo Stagg and Paul Brown. But by searching for clever ways to turn the game's rules to his advantage, Pop Warner played an important role in transforming the rules to the game's advantage.

71

Howard Cosell

"I feel I'm a unique personality who . . . had more impact upon sports broadcast in America than any person who has yet lived."

—Howard Cosell

Perhaps the most impressive thing one can say about Howard Cosell is that he may have been as important as he thought he was. In more than three decades as the dominant voice on the dominant network (ABC) in sports broadcasting, Cosell redefined the role of the man behind the microphone, breathing life into an athletic scene in danger of becoming stagnant.

Along the way, he aroused more emotions than all but a few figures in sports history, becoming famous for his infamy. "There has never been anyone like him in sports," wrote Mike Lupica in *Esquire*. "And there never will be anyone like him again, because no one will have the nerve."

Cosell has been described as "the supreme intimidator" . . . "an emperor in earphones" . . . "an auditory toothache" . . . "The Mouth That Bored." His thunderous voice and slow-motion staccato delivery rank among the most recognized and imitated in history. His style—challenging like a prosecuting attorney (he was once a practicing lawyer)—and his arrogance made him both a self-described pioneer and a self-indulgent villain in the world of sport, two roles in which he reveled.

"THIS . . . IS . . . HOW-WUHD . . . CO-SSSELL," he would begin, as if that statement alone—proud and defiant—was enough to inspire emotions generally reserved for the ninth inning and the fifteenth round. Usually it was. "Cosell's presence turned a game into an event," wrote Tony Kornheiser in *Sport* magazine. "People tuned in to see him. Conversation the next day wasn't about how they played, but about what he did."

"I am the most hated man on the face of the earth."
—Howard Cosell

His audience tuned in for some much-needed escapist fare and left two hours later feeling as though they had just suffered through a lecture—yet they had stayed glued to their television for two hours. Said a former ABC-TV director, "Howard Cosell is much like a comedian who must be funny all the time, except Howard has to be obnoxious all the time."

He became the man sporting America loved to hate—Reggie Jackson, Bobby Knight and John McEnroe were minor leaguers in comparison. When a *TV Guide* poll in the late 1970s revealed that Cosell was both the most and least liked sportscaster in America, it was, explained Kornheiser, "as if none of the others existed, let alone mattered."

He was ridiculed by thousands of homemade banners in stadiums across the nation. Viewers bragged about turning the sound down when Cosell came on. Taverns offered customers a chance to throw a brick through a TV screen bearing Cosell's visage. "I'd come to work Tuesday morning and the office would be filled with sacks of letters demanding that we throw him off the air," said former ABC Sports president Roone Arledge. "And I'm not talking about letters that began, 'In my opinion . . . ,' I'm talking about letters that began, 'We the undersigned . . .' and ended with 300 names."

"I never had any idea that I—that any person in sports—
could become so important in U.S. society. Who would
have dreamed it?"
—Howard Cosell

The son of Polish immigrants, he was born Howard William Cohen on March 25, 1918, in Winston-Salem, North Carolina, his family moving to Brooklyn in 1922. Cosell attended New York University, hoping to become a newspaper reporter, but his parents steered him toward a legal career. He graduated from NYU Law School in 1940 and joined the Army during World War II, quickly advancing to the rank of major.

After the war was over, he opened a labor law practice in New York, and it was his legal career that led him into broadcasting. ABC radio, upon learning, in 1953, that Cosell had written a Little League charter for an American Legion post, hired him as an unpaid host of a radio show featuring Little Leaguers interviewing big leaguers. The show lasted five years; Cosell lasted considerably longer.

When ABC hired him for a $250-a-week radio position, Cosell abandoned his law practice. He began conducting a series of one-hour radio shows exploring issues surrounding sports. By the end of the decade, he had made his way into television covering heavyweight boxing matches.

"I changed the face of television sports."
—Howard Cosell

"The '60s were really my birth, the time of the anti-hero," said Cosell. "The '60s were just right for me." Indeed, Cosell's memorable voice began to permeate sports broadcasting. He was a sports reporter on the nightly news on New York's WABC-TV. He was the voice of boxing, a major leaguebaseball announcer, an Olympic commentator, a reporter for "Wide World of Sports," and producer of several well-received sports documentaries.

And then, in 1970, Roone Arledge created what would become the longest-lasting prime time show on television: "Monday Night Football." Needing something that would "keep people tuned in even for weak games," Arledge hired Cosell, creating for him, according to *Sports Illustrated*'s Bruce Newman, "a position previously unknown in broadcast sports: blowhard."

Cosell would remain onboard through fourteen seasons and 235 telecasts. "Monday Night Football" would change a nation's viewing habits and usher in the era of prime-time sports coverage. The broadcast became at least as important as the game itself, largely because America was tuning in to hear the latest torrent of blasphemy to emerge from Cosell's lips. As Tom Shales, TV critic for *The Washington Post*, explained, "Howard Cosell is not providing commentary for the sporting event; the sporting event is providing commentary for Howard Cosell."

Indeed, in the very first "Monday Night Football" broadcast, when Cosell said of Cleveland's running back, "Leroy Kelly has not been a compelling factor tonight," it was enough to earn an outpouring of criticism from the press and the public. A quarter-century later, it is a remark expected ofcapable announcers. Such was his impact on television broadcasting.

> *"I'm it, and every one of you knows it."*
> —Howard Cosell

Cosell often claimed he was one of the three great men in American television, along with Walter Cronkite and Johnny Carson. He may not have been wrong. "In the late '60s and early '70s, he was a giant, the most dominant figure in sports media—television or radio or print," wrote Mike Lupica. "Whatever explosion happened in American sports during those years, Cosell was in the middle of it."

"Monday Night Football" catapulted Cosell into the kind of celebrity status enjoyed by few sports figures in the 1970s. Cosell became a regular on the banquet and college lecture circuit. He played himself in commercials, comic movies and television sitcoms. He even hosted his own TV variety show, which may have reached rock-bottom when he and Barbara Walters sang, "Anything you can do, I can do better."

In 1976, Cosell's celebrity had risen to such heights that he strongly considered running for a seat in the U.S. Senate. There never would have been an elected official who cared less about public opinion. Cosell never met an unpopular position he didn't like, and he challenged the Establishment at every turn. The most anti-Establishment sports figure in Cosell's early days, of course, was Cassius Clay, and Cosell was one of only a handful of sports commentators who deferred to his request and called him "Muhammad Ali" after he announced his conversion to the Nation of Islam in 1964.

Cosell also became Ali's most vocal defender when Ali refused induction into the military three years later, earning him hate mail addressed to "the nigger-loving Jew bastard." But it also earned him a genuine friendship with Ali, who explained, "We're both number one in our fields." Indeed, both thought they were the greatest; only Ali said it more succinctly.

The two developed a playful repartee, Cosell in the role of the ultimate straight man, a give-and-take described by one observer as "part put-down and almost entirely put-on." Only Cosell could stand toe-to-toe with Ali's wit; only Ali could make Cosell a supporting actor on his stage—like the time he offered $1,000 to anyone who brought him the announcer's toupee.

> *"I tell it like it is."*
> *—Howard Cosell*

Just after the Watergate scandal unfolded in 1974, Robert Daley wrote in *The New York Times Magazine*, "In a country that has been shot through with perjury at the highest level, Cosell maintains a blunt and frequently painful honesty that is all the more shocking because it comes in the otherwise bland arena of sports . . . He persistently infuriates those who think sports and religion are the same, and he defies those who advocate blandness in TV journalism."

Cosell was a no-holds-barred observer in a field populated by "Yes" men. Proclaiming that "the same maladies that exist in the real world exist in sports," he attacked everything—from Major League Baseball's reserve clause to academic abuse in college sports to the commercialization of the Olympic Games.

Of course, not every journalist took comfort in Cosell's crusades. Said *New York Post* columnist Larry Merchant, "He's the only one who makes fun and games seem like the Nuremberg trials."

> *"There are two professions in which one can be hired*
> *with little experience. One is prostitution.*
> *The other is sportscasting.*
> *Too frequently, they become the same."*
> *—Howard Cosell*

Cosell's preference for the unpopular often led his attacks to backfire on him. After all, nobody wanted to agree with Cosell. "So a knock from Howard becomes a boost," wrote *Ball Four* author Jim Bouton, "in the same way that if Idi Amin knocked Ayatollah Khomeini, we'd have to give Khomeini another look."

And when Cosell began to aim his verbal assaults at the entities that made him famous—broadcasting, boxing and football—many observers claimed he had made the transition from hot air to hypocrisy. In 1982, he refused to broadcast any more boxing matches, condemning the sport's corruption. Following the 1983 season, he left "Monday Night Football," claiming that pro football had become

"a stagnant bore." In semiretirement, Cosell became somewhat bitter and bully-
ing, attacking sports from top to bottom and trashing his former associates in an
obsessive quest to tell the truth.

Suffering from cancer, Cosell finally retired from broadcasting completely in
1992, giving up the radio shows he had held for so long—his daily two-minute
broadcast "Speaking of Sports" and his weekly interview program "Speaking of
Everything." He died on April 23, 1995.

For nearly four decades, he had worn his opinions like a badge of honor and
his ego like a crown, turning the small screen into sport's biggest pulpit. Cosell
may have reveled at the sound of his own voice, but he craved the assurance that
at least somebody was listening. "I have often told people," Mike Lupica explained, "that there was nothing more frightening in this world than looking up
as your plane left Kennedy and realizing that Howard Cosell was in the same
cabin. Because he had you there, at thirty thousand feet, a captive audience."

72

Francis Ouimet

America's sporting history has had more than its share of "Shots Heard 'Round the World." There is Bobby Thomson's home run in 1951, Chuck Bednarik's crushing tackle of Frank Gifford in 1960, Hank Aaron's historic blast of #715 in 1974, Keith Smart's jump shot in 1987, George Foreman's right-hand chop in 1994 . . . but the first and arguably the most important "shot" in any one sport was actually a collection of shots in 1913, provided by a 20-year-old golfer named Francis Ouimet.

Ouimet was born in Brookline, Massachusetts, on May 8, 1893, only a few years after the birth of American golf. In 1887, a man named Robert Lockhart had travelled to his native Scotland, where the game originated, and had returned with a set of golf lubs from the Royal and Ancient Golf Club in St. Andrews. Lockhart gave the clubs to a fellow well-to-do Scottish immigrant, John Reid, who lived in Yonkers and lives on as the "father of American golf."

On George Washington's birthday in 1888, Reid grabbed his clubs and his friends and formed a makeshift three-hole golf course out of a nearby cow pasture. There they competed in the first game of golf on American soil. A few months later, after more clubs had been ordered, the group—soon to be known as the Apple Tree Gang—expanded their course to six holes at a different cow pasture. They founded America's first permanent golf club on November 14, 1888, calling it St. Andrew's, unanimously electing Reid as president and devising a set of resolutions which have been described as the "Magna Carta" of American golf.

By 1894, several clubs had sprung up in the East, as well as a few in Chicago. The first national amateur championships were held that year, and the United States Golf Association was formed. But golf was still a fringe sport, very much removed from the lives of the masses. In 1895, *Harper's New Monthly* predicted the game "will fade, like other fashions."

At the time Francis Ouimet arrived on the scene, golf was still considered a pastime reserved for society's elite. President William Howard Taft was enthralled by the sport; the common man was not. But Ouimet was a common man. He was the son of an immigrant French-Canadian gardener who cared nothing about golf, despite the fact that the Ouimet family lived in a modest house across the street from The Country Club in Brookline.

Having grown up in a home overlooking the sixteenth green, Ouimet developed a passion for golf. He started caddying at The Country Club when he was eleven, following in the footsteps of his older brother, Wilfred. In the half-mile walk from his house to school, Ouimet would cut through the golf course, often stopping to watch the golfers play and then later mimicking his favorite swings. He and his brother even constructed a makeshift three-hole course out of the land behind their house, just as Reid had done a generation earlier. When they felt particularly confident, they crept onto The Country Club's course to sneak in a few holes.

By 1909, Ouimet was good enough to take first place in the Greater Boston Interscholastic Championship. The following year, Ouimet decided to enter the U.S. Amateur championships, played at The Country Club, but he failed to qualify in each of the next three years. However, 1913 would prove to be a banner year for the caddy-turned-competitor. He took the state amateur title, the first of eight he would win, and he finally qualified for the U.S. Amateur, though he dropped out in the second round. The U.S. Open was scheduled to be played in Brookline, in his backyard, but Ouimet had to be convinced to enter. It was the competition that scared him.

British stars Harry Vardon and Ted Ray, the Arnold Palmer and Jack Nicklaus of their day, were the tournament's prohibitive favorites. Vardon had already won five British Opens and one U.S. Open; Ray was the 1912 British Open champion and could drive the ball a country mile. "I was an amateur," Ouimet later remembered. "I played for fun. I looked on professionals as magicians who knew all the answers. This was to be a match between Vardon and Ray. I was there by mistake."

It appeared as much when Ouimet arrived on the first tee wearing a rumpled white shirt, woolen knickers and a striped necktie, a young man just out of his teens accompanied by a 10-year-old caddie playing hooky from school. Few people even knew how to pronounce his name (it is "wee-met"), but they would soon learn.

This golfer who didn't seem to belong would show Americans that he—and they—actually did. "Until then it had been an obscure sport pursued mostly by people of means," wrote Marshall Smith in *Life* magazine a half century later. "The masters were mainly English and Scottish, and when one of them condescended to play in an American tournament it was not a question of whether a Briton would win but which one. Ouimet undid all this. He put golf on Page One and hastened the day when golf would be a mass sport with Americans dominating world competition."

At the end of 54 holes, it came as no surprise that Vardon and Ray were tied for the lead with a score of 225. The surprise was that Ouimet was tied with them. The unknown was set to battle head-to-head with the world's most renowned golfers, and as Herbert Warren Wind writes in *The Story of American Golf,* "no man in his right mind could expect to stand up to the enormous pressure of the last round of a major tournament."

Ray was the first to finish his final round, struggling in with a 79 on the rain-soaked links. Vardon followed with the same score, and soon it became clear that Ouimet was the only man left who could catch the duo. At first the pressure seemed to get to him, as he stumbled to a 43 in the first nine holes and then suffered a double-bogey five on the tenth hole. "Francis would have to play the last eight holes in one under," writes Wind, "and under the circumstances that was asking for the impossible."

But he parred the eleventh, bogeyed the twelfth, birdied the thirteenth and then parred the next three. After sinking a historic 20-foot putt for birdie on the seventeenth, Ouimet was faced with a five-foot knee-knocker on the eighteenth green to secure the tie. "Then," writes Wind, "with a complete disregard for the feelings of the spectators, he stepped up to his putt as if he had not the vaguest idea that history was riding with that shot."

When Americans opened up their newspapers the following morning, they were introduced to the amazing feats of Francis Ouimet. Never had so many Americans turned their attention to golf, and never had a golf tournament on U.S. soil generated as much anticipation as the three-man playoff on September 20, 1913.

This time, Ouimet wasn't the only one intimidated by the task ahead of him. "The pressure on them and myself was entirely different," he later recalled. "Their prestige was at stake. It had finally dawned on them how terrible it would be if I beat them."

Each of the three contestants carded a 38 in the first nine holes, then it was not Ouimet who succumbed to the pressure, but his veteran rivals. Three straight pars gave Ouimet a two-stroke lead after the twelfth hole, and when Ray drove into a bunker on the fifteenth and fell four strokes behind, he was out of the game. Vardon was only one stroke back heading into the seventeenth hole, but he, too, found a bunker and had to settle for a bogey. Meanwhile, Ouimet calmly strolled up to an 18-foot birdie putt in front of some 10,000 onlookers and drilled what has come to regarded as *the* shot among Ouimet's many "Shots Heard 'Round the World."

Ouimet finished up five strokes ahead of Vardon and six ahead of Ray. It was an upset of such monumental proportions that one shocked British journalist admitted that "when we may go for weekend golfing trips to Jupiter and Mars, I will perhaps believe what little Ouimet did today."

To Americans, however, Ouimet became a significant symbol. He was a blue-collar champion, an Everyman, who had not only put an end to America's inferiority complex versus the exceptional British golfers but who had also taken the game from the privileged and handed it to the public. Barely 300,000 people played golf in 1913, but within a decade the number had risen to more than two million, as legendary professional Walter Hagen and amateur Bobby Jones built on the boom begun by Ouimet.

Ouimet remained an amateur, opting for a full-time career in a Boston brokerage firm. He never again won the U.S. Open, but he took the U.S. Amateur title in 1914 and repeated as champion again seventeen years later in 1931. Twenty years after that, he was elected captain of the Royal and Ancient Golf Club of St. Andrews, Scotland, the first foreigner so honored.

An original inductee into the PGA Hall of Fame in 1940 and the World Golf Hall of Fame in 1974, Ouimet was still shooting in the 70s well into his 70s, almost up to the day he died on September 2, 1967. To the very end, he claimed that the 1914 U.S. Amateur title was his most exciting moment in golf, but history shows that his greatest impact came one year earlier.

THE PLAYOFF SCORECARD

OUT		IN	
Par	4 4 4 4 4 4 3 4 5—36	Par	3 4 4 4 5 4 3 4 4—35 (71)
Ouimet	5 4 4 4 5 4 4 3 5—38	Ouimet	3 4 4 4 5 4 3 3 4—34 (72)
Vardon	5 4 4 4 5 3 4 4 5—38	Vardon	4 4 5 3 5 4 3 5 6—39 (77)
Ray	5 4 5 4 5 4 3 3 5—38	Ray	4 4 5 4 5 6 4 5 3—40 (78)

73

Martina Navratilova

The adjectives used to describe Martina Navratilova in the first half of her professional career were hardly benign. She was, according to one writer, "the bleached blonde Czech bisexual defector." Her surname was pronounced by many with a derisive flourish, a not-so-subtle dig at the Communist Bloc country that had spawned her and the techno-tennis machine it had produced.

By the time she retired in 1994, however, she was "Martina," a one-word megastar in the mold of Reggie and Bo and Michael, and she was a champion, a beloved American champion. She improved and endured to such an extent that she became arguably the greatest female tennis player of all time. No tennis player has won more matches, more titles or more prize money than Navratilova, who won nine Wimbeldon, four U.S. Open, three Australian Open and two French Open Championships. But it was the evolution of her public reception—from animosity to acceptance to adulation—that became her most profound legacy.

Navratilova's career is about freedom—political freedom, sexual freedom, athletic freedom. The political freedom came first. When she was born on October 18, 1956, Czechoslovakia had been under Russian rule for eight years. Her parents were divorced when she was three, and her father committed suicide a few years later, a fact Navratilova didn't discover until 1980. Her mother remarried, and Martina Subertova became Martina Navratilova. She also became a tennis prodigy.

Navratilova won the Czech championships in 1972, and the following year she was finally allowed to compete in the United States. "For the first time in my life," she wrote in her autobiography, "I was able to see America without the filter of a Communist education, Communist propaganda. And it felt right." When she began winning tennis tournaments, Czech officials began taking large cuts from her earnings and warned her about becoming too Americanized. In a move accompanied by intrigue and anxiety, she responded by defecting following the 1975 U.S. Open, an act that turned her into an overnight celebrity. In 1981, Navratilova officially became an American citizen, and she did not return to her native country until 1986, when she led the U.S. Federation Cup team to victory in Czechoslovakia.

Through one of history's most public defections, Navratilova had put a face on Cold War politics, but only a few days after taking the oath of citizenship, she was forced to brave a crisis of a different sort, an even more personal fight for freedom. "In going from Communist Czechoslovakia . . . to the forefront of the U.S. gay-rights movement," wrote *Sports Illustrated*'s Alexander Wolff, "she simply redirected her indignation."

Soon after defecting, Navratilova had come to realize that she was a lesbian. She didn't come out and announce it, but unlike many athletes, she didn't hide the truth either. She was who she was. "I never felt I would have any image problem," she explained. "I was one of the up-and-coming female tennis players in the world, and I didn't imagine my sexuality would become a major issue to anybody. It seemed like *my* business anyhow."

There are some in women's athletics, both straight and gay, who cringe with every reference to lesbianism, fearing the stereotyping of female athletes. There are others who believe that only openness can stave off the harm of innuendo. In 1981, amid the publicity over Billie Jean King being sued for "palimony" by a former lover, the media reflexively turned to Navratilova, who would suffer through a similar experience a few years later. Confronted by, as Wolff put it, "a moment of truth," she opted for honesty, remembering that when a friend had told her that society wasn't ready for homosexuality, she had responded by saying, "We're society, too."

"Martina was the first legitimate superstar who literally came out while she was a superstar," said Donna Lopiano, executive director of the Women's Sports Foundation. "She exploded the barrier by putting it on the table. She basically said this part of my life doesn't have anything to do with me as a tennis player. Judge me for who I am."

The impact of Navratilova's acknowledgment of her sexuality as she neared the peak of her career cannot be underestimated. It has been said that Jackie Robinson gained full acceptance in the major leagues when he began to get thrown out of ballgames for arguing with the umpire. His color was no longer an issue; just his mouth. Navratilova forced much the same attitude toward her sexuality with a fearless take-it-or-leave-it attitude that seemed to diminish the magnitude of the revelation. She was advised to put men in the friends' box at Wimbledon, but she didn't, saying "I couldn't live with myself if I put up a front like that." And, thus, when a male sportswriter asked, "Martina, are you still a lesbian?" she replied, "Are you still the alternative?"

As Mariah Burton Nelson explains in her book, *Are We Winning Yet: How Women Are Changing Sports and Sports Are Changing Women*, "By quietly acknowledging her long-term relationship, she has forced sportswriters and sports-casters to be equally nonchalant about it. It would be as ludicrous to 'accuse' her of lesbianism as it would to accuse Nancy Lopez of being Hispanic or Jackie Joyner-Kersee of being black."

Yet Navratilova's honesty cost her millions of dollars in endorsement oppor-tunities when corporate homophobia, or at least a fear of their consumers' aver-sion to Navratilova's lifestyle, closed the same doors that were open to the likes of Chris Evert and Jennifer Capriati.

Having caused many Americans to reexamine their attitudes about sexuality and sports, she then began to broaden the definition of femininity in athletics, embarking on a state-of-the-art training regimen and showing that muscle was not confined to the masculine domain. In a 1986 *Sport* magazine tribute to Navratilova, Arthur Ashe wrote that she was "successfully challenging old myths about the place of competitive sport within the changing confines of femininity."

With society historically interpreting sports as a masculine endeavor, many women have been conditioned to almost fear athletic prowess. But Navratilova's success and popularity will undoubtedly go a long way toward end-ing the image of the reluctant female athlete. As she admitted, "The image of women is changing now. You don't have to be pretty for people to come and see you play. At the same time, if you're a good athlete, it doesn't mean you're not a woman."

And Navratilova certainly ranks as one of history's most talented athletes. As a youth she had dreamed of playing at Wimbledon, and in her first appearance at the All-England Club, in 1973, she knelt down and touched the sacred grass. She did the same twenty-one years later in her last appearance, having barely missed out on what would have been her tenth Wimbledon title. By then she was no longer the Czechoslovakian, the defector, the bisexual, the brute. She was just Martina, her biggest victory.

74

Alexander Cartwright

James Naismith, the inventor of basketball, is ranked fourth among *The Sports 100*. Why then is Alexander Cartwright, widely touted as the inventor of baseball, ranked seventy-fourth? Because in his case, fact has been overwhelmed by fiction.

Cartwright is perhaps sport's most underrated and overrated figure. He is underrated because the myth of Abner Doubleday, which has no basis in fact, still retains the luster of truth to the general public. Doubleday's hold on the legend of baseball's creation has obscured Cartwright's very real role in the process.

On the other hand, in an attempt to set the record straight, many historians have given Cartwright far too much credit for designing the modern game. It can safely be said that nobody invented baseball. The game simply evolved, over many years, from a British game called rounders—also known (in various forms) as town ball, goal ball, stool ball and old cat. Giving Cartwright credit for its invention is part oversimplification and part jingoism. As baseball historian John Thorn claims in the 1993 edition of *Total Baseball*, Cartwright, like Doubleday, has become "a tool of those who wished to establish baseball as the product of an identifiable spark of American ingenuity, without foreign or Darwinian taint."

That is not to say, however, that Cartwright wasn't important. He has been included in this book for one basic reason—he suggested the formation of the Knickerbocker Base Ball Club of New York, the team that essentially marks the beginning of organized baseball.

Cartwright, born in New York, on April 17, 1820, descended from a long line of sea captains, but by the 1840s he was a volunteer firefighter and bank teller, as well as a 6-foot-2, 210-pound sports enthusiast. Beginning in 1842, a group of men had consistently gathered at the corner of 4th Avenue and 27th Street in

Manhattan to play baseball. It was Cartwright who suggested the group organize itself into a club, and on September 23, 1845, the Knickerbockers were born. The club recruited more members and moved its games to Elysian Fields in Hoboken, New Jersey.

The Knickerbockers produced a constitution and baseball's first set of formal playing rules, which included several distinct differences from the many forms of town ball popular in the East. According to historian Harold Seymour in *Baseball: The Early Years*, "Baseball's rules have been refined and polished over the years, but the hard Knickerbocker core had remained central. The four-base diamond; 90-foot base paths; three out, all out; batting in rotation; throwing out runners or touching them; nine-man teams, with each player covering a definite position; the location of the pitcher's box in relation to the diamond as a whole—these are fundamental in baseball."

The Knickerbocker rules came to be known as the New York Game, which surpassed the Massachusetts Game with its smaller ball, ten to fourteen to a side, wooden stakes instead of bases and 100 runs needed to win. The Knickerbockers played a pivotal role in standardizing the rules and inspiring the formation of additional clubs. On March 10, 1858, nearly two dozen such clubs formed the National Association of Base Ball Players (NABBP), using primarily the Knickerbocker rules. Within eight years, the Association included more than 200 clubs from seventeen states.

"The Knickerbockers blazed a path others were to follow," Seymour contends. "If any individual or group must be singled out as the founder of modern baseball, the credit has to go to Alexander Cartwright and his friends. Theirs was the first step in the evolution of an important entertainment business which in a matter of decades became commercialized on a nationwide scale."

Certainly, Cartwright and his friends should be credited with getting the ball rolling, but to what extent? And more importantly, what do we know about Cartwright's role? The answer to the latter question is, not much. The plaque honoring Alexander Joy Cartwright, Jr., in Cooperstown reads, "'FATHER OF MODERN BASEBALL.' Set bases 90 feet apart. Established 9 innings as a game and 9 players as team." None of it is actually true.

First, many men have been credited with "fathering" baseball, and four of them—Albert Spalding, Harry Wright, William Hulbert and Henry Chadwick—are ranked far higher than Cartwright among *The Sports 100*. Second, Cartwright was not solely responsible for the creation of the original Knickerbocker rules. He was simply one of four men on the rules committee.

The most important innovations included in the club's original rules were actually the concepts of foul territory, a baseball diamond instead of a square and the notion of tagging a runner or a base instead of throwing the ball at him. Nine innings, nine players and ninety feet came later. The 1845 rules specify only that the bases be placed forty-two paces apart, which Thorn estimates produced approximately 75-foot basepaths, and many of the early games were played with eight, ten or eleven players to a side.

Even in what has been called baseball's first game between two different teams—when the Knickerbockers faced the New York Base Ball Club on June 19, 1846, at Elysian Fields—the game lasted only four innings. The "road team" beat the Knickerbockers 23-1 in four innings because, according to the new rules, they were the first team to reach 21 "aces" or runs. Many references to that game have named Cartwright as baseball's first umpire, but the scorebook from the game lists no umpire.

Though the Knickerbocker contribution of set positions was a vital innovation, it may have been another Knickerbocker besides Cartwright, a man named Daniel Lucius Adams, who created the position of shortstop. In fact, Adams may even be more responsible than Cartwright for the 90-foot basepaths, nine men to a side and even a subsequent rule change that finally required that a ball be caught on the fly to register an out.

The Knickerbockers were clearly an influential force in the evolution of baseball, and their creation, inspired by Cartwright, represents a seminal moment in the development of the game. But there is even evidence that several ballclubs, including the New York Club, may have preceded the Knickerbockers.

In addition, the Knickerbockers became almost obsolete within a decade. They tried—and failed—to restrict the game to what they considered their higher social class. By the time the NABBP was formed in 1858, no Knickerbockers were among the first elected officers of the organization. Seymour explains that "as the scene changed, the Knickerbockers were increasingly reluctant to participate in the great growth of baseball interest, so the show simply passed them by."

As for Cartwright, unlike other sporting pioneers such as James Naismith, Walter Camp, George Halas and Bill France, Sr.—men who continued to watch over their creations long after laying the foundation—he left the scene rather abruptly. In 1849, only four years after the Knickerbockers were formed, Cartwright left New York for the California gold rush.

Historians have often stated that he organized baseball games during the long trip West, introducing the New York Game everywhere from Pittsburgh to St. Louis to San Francisco. But he stayed in California for only a few days, moving to Hawaii and never returning to the continental U.S. By the time he died on July 12, 1892, he was better known as a civic figure in Honolulu than a man who had anything to do with the origins of baseball.

For spurring the organization of the Knickerbockers, Cartwright has earned a spot in *The Sports 100*. But to place him any higher would be to substitute comfortable legend for the complexities of fact.

SO WHO'S ABNER DOUBLEDAY?

Abner Doubleday was not the inventor of baseball; he was the invention of baseball people. In fact, Doubleday was nothing more than a convenient creation to satisfy a few Americans' insecurities about America's game.

The Doubleday myth grew out of a friendly feud between two of baseball's most influential figures, pitcher-turned-executive Albert Spalding and journalist Henry Chadwick. Chadwick was certain that baseball had originated in his native England, having evolved from the game of rounders. Spalding, like most observers, had accepted Chadwick's arguments through the nineteenth century, but time changed his perspective. By 1905, he was using the pages of his annual baseball guide to attack Chadwick's contentions. He sought to prove that the most American of games was American in origin.

To do so, Spalding formed a seven-man commission, which relied on a letter from an elderly mining engineer named Abner Graves, who stated that baseball was invented in 1839 in Cooperstown, New York, by a future Civil War hero named Abner Doubleday. On December 30, 1907, the commission concluded that baseball originated in the States and was first designed by Doubleday. It was later discovered that Doubleday was at West Point in 1839 and that none of his writings ever even mentioned the game, but the commission's ruling came to be accepted as fact.

75

Gary Davidson

"What man, more than any other, has had the greatest impact on professional sports in America?" wondered a 1977 editorial in *The Sporting News*. "You'd have to say Gary Davidson."

Hindsight renders the statement humorous, but at the time it was no laughing matter. Davidson's influence on professional sports in the 1970s was dramatic, if brief, and while his name has faded into the background, for a moment he was at the forefront of a sporting revolution.

Who is Gary Davidson? In 1967, the 10-team American Basketball Association was formed as a challenger to the 21-year-old NBA. Davidson was the league's founder and president. In 1972, the 12-team World Hockey Association initiated a league war against the 56-year-old NHL. Davidson was the league's founder and president. In 1974, the 12-team World Football League took on the 55-year-old NFL. Davidson was the league's founder and president.

Before all of this, Davidson had simply been a tax and finance attorney in Orange County, born August 13, 1934, a graduate of UCLA law school who had paid his way by working in a mortuary. Suddenly, however, when he and co-founder Dennis Murphy hatched the idea for the ABA, Davidson took on the role of sports mogul.

His upstart leagues were hardly something to sneeze at. They attracted stars and spawned stars. They had Bobby Hull, Rick Barry, Calvin Hill and Spencer Haywood; Connie Hawkins, Julius Erving, Gordie Howe and Larry Csonka; Artis Gilmore, Paul Warfield, Ken Stabler and Wayne Gretzky. Davidson formed the teams, the teams recruited the stars, the stars made the leagues, and the leagues made a difference.

Davidson was no long-term visionary. He was, in fact, known for keeping one franchise in each league for himself, selling out at an enormous profit, and then moving on to his next venture. His fifteen minutes of fame lasted about a decade, and in that time, his impact on sports was essentially a smaller version of that produced by several figures in *The Sports 100*.

Davidson was part Walter O'Malley. As O'Malley had opened up the sporting landscape by moving Major League Baseball to the West Coast, Davidson did so by creating a new notion of what constituted a "major league" city. All he had to do was turn on his considerable charm for a select group of millionaires and appeal to their vanity, their desire to be famous as well as rich. Suddenly, there were major league franchises in places like San Diego and Charlotte, Miami and Memphis, Indianapolis and Oakland.

Davidson was part Marvin Miller, a maverick interloper whose actions rearranged the salary structures in the established leagues. Nothing inflates salaries like bidding wars, and nothing initiates bidding wars like two leagues fighting for superiority. During the life of the ABA for instance, the average NBA salary quadrupled due to the inter-league competition for players. By 1970, forty-four pro basketball players, fifteen in the ABA, enjoyed salaries of at least $100,000, a number reserved for only Bill Russell and Wilt Chamberlain a few years earlier. Like Miller (and Curt Flood), Davidson also challenged the reserve clause. He directed his teams to draft any player with an expiring NHL contract, claiming the reserve system was illegal.

Davidson was part Bill Veeck, a man allergic to the accepted order of things and fully aware of the power of publicity. His rebel leagues, according to Rushin, "were designed to be the *mod* alternative to the *square* professional sports Establishment." The ABA was famous for its red-white-and-blue basketballs; the WFL boasted gold-and-orange striped footballs; the WHA used dark-blue hockey pucks.

Davidson was part Pop Warner. Much like the legendary football coach's frequent attempts to find strategic loopholes had spurred college football's rules committee to refine the game, Davidson's leagues provoked responses as well. After the World Football League placed goalposts at the back of the end zone, the NFL followed suit. Likewise, the ABA gave the NBA the three-point shot and the All-Star slam-dunk contest.

In fact, with the slam-dunk contest and with players like Hawkins, Erving and a rookie named David Thompson in 1976, the ABA played a significant role in taking the game above the rim. By featuring Hawkins and Spencer Haywood, two men who hadn't finished college, the league also set the stage for the early entry process, which has become so standard that it is now bigger news when a top player actually stays in school.

Davidson was part Branch Rickey. Just as Rickey's attempts to start a third major league, the Continental League, had spurred Major League Baseball to expand in the early '60s, Davidson's organizations produced the same effect on the NBA and the NHL. During the ABA's nine-year run, the NBA added the San Diego (later Houston) Rockets, Seattle SuperSonics, Milwaukee Bucks, Phoenix Suns, Portland Trail Blazers, Cleveland Cavaliers, New Orleans (later Utah) Jazz and Buffalo Braves, who became the L.A. Clippers. During the WHA's seven years of existence, the NHL added the New York Islanders, Atlanta (later Calgary) Flames, Washington Capitals and Kansas City Scouts, who became the New Jersey Devils.

And finally, Davidson was part Lamar Hunt. While Hunt's American Football League survived to be part of a true merger with the NFL, Davidson's creations were involved in something closer to absorption—but it was something, nonetheless.

In 1976, while the rest of the league folded, four ABA teams—the Denver Nuggets, Indiana Pacers, New York (soon to be New Jersey) Nets and San Antonio Spurs—joined the NBA. And then in 1979, four WHA clubs—the Winnipeg Jets, Edmonton Oilers, Quebec Nordiques and New England (Hartford) Whalers—joined the NHL.

Only the World Football League was a complete failure. It already suffered by going against perhaps the nation's most powerful league, one that had already expanded from twelve to twenty-six teams only a few years earlier, and it would lose $20 million in its first season. In fact, 1974 turned out to be its only full season. The league's first title game, World Bowl I, would come to be called World Bowl I-and-Only.

After the WFL folded midway through the 1975 season, as the ABA and WHA prepared to merge, and after his wife and much of his money were suddenly gone, Davidson traveled to Haiti, where he lived in self-imposed exile. The man who *Sports Illustrated* had called "one of the most influential figures in the history of professional sport" in 1975 was largely forgotten. But Davidson eventually returned to California and developed retirement communities, making all his money back and more. He is no longer famous, no longer the mod maverick of sports, but his influence lingers.

76

Julius Erving

"There have been some people better off the court—like a few mothers and the pope," Pat Riley once said about Julius Erving. "But there was only one Dr. J, the player."

Erving's most significant influence came in his role as a transitional figure. He was, essentially, a bridge to prosperity during a period when professional basketball teetered on a precipice. Expansion had diluted the impact of rivalries; drug rumors had tarnished the NBA's image; an apparent backlash from the white public against an increasingly black game presented the league with an uncertain future. But with Erving as the game's ambassador, pro basketball would survive and then thrive.

"Erving," writes Nelson George in *Elevating the Game*, "seemed an irresistible force of nature, an embodiment of all that was innovative and exciting, of the ability to intimidate through his improvisations." On the court, he was a descendant of Elgin Baylor and Connie Hawkins, a forerunner to Michael Jordan and Scottie Pippen. But he was the vital link between the two generations.

He was among the first basketball figures to blur the line between athleticism and artistry, a dichotomy that became one of the most appealing facets of the game. Erving didn't only do things well: he did things nobody thought could be done. He took the game higher, literally and figuratively.

"I always had the feeling," said St. John's University coach Lou Carnesecca, "that one time he would lift off and rise through the glass, out of the arena, and disappear into space." Hang time became a marketable product, with Erving as its most expert practitioner. Each time the 6-foot-7 forward rose toward the basket, a ball cradled in his enormous hands, hopes for the future of pro basketball clung to his cape.

Off the court, Erving was just as important. He was smart, articulate, friendly. He was, as a poll of the sports media later revealed, the nicest guy in sports. In short, he was everything the "new breed" of hoops star was not supposed to be. To disenchanted white fans, he made them think twice about disregarding the game. To eager black players, he was the ideal. As David Halberstam explains in *The Breaks of the Game*, "Erving, both as an athlete and as a man, intelligent, proud, respected, was so important to black players, he was to them an almost mythic figure, the epitome of the black game."

Yet, the man who helped bring playground excitement to professional basketball was born into a middle class family in Roosevelt, New York, on February 22, 1950. He was Julius Winfield Erving II, a child of Long Island, not quite the pedigree expected to produce the man who would later personify basketball's playground aesthetic. He would attract and discard a handful of nicknames— Jewel, The Claw, Black Moses—until finally "The Doctor" caught on. An ABA teammate would later cap it off with an initial: Dr. J.

Erving attended the University of Massachusetts, averaging more than 26 points and 20 rebounds per game. Hoping to pay his mother's medical bills, he left college early and signed a $500,000 contract with the Virgina Squires of the upstart ABA in 1971. The team's management had never seen him play when they signed him.

The Doctor spent five years in the ABA, two with Virginia and three with the New York Nets, the latter being one of four teams to be absorbed by the NBA following the 1976 season. Erving led the ABA in scoring three times, he was named league MVP three times, and he won two championships with the Nets. In 1974 and 1976, he accomplished all three feats.

The ABA had no television contract when his skills were unveiled at the professional level, yet the word spread that Erving had a look (bushy Afro, goatee, enormous hands and kneepads) and a style (one-handed, airborne) all his own. He was the image of professional basketball's above-the-rim destiny; he made the ABA shine and the NBA salivate.

As Alexander Wolff wrote in *Sports Illustrated*, the NBA "had the tradition, the major markets, the network contracts, but unless you bought a ticket to an ABA game, you couldn't see *the Doc-ta*. If Erving didn't actually force the 1976 ABA-NBA merger, he was surely the most valuable asset the young league brought to the table."

Erving's peak came in the relative obscurity of the ABA, yet he still seems to have been to hoop highlight films and instant replays what Mickey Mantle was to bleachers and tape measures. His career was defined by moments in which he seemed to push the envelope of accomplishment on the court, as if to present a sneak preview of the entertainment bonanza awaiting NBA fans in the ensuing years.

There was the first-ever slam-dunk contest at halftime of the 1976 ABA All-Star Game in Denver. On his final attempt, Erving outpointed his opponents by taking off from just inside the free throw line and finishing off with a windmill slam. It remains the dunk that spawned all others.

There was his six-game peformance in the 1976 ABA Finals, when his Nets beat the Denver Nuggets thanks to Erving's 226 points and 85 rebounds. Bobby Jones, the man who defended him and who later teamed with him on the Philadelphia 76ers, remarked, "He destroys the adage that I've always been taught—that one man can't do it alone."

After a contract dispute led New York to sell Erving to Philadelphia in October 1976 for a reported $3 million, the 76ers made it to the 1977 NBA Finals, but blew a two-game lead to the Portland Trail Blazers. They were runners-up again in 1980 and 1982, finally redeeming themselves six years later when, with the help of Moses Malone in the middle, they lost only one playoff game en route to the title. An Erving jump shot late in Game 4 clinched the championship. Said the Doctor, finally feeling vindicated as an NBA player, "I didn't find that shot. It found me."

It proved to be Erving's only NBA title, and in 1987 he finally called it quits after averaging 24.2 points, 8.5 rebounds, 4.2 assists, 1.9 steals and 1.7 blocked shots per game over his pro career. Only a few weeks before his retirement, he threw in 38 points en route to joining Kareem Abdul-Jabbar and Wilt Chamberlain as basketball's only 30,000-point scorers. Moses Malone has since joined the list; Erving remains the only noncenter.

In the latter half of Erving's career, he was somewhat overshadowed—by the rivalry between Larry Bird and Magic Johnson, by the sustained excellence of Abdul-Jabbar, by the emergence of Michael Jordan. The NBA became the best-marketed product this side of Disney World. But, as thearchitect of the '80s, NBA commissioner David Stern, pointed out, "The guy who really started it was Julius Erving, who was a public relations genius." What Jordan became, Erving began. Jordan was Eddie Murphy to Erving's Richard Pryor.

He was "a rare figure," wrote Wolff, "someone who embodied the most old-fashioned virtues while performing the most futuristic and apparently super-human feats." Basketball was in dire need of projecting an aura of stability yet excitement, class yet creativity. The Doctor provided it all, giving the game a much-needed blood transfusion.

77

Bobby Hull

Robert Marvin Hull was born on January 3, 1939, in Point Anne, Ontario, a town of 1,000 people. But this one-in-a-thousand child grew up to be a one-in-a-million man for the National Hockey League. The NHL, when he first joined the Chicago Blackhawks in 1957, was vastly different from the NHL when he played his last game with the Hartford Whalers in 1980. And Hull was more responsible for that change than any other hockey figure.

He was the sport's poster boy, the "Golden Jet," described by one Chicago society page columnist as "a statue come alive from the Golden Age of Greece, incredibly handsome even without his front teeth." He was the fastest skater in the game—reaching speeds of 28.3 miles per hour with the puck, 29.7 miles per hour without it. And he had hockey's hardest slapshot—clocked at 118.3 miles per hour, nearly 35 miles per hour faster than the league average.

The end result was a scoring machine. In Hull's twenty-three seasons in professional hockey, he collected 913 goals and 895 assists for 1808 points, a total bested only by Wayne Gretzky and Gordie Howe. He started off slowly with 13 goals in his rookie season and 18 the following year, but he exploded for a league-leading 39 goals in 1959–1960 and he wouldn't tally less than 30 for another sixteen years.

After leading Chicago to its only Stanley Cup victory in the last half century in 1961, Hull became only the third person to reach the 50-goal plateau the following year, totalling exactly that to match the single-season mark. Five years later, he embarked on a Roger Maris–like quest to break the 50-goal barrier. He recorded his 50th in the 57th game, and his effort to collect number 51 became the biggest sports story of the year. He finally notched it in his 61st game in front of a packed house at Chicago Stadium. He would finish with 54 goals in the 70-game season and then lead the league three more times over the next three seasons, setting a new mark with 58 goals in 76 games in 1968–1969.

In all, Hull received the Art Ross Trophy as the league's top goal-scorer a record seven times. He also twice received the Hart Trophy as NHL MVP (1965 and 1966), but a more important honor came in 1969 when he received the Lester Patrick Trophy for outstanding service to hockey in the United States. It wasn't a nod to the way he carried a team; it was a reflection of the way he carried the league.

Sports Illustrated's E. M. Swift wrote that Hull "may be the player most responsible for hockey as we know it today. As great as Howe was, as great as Orr, Esposito and Beliveau were, they didn't have Hull's charisma. His style of play matched his personality—open, dramatic, uncompromising and utterly joyful.

Hull generated excitement and attention as, according to historian Stan Fischler, he became "the symbol of the modern, flashy, hockey player. Unlike Bobby Orr, who was injury prone, Hull wasn't. And he was much more gregarious, a terrific salesman for the game. He, more than anybody, inspired the big expansion of the NHL. Just like Howie Morenz was in the '20s, that's the way Hull was in the '60s."

The NHL had not been challenged by a competing league since 1926, and by Hull's rookie season it had settled into a six-team circuit with franchises in Montreal, Toronto, New York, Boston, Detroit and Chicago. But by the time Hull retired, the league boasted more than three times as many teams. Six teams were added in 1967 and two more every other year from 1970 through 1974. Two teams merged into one in 1978, and four more were added in 1979, bringing the total to twenty-one heading into the '80s.

While Hull's performance may have led to NHL expansion in the '60s, the league's growth in the '70s was primarily a reaction to its first challenge in nearly five decades—from the World Hockey Association. And just as Joe Namath's three-year, $400,000 deal with the New York Jets in 1965 had immediately brought much-needed publicity to the American Football League, Hull's $1.75 million deal with the WHA's Winnipeg Jets in 1972 not only made him hockey's richest player, it also legitimized a league.

He wasn't the only big-name defector. In fact, Gordie Howe would even come out of retirement to play with his sons on the WHA's Houston Aeros. But the "Golden Jet" and the Jets were still the league's biggest draw. As Fischler explained, "Hull's defection from the National Hockey League was the major reason for the WHA's ability to become the game's second major hockey league overnight."

The NHL initiated lawsuits in an attempt to prevent Hull from skipping town. As a result, he missed fifteen games, yet he still reached the 50-goal plateau for the sixth time at the age of thirty-four. He added 52 assists to his 51 goals to finish fourth in the league scoring race in only sixty-three games. The Jets won the West Division title; Hull was named league MVP.

He would win the MVP award again in 1975 after scoring 77 goals, a professional record since surpassed only by Wayne Gretzky, Mario Lemieux and Hull's son, Brett. He remained a Jet for each of the WHA's seven seasons of existence, but the finale to his career would occur in the NHL, as the league absorbed four WHA teams, including the Jets.

Hull scored six times in the 1979–1980 season, spending his last few games with the Hartford Whalers and retiring as the highest-scoring left wing in hockey history. He had come full circle. He was back with an American team in what was, once again, professional hockey's only major league. But largely due to Hull, the NHL in his first season and the NHL in his last were leagues apart.

A Goalie's Worst Nightmare

The two men most often given credit for introducing the slapshot to hockey in the 1950s are Bernie "Boom-Boom" Geoffrion of the Montreal Canadiens and Andy Bathgate of the New York Rangers. But it was Bobby Hull's success with the shot, in particular, which led to its becoming the weapon of choice, permanently altering offensive and defensive strategy on the ice.

A few years after unveiling his slapshot, Hull transformed hockey offense once again when he and longtime linemate Stan Mikita accidentally discovered the wonders of the banana blade. Upon discovering a warped stick with a curved blade, the duo found that it turned an innocent shot into an unpredictable one. Hull and Mikita were hooked, so to speak, and soon the curved blade was so popular—and so potentially dangerous to goalies—that the league was forced to legislate that the curve be limited to a certain size.

So what did a goaltender have to contend with? With Hull, it was probably something like facing a Nolan Ryan fastball that moved like a Hoyt Wilhelm knuckleball.

78

Roberto Clemente

Baseball from the mid-1950s to the mid-1970s was the playground of any number of icons—Willie Mays, Henry Aaron, Mickey Mantle, Ernie Banks, Bob Gibson, Sandy Koufax—but none, as it turns out, made more of a transcendental impact than Roberto Clemente.

He was, in many ways, a Hispanic Jackie Robinson, a man of courage and conviction, a peerless talent, fearlessly outspoken and, most importantly, a symbol for hundreds of players who followed his lead and turned major league baseball into an ever-increasing international stage. As *Sports Illustrated*'s Steve Wulf wrote in 1994, "Today, one in every seven major league players is a Latin American, and for virtually all of them, Roberto Clemente stands as their most beloved pioneer."

He was certainly not baseball's first Latin American player. Light-skinned Hispanics had appeared in the major leagues just after the turn of the century. And he was not the game's first Latin American star. Dark-skinned Minnie Minoso from Cuba began a brilliant career in 1951 that would have landed him in the Hall of Fame had he been allowed entry to the big leagues before his late twenties.

Nor was Clemente a lone Hispanic standout during his lengthy career. Among the others were Mexican Bobby Avila, Dominicans Juan Marichal and the Alou brothers, Cubans Tony Oliva and Bert Campaneris, and Vic Power and Orlando Cepeda from Puerto Rico. In fact, Cepeda was the first of Clemente's countrymen to achieve big league stardom, winning the Rookie of the Year Award in 1958.

But it was Clemente who came to represent the Hispanic players' struggle for acceptance and who became the voice of that struggle. He began as "Bob" Clemente, misunderstood and stereotyped; he became Roberto Clemente, respected by baseball figures, revered by baseball fans.

Roberto Walker Clemente was born on August 18, 1934, in a barrio of Carolina, Puerto Rico. Having watched his father toil in the sugarcane fields, he dreamed of an escape through baseball. At age fourteen, Clemente earned a tryout with a company softball team, and two years later he began to play for Juncos in the Puerto Rican Double-A League. He also starred as a track athlete. In fact, he was a viable candidate for the 1952 Summer Olympic team, but he chose to sign a professional baseball contract instead.

Clemente, by now a rightfielder, had been invited to an open tryout held jointly by the Puerto Rican League's Santurce Cangrejeros (Crabbers) and the Brooklyn Dodgers. The Dodger scout, ironically, was Al Campanis, whose racist remarks thirty-five years later would trigger a reexamination of prejudice in the game. Enthralled by Clemente's potential, Campanis was unable to sign him until he finished his final year of high school, so Clemente played with Santurce and played so well that, by 1954, he was no longer a secret known only to the Dodgers.

After a bidding war between the Dodgers and the Giants, Clemente chose Jackie Robinson's team, signing for a $5,000 salary and a $10,000 bonus. However, Brooklyn, possibly adhering to an unspoken racial quota, was less interested in playing Clemente than in preventing him from playing with Willie Mays and the Giants. He was assigned to the Dodgers' top farm club, the same Montreal Royals team Robinson had broken in with but he played sparingly, recording only 148 official at-bats. "The idea was to make me look bad," Clemente recalled. "They wanted to make me mad enough to go home."

Clemente was on the verge of packing his bags and returning home, until the Pittsburgh Pirates made it known to him that they were eager to choose him in the postseason draft (as a bonus player, he was eligible). More irony: Pittsburgh's general manager at the time was Branch Rickey. The Pirates drafted Clemente in the first round, and though at the time he didn't even know where Pittsburgh was, he and the city soon became synonymous.

The Pirates had lost more than 100 games in three straight seasons, and so they were willing to give Clemente an opportunity to play early in the 1955 season, Ironically again, his first start came against the Dodgers, and the man he replaced in right field was a Latin American, Roman Mejias. The 20-year-old batted .255 in 124 games as a rookie, and though his hitting would improve with age he was already displaying what many consider to be perhaps the greatest throwing arm in big league history. He recorded 10 assists in his first 50 games, and even though runners quickly learned not to go for the extra base against Clemente, he would still go on to lead the league in assists five times.

Clemente batted over .300 only once in his first five seasons, experiencing some difficulty adjusting to life in Pittsburgh. His fiery temper often got the best off him, and he took it out on batting helmets, on umpires and, increasingly, on the media. Unschooled in gee-whiz modesty, and unwilling to ignore perceived slights, Clemente rarely saw eye-to-eye with ethnocentric writers who insisted on calling him "Bob" or "Bobby" in print.

"It became easier to ignore Clemente than to hear what he had to say," writes biographer Thomas W. Gilbert. "As a result, he became almost invisible in the sports pages. A reader can go through back issues of *The Sporting News* from the late 1950s to the early 1960s and find countless articles on Groat, Hoak, Law and Mazeroski but hardly run across any mention of Clemente."

Prejudice seemed to rear its ugly head following the 1960 season, during which Clemente had batted .314 with 94 runs batted in, as the Pirates beat the formidable Yankees on Bill Mazeroski's World Series–winning home run. Shortstop Dick Groat, who hit .325 with 50 RBIs, was voted National League MVP. Clemente finished eighth, behind three teammates.

Proud and sensitive to criticism, Clemente was hurt by the outcome of the voting, his relationship with the press—who described him in mildly racist terms ("chocolate-colored islander") and quoted him in broken English ("I no play so gut yet")—continuing along its stormy path. "The Latin American player doesn't get the recognition he deserves. Neither does the Negro player, unless he does something really spectacular, like Willie Mays," Clemente would say. "I am an American citizen. But some people act like they think I live in the jungle someplace. To those people, we are outsiders, foreigners."

Clemente took great pains to never appear as if he were a foreigner in his native Puerto Rico, returning to play winter ball for the bulk of his career, even as he totalled more than 9,000 major league at-bats. Yet, in America, he had earned a reputation as a hot dog and a hypochondriac. Said his former manager, Danny Murtaugh, "He was such a truthful man, it backfired on him sometimes. If you asked him if his shoulder hurt, he'd say, 'Yes, it does.' Then he'd go out and throw a guy out at the plate. That's how he got the hypochondriac label."

But as the 1960s progressed, Clemente's performance began to rank him with baseball's best, and doubts about his motivation began to be replaced by respect for his accomplishments, on and off the field. In 1961, his peers voted him an All-Star, the first of twelve such selections, and he responded with a game-winning hit in the exhibition. He batted .351 that year, taking his first batting title, and added a league- and career-best 27 outfield assists to win the Gold Glove Award, also the first of twelve. That same year, Orlando Cepeda led the National League with 46 home runs and 142 RBIs, and both returned home to their native Puerto Rico to a cheering throng of thousands.

Clemente's lunging hitting style was unorthodox—Lou Boudreau called him "one of the worst-looking great hitters I've ever seen"—but it was remarkably potent. From 1961 through 1972, he averaged .331 with 17 homers and 81 RBIs. He won his second batting title in 1964 (.339) and his third in 1965 (.329), following those performances with a .317-29 homer-119 RBI campaign in 1966. This time, Clemente was voted N.L. Most Valuable Player, the first Hispanic to receive the National League award. He narrowly beat out Sandy Koufax, who had pitched the Dodgers to a pennant by going 27-9 with a 1.73 ERA, but who had described how to pitch to Clemente by saying, "Roll the ball."

In accepting the MVP Award, Clemente was typically self-confident and, also typically, aware of the significance of his role. "When I was a kid I felt that baseball was great to America. Always, they said Babe Ruth was the best there was . . . but Babe Ruth was an American player," he said. "What we needed was a Puerto Rican player they could say that about, someone to look up to and try to equal . . . I've had many good years. I've won the batting title three times and now I've won the MVP. This makes me happy because now the people feel that if I could do it, then maybe they could do it."

He followed his MVP season with perhaps his best campaign in 1967, winning his fourth batting title (.357) and adding 23 home runs, 110 RBIs and 103 runs. This time, his countryman, Cepeda, won the trophy. Clemente would bat over .340 three more times, but it was his performance in the 1971 World Series, at the age of thirty-seven, that became the final feather in his cap.

The Pirates had won their first pennant since 1960, but the defending champion Baltimore Orioles had averaged 106 wins over the previous three seasons and were prohibitive favorites. After the Orioles won the first two games, one writer announced, "The World Series is no longer a contest. It's an atrocity; it's the Germans marching through Belgium."

But it became Clemente's march toward immortality, as a national television audience watched him lead the Pirates to a seven-game triumph with what Roger Angell described as "a kind of baseball that none of us had seen before—throwing and running and hitting at something close to the level of absolute perfection, playing to win but also playing the game as if it were a form of punishment for everyone else on the field." Clemente batted .414 with 12 hits, two home runs and a .759 slugging percentage, earning the World Series MVP Award.

Clemente capped off his career with his 3,000th hit, a double off the wall in his final at-bat of the 1972 regular season. It actually would have been his 3,001st hit, but a smash off the opposing second baseman's glove a day earlier was quickly changed from "H" for hit to "E" for error on the scoreboard even as umpires were retrieving the ball for the slugger.

The decision would contribute to the Clemente legend, as his 3,000th hit proved to be his last. Two days before Christmas, in 1972, a severe earthquake devastated the capital city of Managua, in Nicaragua. Adding to his endless list of charitable crusades, Clemente volunteered to serve as chairman of the Puerto Rican relief effort, piling supplies into an old DC-7 and preparing to go there himself, in part to make sure the relief would go to the earthquake victims instead of to Nicaraguan dictator Anastasio Somoza's army.

The airplane took off just after 9 P.M. on New Year's Eve, but it never arrived, crashing into the ocean after developing engine trouble. The Coast Guard found the pilot's remains, but Clemente's body was never found.

Clemente can still be found, however, in the faces of the thousands of children he touched, in the memories of Pittsburgh fans and Puerto Rican citizens (to whom he is close to a deity) and in the hearts of the many Latin American major leaguers he inspired. As one letter of condolence to Clemente's wife, Vera, put it, "He fell into the water so that his spirit could be carried by the ocean to more places."

While it is often said that Roberto Clemente disappeared without a trace, nothing could be further from the truth.

PUERTO RICAN PIONEER

Roberto Clemente's death, on December 31, 1972, inspired an outpouring of grief (Puerto Rican citizens could be found wading in the waves for days, hoping to find his body) and an unprecedented honor (less than four months later the baseball writers waived the traditional five-year waiting period and granted him immediate induction into the Hall of Fame).

Perhaps most important of all, however, his untimely demise spurred donations to Ciudad Deportiva, or Sports City, a dream of Clemente's that became a San Juan–based reality under the direction of his wife, Vera. The Sports City's baseball program has assured that Clemente's legacy lives on in the performance of some of baseball's biggest stars. Among the talent it spawned: Ruben Sierra, Juan Gonzalez, Carlos Baerga, Roberto and Sandy Alomar, Benito Santiago and Ivan Rodriguez.

79

Tony Hulman

It may be that the four most famous words in sport aren't "Strike three, yer out!" or "He shoots, he scores!" or "He missed the tag!" or even "I am the greatest!" They are four words which were spoken by Anton Hulman, Jr., for more than a quarter-century, a command that made him so nervous he was known to actually have read them from an index card every Memorial Day, and to have worked with an announcer to get his inflection just right. They are four words that mark the start every year of what many have called the greatest sporting event on earth.

"Gentleman, start your engines . . ."

Tony Hulman did not build the Indianapolis Motor Speedway. He did not create the Indy 500. But he saved them both, and turned them into the Rose Bowl of Racing, the Super Bowl of Speed. In the process, Hulman became, according to one writer, "one of those priceless characters who are bigger than life, not men but institutions."

Indianapolis Motor Speedway was originally constructed in 1909 by four prominent Indianapolis businessmen, a group led by car dealer Carl G. Fisher. At the time, Indianapolis was staking its claim as the nation's car manu-facturing capital, and the Speedway was conceived as a test and competition center, a "great outdoor laboratory." In August of its first year, the track hosted its first racing event, a three-day program of competition in which turn-of-the-century racing legend Barney Oldfield set a new world record by averaging 83.2 miles per hour over one mile.

By the third day of the event, however, the track was disintegrating considerably. Officials of the American Automobile Association put an end to the final 300-mile race about three-fourths of the way through it. It was then that the Speedway's owners decided to resurface the course with 3.2 million paving bricks. The Speedway soon became known as The Brickyard.

Fisher and his associates also decided to focus on one major event each year, then called the Indianapolis 500-Mile Race and first held on May 30, 1911. They chose to make it an annual Memorial Day affair in part because local farmers would be less busy and more likely to attend. As Robert Shaplen explained in *Sports Illustrated* forty-seven years later, it was the birth of a legend. "People who can't tell a Buick from Bugatti know that Indianapolis means automobile racing," he wrote.

The first Indy 500 champion, Ray Harroun, averaged just under 75 miles per hour. Seventy-nine years later, Arie Luyendyk averaged nearly 186 miles per hour, a track record. But Harroun was somewhat of a revolutionary, discarding the usual two-seater vehicle for a single-seat Marmon Wasp. The other drivers were accompanied by a riding mechanic, whose job included looking out for traffic approaching from behind. Harroun? He simply rigged his car with something called a rearview mirror.

In 1927, Fisher and Co. sold the Speedway to Captain Eddie Rickenbacker, a former Indy driver and World War I flying ace. The onset of the Depression two years later left Rickenbacker barely able to meet the track's most basic needs, much less provide funds for improvements. When all racing activity was suspended during World War II, the Speedway began to deteriorate. In 1945, three-time winner Wilbur Shaw embarked on a mission to find a buyer to save the Speedway. He found his savior in Tony Hulman.

Shaplen described Hulman as "self-effacing to the point of self-obliteration . . . sort of Walter Mitty in reverse, doing his best to live down a glamorous past." He was born in Terre Haute, Indiana, on February 11, 1901. His father owned Hulman & Company, a successful baking soda manufacturer and grocery dry goods distributor founded in 1849. Anton Hulman, Sr., had been a state champion bicyclist in the heyday of two-wheelers.Once auto racing became the rage, the Hulmans made frequent trips to Indianapolis—or, technically, to a town six miles northwest of the state capitol, a town called Speedway. Tony Jr. saw his first Indy 500 in 1914.

Hulman attended prep school out East and became an all-around track and field star. He continued his track career at Yale, earning ten medals for pole vaulting and hurdling as a freshman. He also starred for the undefeated 1923 Yale football team. Hulman graduated in 1924 with a degree in administrative engineering and joined the family business. Upon inheriting the company, he began to acquire other holdings—from breweries and banks to refineries and real estate—turning a fortune into even more.

Hulman's most dramatic acquisition was the Indianapolis Speedway, and despite his immense wealth, his purchase of the aging track—for $750,000, just $50,000 more than Rickenbacker had paid two decades earlier—raised eyebrows. The Speedway was in disrepair, with sagging grandstands, splintered boards, curling paint and weeds sticking up between the cracks of the bricks. "Capt. Eddie has sold the Hoosier white elephant," claimed one newspaper reporter. Said another, "Either Tony had the vision of what the Indianapolis Motor Speedway could look like some day or Wilbur and Eddie pulled off one of the greatest sales jobs of all-time." Even the ever-optimistic Hulman later recalled, "I began wondering what would happen if I held a race and nobody came."

He needn't have worried. Only a few months after purchasing the track, he had improved it enough to reopen it in May of 1946. Within a few short years, Hulman had turned the dilapidated course into a state-of-the-art facility, transforming an event on the verge of extinction into a magnificent American sporting spectacle.

He replaced the wooden grandstands with steel and concrete, and rebuilt "Gasoline Alley" following a 1941 fire. He added a control tower and an electric scoring pylon in the late '50s, during which he was also instrumental in forming the U.S. Auto Club, which took over for the American Automobile Association. By 1961, Hulman had replaced the Speedway's grandstands once again and had covered The Brickyard's millions of bricks with asphalt, though he gave a nod to tradition by leaving the now-famous "Yard of Bricks" at the start-finish line. He also built the Speedway Motel and began the construction of what became ninety-two executive suites in three complexes alongside the track. Hulman died on October 27, 1977. Ten years later, Indianapolis Motor Speedway was named a National Historic Landmark.

It has been estimated that close to one million people enter the Speedway during the month of May—for practice, qualifying and the big race itself. The day of the race is said to be the world's largest one-day sporting event. When Hulman bought the track, the grandstands held 70,000. Today, more than 350,000 people flock to Indianapolis each Memorial Day. Hulman offered $25,000 in prize money in 1946. Today, thirty-three drivers compete for a purse of some $7.5 million.

The Indy 500 began as a race. It became an event. It emerged, thanks to Hulman, as part of the fabric of American sport.

80

Walter Hagen

It seems backward to call Walter Hagen the Arnold Palmer of the early twentieth century, because, in reality, Palmer was cut in the mold of Hagen. Indeed, it was Hagen, more than any other person, who signalled and demanded the arrival of professional golf.

"When Hagen first started playing the game, golf was dominated on both sides of the Atlantic by gifted amateurs—in England by aristocrats, in the U.S. by the socially prominent. Clubhouses were sanctuaries for the members and strictly off-limits to the club professionals. The pro in those days was little more than a servant, an instructor to the rich," wrote Ron Fimrite in *Sports Illustrated*. "And then along came Sir Walter . . . His colleagues had only to ride his gaudy coattails to respectability."

Born December 21, 1892, in Brighton, New York, a suburb of Rochester, Hagen was the son of a blacksmith who earned $18 a week. At the age of ten, Hagen took work as a caddie, making 10 cents a round. He would later earn quite a bit more for an 18-hole journey.

Hagen quit school at the age of thirteen and then worked as a garage mechanic, a taxidermist, a piano finisher and an apprentice to a mandolin maker before becoming an assistant golf pro at The Country Club of Rochester. At the age of nineteen, Hagen competed in his first tournament, the Canadian Open. He finished thirty-sixth. The following year, while 20-year-old Francis Ouimet captured America's fancy by winning the U.S. Open, 20-year-old Walter Hagen finished three strokes back. He won the event the next year, carding a record-tying 290 and winning $300 for his efforts.

His next major triumph didn't come until 1919. By now a full-fledged pro at Oakland Hills, outside of Detroit, Hagen won his second and last U.S. Open title. Afterward, he announced his intention to become the first full-time touring professional, unattached but paid handsomely. His subsequent successes made it work.

Though he never won another national crown, Hagen placed in the top ten 15 times in his 21 U.S. Open appearances. He became the first American-born British Open champion in 1922, and added three more British titles in the next seven years. To that total he added five PGA Championships—in 1921 and each year from 1924 to 1927. In all, Hagen won more than sixty tournaments and at least one major title in nine of the eleven years between 1919 and 1929.

Only Jack Nicklaus has surpassed his total of eleven major professional victories, but even in his own era, Hagen essentially played second fiddle to the sport's maestro. Bobby Jones, who almost always seemed to win when he deigned to play, was the sport's seminal figure in the 1920s. Hagen, basically, was Lou Gehrig to Jones's Babe Ruth. In the only one-on-one match between the two, when both were near their peak in 1926, Hagen beat Jones handily. But over the last decade of Jones's career, Hagen never won an Open championship in which his rival was entered.

In fact, Hagen and Jones were strikingly dissimilar figures. Unlike Jones, Hagen was not averse to intimidating his opponent or using an obscure rule to his advantage; he was more than willing to make mounds of money off of his golf expertise; and he considered crowds his own, rather than a necessary evil. Jones was self-deprecating; Hagen was self-promoting. Indeed, Hagen's personality was more important to golf than his prowess. While Jones was the more Ruthian figure, Hagen was much more cut out of the Ruthian mold. In essence, he was a Bambino in knickers.

Hagen was famous for having a taste for expensive clothes and attractive women, a disregard for convention and a flair for the dramatic. A teetotaler in his younger days, he drank enough scotch during Prohibition to dry up the nineteenth hole. He was the kind of a man who would arrive late to an important match still wearing his tuxedo from the previous night's party, who would meet a woman on the fifteenth hole and have a date set up by the end of the round, who would net the unheard-of sum of $23,000 on an exhibition tour and then return home too broke to do his laundry. Said one observer, "In the credit card age, he might have broken American Express."

Hagen's golf game was certainly a clone of his personality—bold, exciting, unpredictable. His style has been described as "an almost endless spectacle of self-inflicted damage followed by redemptive acts of Herculean proportions." He never developed a classic swing, and his long game was short on consistency. As a result, he often found himself in troubling places on the golf course, but he usually found a way to make a success of it.

It was this unpredictability, along with his unsurpassed showmanship, that drew crowds to him and, thus, to the game. "He made golf look difficult," Mark McCormack writes in *The Wonderful World of Professional Golf*, "and because most golfers find the game difficult they were able to identify with Hagen just as they identify with Palmer, although accepting the gulf that exists between their own play and that of the masters."

But it wasn't the gulf between duffers and masters that most concerned Hagen; it was the chasm between the respect accorded amateurs and professionals. During the '20s and '30s, Hagen embarked on exhibition tours all over the world, averaging more than 125 matches a year. But not only did he prove that the life of an independent professional could be remarkably lucrative, he made certain the fame and fortune translated into acceptance—for him and for all professionals.

When he travelled to his first British Open, in 1920 (accompanied by four trunks stuffed with clothes, a press agent and an advisor), he learned that the amateurs were to dine in the clubhouse, while he and the other pros were relegated to a tent. Hagen responded by arranging an elaborate luncheon beside his limousine in full view of club officials. Three years later, after finishing runner-up in the British Open, he declined an invitation to the clubhouse for the presentation ceremony because the professionals hadn't been allowed to enter it during the week. Instead, Hagen invited everyone to the pub.

In many respects, by demanding access to clubhouse and locker room facilities, and by elevating the status of the pro golfer, Hagen was to professional golf what Red Grange was to professional football. And the men who came after him knew it. "Golf has never had a showman like him," another golf great, Gene Sarazen, would say. "All the professionals who have a chance to go after the big money today should say a silent thanks to Walter each time they stretch a check between their fingers."

Hagen died on October 5, 1969, but not before his modern reincarnation, Arnold Palmer, was able to put Hagen's influence in appropriate perspective. At a testimonial dinner given by a group of professionals in the 1960s, Palmer told him, "If it were not for you, Walter, this dinner would be downstairs in the pro shop and not in the ballroom."

81

Bobby Orr

There is something remarkably precocious about young athletes named Bob. By the age of twenty-two, Bobby Jones had won U.S. Amateur and U.S. Open titles; Bob Feller had recorded 82 wins and 973 strikeouts; Bob Pettit had been named NBA Rookie of the Year; Bobby Hurley had led Duke University to two straight NCAA basketball titles. But there has arguably never been a young athlete with an impact quite like Bobby Orr's.

Orr turned twenty-two in 1970. He also turned the National Hockey League on its head. A defenseman, he recorded 33 goals and 87 assists for a league-leading 120 points, the second-highest total in history and the first time a defenseman ever led the NHL. He won the Hart Trophy as the league's MVP; he won the Norris Trophy as its top defenseman; he won the Art Ross Trophy as its leading scorer; and he won the Conn Smythe Trophy as playoff MVP.

When *Sports Illustrated* named Orr its 1970 Sportsman of the Year, making him the first hockey player so honored, writer Jack Olsen declared, "Let it be said and done with: by acclamation Bobby Orr is the greatest player ever to don skates . . . To the students of Bobby Orr, the spectacular has become the routine, and the routine has become unacceptable."

With a game-winning goal in the final contest, Orr led the Bruins to the 1970 Stanley Cup championship, their first title since 1941. It was a fact not lost on Scotty Bowman, then coach of the losing St. Louis Blues. "They say the Bruins started rebuilding that year," he said. "I don't believe that. I think they started rebuilding in 1948—the year Bobby Orr was born."

Orr was born on March 20 of that year, in Parry Sound, Ontario. The Bruins discovered him when he was a 12-year-old playing midget hockey. By the time he was fourteen they had moved him into junior hockey, where he averaged 33 goals per season over three years as a teen defenseman. By the time he was sixteen, Orr's picture had appeared on the cover of Canada's national magazine, *Maclean's*. By the time he was eighteen, Orr was in the NHL.

He had signed an unprecedented (for hockey) bonus contract for $75,000 over two years and went on to earn Rookie of the Year honors in 1966–1967. However, he didn't receive the James Norris Trophy as the league's best defenseman. That went to Harry Howell of the Rangers, who said, "I'm glad I won it now because it's going to belong to that Orr from now on."

Howell was right. Orr would go on to win the Norris Trophy a record eight straight times from 1968–1975. He would be the first to win the league MVP Award three straight times (1970–1972), leading the Bruins to another championship in '72. After becoming the first defenseman to lead the NHL in scoring in 1970, he would do it again five years later, when he recorded a career-best 135 points.

Before Orr, the last defenseman to score at least 20 goals in a season did it during World War II; Orr exceeded 30 three times and scored 46 in 1974–1975. Before Orr, no defenseman had ever led the NHL in assists; Orr did it five times, including 1971, when he became the first person to break the 100-assist mark. At a time when two of hockey's finest, Gordie Howe and Bobby Hull, were still roaming the ice, Orr was generally given the nod as the game's best player. Said Bruins coach Harry Sinden, "Howe could do everything, but not at top speed. Hull went at top speed, but couldn't do everything. Orr can do everything, and do it at top speed."

Perhaps Orr's only rival as hockey's greatest talent is the only man to surpass his total of five assist titles, and likely the only hockey player more precocious than he: Wayne Gretzky. "It's not necessary to get into who may be better, Orr, the defenseman, or Wayne Gretzky, the center," wrote Frank Deford, "except to note that Orr did something that Gretzky had no opportunity to do, and that was change the very nature of the game."

Indeed, while Gretzky carried offensive hockey to new levels, Orr brought it to new dimensions—and that was his most significant impact. Lester Patrick had first demonstrated the offensive potential of defensive players at the turn of the century, but since then there had been only a handful of defensemen who were talented enough to make their mark in the scoring column. And none had the ability to take over a game like Orr could.

"He changed the sport by redefining the parameters of his position," wrote E. M. Swift, in *Sports Illustrated*. "A defenseman, as interpreted by Orr, became both a defender and an aggressor, both a protector and a producer. Orr was much more than an opportunist: He *created* opportunities."

Just as Patrick Ewing and Alonzo Mourning were spawned by Bill Russell, Orr's style generated a new wave of offensive-minded blue-liners, players like Denis Potvin, Paul Coffey, Ray Bourque and Brian Leetch. Of course, whether or not this is a positive trend is still a matter of perspective. Said hockey historian Stan Fischler, "Now if you find a defenseman who can play defense, it's like finding a jewel in a mud heap."

But Orr could do it all. He had an explosive and accurate shot; he displayed remarkable quickness; he was a ferocious bodychecker, a fearless defender, a tough fighter. And woe to the team that allowed Orr to get ahold of the puck in a penalty-killing situation. "Whenever you do that, you can just kiss it goodbye," lamented one opposing coach. "That's just another part of the game Orr has spoiled for everybody."

But as much as Orr's skills revolutionized the game, they may have been more important as a marketing tool at a time when expansion would double the size of the NHL. Former Bruins coach Tom Johnson explained it best, telling Olsen, "If you're looking at your first hockey game—and lots of people are nowadays—all you do is watch Orr and you catch on fast."

But off the ice, despite being blond-haired, blue-eyed and Boston's own, Orr didn't have quite the same effect as some other hockey legends. He didn't have the pioneering influence of Lester Patrick, the public-relations value of Howie Morenz, the charisma of Bobby Hull or the transcendental impact of Wayne Gretzky, and so he is ranked below them in *The Sports 100*.

Olsen had predicted that Orr would be the "personality around whom the entire sport will coalesce in the decade of the '70s, as golf once coalesced around Arnold Palmer, baseball around Babe Ruth." Orr had arrived as a professional at about the same time as Joe Namath, and it was expected that he would do for the NHL what "Broadway Joe" did for the AFL. But, for the most part, Orr didn't have Namath's personality; he just had his knees.

Six operations on his left knee alone were enough to guarantee that Orr's career would be all too brief. After ten seasons in Boston, he signed a five-year, $3 million deal with the Chicago Blackhawks in 1976, but after two injury-plagued seasons he retired from the game. He was elected to the Hockey Hall of Fame in 1979, at the age of thirty-one, still precocious enough to fit right in.

82

Don Hutson

"People always ask me who was the greatest player of all-time," football historian Bob Carroll explained. "My standard answer is Don Hutson." Carroll is not alone. As a receiver, Hutson was as far above his contemporaries as Babe Ruth, Wilt Chamberlain and Wayne Gretzky were each superior in their own respective sport. In football, perhaps, only Jim Brown compares, and even then, there were running backs closer to Brown's skill level.

"If you rated every pass catcher when Hutson was playing on a scale of 100, and you started with Hutson as 100, the next highest guy would be about a 40. He's just that much ahead of anybody else," Carroll insisted. "Jerry Rice might be a better pass receiver, but if Jerry Rice is rated a 100 today, there are a lot of guys in the 90s."

Hutson's talent translated into remarkable numbers and dozens of league records in his eleven seasons with the Green Bay Packers. Arthur Daley of *The New York Times* once wrote that "whenever anyone erases some Hutson statistics, it seems as sacrilegious as a baseball player breaking a record which belonged to Ty Cobb." And like Cobb's, some of Hutson's records seemed all but unbreakable. He caught 99 touchdown passes in an era when the touchdown pass was a novelty, a record that remained through the aerial revolution of the next four decades until Steve Largent broke it in 1989. Even today, only Largent and Rice have recorded more scoring grabs than football's first truly spectacular receiver.

According to *Sports Illustrated*'s Paul Zimmerman, Hutson "came to the game in 1935 like an emissary from another planet." On the first play of his first professional game, he caught a pass and raced 83 yards for a touchdown. In his last game, in 1945, he set a league record by scoring 29 points (four touchdowns, a field goal and two extra points) in the second quarter alone.

By the time Hutson retired he had collected 488 receptions, 298 more than anybody else, and a record 7,991 receiving yards. He had led the NFL in receptions eight times (no one else has done it more than five times) and had led the league in scoring from 1940 through 1944, totalling more points (823) than anyone else who had ever played the game.

Hutson averaged 24.9 yards per reception in 1939, by far the most ever for a league-leader. He caught passes in 95 consecutive games, scored in 42 straight games, made the all-league team nine times and became a charter member of the Pro Football Hall of Fame. "Hutson is so extraordinary," Chicago Bears owner George Halas once said, "that I concede him two touchdowns a game and just hope we can score more."

In his best season, 1942, Hutson had the advantage of a diminished talent level in the league due to World War II. He responded with 17 touchdowns in the 12-game season, a record that lasted more than four decades, and 138 points, a total not bested for another eighteen years. He set a new mark with 1,211 receiving yards and 74 receptions, more than the entire total of four NFL teams.

And the "Alabama Antelope" did it all before the two-platoon era, playing 60 minutes of every game. Just 6-foot-1 and 185 pounds, he began his NFL career as a rather inadequate defensive end when the other team had the ball. But he was soon switched to the secondary, where he made use of his near–world class speed and intercepted 23 passes in his last four seasons. "Too bad the two-platoon system wasn't used when I was with the Packers," Hutson would later say. "If I could have played only offense I'd probably still be playing."

But Hutson's enduring impact on pro football was not the fact that he dominated to such an extent: it was his influence on the revolution of the passing game. The art of passing came of age in the 1930s and 1940s, the result of several factors, among them the advent of the T-formation, the free substitution rule, the institution of penalties for roughing the passer, and the use of slimmer balls that were easier to throw. Several quarterbacks contributed to the revolution, including two converted halfbacks, Sid Luckman and Sammy Baugh. Baugh, who joined the NFL two years after Hutson, eventually finished his 16-year career with more attempts, completions, touchdown passes, yards and a better completion percentage than anyone in league history.

But even "Slingin' Sammy" didn't dominate like the "Greyhound from Green Bay." Hutson had been placed in an environment perfectly suited to his skills. His coach, Packers founder Curly Lambeau, was football's first pass-oriented coach, and his quarterbacks, Arnie Herber in the '30s and Cecil Isbell in the '40s, were two of the league's best. But Hutson, more than anyone else in the era, was responsible for elevating the passing game, and he did it through a unique combination of talent and technique.

"Hutson virtually invented modern pass receiving," said Carroll. "He invented moves, routes, practice techniques. It wasn't that they didn't run patterns before then, but it was basically down-and-out or down-and-in. He invented the change of pace and possibly the button-hook. He even had passers throw bad passes to him, so he could work on that." It wasn't until Hutson came along that defenses ever felt the need to double- or even triple-team a receiver. And it was essentially Hutson who, as a student of the game, did much to transform the passing game from a rather primitive game of catch to a precise craft.

It wasn't until his senior year in high school that Hutson even played the game he would later alter so profoundly. Born January 31, 1913, in Pine Bluff, Arkansas, the son of a conductor on the Cotton Belt Railroad, he was not even considered the best athlete in his family. Though he did become an all-state basketball player in high school, he only tried the gridiron in his final year, and reportedly only earned a scholarship to the University of Alabama because the school was interested in a teammate of his.

But Hutson, who also played baseball (later even spending three years in the minor leagues), and consistently broke 10 seconds in the 100-yard dash as a track athlete, became an All-American end at Alabama (the other end on the team was Hutson's best friend, Paul "Bear" Bryant). Hutson capped his collegiate career with two touchdowns in a 29-13 Rose Bowl upset of Stanford and then turned to the professional game. The NFL was planning to institute its college draft in 1936, so 1935 represented the last year of unrestricted free agency for collegiate stars. As the most coveted prospect available, Hutson eventually signed for what was then the impressive sum of $300 a week, though he would eventually earn a $15,000 salary.

But he also signed with two teams—the pass-happy Packers and the run-oriented Brooklyn Dodgers. NFL president Joe Carr solved the problem by ruling that the team that mailed its contract first would be awarded the rights to Hutson. In another lucky break for Hutson, the Packers contract had been postmarked 8:30 A.M., the Dodgers at 8:47 A.M.—seventeen minutes that may have changed the course of football history.

83

Charlie Finley

In twenty years as a sports team owner, Charlie Finley may have earned more media attention than any owner before him. He also earned some of the least flattering characterizations ever heaped upon a sports mogul. He was the "Abominable Showman" . . . "his own worst press agent" . . . "one of the most disreputable characters ever to enter the American sports scene." Wells Twombly wrote in *People* magazine that Finley "disturbs the bile of every man who has ever revered the game of baseball."

He wore a trademark Alpine hat, but it may as well have been black as coal. Everybody, it seemed—his players, fans, journalists, many of his fellow baseball owners, three different baseball comissioners—hated Charlie Finley. But it was his maverick personality, his insatiable ego and fearless disregard for tradition that allowed Finley to play an integral part in transforming baseball in the 1960s and 1970s. The "O" in Charlie O. might have stood for outrageous, obnoxious, outspoken, outlandish, overbearing, obstinate, obtrusive and offensive, but Oakland's owner was also an open-minded, opinionated original—and just what baseball needed.

Born on February 22, 1918, in Ensley, Alabama, Finley served as a bat boy for the Birmingham Barons as a youth, before his family moved to Gary, Indiana, in 1933. He played baseball and boxed in local Golden Gloves tournaments, attended Gary Junior College and then Indiana University, and then entered the insurance business.

Finley's life turned on a near-tragedy, when he spent twenty-seven months hospitalized for tuberculosis following World War II. While losing nearly seventy pounds, he gained insight into the future of disability insurance. Discovering that few doctors carried health insurance, he developed the idea of selling group insurance to the medical profession, and got in on the ground floor of an industry that would make him a multi-millionaire.

With money to burn, he pursued a dream of owning a baseball team, and reveled in the recognition that came with it. After failed bids to purchase the Philadelphia Athletics in 1954, the Detroit Tigers in 1956, the Chicago White Sox in 1958 and the expansion Los Angeles Angels two years later, he finally found himself owning 52 percent of the last-place Kansas City Athletics late in 1960, buying the remainder of the team's stock soon after. Within a dozen years, one of his stars, Joe Rudi, would be saying, "Ours is the only franchise I know that has people talking more about the owner than the players."

Almost immediately, Finley began to unveil the monster baseball had created by allowing him into the fold. He fired manager Joe Gordon midway through the 1961 season and did the same to his general manager soon after, taking over the job himself. He unveiled promotional gimmicks in the Bill Veeck mold—a mechanical rabbit handed baseballs to the umpire; an air vent dusted off home plate; sheep grazed beyond the outfield fence; there were fireworks, ball girls, Bald-Headed Day, Hot Pants Day.

It was Finley who introduced color uniforms in 1963, saying, "It used to be that all cars were black. Now you almost never see a black car. The colors don't make cars run better, but they sure sell better." When he later paid his players to grow their hair long, he claimed the same motivation that led him to spearhead the change to night World Series contests—the fans and the good of the game. "Do you realize what a shot-in-the-arm that was for baseball?" he said of his players' mustaches. "All the people in this modern generation identified with the Athletics. They saw us as a mod team. We were their symbol."

Indeed, Finley considered himself a fan's owner and was an admirer of Veeck, certainly to a greater extent than his colleagues. But there was an important difference between the two. While Veeck was beloved by most of his players, Finley fostered what became a common attitude on all his teams: a joint hatred of the man paying their salaries. By 1967, his Kansas City players were so disenchanted with him that they filed a complaint of unfair labor practices with the National Labor Relations Board. Events in Oakland a few years later were even more contentious. Bitter contract disputes with Reggie Jackson and Vida Blue led Blue to declare that Finley "treats all of his black players like plantation niggers." To which catcher Dave Duncan replied, "Do you honestly think he treats his white players any different?"

But something about Finley's role led his Oakland teams to greatness. The A's won world championships in 1972, 1973 and 1974, the first team to three-peat since the Yankees of the '50s. As former A's first baseman Mike Epstein explained, "In Finley, I see a man who tries to generate so much hate against himself by the ballplayers that they'll play better. A team with a common enemy has better unity."

Finley had moved the A's to Oakland following the 1967 season, leading Missouri senator Stuart Symington to describe Oakland as "the luckiest city since Hiroshima." The move, particularly the American League's desire to find a replacement team in Kansas City, hastened expansion of both leagues and the change to a two-decision, playoff format in 1969.

In 1970, Finley added to his sporting interests by purchasing the NHL's Oakland Seals, promptly adding white skates and gold and green uniforms, and changing the team's name to the California Golden Seals. Finley was stopped short of instituting colored sticks, orange pucks and a green ice surface, but he added a red-white-and-blue ball to his collection in 1972 when he purchased the ABA's Memphis Pros as the franchise was about to fold. Within two years, however, Finley was out of hockey and basketball, having been bought out by both leagues for a tidy profit.

Meanwhile, back in baseball, Finley had unwittingly helped to spawn the era of free agency when Oakland's best pitcher, Jim "Catfish" Hunter, technically became the first-ever free agent, following the 1974 season. By neglecting to direct half of Hunter's salary to an annuity during the season, Finley had violated his contract, and when an arbitrator ruled Hunter a free agent, he went from making $100,000 a year with the A's to earning $3.75 million over five years with the Yankees.

Suddenly, the players were confronted with not only the possibility of free agency, but also its potential rewards. Andy Messersmith and Dave McNally challenged the reserve clause a year later, and won. Free agency meant an end to the Oakland dynasty, as the A's failed to win another division title before Finley sold the club in 1981.

Before leaving baseball, however, Finley had been able to push through a rule change that has proven to be his most dramatic impact on the game: the designated hitter. Like many of Finley's innovations, the DH (originally called the designated pinch hitter) was condemned by baseball's traditionalists. But the question of whether or not a pitcher should bat is actually even older than Finley himself. In fact, an article published in a 1906 issue of *Sporting Life*—entitled "Why the Pitcher Ought to Bat"—debated the contention, by one Connie Mack, that a substitute player should be sent up to hit. National League president John Heydler came close to convincing league owners to try a "10th man" experiment during spring training twenty-three years later, but—like Mack—he failed in the end.

A California amateur league used a DH-rule in 1940, with several other amateur leagues following suit. When pitchers became too dominant in the professional leagues of the late '60s, the pros then considered the idea. After the Year of the Pitcher, in 1968, the major leagues lowered the mound and changed the strike zone. Baseball also began using the DH in American League exhibition games, and the Triple A International League used it during the 1969 season before discontinuing the rule one year later.

Only the American League was left to keep the idea alive, and many owners felt something had to be done, because the league was lagging behind its National League counterparts in run production and—more importantly—in attendance. Though Finley had not come up with the idea of a designated hitter, he championed it from a position of power. "I pushed the DH for three years," he said. "They thought I was nuts but after continuously harping, I finally woke them up."

On January 11, 1973, the American League owners voted 8-4 to try a three-year experiment with the rule. Less than three months later, Ron Blomberg of the New York Yankees officially became baseball's first designated hitter, the beginning of perhaps the most significant rule change in baseball in the past century. Pitchers had batted .145 in 1972; designated hitters batted .257 in 1973. In fact, the entire league batting average went from .239 to .259, with the league earned run average increasing from 3.07 to 3.82

The DH lengthened the careers of several marquee players, which in turn increased the league's attendance. In fact, American League attendance jumped by more than two million in 1973 alone. Of course, National League representatives and fans claim to dislike the rule, but one man claims to know why. "The reason the National League doesn't like the DH is that the American League beat them to the punch through the forethought of Charlie Finley," says Charlie Finley.

DH AND ERA

In the five years preceding the American League's adoption of the designated hitter, the average ERA in the National League (3.51) was higher than that in the American League (3.37). In the twenty years following the DH, however, the average American League ERA was 32 points higher than the average National League ERA (3.96 to 3.64). In fact, though the National League recorded a higher league batting average in the nine years preceding the DH, the American League average has been higher every year since.

84

Red Auerbach

The rationale for Red Auerbach's inclusion in *The Sports 100* is relatively simple. Every major professional league seems to have one franchise that has emerged as the backbone of the league. The Boston Celtics are that franchise in the National Basketball Association. And for nearly half a century, Red Auerbach has been the Boston Celtics.

A statue of Auerbach stands in Boston's Quincy Market, facing Boston Garden, his lair for more than four decades. The statue is carrying a rolled-up program in its left hand, a cigar in its right. Much more often than not, that cigar would be lit as the game wound to a close, a performance Bob Cousy once described as "the single most arrogant act in sports."

In twenty seasons, Auerbach lit 938 regular-season victory cigars, a victory record only recently broken by Lenny Wilkens, who promptly lit up in a tribute to Auerbach. Wilkens's coaching résumé includes only one NBA championship; Auerbach's includes nine, along with seven more as the team's general manager and then president. Auerbach coached the Celtics to their first title, in 1957, and then to eight straight between 1959 and 1966, when he abruptly stepped down at the age of forty-eight. No other coach has recorded more than five titles; only three other coaches have recorded more than two. In 1967, the NBA christened the Coach of the Year award the Red Auerbach Trophy, a decision as obvious as baseball's Cy Young Award.

Certainly, Auerbach had the players—Bob Cousy, Bill Russell, John Havlicek, Dave Cowens, Jo Jo White, Larry Bird, Kevin McHale, Robert Parish. But the Celtics won two titles in the '50s, nine in the '60s, two in the '70s and three in the '80s. The only constant throughout was the man with the cigar. The franchise even went through seven different owners from 1963 to 1969, during which the Celtics won six championships. In fact, Auerbach has even outlasted Boston Garden.

Success spawned the "Celtic mystique," words easy to come by when surrounded by sixteen championship banners and nineteen retired jerseys. "There has been no franchise like the Celtics in American sports," wrote Frank Deford in *Sports Illustrated*, "and no guardian of franchise ever like Auerbach." It is as if the New York Yankees or the Montreal Canadiens, as important as those franchises were to their respective sports, had a guiding hand throughout the years—one man calling the shots, his influence reverberating throughout the league.

Arnold J. Auerbach was born on September 20, 1917, and raised in Brooklyn. He played guard on his high school basketball team and at George Washington University, where he averaged 10.6 points per game as a senior, but he was destined to coach. He majored in physical education in college, coached high school ball for a couple years, earned a master's degree by producing a thesis on physical education programs for junior high schools, and then joined the U.S. Navy from 1943–1946, where he directed intramural sports.

In 1946, a pro basketball team was formed in Washington, D.C., and Auerbach talked his way into the head coaching job. The Washington Capitals went 49-11 in his first season. After two more seasons, Auerbach moved to the Tri-City Blackhawks of the newly formed NBA. The team's 28-29 record marked the only losing campaign of his career, and when the Tri-City owner made a trade without consulting Auerbach, he quit in protest. Soon after, on April 27, 1950, he was hired by Walter Brown, owner of the Boston Celtics. He has been there ever since.

The Celtics had finished in last place the year before Auerbach arrived. They would improve immediately, thanks to a neat piece of luck. Auerbach had passed on Bob Cousy from local Holy Cross in his first draft, calling him a "local yokel." Cousy was sent to the Chicago Stags, who promptly folded. The team's top players were dispersed, and the luck of the draw brought Cousy to Boston, where he turned in a Hall of Fame career.

The Celtics finished second in the Eastern Division four times over the next six years, and then, when Russell joined the team in 1956–1957, Auerbach and the Celtics won their first title. For the next decade, there was no stopping them, and Boston became the league's biggest road attraction when it most needed to attract fans.

Much of the team's success was due to Auerbach's willingness to build his team around African-American standouts. Just before he was officially introduced as Boston's head coach, in 1950, the Celtics became the first NBA team to draft a black player, Chuck Cooper. In 1957, Auerbach maneuvered to obtain Russell, and built his team around him. By 1963, Russell was joined by three other black starters—K. C. Jones, Sam Jones and Tom Sanders. In 1964, Boston acquired Willie Naulls from the New York Knicks and became the first team with five black players on the floor at one time. Two years later, Auerbach stepped down as coach and handed the reins to Russell, making him the NBA's first black head coach.

Of course, for Auerbach, this had nothing to do with good intentions. It was simply good business, just another way to keep a step ahead of the rest. "[He] was no leader of civil rights," Cousy would later explain. "But show him a polka-dotted seven-footer who can dunk and he'll put him on the team . . . He was completely one-dimensional; his entire life was *win*."

Auerbach was described as "so far ahead of everyone else that the pack couldn't sniff his cigar smoke," and that goes beyond simply merging Russell's defensive skills with a fast-break offense, utilizing John Havlicek as history's finest sixth man, assuring his team would get Larry Bird by drafting him a year early.

No detail escaped Auerbach's gaze. He was the kind of guy who dressed his players in black shoes because white ones became dirtier faster and who pointed out that players should be measured not from head to toe but with their arms raised over their head, from fingertip to toe. He was also the kind of guy who asked for his championship watch to be engraved on the clasp, rather than on the back. After all, who wants to take off a watch to display the engraving?

It is perfectly logical, somewhat obvious, and something nobody else would think of—only he was the one who thought of it, which is why he owns so much championship jewelry.

Dynasties

The following are the most successful franchises in sport through 1995:

- Football: Green Bay Packers   11 of 75 NFL titles (15%)
- Baseball: New York Yankees   22 of 90 World Series titles (24%)
- Hockey: Montreal Canadiens   23 of 77 Stanley Cup titles (30%)
- Basketball: Boston Celtics   16 of 49 NBA titles (33%)

85

Danny Biasone

Basketball was the invention of James Naismith, but, according to Harvey Araton of *The New York Times*, it was "reinvented into its current popular form by an irascible fellow named Daniel Biasone."

Biasone's contribution was as revolutionary as it was simple: a shot clock. When Biasone introduced his 24-second clock, in 1954, he saved the game from itself. Nearly a decade later, *The Sporting News* called the clock "no less important to pro basketball than a tracking station is to an astronaut." Twenty years after that, *Sports Illustrated* said it was "as basic to the professional game as ball and rim, net and court and moon-boot sneakers."

Pro basketball before Biasone was rather boring. In the early days of the NBA, the professional game was on the verge of extinction due to inaction. The stall was the most potent weapon in the game—and the least attractive. As the contest wore on, the team with the lead would simply hold the ball. Talented guards like Bob Cousy would dribble away from their opponents and then head to the foul line when the opponents grew restless. The low point came on November 22, 1950, when the Fort Wayne Pistons held the ball for most of the game against the more talented Minneapolis Lakers. The strategy worked, but the game suffered. The final score was 19-18.

The NBA attempted to respond to the problem, quickly instituting a rule calling for a technical foul for obvious stalling. Before a contest in March 1954, Boston Celtics coach Red Auerbach admitted, "If we're eight points ahead or so at the half, we'll hold that ball, and hold that ball for the longest stretches."

The game hardly resembled today's made-for-TV version, and crowds grew weary of the tactics. By 1954, the league was in trouble. "Things went from bad to worse," recalled Maurice Podoloff, the NBA's first commissioner. "The games were interminable. Attendance was suffering. We were in a desperate situation."

But of all the saviors—a 5-foot-6 Italian immigrant who owned a bowling alley in Syracuse, New York?

Born on February 22, 1909, in Italy, Danny Biasone came over to the United States at the age of ten. Despite his height limitations, he became a star quarterback at Syracuse's Vocational High School. After a series of jobs, he and a partner opened a restaurant in 1936. Five years later, Biasone bought a property that became a bowling alley, which he operated until his death on May 26, 1992.

In 1946, Biasone scraped together $1,000 to start a team in the National Basketball League. Three years later, the NBL merged with the Basketball Association of America to form the NBA, and the Syracuse Nationals survived. Over the years, NBA executives made repeated attempts to convince Biasone to move his franchise, as Syracuse represented the league's last small-market outpost. Finally, in 1963, he acquiesced. He sold the club for $500,000, and the team was moved to Philadelphia. The league had become too big for a smallish city like Syracuse, and, ironically, Biasone had much to do with that.

"I'm no expert on the game. I never claimed to be. But I knew fans weren't paying to see the ball being dribbled around all night," said Biasone. "I'm not a genius. I'm not a savior or a strategist. What I really am is a fan."

He had begun trying to sell the idea of a shot clock to league owners in 1951, but it wasn't until August 10, 1954, that he was able to put on an exhibition of the device for the league's power brokers. Biasone's fellow owners, having seen into the future, agreed to try the rule during the 1954 exhibition season, and it was so successful that it was adopted for the 1954–1955 regular season.

The number twenty-four, incidentally, had been arrived at through a mix of approximation and calculation. "Teams were taking about 60 shots a game if nobody screwed around," said Biasone. "I figured if the teams combined for 120 shots and the game was 48 minutes long, I should divide 120 into 2,880 seconds. The answer was 24."

In the early days of the shot clock, there were frequent malfunctions, accusations of slow-fingered timers and even instances of fans short-circuiting the clock by tripping over exposed wires. However, the impact of the 24-second clock was immediate. At the same time, a rule had been enacted limiting each team to six fouls in any quarter. The two rules complemented each other perfectly, and professional basketball was ushered into the modern era. A running game became the rule, rather than the exception, increasing the entertainment value of the game immeasurably. Scoring increased by eighteen percent; the Boston Celtics averaged 101.4 points per contest.

Though Bob Cousy once estimated that he had lost as many as ten points per game (in foul shots) because of the shot clock, he has nothing but praise for Biasone's invention. "I think it saved the NBA at that time," he said. "It allowed the game to breathe and progress." Of course, it was a bit of a why-didn't-I-think-of-that contribution, but as another Hall of Famer, Dolph Schayes, explained, "Someone else would have done it eventually—like Columbus discovering America—but he was the one who did it." Schayes played for Biasone for fifteen years, and he thought enough of the man to name his NBA-caliber son after him.

The basketball played by Danny Schayes in the '90s hardly resembles the game his father played in his early years as a pro, and Biasone's shot clock—since imitated at every level of the game—is a major reason. "If it wasn't for the 24-second clock, we never would have had TV; the games would have dragged on too long with no excitement at the end," said Podoloff, who called Biasone "the patron saint of the NBA." Podoloff claimed the league wouldn't have lasted another five years if not for his invention.

Biasone is noticeably absent from basketball's Hall of Fame. However, there is a special exhibit devoted to Biasone's invention. And besides, Biasone's reward actually came at the end of the shot clock's first season. In the seventh game of the NBA Finals, the final seconds of the game were free from stall-and-foul tactics. Instead, there was a dramatic come-from-behind victory—and the Syracuse Nationals won their only NBA championship.

SOARING SCORING

The following represents the average score per team per game in the years preceding and following the advent of the 24-second shot clock in 1954:

1948–1949: 80.0	1954–1955: 93.1
1949–1950: 80.1	1955–1956: 99.0
1950–1951: 83.9	1956–1957: 99.6
1951–1952: 83.7	1957–1958: 106.6
1952–1953: 82.7	1958–1959: 108.3
1953–1954: 79.5	1959–1960: 115.3
average: 81.7	average: 103.7

86

Matt Winn

"Of all the thoroughbred racing tracks in the nation, from stately Belmont in New York to balmy Santa Anita in California, only Churchill Downs is an authentic American sporting shrine," wrote *Sports Illustrated*'s William F. Reed. "Churchill Downs is to racing what Yankee Stadium is to baseball and August National is to golf."

Yet the aura surrounding Churchill Downs is not the product of its famous twin spires or its mint juleps; it comes from the pageantry of the Louisville race track's featured attraction: the Kentucky Derby. The Derby was launched in 1875, but at the time the man who would become the most important person in the making of America's most important horse race was just thirteen years old. Matt Winn watched the first Derby from the back of his father's grocery wagon, and, by the time he saw his last Run for the Roses, seventy-four years later, Winn had, in the words of Frank Deford, "made himself and the Derby national institutions."

Churchill Downs was created to meet a need. In the early 1870s, horse breeders in Kentucky were considering closing their farms because the state did not offer large stakes races to sustain their efforts. In response, Colonel M. Lewis Clark made plans to build a track in Louisville and establish a stakes race attractive enough to keep the breeders breeding. Clark leased 180 acres from Louisville's Churchill family, and gathered $100 each from 320 patrons to form the Louisville Jockey Club.

The first race at the new track, held on May 17, 1875, was the first Kentucky Derby, a stakes race modeled after England's Epsom Derby. The races that were to become the other two jewels in thoroughbred racing's Triple Crown for three-year-olds had been established only a few years earlier—the Belmont Stakes in 1867 and the Preakness Stakes in 1873.

Aristides, ridden by black jockey Oliver Lewis, won the first Derby, which was then a one and one-half mile event, taking a purse of $2,850 in front of some 10,000 spectators. In 1895, Churchill Downs unveiled a new grandstand, including its famous twin spires, and the following year the Derby was shortened to one and one-quarter miles. But by the turn of the century, poor management had placed the track on the verge of folding—until Winn turned around the losing proposition.

Martin Joseph Winn was born in Louisville on June 30, 1861. He graduated from business school, became a travelling salesman for a grocery firm, and then started a successful tailoring business. His only tie to horse racing was as an enthusiastic bettor. "All I knew about racing," he later admitted, "was that sometimes a man could make money betting the right horse in the right race."

But, in 1902, with Churchill Downs nearing bankruptcy, Winn was asked to head a group which would buy the property for $40,000. Late in the year, he was elected vice-president of the Louisville Jockey Club; two years later, he became general manager. Winn felt that the Western Turf Association, which allotted racing dates, favored other tracks and left his at a disadvantage. So he gathered nine other dissatisfied track owners and formed the American Turf Association, eventually emerging victorious after a two-year confrontation. The war resulted in the creation of the Kentucky State Racing Commission in 1906, which became a blueprint for governing the sport.

Two years later, when a reform movement banned track bookmakers, Winn found a bit of a legal loophole and provided perhaps his most profound contribution to horse racing. He discovered that, while Kentucky law barred gambling machines, it specifically allowed "French pools" or parimutuels. Four parimutuel machines had been in operation at Churchill Downs two decades earlier, and Winn initiated a frantic search for the old machines. One was uncovered in the bowels of the track, another was owned by a collector, a third was found at a pawnshop, and the fourth was recovered piece by piece. The 1908 Derby brought in $50,000 through the machines, and what was originally thought to be a temporary measure became a revolutionary staple of the sport.

As for the Derby itself, it really arrived a few years later, after several fortuitous races—a record winning payoff in 1913, a track record in 1914, the first filly to win in 1915—allowed Winn to maximize his talents at publicity, which were considerable. By then he was known as the Colonel, a strictly honorary title.

"The Colonel knew everybody everywhere," Brownie Leach, Winn's PR man at Churchill Downs in his last years, told Deford. "There were few outstanding people in the country he was not friendly with. I knew his thinking: you get the ladies and gentlemen, and the ordinary people will beat the doors down to get in. From 1920 through the Second World War, anybody who was anybody—social leaders, business leaders, political leaders—were at the Derby . . . The Colonel made the Derby class."

Indeed, Winn made the Derby appeal to the highest classes and the zealous masses, offering $100 boxes with $2 mint juleps and $5 lunches as well as a

50-cent grandstand section with dime sandwiches and dollar bets. He also made the Derby thrive, even in times of crisis. During World War I, he kept the track open by selling carnations grown in the infield to benefit the Red Cross. During World War II, the government threatened to put a halt to the Derby and a travel embargo threatened to do the same. Winn simply handed over Derby tickets to soldiers stationed in Louisville, insisting that the show would go on "even if there is only one starter and the only spectators are the trainer, the owner, and myself."

Like Roy Hofheinz, the man who created the Astrodome, Winn made his monument a home, living in a six-room apartment at Churchill Downs from the 1920s until his death. Also, like Hofheinz, Winn was often compared to P. T. Barnum. Wrote Arthur Dailey of *The New York Times*, "He could give cards and spades to Barnum and still win."

Winn died on October 6, 1949, a few months after enjoying his seventy-fifth Kentucky Derby. In the nearly half-a-century during which Winn controlled, nurtured and promoted the race, he saw it evolve from a regional event with a purse of $6,000 and even fewer spectators into a national event with the winner's share—and the crowd—exceeding 100,000. The modern Derby has been transformed into a 10-day Kentucky Derby Festival, featuring steamboat and hot-air balloon races, parades and fairs, dances and Derby queens, all of it a manifestation of Winn's dream and his efforts to make the Derby more than just another horse race.

Nearly five decades after his death, the Derby remains the foremost jewel in the Triple Crown, and Churchill Downs, on the first Saturday in May, remains the spiritual embodiment of the sport in America. As Deford explained, "Under the twin spires, in the aura of the bluegrass spring, any good man will cloud up when they play *My Old Kentucky Home* and cry outright when he realizes he is standing in one of those rare places where beauty and history bisect for an instant."

87

Sonja Henie

The CBS broadcast of the women's technical program in the 1994 Winter Games was watched by more than 45 million U.S. households, second in history only to the last "M*A*S*H" episode. More than 41 million households took in the women's long program two days later. Certainly, viewers weren't tuned in only to see figure skating; they were drawn to the final act of the Nancy Kerrigan–Tonya Harding debacle. But would the event have aroused America's curiosity and dominated newscasts for weeks had it been a conflict between, say, two bobsledders or two cross-country skiers? No chance.

Even back in 1992, figure skating's television ratings surpassed every sport other than pro football. Indeed, at least for Americans, it has firmly established itself as the glamour sport of the Winter Olympics. The events of 1994 only affirmed that. And Sonja Henie is the primary reason why an obscure diversion in outdoor rinks became the sport that crowns the quadrennial Olympic princess.

It was in the 1860s that an American man named Jackson Haines turned what had been a rather rigid, robot-like skating routine into a stylish combination of music and movement. Haines's version became widely accepted in Europe, but still the sport remained on the periphery of the world's interest—until Henie revolutionized figure skating on and off the ice.

Henie burst on the international athletic scene as an underage pixie, emerged as a champion, took America by storm, and then became one of Hollywood's biggest stars. She could be extremely temperamental and self-centered, she could swear like a truck driver, and she was as ostentatious as she was rich. In short, she may have been a combination of Harding, Shannen Doherty and Zsa Zsa Gabor—if you can imagine that. But she was also, indisputably, the most important person in the history of figure skating and one of the most significant female athletic

3 5 5

figures in American sport. Henie made possible America's passion for its Olympians on ice, from Peggy Fleming and Dorothy Hamill to Kristi Yamaguchi and
Nancy Kerrigan.

On the ice, her technical and artistic innovations established standards that
altered the sport's focus. She made the sport both more athletic, adding primitive
jumps and spins, and more artistic, incorporating aspects of ballet. She merged
style with skill, dance with daring, and inspired thousands of young women to
take up figure skating. Along the way, she won ten straight world championships
and three straight Olympic gold medals. Only one other woman skater, Katarina
Witt, has even won two gold medals in a row.

Off the ice, Henie has been called "Norway's greatest export since sardines."
After retiring from competition, she conquered America with her ice shows, which
created the modern aesthetic for figure skating entertainment, and became a Hollywood box-office bonanza. She was, essentially, Arnold Schwarzenegger on skates.

"If those favored by fortune are born with silver spoons in their mouths,"
The New York Times would later claim, "it can be said with equal truth that Miss
Henie was born with skates on her feet." Of course, the spoon was there, too. On
April 8, 1912, in Oslo, Norway, Henie was born into both wealth and athleticism
(her father, owner of Norway's largest fur company, had been a two-time world
bicycling champion in the 1890s).

Henie received her first pair of skates when she was five. She went on to win
the Oslo children's figure skating championship at age eight, the junior national
title at age nine and the national figure skating championship of Norway at age
ten. The following year, she participated in the Winter Olympics in Chamoix,
France, placing dead last out of eight competitors, though the free skate portion
of her program was good enough for third place. Two years later, she had improved enough to place second at the world championships. From then on, she
would never fail to finish first.

In 1927, Henie took the first of her ten straight world championships on her
home ice in Oslo. Of the five judges, the three from Norway voted for Henie,
while the other two (from Austria and Germany) voted for her top competitor.
Henie won, but the controversy surrounding the judging led the International
Skating Union to mandate only one judge per country in international meets.

The following year, she won her first gold medal at the Winter Games in St.
Moritz, Switzerland. By then she had introduced meticulous choreography to the
sport, turning what had been a series of disconnected technical feats into a smooth,
holistic approach. Henie had seen famed ballerina Anna Pavlova dance in London
and had been hooked. She soon came to be known as the "Pavlova of the Ice."

She made her first visit to the United States in 1929, when she traveled the
country on an exhibition tour, capped by a world championship in New York
City. In 1932, Henie returned for the Winter Olympics in Lake Placid, New York,
winning her second gold medal, this time as a unanimous choice. By then the
5-foot-2, blond-haired "Norwegian Doll" was one of the world's most famous
athletes, besieged by lucrative offers to turn professional.

Henie's performances in Lake Placid drew so many spectators that standing-room-only tickets sold for $5 apiece—and this at the nadir of the Depression. Indeed, at a time when the Winter Games were still on the brink of being dropped from the Olympic slate, Henie was a vital factor in their survival. Figure skating had first been sanctioned as an event at the 1908 Summer Games, reappearing for a second time in 1920. The first separate Winter Games had coincided with Henie's first appearance in 1924, and thus, there had not yet been a Winter Olympics without her as one of its stars.

At about the same time Henie won her second gold medal, her most avid admirer came to power in Germany. According to Raymond Strait and Henie's older brother, Leif, authors of *Queen of the Ice, Queen of the Shadows*, Adolph Hitler had never met Henie at that point, but he felt "she epitomized his vision of a pure, blond Aryan race." The two would become mutual admirers. Henie was known to have given Hitler the Nazi salute, lunched with him, and visited his hideaway in the mountains. When Norwegian newspapers wondered, in the early '30s, "IS SONJA A NAZI?," she feigned indignation, claiming that she had simply been honoring Germany by showing respect to its leader. Yet, according to her biographers, Henie "did share some of [Hitler's] ethnic and racial views."

In the mid-1930s, however, Henie's affinity for fascists didn't dim her popularity. Virtually everywhere she performed exhibitions—from Prague to New York City—she required a police escort. There had long been rumors that she was the "richest amateur in sports," having received hefty under-the-table appearance fees for years. After winning her third Olympic gold medal—in Germany in 1936—and her tenth straight world title, she retired. Having accumulated nearly 1,500 medals and trophies in her career, she then began the process of accumulating money.

She signed a contract for $70,000 up front plus a percentage of gate receipts, and toured the eastern U.S., making eighteen exhibition appearances, beginning with "Sonja Henie Night" at Madison Square Garden. For her eighteenth appearance, she traveled to a rink in Hollywood with her sole intention being to impress movie moguls.

As the Hollywood correspondent of the *New York World-Telegram* reported, "The next morning . . . Sonja Henie was the talk of the town. Studios were cooing at her." One executive in particular, Darryl F. Zanuck of 20th Century Fox, was so enthralled with her that he signed her to a five-year movie deal for a series of skating films at $125,000 per picture. Having made the transition from gold medals to the silver screen, Henie announced, "I want to do with skates what Fred Astaire is doing with dancing."

Henie's first film, *One in a Million*, a 1937 release about a Swiss innkeeper's daughter who becomes an Olympic skating champion, was an enormous box office success. She would go on to star in ten more movies, and soon only Clark Gable and Shirley Temple were bigger stars in the Hollywood constellation. In the days when female athletes were disparaged more often than not, sportswriters were calling her "the greatest box-office draw in the history of sport."

At the same time, Henie was matching her millions in movie salary with at least as much profit from her ice shows. She filmed during the summer and toured the country in skating exhibitions during the rest of the year. In 1940, she and Chicago Stadium owner Arthur Wirtz created her Hollywood Ice Revue, which consistently played before sold-out crowds.

The Ice Follies had been formed a few years earlier, but it was largely Henie's show that ushered in the age of "ice theater," further transforming figure skating into a national phenomenon. By 1947, it was estimated that 15 million people had paid $25 million to see her skate in the past decade. Artificial ice rinks now dotted the country; Henie had sparked a figure skating boom at the grass-roots level and at center stage.

Off stage, however, Henie had her dark side. As age limited Henie's acting and skating opportunities, she became a caricature of the self-obsessed, filthy-rich has-been film star. She had become bulimic and alcoholic, married and divorced two American millionaires before wedding her childhood friend, sued her own brother, and disinherited her family from her will. She was reported to have travelled around carrying a dilapidated suitcase filled with more than $1 million in jewelry from her extensive collection.

Henie was only fifty-seven when she died of leukemia on October 12, 1969. She was worth $47 million at the time, but her true legacy was found in the fortunes of figure skating.

88

Richard Petty

Say all you want about Elvis, but there are a good many racing fans who don't think of "Hound Dog" when somebody mentions The King. They think of a blue-and-red blur, #43, a winning smile, an oversized hat and dark sunglasses—images as vivid to them as Magic Johnson's grin, Kareem Abdul-Jabbar's goggles, Babe Ruth's stutter-stepped trot and Red Grange's #77 were to others. They think of the ambassador of stock car racing for thirty-five years, Richard Petty.

Petty combined the long-lasting dominance of Jack Nicklaus with the charisma of Arnold Palmer. He had Wilt Chamberlain's hold on the record books and Michael Jordan's following. For more than three decades, a sport colored by passion perhaps more so than any other was awash in Petty Blue. "Stock car racing fans are the most intensely brand-loyal in all of sports, devoting themselves early in life to the fortunes of one driver," wrote Bruce Newman in *Sports Illustrated*. "For most of a generation, that driver was Richard Petty."

Petty collected more than $7 million in career earnings after earning a total of $760 in his first year. He won seven driving point (Winston Cup) championships. He became the first man to repeat as Daytona 500 champion, and then proceeded to win it five more times. He won in Oldsmobiles, Plymouths, Fords, Dodges, Chevrolets, Buicks and Pontiacs. He won in the '50s, '60s, '70s and '80s. His 200 victories on the NASCAR circuit are nearly twice as many as any other driver. He also finished second 158 times.

Petty Enterprises, in Level Cross, North Carolina, has been home to three generations of NASCAR stars—from Lee Petty, Richard's father and among the first household names in organized stock car racing, to Kyle Petty, Richard's son and one of the top drivers of the past decade. Level Cross, where stock car racing's greatest figure was born on July 2, 1937, is now also home to the Richard Petty

Museum, which draws thousands of fans each year, many of them regarding it as an almost spiritual journey.

Richard's father was a three time Grand National champion, his record of 54 NASCAR victories lasting until his son shattered it and left it a distant image in his rearview mirror. The father wouldn't let the son race as part of Petty Enterprises, however, until he was twenty-one. When he finally competed in his first race in July 1958, he finished sixth. Of his first nine races, that was the only one he managed to finish. His father's continued success allowed him the opportunity to strive for the same, but Petty was adamant that if he succeeded in racing, "I wanted to do it on my own." So his father let him. It was Lee Petty who knocked Richard Petty out of an early race on his way to first place. And after Richard apparently won his first race in 1959, it was Lee who was awarded the victory after protesting that the checkered flag had been waved one lap early.

Daytona International Speedway opened in 1959, with Lee Petty winning the inaugural race, while his son lasted only eight laps before blowing an engine. But the event marked the beginning of the superspeedway era, conveniently timed to coincide with the launch of Petty's career. "If I was any good," he said, "I could grow along with the sport."

Petty wound up earning NASCAR Rookie of the Year honors in 1959. The following year, he won three races and $35,000, placing third at Daytona (just ahead of his father) and second in the Grand National point standings. By 1962, his father's career had ended with a near-fatal crash, but the Crown Prince of NASCAR was about to evolve into the King.

Petty won six races in 1962, 13 in 1963, and his first Daytona 500 in 1964. In 1965, a controversy over the size of his engine led him to withdraw from stock racing to try drag racing. He crashed in Georgia, killing an eight-year-old boy, and returned to the NASCAR circuit. The following year, he became Daytona's first two-time champ.

In 1967, Petty produced stock car racing's version of Wilt Chamberlain's 50-points-per-game season, Mickey Mantle's triple crown performance and O. J. Simpson's 2,000-yard campaign. Not only did he pass his father as NASCAR's most successful driver with his 55th career victory, he also won 27 of 48 races, placing in the top five in 38 and winning 10 in a row.

It was a performance as valuable to stock car racing in the '60s as Palmer's was to golf, both having captured the imagination of the spectators during vital transitional periods. And just as Palmer tended to have the fans on his side in his battles against Nicklaus and Gary Player, Petty had much the same appeal as he went fender-to-fender with David Pearson and Bobby Allison.

Pearson's 105 NASCAR victories are second on the all-time list, yet 95 behind Petty. The duo finished 1-2 a total of 63 times between 1963 and 1977, and Pearson actually won 33 of them, but he was always somewhat of a supporting actor on Petty's stage. Said Darrell Waltrip, himself a NASCAR legend, "Particularly in the early years, it was as if Richard had written the script and NASCAR just helped him to play it out. And anybody else who tried to come in, tried to get a leading role, had to be the bad guy."

Petty's image as the man in the white hat, however, was largely a product of his accessibility, where, again, he took after Palmer. "Few figures in American sports have appreciated their fans as much as Petty has; few, if any, have reciprocated as thoroughly by mingling with the crowd," wrote Ed Hinton in *Sports Illustrated.* "Petty does not tower over his followers as much as minister to them." And so it was not all that uncommon for a Richard Petty Fan Club convention to outdraw most sporting events.

The 1970's brought Petty five more Winston Cup titles and four more Daytona championships. His most famous appearance at Daytona, however, was the one he barely lost in 1976, when he and Pearson collided just before the finish and Pearson sputtered past the checkered flag.

Petty had 40 percent of his stomach removed in 1978 due to ulcers—"likely the price," according to Hinton, "of being too nice to too many people for so long." He came back to win Daytona and another Winston Cup championship the following year, but the '80s were less kind to The King. His last victory, the 200th of his career, came on the Fourth of July in 1984, at the Firecracker 500—at Daytona, no less, and with President Ronald Reagan in attendance. The winning #43 Pontiac was sent to the Smithsonian.

The winless seasons that followed fueled persistent rumors about Petty's impending retirement, but he would only say, "One of these days when they have a race and I don't show up, then everybody will know I've retired." In 1992, however, he announced it would be his last year on the circuit, leading to a farewell tour filled with the kind of sentiment that surrounded Palmer at the eighteenth green of his final U.S. Open.

No matter that Petty had run out of gas, figuratively speaking, eight years earlier. Legends can get by on fumes.

89

Cap Anson

No single person was responsible for professional baseball's color barrier. It was a manifestation of widespread racism, a product of misguided elitism. Yet there was a time when professional baseball was by no means an impenetrable fortress. Some sixty years before Jackie Robinson became the twentieth century's first black professional, a handful of nineteenth century blacks could be found playing alongside their white counterparts. It was only gradually that the notion of an all-white game took hold, which, in itself, was representative of the country's changing attitudes.

But the culture of athletics hasn't always followed in lock-step with the culture of its surroundings, and it is not unreasonable to think that the efforts of a few good men might have overcome the growing specter of Jim Crowism in America and turned baseball into an agent of enlightenment. Instead, the opposite happened, and if one man can be blamed for instigating baseball's segregated system, that man would be Cap Anson.

Adrian Constantine Anson was baseball's first superstar, perhaps the greatest player of the nineteenth century. His upbringing leaves no clue as to the origins of his bigotry. He was born ten years before the Civil War, on April 11, 1852, in Marshall-town, Iowa. He was, in fact, the first white child born in Marshalltown, which was founded by his father. In the land surrounding the Ansons' log cabin were dozens of Pottawatomie Indian tepees, whose young inhabitants became his playmates. It is anything but a textbook recipe for nurturing intolerance.

Anson led his high school to the state baseball championship in 1867 and then attended the University of Notre Dame in 1870, where he is credited with organizing its first baseball team. One year later, he joined the Rockford club of baseball's first pro league, and he later joined the Philadelphia Athletics. When the National League was created in 1876, Anson jumped to the Chicago White Stockings.

In 1879, he was named the team's captain and manager (hence the "Cap" nickname), and he led Chicago to five pennants in his nineteen seasons as player-manager. He became so associated with the team that, after he was fired in 1897, the club became widely known as the Orphans. Not until 1900 were they re-named the Cubs.

Anson hit .329 in his National League career, batting over .300 a total of 19 times. At the age of forty-seven in 1897, he recorded his 3,000th and final hit, the first man in professional baseball history to reach that plateau. He was considered one of the game's first managerial geniuses, an early proponent of spring training, base coaches, basestealing, pitching rotations and the hit-and-run. Anson actually made claims of morality, barring his players from drinking and smoking, even though he had once spent a night in jail for drunkenness and was renowned for his use of vile language, his tendency to complain and his venomous racism. And so he also led the league in hypocrisy.

It was the Hall of Fame hypocrite in Anson, rather than the Hall of Fame talent, that earned him a spot among *The Sports 100*. Anson debuted profession-ally in 1871, at about the same time as the first African-American professional, Bud Fowler. Baseball's first league, the amateur National Association of Base Ball Players, actually had a written ban against black players, with the league denying admission to any teams "composed of one or more colored persons." When the game's original major pro leagues were created, the agreement took the form of an unwritten code. But the majors could not impose their will on the myriad other leagues that began to pop up, and so Fowler found the opportunity to play the game at which he so excelled.

Over the first dozen years of his career, he competed on teams like Stillwater of the Northwestern League and Keokuk and Topeka of the Western League. Fowler's career began to earn him a mixture of praise and pity. "The poor fellow's skin is against him. With his splendid abilities he would long ago have been on some good club had his color been white instead of black," an article in *Sporting Life* declared in 1885. "Those who know say there is no better second baseman in the country."

All told, as many as sixty African-Americans played on pro teams in the 1870s and 1880s, including star pitcher George Stovey and second baseman Frank Grant, who led the International League with a .366 batting average in 1877. Catcher Moses Fleetwood Walker and his brother, Weldy, even became the game's first black major league players, in 1884, when their Toledo club joined the American Association, at the time the National League's rival.

But there were unmistakeable signs that Jim Crowism was beginning to cross the white lines, thanks primarily to baseball's biggest star. When Anson brought his pennant-winning White Stockings to Toledo for an exhibition game in 1883, he threatened to cancel the game if Moses Walker played. Though Walker hadn't even been scheduled to play, the Toledo manager deliberately called Anson's bluff by playing him. Anson chose not to forego the game's gate receipts, but his threat had sounded an ominous tone.

The beginning of the end of black acceptance in pro baseball came four years later, in 1887. The League of Colored Base Ball Clubs had been recognized as a minor league, and it would have provided opportunity for advancement to the majors, but it folded before the season began. Then members of the International League's Syracuse Stars took matters into their own hands, so to speak, intentionally making errors when black pitcher Bob Higgins was on the mound and then refusing to pose with him for a team picture. On July 14, the league announced it would accept no further contracts with black players because "many of the best players in the League were anxious to leave on account of the colored element."

The final straw, not surprisingly, came when Cap Anson entered the scene a few days later, on July 19. It was another exhibition game between Anson's major leaguers and an International League club, this one from Newark. George Stovey, Newark's best pitcher, was scheduled to start. In his *History of Colored Base Ball*, published in 1907, former black player Sol White claims that the New York Giants had been on the verge of buying Stovey's contract earlier, but Anson had objected so vehemently that the National League team backed down. Now Anson, once again, threatened not to play, and this time it worked. Stovey was pulled from his scheduled start.

The barrier was raised. Newark released Stovey, a 33-game winner, at the end of the year. Bud Fowler, who had been hitting .350 with 30 stolen bases for the International League's Binghamton club, was also dropped. By 1889, Bob Higgins, Frank Grant and Weldy Walker were no longer in the International League. Moses Walker, the first black major leaguer, became the last black professional in the nineteenth century. He batted .216 for Newark that year and was not invited back. By the turn of the century, the only appearances made by black men in pro baseball were as team mascots.

So what was Anson's role in the sequence of events? It is obvious that racism and segregationist fervor were commonplace at the time, fed by any number of cultural factors, and without Anson's distasteful attitude blacks would quite likely have been banned from organized baseball anyway. Indeed, targeting Anson as the primary force for baseball's racist policies is a means of personalizing what was really institutional in nature.

In addition, right up until the days of Jackie Robinson, baseball's owners tended to blame fans, players, managers, everyone but themselves for racial segregation in baseball. However, Anson was more than just a symbol of the country's growing segregationist policies. He was one of the game's most influential figures, and his intolerance translated to a color barrier which lasted more than two decades after Anson's death on April 14, 1922. As Sol White wrote, "His repugnant feeling, shown at every opportunity, toward colored ball players, was a source of comment throughout every league in the country, and his opposition, with his great popularity in base ball circles, hastened the exclusion of the black man from white leagues."

One can only wonder what might have happened had his energy been channeled in the opposite direction. Instead, he went out of his way to draw a color line in the dirt, and he dared anyone to step over it.

THE FIRST JACKIE ROBINSON

The first black man to play Major League Baseball was as well suited for the job as Jackie Robinson was some sixty years later, but Moses Fleetwood Walker was the right man at the wrong time. Walker was born in 1857, in Mount Pleasant, Ohio, which happened to act as a way station along the Underground Railroad to assist escaped slaves. The son of a physician, at age twenty he enrolled at Ohio's Oberlin College.

In 1881, he became the catcher on the university's first baseball team, but the following year, he transferred to the University of Michigan, where he played for two seasons. Walker became a professional player in 1883, and then a major leaguer the following year. He was met with a mixed reception, the worst being a death threat in Richmond, Virginia.

Walker had attended integrated schools and played on integrated teams throughout his life, but after his baseball career was derailed by racism, his attitude changed. Walker became a businessman, newspaper editor, author and inventor, but by the end of his life he was also a separatist. Perhaps soured by his experience in America's game, he called for the emigration of African-Americans back to Africa.

90

Pelé

Soccer has plenty of detractors. The game may be a global passion, they say, but in the U.S. it falls—both alphabetically and in popularity—somewhere between bowling and water polo. Indeed, while soccer came over with the first English settlers, it soon fell victim to the same kind of Americanization that turned rounders into baseball. In fact, if anyone is to blame for soccer's lack of progress in America, it is the men responsible for the advent of the game's cousin—American football.

Until the 1994 World Cup, America's only impact on the international soccer scene came when it reached the semifinals of the inaugural World Cup in 1930, and when it produced a shocking 1-0 victory over England in 1950. That's it, and as Paul Gardner explains in *The Simplest Game*, both events "were remarkable precisely *because* the United States was regarded as a lightweight in world soccer competition."

But, while soccer-bashing has become fashionable, it is not quite factual. At the professional level, the game has a history of failure in the U.S., but soccer officials are hoping to use the 1994 World Cup as a springboard to financial success with the launch of Major League Soccer in 1996. At the grass roots level, however, the game has been thriving since the 1970s, when a soccer boom began whose participants are only now beginning to make an international impact. According to World Cup USA figures, nearly 16 million Americans play soccer, the second most popular youth sport in America. U.S. high school participation has more than doubled since 1980, and college soccer teams now outnumber football teams.

Having almost none of the history that fuels the sport around the world, U.S. soccer has largely had to grow by bringing the world's passion to the American stage. Appropriately then, the most important figure in American soccer history is not an American at all. It is Edson Arantes do Nascimiento, known to the world as Pelé.

Tres Coracoes, the Brazilian village where Edson was born, on October 23, 1940, is located in one 2of the country's most impoverished sections. Edson's father was a professional soccer player of some renown, playing for less than $5 a game until a knee injury ended his career and caused Edson to drop out of school in order to earn money for his family. His mother warned him against a soccer career, but, by then, the game had consumed him and a nickname, Pelé, had stuck to him.

By the time he was fourteen, he had led a junior soccer team to three regional championships, which earned him a spot on the Santos team, his home for the next two decades. In his first regular first division game he scored a goal, and in his first season as a starter he scored 65 of them.

At the age of seventeen, in 1958, Pelé led Brazil's national team to its first-ever World Cup victory. The boy who had grown up using a grapefruit as a soccer ball returned home and renegotiated his contract to make him the world's highest paid team-sport athlete.

Brazil repeated as World Cup champion in 1962, though Pelé missed much of the tournament with a torn thigh muscle. By then, however, he had become a worldwide phenomenon. Cities declared national holidays and countries literally put wars on hold when he came to play. He scored the 1,000th goal of his career on November 19, 1969, in dramatic fashion, with some 80,000 spectators and a Brazilian national television audience watching, as he lofted a penalty kick past the goalkeeper.

But Pelé's finest moment came in 1970, when he returned for one last romp in the World Cup, and his beloved Brazil became the first nation to win three Cup titles. Pelé then retired from the national team—on July 18, 1971—at his peak. Neither 180,000 fans yelling "Fica! Fica!" ("Stay! Stay!") nor a petition signed by 100,000 children would change his mind. Three years later, he retired from the Santos team as well, having scored 1,219 goals in 1,254 games. The Pelé era in world soccer was over, but for American soccer, an era was about to begin.

Professional soccer had neither played well nor been played well in the U.S. The first pro league, the American Soccer League, had been born in 1921, and had died nine years later. But in 1960, the International Soccer League was formed, composed of eleven foreign teams and one American squad. The league's occasional ability to draw impressive crowds led to a soccer boom of sorts—in the form of eager investors.

This led to two warring organizations vying for control of pro soccer in America. The United Soccer Association (USA) was led by the likes of Lamar Hunt, Roy Hofheinz and Jack Kent Cooke. However, its rival, the National Professional Soccer League (NPSL), boasted a $500,000 television contract with CBS. The NPSL's inaugural season, in 1967, featured 179 players from thirty-eight countries—and six Americans. The rival league countered by importing entire foreign teams. The end result was success for neither organization, and the two leagues merged at the end of the year to form the 17-team North American Soccer League (NASL).

The first year of the NASL threatened to be the last. Every team lost money, CBS departed, and only 336 fans showed up to one contest, leading one coach to suggest that most of his team's crowds "arrived in the same cab." Only five teams started the 1969 season.

Hunt convinced his colleagues to hire former British star Phil Woosnam as league commissioner. Woosnam promptly hired an assistant, Clive Toye, who had headed the league's Baltimore franchise, leaving his job covering soccer for the London *Daily Express* to do so. Woosnam and Toye figured what the league needed was a New York franchise and an American feel.

In 1971, they convinced Warner Communications to finance the New York Cosmos, and Toye became the team's general manager. The next year, a rule was passed creating quotas of American players, and a college draft was instituted, but the league still struggled. America needed a superstar. It needed Pelé.

It took several years, hundreds of phone calls, thousands of commuting miles—and a three-year, $4.5 million contract—for Toye to snag Pelé. On June 10, 1975, Brazil's retired national treasure signed with the New York Cosmos, taking the world's most refined soccer skills to the soccer outback. It was as if Michael Jordan went off to play basketball in France after being promised the Eiffel Tower. Pelé simply explained, "I looked and saw another mountain to climb."

Suddenly, NASL press boxes were full, and Pelé could be found everywhere from the "Tonight Show" to the White House. Before Pelé, the typical attendance at a Cosmos game was somewhere in the low thousands. Now, there were capacity crowds everywhere they played. "Pelé is not so much promoting U.S. soccer," wrote *Sports Illustrated*'s Jerry Kirshenbaum, "as exposing it." The league drew over two million fans in 1976, as well as some of the world's top players. Pelé was the league MVP. The Cosmos embarked on a world tour and then won the NASL championship in 1977, after drawing nearly 78,000 fans to one playoff game.

Had the NASL continued to grow, and had professional soccer emerged as a major U.S. sports attraction, Pelé's place among *The Sports 100* would probably be uncontested. However, just as the league was expanding, its savior retired for good. His last match was an exhibition between the Cosmos and Santos, witnessed by 75,000 fans and 650 journalists and broadcast to thirty-eight nations on television. He played with the Cosmos in the first half, with Santos in the second. But after Pelé left the scene, the NASL quickly lost ground. By 1982, there was no longer a TV contract. By 1984, there were nine teams remaining. By 1985, the league was finished.

So why does Pelé still merit a spot in this book? Because his legacy was not tied in with the league but with the game. His influence can be seen in many places. The number of players registered with the U.S. Soccer Federation quadrupled from 100,000 to 400,000 during Pelé's twenty-seven months with the Cosmos, and today it closes in on two million. There are an estimated six million youths under the age of twelve playing soccer in some form, making it second only to basketball in that age group. College soccer also came of age, evident not only in the increase in the number of men's teams, but in the arrival of and explosion in the collegiate women's game.

Is Pelé, alone, responsible for all of this? Of course not. But he deserves more credit than anyone else for America's growing interest in the world's favorite game. Ask just about any American to name a great soccer player, and they'll name Pelé. He played here for only three years, but his influence lives on. As the man himself once explained, "Edson is a man like other men. Edson is going to die someday . . . But Pelé doesn't die. Pelé's immortal."

THE LOBBYIST

"The showcase event of the world's most popular sport held in a country where football was a game played with an oblong object, and strikers were people who walked a picket line?" *Sports Illustrated* wondered. "Lunacy."

But Pelé had a vision, and in 1983, he began a campaign to bring the World Cup to the United States. When his efforts to snare the 1986 Cup failed, he concentrated on 1994, even lobbying for the U.S. over his native Brazil, which earned him the wrath of his countrymen. When the U.S. was awarded the prize, Alan Rothenberg, head of the U.S. Soccer Federation, called him "the single most important person in bringing the World Cup to the U.S.A." Being that the summer of 1994 may have been the most important event in American soccer history, Pelé only continues to further his legacy.

91

William Randolph Hearst

For most of the people profiled in *The Sports 100*, their legacy in sports was largely their legacy in life. For William Randolph Hearst, his sporting contribution was among his least important—not because it left a minor imprint on sports, but because he led such a remarkable life. In fact, at the peak of his powers, Hearst ranked as one of the most influential figures in the United States in any endeavor.

"The rich have always seemed to have more money than fun. William Randolph Hearst was the great and memorable exception," *Life* magazine editorialized on the occasion of Hearst's death on August 14, 1951. Hearst had died (or as *Time* magazine put it, "stopped the presses for the last time") in a manner befitting an eccentric, fabulously wealthy American demagogue—at the age of eighty-eight, in the Beverly Hills home of his longtime mistress.

More than 1,500 people attended his funeral, the honorary pallbearers ranging from Herbert Hoover to Douglas MacArthur to Earl Warren. The *New York Journal-American*, the newspaper responsible for turning Hearst from merely an heir to a fortune into the guardian of an empire, announced that the world "has lost a colossus . . . such a man as he, who became a legend within his lifetime, we will not see again." Whether that was good or bad was a matter for debate.

Hearst had been a heir to $30 million. At his death, even after coming close to financial collapse during the Depression, his fortune, most of it vested in the monolithic Hearst Corporation, was estimated to be at least $200 million. He had started with one newspaper, the *San Francisco Examiner*. Through a combination of fearlessness and ruthlessness, he had parlayed it into the world's largest publishing business, including—at its peak—thirty-two newspapers (from Boston to Los

Angeles) and a stable of the nation's most widely read magazines (from *Popular Mechanics* to *Good Housekeeping*).

He owned radio and television stations, hotels and mines. He had gathered one of the world's foremost art and antique collections. He employed some 40,000 people. His opinions and prejudices, through a newspaper syndicate geared to his personal tastes, may have reached more people than those of any other non–world leader in history.

Hearst had spent two terms in the House of Representatives and had failed in repeated attempts to run for mayor of New York City and governor of New York. He had positioned himself for a run at the presidency so often that his detractors began calling him "William Also-ran-dolph Hearst." As it was, he simply turned his empire into a publicity machine for the candidate of his choice.

He had poured millions into his palatial estate overlooking San Simeon Bay, which included 240,000 acres of land, fifty miles of property along the ocean and four castles—a monument to himself described by George Bernard Shaw as "what God would have built if He had the money." Hearst had been, according to *Fortune* magazine, "the nation's No. 1 spender." He had been the model for a 1941 film by Orson Welles, an epic study of ambition and power called *Citizen Kane*.

In the beginning, however, Hearst had just been a young man with a wild streak, and a family fortune large enough to allow him to take advantage of it. Hearst's father, George, was a Missouri farmer who made himself into a California mining millionaire and a U.S. senator. "Willie" was his only child, born April 29, 1863, in San Francisco. After he was kicked out of an Eastern prep school, his father used his influence to get him into Harvard, where Hearst was expelled once again for playing a practical joke on his professors.

In his brief stay at Harvard, Hearst had become the business manager of the university's satirical magazine, *Lampoon*. After leaving school, he took a job as a reporter for the *New York World*, owned by another newspaper legend, Joseph Pulitzer, who would become both Hearst's biggest influence and biggest rival. George Hearst had hoped his son would explore a more lucrative and less unstable field. When he realized his son was not to be denied, he gave him a gift—his first newspaper, the *San Francisco Examiner*.

By the time George Hearst died four years later, in 1891, his son had nearly tripled the size of the *Examiner*, turning it into the biggest and most powerful paper in the West. He did so by recreating the rag in the image of Pulitzer's *World*, the pioneer of "yellow journalism." Hearst's headlines were bigger, bolder, inflammatory. He highlighted stories about tragedy and romance, fires and fugitives, orphans and opium dens. The newspaper didn't make money, nor did it make many friends, but it made Hearst.

In 1895, he turned his ambitions eastward and purchased his second newspaper, the *New York Morning Journal*, for $180,000. The *Journal* had a circulation of about 30,000; the *World*'s circulation had reached 500,000, three times that of any other newspaper. By the turn of the century, however, Pulitzer's protégé would become his greatest competitor. Pulitzer had invented yellow journalism; Hearst would perfect it.

Hearst doubled the paper's size, slashed its price to a penny to cater to the masses, outbid Pulitzer for his best reporters, and tripled the Journal's circulation in less than two months. He built his empire by pouring money into his papers and using the profits to buy more. By doubling and even tripling their salaries, he recruited reporters and columnists who were celebrities in their own right. With no stockholders to answer to, no editors bold enough to question his judgment and no end to his ambition, Hearst, through the *Journal*, became the ultimate crusader, often taking a stand opposite that of the rest of the Eastern press.

He championed union labor, the building of the Panama Canal, a stronger U.S. Navy. In 1898, Hearst and the *Journal* declared the nation at war with Spain three months before the U.S. government did. One story, probably apocryphal, had Hearst telling one of his employees, "You furnish the pictures, I'll furnish the war."

By the end of the war, the *Journal* (later known as the *Journal-American*) had reached a circulation of 700,000, and it would soon pass the *World* in readership. In only a few dozen months, Hearst had become one of the most pugnacious and powerful people in America. His perspective would evolve—he went from a progressive to a socialist Democrat to a staunch anti-Communist Republican, from a war hawk to an isolationist—but, while his attitudes would change, his style would not.

With banner headlines, a splash of color, cartoons, shocking photographs, investigative vigor and a whirlwind of sex, murder and political corruption, his newspapers were part reform and part sensationalism. They appealed to the highest of morals and the lowest of curiosities. And when there seemed a lack of news, Hearst would somehow create it. "Hearst Journalism, in its oldest and yellowest days, may have struck some readers as undignified and phony," *Life* magazine stated, "but it never struck some readers as dull."

But what about sports? With regional passions, the spice of competition, the attraction of celebrity and the occasional scandal, it was ripe fodder for yellow journalism. Of course, Hearst didn't create sports coverage by any means. The first sports newspaper in the United States had been founded back in 1829. The *American Turf Register*, devoted to horse racing, lasted fifteen years. Its founder, William Trotter Porter, began editing a second major sports publication in 1831. The *Spirit of the Times* survived for seventy years. Sports weeklies such as *Sporting Life* and *The Sporting News* would arise half-a-century later, but it was predominantly the daily newspaper that would bring the games to the masses.

In the mid-1800s, there were occasional horse racing, wrestling and prizefighting accounts in newspapers, but sports reporting rose to prominence in the latter part of the century for several reasons. First, there was the arrival of a bona fide sports celebrity, boxer John L. Sullivan, and a bona fide American passion, baseball. Second, there were numerous technological advances which boosted all types of reporting dramatically, including the typewriter, the telephone and the telegraph. In fact, the first news report transmitted over a wireless telegraph concerned an international yacht race.

Finally, there were newspaper publishers like Richard Kyle Fox, who built the circulation of the *Police Gazette* around super-sensationalism and sports coverage; James Gordon Bennett, who sponsored a wide array of sporting events through the *New York Herald*; and Joseph Pulitzer himself, who is said to have organized the first sports department at the *World*.

But it was Hearst who took the most important step toward the publicity, legitimacy and maturity of sports journalism. At the *Journal*, he recruited a staff of expert reporters—Paul Armstrong on boxing, Charles Dryden on baseball, Ralph Paine on rowing. Another Hearst employee, Robert H. Davis, may have been the first to serve as a ghost writer for sports celebrities. However, it was in an early memo to the newspaper's editors that he unveiled his most important innovation. An unabashed baseball fan, he was tired of having to leaf through pages to locate scattered sports results. "It should be," he wrote, "that the sports can be found in one orderly grouping." Since he was "the Chief," he made it so, and soon every newspaper in the country was doing the same.

William Randolph Hearst, the man who had started wars, created and destroyed presidencies, and turned a newspaper empire into a personal pulpit, had added yet another item of lasting significance to his résumé: He had invented the sports section.

92

John Wooden

Until John Wooden turned the UCLA Bruins into college basketball's Goliath, we had a mistaken sense of just what a dynasty was. We thought to repeat was a feat. Wooden made it a starting point.

It was a horse race every year, but the bespectacled Indiana farm-boy-turned-sports-professor always seemed to find his way to the winner's circle. In fact, his former assistant, Louisville coach Denny Crum, called him "the Man o' War of coaches, the Secretariat of men." Historian Wells Twombly wrote that he "taught like a professor and coached like a dictator." Former star player Mike Warren ascribed to him "the discipline of a monk but the will of a hurricane."

One thing is certain. The Wizard of Westwood ranks as the most successful coach in sports history, bar none. He was chosen UPI college basketball Coach of the Year six times; nobody else has received the award more than twice. Six coaches have recorded more overall victories than Wooden, and three own a better winning percentage, but since the NCAA Tournament began, in 1939, nobody has even touched his postseason record.

Wooden towers over college basketball as no other coach towers over his sport. Casey Stengel managed seven World Series champions, but so did Joe McCarthy. Bear Bryant totalled six college football national titles, but Woody Hayes and Bernie Bierman produced five apiece. Perhaps only the success of Vince Lombardi, Toe Blake and Red Auerbach can compare to that of Wooden. Lombardi won five NFL titles in a 10-year career with the Green Bay Packers. Blake coached the Montreal Canadiens to eight Stanley Cup championships in 13 seasons. Auerbach won nine NBA crowns in his career over a 10-year span. But even Lombardi's total was fewer than that of Curly Lambeau and Paul Brown. Blake's eight titles are just two more than Scotty Bowman. And Auerbach had the luxury of fine tuning his club around Bill Russell.

But not Wooden. He won 10 NCAA Tournament titles over a 12-year span. Adolph Rupp, his most renowned contemporary, and the man with the second most tournament titles in history, won only four. Wooden rolled to seven straight NCAA titles from 1967–1973, and in doing so he wasn't allowed to do what even the great Stengel and Auerbach teams could do—lose a postseason game here and there. He recorded four perfect 30-0 seasons, a record 88-game winning streak, a 47-game streak, a 41-game streak. In the process, he created interest in college basketball, sowing the seeds of March Madness.

Certainly he was blessed with some excellent players, but as Wooden himself admitted, "No one can win without material. But not everyone can win with material." And particularly when the material changes form every few years. Wooden won his first two championships (in 1964 and 1965) with a small, guard-oriented squad. He won his next three (in 1967, 1968 and 1969) with Lew Alcindor (Kareem Abdul-Jabbar) in the middle. He won with star forwards in 1970 and 1971 and then with another dominant center, Bill Walton, in 1972 and 1973. Finally, in 1975, after announcing his retirement two days earlier, he won with a team nobody expected to win at all.

"I don't buy the proposition that UCLA has risen above the general level of college basketball," Wooden would claim. "We've been more consistent, come closer to our natural ability more often than others." That, of course, is the product of good coaching, which is why the statement was one of several made to *Sports Illustrated* in 1972 when Wooden became the only coach to win Sportsman of the Year honors in the first forty years of the award.

Ironically, the era in which UCLA consistently dominated college basketball also just happened to be the most turbulent years ever to hit college campuses. And, on the surface, Wooden seemed an unlikely success story, as he reeked of Establishment sensibilities in a decidedly anti-Establishment environment.

His was a Midwestern, small-town upbringing. Born on an Indiana farm on October 14, 1910, he grew into a three-time All-America guard at nearby Purdue University in the early '30s. In fact, Wooden was good enough to earn selection to the Hall of Fame in 1960, before his run of championships led to his enshrinement as a coach a dozen years later. He remains the only person honored twice.

Wooden coached high school ball for several years, amassing more than 200 wins in Indiana and Kentucky before taking over the reins at Indiana State in 1947 and then UCLA in 1949. Throughout his tenure at UCLA, Wooden retained his small-town values. He was about as un-hip as an educator could be in the '60s. He installed rigid dress and appearance codes just as long hair was becoming a status symbol and spoke in cliché philosophies. Yet his two biggest stars, Alcindor and Walton, were also two notorious activists, and somehow Wooden merged his counterculture kids into champions.

Wooden won, said *Sports Illustrated*'s Alexander Wolff, "largely by getting back to basics, by teaching the game and not dealing with all the Jim Valvano–type stuff that college basketball coaches deal with today—speaking engagements and videos and careers hosting 'Saturday Night Live.'"

Wooden was clearly the last of a breed. And yet, in many ways, he was also ahead of his time, particularly as a coach who integrated black and white players into a dominant unit. By the mid-'60s, UCLA already boasted an impressive tradition of African-American sporting excellence, from Ralph Metcalfe and Rafer Johnson to Jackie Robinson and Arthur Ashe. The school's history and its setting enabled Wooden to attract black stars, and he largely built his teams around them.

In some respects, this put Wooden nearly alone among NCAA champion coaches. Adolph Rupp at Kentucky, for example, was notorious for his prejudice. And even the Texas Western title-winning team of 1966, with its first-ever all-black starting five, graduated none of its black players, using and discarding them like equipment. But Wooden's was integrated success with a foundation. Black players were more than just temporary window dressing.

Still, the question remains. What was so important about John Wooden? The kind of figure included in *The Sports 100* is generally one who was not merely successful but influential, preferably the first of his kind rather than the last. So what did Wooden leave behind?

In a word: standards.

"Turnovers" was once the dirtiest of words to college basketball coaches; now it is "turnover"—the job-security kind. Wolff explained, "In a way, he's probably helped create all the pressure that gets all these coaches fired. God forbid you don't make it to the NCAA Tournament a couple years in a row. Well, John Wooden won the whole tournament seven years in a row. He created that culture of expectation, and that's probably his most poisonous legacy, but it certainly is a legacy."

And so, while he claimed to abhor the trappings of big-time college basketball, John Wooden played a pivotal role in ushering in just that.

93

Harry Edwards

In many respects, 1968 was the year America grew up. Never before had so much conflict, so much anger, so much frustration erupted in so many places. Peace and patriotism butted heads; youth and power stared each other down; the white Establishment met its match in black dignity.

The Tet Offensive in January turned the psychological tide of the war in Vietnam, causing many Americans to wonder whether, if not unjust, it was at least unwinnable. In March, a weary President Lyndon Johnson elected to step down, ostensibly in the name of national unity. The assassinations of Martin Luther King, Jr., and Robert Kennedy in April and June turned hope into cynicism; cynicism turned to violence with riots stretching from Newark to Los Angeles.

Always, however, sport was supposed to be immune to it all, the escape, the toy department. But, in 1968, the athletic fields became a political battleground. Reality invaded the games. And the person most responsible for the revolution was Harry Edwards.

In the '60s, Edwards was the very picture of black militancy, described by a friend as "Nat Turner, Malcolm X and Paul Robeson all rolled into one." He wore a beret and dark sunglasses. He huddled with Stokely Carmichael and H. Rap Brown. For a time, he was a member of the Black Panther movement and was under FBI surveillance. He was also an assistant professor of sociology at San Jose State College and a man with a mission: to strip away the myth of sport as a haven of racial equality and to use the athletic arena as a means of social protest. He was remarkably successful on both counts.

In the '90s, Edwards, sans beret, is a full professor of sociology at Cal-Berkeley and a consultant to the San Francisco 49ers. But his mission remains the same. "The establishment has changed to the extent that they decided to invite me in," Edwards explained. "But I'm like the Statue of Liberty. I've been in the same position since Day One."

Said Robert Lipsyte, former columnist for *The New York Times*, in 1987, "Twenty years ago he was considered a dangerous radical who was going to pull down the republic. Instead, he has worked within the system and has become the most important sports activist we've had in our lifetime."

He is certainly a success story, because on November 22, 1942, when he was born into poverty in East St. Louis, Illinois, renown of any kind must have seemed remote. Edwards was raised in a house with broken windows, holes in the roof and an outhouse in the back, sharing the squalor with seven brothers and sisters and countless rats and roaches. His mother abandoned the family when he was eight. His brother was sent to Iowa State Penitentiary, and Edwards himself was jailed for repeated juvenile offenses. His father, an ex-convict with a third-grade education, raised his children in a community that expected little more.

Edwards was often told by his father that sports were the only ticket to success, a notion he has spent his life trying to refute, contending that "to tie the aspirations of 30 million people to fewer than 2,000 jobs in three professional sports is an inhuman mockery." Ironically, though Edwards was insightful enough not to count on a professional career, his athletic prowess did serve as a springboard out of the ghetto.

A 6-foot-8 center and an excellent discus thrower, he would earn athletic scholarships in basketball and track, first at Fresno (California) City College, and then at San Jose State, where he received his undergraduate degree. He would go on to earn a master's and Ph.D. at Cornell University, receiving an equally important education on weekends by travelling by bus to New York City, where Malcolm X held court.

The revolutionary events of 1968 actually began in 1967 at San Jose State. Sixty of the school's seventy-two black students called on Edwards, by then an assistant professor, to assist them in airing complaints about discriminatory practices in housing, athletics and academics. Edwards led a rally on the opening day of classes and oulined a list of demands, threatening to disrupt the season-opening football game if they weren't met. Ronald Reagan, then governor of California, responded by threatening to call out the militia and labelling Edwards a lawbreaker who was unfit to teach. Edwards, in turn, called Reagan "a petrified pig, unfit to govern." In the end, the football game was cancelled, but the college administration met the black students' demands.

"So we had carried the confrontation," Edwards would write two years later in his first book, *The Revolt of the Black Athlete*. "But more than this, we had learned the use of power—the power to be gained from exploiting the white man's economic and almost religious involvement in athletics."

At almost the same time, a San Jose State student-athlete, world class sprinter Tommie Smith, had caused an uproar by casually mentioning in an interview that some black athletes had discussed the possibility of boycotting the upcoming Olympics, a notion that had first been suggested by comedian and activist Dick Gregory in 1964.

In October, Edwards, Smith and a handful of others gathered to form the Olympic Committee for Human Rights (OCHR) and its segment devoted to planning a possible boycott, the Olympic Project for Human Rights (OPHR). Six weeks later, Edwards chaired a workshop involving dozens of black athletes, including Smith and UCLA basketball star Lew Alcindor. The result was a pro-boycott endorsement and a list of six demands, including the restoration of Muhammad Ali's titles; the removal of International Olympic Committee chairman Avery Brundage, whom the OCHR considered racist and anti-Semitic; and the continued exclusion of teams from apartheid South Africa and Rhodesia in U.S. and Olympic athletic events.

The OCHR also called for the desegregation of the New York Athletic Club, which had no black or Jewish members and which had an indoor track meet scheduled for February 15. All but nine black athletes withdrew from the meet, most echoing the sentiments of O. J. Simpson, who said, "I wouldn't run that weekend if my mother was holding the meet." The black protesters were joined by several white athletes and many college teams. Edwards would later write that the series of events "marked the end of an age when Afro-American athletes would compromise black dignity for a watch, a television set, a trophy, or merely the love of competition."

On the same day as the track meet, however, it was announced that South Africa, which had agreed to integrate its Olympic team while still practicing official racial segregation at home, was being readmitted to the Olympic Games. In response, most African nations withdrew from the Games and Edwards declared, "Let whitey run his own Olympics." He announced plans for a second set of games to be held in Africa and involving black athletes. The decision to readmit South Africa was quickly reversed.

With Edwards's lead, 1968 became a watershed year in the relationship between race and sports, as long-suffering African-American athletes were moved to denounce widespread discriminatory practices. Black athletes at dozens of colleges revolted, as did many of their professional counterparts, particularly on the NFL's St. Louis Cardinals and Cleveland Browns. Stars like Arthur Ashe also began to take more public stands. "What has happened is that the black athlete has left the facade of locker room equality and justice to take his long vacant place as a primary participant in the black revolution," Edwards explained.

The publicity led *Sports Illustrated* to publish a five-part series entitled "The Black Athlete—A Shameful Story" in which author Jack Olsen stated, ". . . like it or not, face up to it or not, condemn it or not, Harry Edwards is right." Edwards was mentioned or quoted in the series nineteen times.

Edwards's biggest moment was still to come, but reaction to the proposed boycott of the Olympic Games was as diverse as it was spirited. Said long jumper Ralph Boston, "If we decide on some kind of protest, I'd be less of a man not to participate. I'd be letting myself down, my family, my race." But older former Olympians like Jesse Owens and Rafer Johnson spoke out against it, labelling the protest noble but misguided and pointing out that the Olympics had been the best thing that had ever happened to them. Many prospective competitors agreed, including high jumper John Thomas, who asked, "How much pride can you lose by emerging an Olympic champion?"

Edwards's perspective: "Grinning black faces atop an Olympic victory stand only mock kids smothering in slums, old women dying of malnutrition, bombed-out churches, the bodies strewn along the path of riot . . . If the fastest among us can show that our sense of personal worth and obligation outweighs any rewards offered us and that we represent the many, something may be accomplished."

As it turned out, Edwards's boycott never happened and most of the O.C.H.R. demands were ignored, but his ultimate mission—to draw attention to the plight of African-Americans—was still essentially successful. At the Olympic Trials, less than half of the black athletes voted to support a boycott, so it was decided that each athlete would choose his or her own form of protest. Still, some athletes, including Tommie Smith and fellow San Jose State sprinter John Carlos, had to be convinced to compete; others, such as Lew Alcindor, never competed at all.

For his own safety, Edwards had been warned against attending the Games in Mexico City, and so he watched on television as Smith set a world record in the 200-meter dash finals and Carlos finished third. Just before the medal ceremony, Smith pulled two black gloves from his bag and handed the left one to Carlos. Each wore long black socks and no shoes; Smith tied a black scarf around his neck. During the playing of America's national anthem, they raised their black-gloved fists straight above their bowed heads in a protest as dramatic as any Edwards had hoped for.

Smith later explained, "My raised right hand stood for the power in black America. Carlos's raised left hand stood for the unity of black America. Together they formed an arch of unity and power. The black scarf around my neck stood for black pride. The black sock with no shoes stood for black poverty in racist America. The totality of our effort was the regaining of black dignity."

But Avery Brundage and the IOC believed it stood only for insubordination and a mockery of the Olympic ideal. Smith and Carlos were immediately suspended from the U.S. Olympic team and sent home, where they found many doors closed to them as a result of their silent protest. Of course, they were also heroes to many black Americans and to many Third World athletes, as was Edwards, who received a silver medal as a gift from the Cuban 400-meter relay team. Of course, it being Cuba, it only earned Edwards further contempt from the Establishment.

For better or for worse, the Olympic Games would never again pretend to be above the fray. In 1972, Palestinian terrorists would murder eleven Israeli competitors. In 1976, twenty-seven African nations would withdraw from the Games. For the Moscow Olympics in 1980, Jimmy Carter would engineer a boycott of more than forty countries to protest the Russian invasian of Afghanistan, leading Edwards to comment, "I find it ironic that 12 years after I was denounced for calling for a boycott of the Olympics, the President of the United States has called a boycott—proving unequivocally that sports are indeed political."

As for Edwards, he would continue to pioneer in the field of sports sociology, authoring *The Sociology of Sport*, in 1973, described as "the first comprehensive

analysis of the connection between the world of athletics and American society."
In the '80s, he even turned himself into something of a cottage industry, joining
the 49ers and later the Golden State Warriors as a consultant to help athletes in
their struggles to cope with life on and off the playing surface. In 1987, he was
hired by Major League Baseball to improve the game's record on minority hirings,
particularly in coaching and front office positions.

But the ultimate sports activist plods on. "I know that I'm not going to get
everything done. My grandchildren are going to be fighting this battle," he has
said. "But my grandchildren and my children shouldn't have to fight battles that I
should have fought."

94

Peter Ueberroth

Ueberroth means "above red" in German. And so it seems entirely appropriate that, after so many years of Olympiads in the red, when the 1984 Summer Olympics in Los Angeles emerged as the most profitable sporting event in world history, the man responsible for the success of the Games would be named Peter Victor Ueberroth.

Ueberroth's subsequent five-year reign as commissioner of baseball met with decidedly more mixed reviews, yet few sports figures have been as influential over the past fifteen years as the man with the golden name. Though he was once described as being "a man so laid back he's almost supine," Ueberroth's success, much like Peter the Great's, was due in part to a healthy dose of ruthlessness. And like the fisherman-turned-apostle Saint Peter, he rose from humble beginnings to sainted status.

He was born September 2, 1937, in Evanston, Illinois. His mother died when he was four; his father was a roaming aluminum siding salesman. As a result, before the family eventually settled in Burlingame, California, Ueberroth attended six different elementary schools and two high schools in five states. He mowed lawns, worked a paper route, caddied, worked on a chicken farm; he was an entrepreneur in training. Ueberroth was also an athlete, earning letters in four sports in high school and then an athletic scholarship to San Jose State College as a water polo player. Though he led the league in scoring in his final two seasons, he missed the cut to make the 1956 Olympic squad.

His business career would meet fewer failures. In fact, he became a self-made millionaire. By the time he was twenty-two, he was a vice-president and shareholder of Trans International Airlines. By age twenty-six, he had started his own travel services company, the First Travel Corporation. By 1978, it had become the second largest travel company in North America. It was then, soon after Los Angeles made a successful bid to host the 1984 Summer Games, that Ueberroth found a new job.

Los Angeles had hosted the Summer Olympics fifty-two years earlier, producing an extravagant event, even by Hollywood standards, that set the Games on a course of irresponsible spending for years to come. In 1976, for instance, the Montreal Games left the city $1 billion in debt. In 1980, the Moscow Games cost the Soviet Union nearly $9 billion. The Olympics had become a losing proposition, and seemed to be at a crossroads. Whereas cities had once clamored to host the Games, Los Angeles was the only city even to make a realistic bid for 1984.

A poll of Los Angeles citizens in the late '70s revealed that eighty percent were in favor of hosting the games, but only if the city wasn't forced to spend a dime. In 1978, those same citizens voted to put that sentiment into law, making it a city charter amendment. Consequently, the Southern California Committee for the Olympic Games (SCCOG) then approached the IOC with a novel concept—the Games would be run by a private corporation with no government funding. It took seven months of negotiations, but once the IOC yielded, the SCCOG began to search for the man to make it work.

Said one committee member, "We wanted someone to run the Games; we didn't want the Games to run us." The SCCOG chose Ueberroth, described by *Sports Illustrated* as "prince of the private sector, the golden boy with the miser's touch." Ueberroth became president of the Los Angeles Olympic Organizing Committee (LAOOC).

"We're not trying to be bigger, better, grander," Ueberroth announced. "We're clearly trying to put on a Games that goes back to the early, easy principles of the Olympics, to celebrate sport." Translation: fiscal responsibility and what has been called the first corporate Olympics.

While previous Olympics had been supported almost entirely through government funding, Ueberroth and the LAOOC funded the $500 million 1984 Games primarily through television contracts, commercial sponsorships, and ticket sales. No longer would radio rights to the Games be free of charge, no longer would Olympic officials have the luxury of free limo service. Nearly half of the nearly 70,000 people who assisted Ueberroth were volunteers.

The first key to the Games was the television package, and Ueberroth played a key role in securing an unprecedented $225 million offer from ABC, which was about equal to that paid for all previous Olympic Games combined. In researching previous Games, Ueberroth also discovered that "if you took one item, one line off the cost of an Olympics—construction—they all would've made money." And so he kept construction costs down by using existing facilities and by asking corporate sponsors to provide new ones.

Ueberroth also limited sponsorship to a few select product categories and a handful of top corporations, creating an appearance of exclusivity and increasing the value of sponsorship. At the Winter Olympics four years earlier, in Lake Placid, more than 380 corporate sponsors had participated, but they provided only $9 million. The Games finished $6 million in debt. In Los Angeles, with less than one-tenth as many sponsors, Ueberroth took in more than ten times as many sponsorship dollars.

Still, many predicted failure for the big event, and even as the 23rd Olympic Games approached, the specter of potential disaster hovered. But a little luck and a lot of foresight translated into an unqualified success.

The Soviet Union and seventeen other nations boycotted the Olympics just two months before they were to begin, which some predicted would bring financial ruin to the Games. But Ueberroth embarked on a campaign to convince wavering countries to participate, notably Rumania, which made the trip to Los Angeles and returned home with fifty-three medals.

Security was also a potential nightmare, and indeed, four men carrying shotguns were caught storming Ueberroth's house, two of his dogs were poisoned and there were about eighty investigations of bomb scares. However, Ueberroth had mustered twenty-nine different police forces, and there were no major incidents.

Others feared the detrimental effects of Los Angeles's smog and traffic, but there were blue skies through much of the fortnight and most Angelenos remained parked in front of their television sets. Even former decathlete Rafer Johnson, whom Ueberroth chose to light the Olympic flame, developed shin splints, but he and the torch prevailed, as did the Games. More than 7,000 athletes from 140 countries competed in front of nearly six million spectators, and more than 180 million American television viewers.

The acclaim given Ueberroth was virtually universal. In naming him the first-ever sports figure to be named its Man of the Year, *Time* magazine announced, "The Los Angeles Olympics became a spectacular dramatization of a renascent American entrepreneurial energy and optimism . . . Not since Neil Armstrong's walk on the moon has America had such an opportunity to lift its best face to the world. Ueberroth arranged the showing."

Weeks before the game, Ueberroth had quietly predicted at least a $15 million surplus, an announcement greeted with widespread skepticism. In the end, the surplus exceeded $220 million, all of it going to boost amateur sports in Southern California and the rest of the nation. Of course, there were observers who claimed that a profit doesn't necessarily translate into success, that it really means perhaps ticket prices should have been lower or more money should have been invested in the event. Regardless, Ueberroth's legacy is a demonstration of potential—that the Olympic Games were a potent marketing vehicle and that they could be used to publicize not only countries, but cities, as well.

From the personal tragedies of Munich to the financial tragedy of Montreal to the political tragedy of Moscow, a dark cloud seemed to have been forming over the Games. But, as longtime *Los Angeles Times* reporter Kenneth Reich wrote in *Making It Happen*, an account of the 1984 Games, "The Olympics, in the end, breached this newspaper reporter's cynicism and reawakened my idealism, and I thought that was no small achievement."

THE COMMISH

Riding the wave of popularity from the 1984 Olympic Games, Peter Ueberroth became the sixth commissioner in baseball history on October 1, 1984, taking over for Bowie Kuhn. According to *Sports Illustrated*, after five years and three months as baseball's top man, Ueberroth "left the game in much better shape than when he arrived."

He was occasionally criticized for preferring style over substance, and was suspected of using the position to posture for a run at political office, but he still made a significant impact on the game. Baseball had experienced a rash of drug investigations and revelations in the early '80s, and Ueberroth's influence on drugs in baseball was much like Kenesaw Mountain Landis's on gambling. He didn't necessarily stop the threat, but he stopped it from threatening the game's integrity.

Ueberroth also reinstated Mickey Mantle and Willie Mays (whom Kuhn had banned from the game for taking jobs with Atlantic City casinos), made a concerted effort to increase minority hirings, helped to bring an end to the brief 1985 players' strike, signed lucrative TV contracts with CBS and ESPN, and initiated the probe into gambling allegations against Pete Rose.

When Ueberroth first took office, twenty-one of the twenty-six big league clubs were said to be losing money; five years later about the same amount were at least breaking even. However, as it turns out, much of the owners' newfound financial stability was due to collusion. That is, under Ueberroth's orchestrations, the owners were violating baseball's labor agreement by refusing to bid on free agents.

The players association filed three grievances, and after Ueberroth left office, the owners agreed to pay $280 million in damages to the players—more than Ueberroth made on the entire 1984 Olympics.

95

Charles McNeil

The final seconds were closing in on Super Bowl XXIX, January 29, 1995 and the San Francisco 49ers held on to a 49-26 lead over the San Diego Chargers. The game had long been over, decided in the opening minutes when the 49ers scored two touchdowns on their first two possessions. Yet, as the Chargers tried one desperate final attempt, a "Hail Mary" toss into the end zone, millions of viewers remained on the edge of their seats. The reason: the point spread.

San Francisco was an 18½-point favorite. A last-second touchdown by San Diego would have cut the victory margin to 17 points. Long after the game had been decided, one lone quarterback essentially was deciding the fate of millions of bettors wagering in excess of $1 billion. The situation, in a nutshell, reveals the three most obvious ways in which the point spread has influenced sport—more interest in the games, more betting on the games and more opportunity for scandal—and, thus, it reveals the influence of the man whom many consider most responsible for its emergence: Charles McNeil.

The point spread is a relatively recent phenomenon in sports betting, as is the emergence of professional football as the bettors' primary focus. For more than a century, bookmakers were primarily associated with horse racing. In the first part of the twentieth century, baseball topped the list among team sports wagers. But as betting at the track was gradually legalized and, most important, thanks to the revolutionary appeal of the spread, football became the bookmaker's bread-and-butter.

A central question bookies and bettors had been faced with for years was how to deal with an event in which one competitor was far superior to another. Early horse races featured different weights assigned to different horses, the favored entry having to carry more pounds. Soon, the practice of establishing odds became commonplace in sports betting of every kind. Lucky Louie would be a 6-to-5 favorite in the sixth race; the odds would be 2-to-1 that Minnesota would beat Illinois. A bettor might have to bet $5 to make $1 if wagering on the favorite, or his return might be $4 on a $1 bet if an underdog or longshot prevailed.

Modeled on baseball, the system was applied to football and basketball, but it didn't work as effectively. The odds system still engendered hesitation on the part of the bettor. Bet on the favorite, and you're risking a lot to earn a little. Bet on the longshot, and your bet is smaller but success seems remote. Then sometime before World War II, the point spread arrived, and sports betting's appeal increased considerably.

The new system was most amenable to football and basketball. Instead of offering odds, bookmakers offered points. They rated each team and estimated by how many points the favored team would win. The Rams, for instance, would be 10-point favorites over the Steelers. All wagers were placed at even money, with the bettor simply staking $11 to win $10. The $1 difference went toward the bookie's commission.

But while the point spread is simple, its origins are a bit more complex. There are certainly references to the point spread before Charles McNeil became a dominant figure on the scene. Some sources contend the spread was used in Minneapolis as early as the 1930s. But the person most often credited as the major force behind the popularity, if not the invention, of the point spread is McNeil.

Mort Olshan, editor of *The Gold Sheet*, the nation's most respected handicapping publication, explained, "McNeil might not have invented the point spread, but he certainly refined it." Kentucky bookmaker Ed Curd, another seminal figure in sports betting history (and Mafia boss Frank Costello's personal bookie), called McNeil "the greatest handicapper in my lifetime . . . There might be one as good somewhere, but none better." And Robert H. Boyle, former senior writer at *Sports Illustrated* and an acquaintance of McNeil, said his friend "did for sports what Adam Smith did for economics."

Information about McNeil is sketchy, which is not surprising since he even kept his bookmaking and betting habits a secret from one of his good friends, University of Chicago football coach and athletic moralist Amos Alonzo Stagg. Born in Chicago, in 1903, McNeil graduated from the University of Chicago, where he befriended Stagg, in the mid-1920s. One source refers to him as an economics major, another claims he was a math major, a third that he was a history major. Regardless, by all accounts he was brilliant, particularly when it came to numbers.

McNeil taught math for several years after graduating, before taking a job as a securities analyst for a Chicago bank. Because the job coincided with the worst years of the Depression, McNeil pointed out that "if that didn't teach you to play the angles, nothing would." And McNeil became increasingly enchanted with playing the angles, betting on anything and everything, even placing bets with office colleagues on how much longer the bank's executives would hold on to their jobs. When the bank president found out that his odds has fallen to 3-to-1, he fired McNeil instead. "At the time," McNeil recalled, "I had 8-to-1 on myself."

McNeil turned to gambling full-time, and, in the late 1930s he was one of four partners who opened the Gym Club, which became Chicago's top bookmaking joint. Two vital ingredients in the Gym Club's success were McNeil's point spread system, which he called "wholesaling odds," and his ability to establish just the right line.

McNeil seems to have been viewed as something of a betting professor. He not only legitimized the point spread as a viable betting tool, but he also became an arbiter of national disputes involving sports betting and a force against the unsavory tangents to his profession. He had an uncanny ability, for instance, to sniff out a "fix."

However, by the 1950s, McNeil had decided to concentrate only on making bets instead of taking them, explaining, "Bookmakers go to jail. Bettors do not go to jail." He is said to have turned from oddsmaking to gambling when the Mob wanted to use his mind for their profit. "There are three things a gambler needs: money, guts and brains," he once said. "If you don't have one, you're dead. I have all three." That being the case, he estimated that he bet an average of $200,000 a week on college football, winning nearly two-thirds of the time and earning more than $300,000 a year.

Eventually, his gambling earnings allowed him to buy into several small businesses, and largely retire from the betting business. He moved to Fort Lauderdale in his later years, residing there until his death in 1981.

Did Charles McNeil invent the point spread? It is difficult to say, which is why McNeil is ranked #95 instead of much higher. Boyle is certain he did; others claim the point spread was a phenomenon that arrived gradually in several places at the same time. It is quite apparent, however, that McNeil was an instrumental figure in making the point spread an accepted feature—indeed, the primary feature—of sports betting.

"I can't imagine doing business without it," said Michael "Roxy" Roxborough, president of Las Vegas Sports Consultants, which sets the betting line for 75 percent of the legal market. "The point spread is the handicap that supposedly makes everything equal, and that's why we can almost make betting odds on any two teams, regardless of the disparity in talent. If there was no such thing as a point spread, if for some reason nobody was smart enough to think of it, there would be hardly any gambling at all on pro football. It would be about 10 percent of what it is now."

What it is now is an industry in which it has been estimated that $2 billion is legally wagered in Nevada and as much as $75 billion is illegally wagered across the nation. The 1995 Super Bowl alone took in $69 million legally, perhaps fifty times as much illegally.

The point spread stimulates betting by increasing the appeal of uneven games that would normally draw low betting volume, but it also promotes gambling by simplifying the process. "Try this test," explained Lang, who is associate editor of

Gaming Today. "Enter a crowded room and casually remark that the Giants, in your estimation, are 7 to 2 to beat the Eagles. Odds are that this comment will pass without rebuttal. At another gathering, remark casually that the Giants are nine points better than the Eagles. Invariably, someone will counter with a different number."

As much as the point spread has increased the appeal of watching and betting on the games, it has increased the possibility of fixing them, too. A team can win a game but fail to beat the spread, meaning players can shave points to benefit those who bet on the other side.

The fallout from the point spread was immediate and dramatic. In 1945, a basketball game between Brooklyn College and Akron was cancelled due to rumors, later confirmed, that Brooklyn players had agreed to shave points. The following year, two players were suspended indefinitely from the NFL after failing to report an attempted fix of the 1946 Championship Game. Five years after that, a college basketball point-shaving scandal was uncovered involving thirty-two players and seven schools between 1947 and 1950. A decade later, thirty-seven players from twenty-two schools were implicated in point-shaving scandals masterminded by former Columbia basketball star Jack Molinas. Since then, point-shaving attempts have also been uncovered at Boston College (in 1978–1979) and at Tulane University (1984–1985).

Perhaps Arthur Daley of *The New York Times* had the right idea in 1951, when he wrote that the "gambling craze has swept the country with the avariciousness of a prairie fire. The flames are out of control . . . [fed by] the satanic gimmick of the point spread."

96

A. J. Foyt

Anthony Joseph Foyt, Jr., son of Anthony Joseph Foyt, Sr., and father of Anthony Joseph Foyt III, made a name all for himself as the World's Greatest Racecar Driver. For some four decades, he roamed America's tracks, winning in almost every type of car in every type of race—and continuing to win long after becoming a living legend. In fact, of four athletes who were honored with Sports Legend awards in 1986, three—Joe DiMaggio, Red Auerbach and Bobby Orr—were long retired. The fourth was A. J. Foyt.

Foyt is included among *The Sports 100* because, like Jack Nicklaus in the 1970s, his performance gave him mythical status, and his mythical status carried his sport. Nicklaus personified golf; Foyt personified speed. *Sports Illustrated*'s Bob Ottum described him as "part of the national subconscious," adding that "years ago, all other drivers were compared to Barney Oldfield; now A.J. is the bench mark."

Of course, Oldfield was renowned for going a mile a minute at the turn of the century; Foyt reached that level when he was about five. Born January 16, 1935, in Houston, Texas, Foyt was the son of an auto mechanic. He spent most of his childhood under the hood of a race car before spending forty years of his life behind the wheel. When he was five or six, his father presented him with a midget-type racer and pitted him in an exhibition against a leading adult driver of the day. Foyt won.

A dozen years later, he dropped out of school to race competitively, and he quickly became known, according to *Sports Illustrated*'s William Nack, as a "hard-charging, bandanna-flying damn-the-torpedoes kid who could drive the paint off the midgets and the sprint cars." From his arrival in the '50s, throughout his heyday in the '60s and '70s, then his twilight in the '80s and the finale to his career in the early '90s, Foyt, along with Richard Petty, was the face of auto racing—even if it was hidden beneath a helmet zooming by at 150 miles per hour. No career in motorsports—indeed, few in any athletic endeavor—combined dominance, diversity and distance like Foyt's.

Dominance? He was the first man to win the Indy 500 four times, doing so in 1961, 1964, 1967 and 1977. Two drivers, Al Unser and Rick Mears, have since matched the total; nobody has surpassed it. Foyt collected a record 67 Indy Car victories, 15 more than Mario Andretti and 40 percent more than anyone else. He won seven USAC (U.S. Auto Club) championships, his first in 1960 and his last in 1979. No other man has won as many as five. In 1964, Foyt competed in 13 Indy Car races. He won 10 of them.

Diversity? Besides ranking as history's top Indy car driver, he won seven NASCAR Winston Cup races (including the 1972 Daytona 500), seven sports car events, and more than 90 USAC stock car, sprint car, midget and dirt car races. Of the USAC's four major categories—Indy cars, stock cars, sprint cars and midgets—Foyt is the only man to claim at least 20 victories in each. No man recorded a long-lasting dominance over the Indy car circuit to match Foyt's, yet he admitted that until the 1980s, he lived solely on his stock car and midget racing income, investing the remainder. Wrote Ottum, "That's like Reggie Jackson living on the royalties from his candy bar and socking away everything else."

Foyt is the only man to win a USAC stock car and Indy car championship in the same year (1979). In the first endurance race he ever entered, the 24 Hours of Le Mans, he and his partner, Dan Gurney, became the first Americans ever to capture the prestigious event. Foyt also won the 24 Hours of Daytona twice, as well as the 12 Hours of Sebring. He won on dirt tracks, on road courses, on speedways. He won with engines mounted in front of him and with engines mounted behind him. He won 100-mile races, 500-mile races and just about every distance in between.

Distance? Few athletes can match Foyt's longevity. He won his first legitimate race in 1953. He announced his retirement from Indy car racing on May 15, 1993, on the day he qualified for his record thirty-fifth straight Indy 500. When he began racing, Indy drivers wore slacks, a T-shirt and an open-faced helmet; Indy cars were 2,500-pound front-engine roadsters costing an estimated $25,000; and Foyt could qualify by reaching 143 miles per hour. By the time he retired, drivers were encased in fire-retardant one-piece suits and helmets; Indy cars were rear-engine imports, barely half as heavy but nearly twenty times as expensive; and Foyt, almost sixty years old, was qualifying at speeds beyond 220 m.p.h. Foyt won $2,171 in his first season on the Indy Car circuit; he won $578,744 in his thirty-fourth season.

That Foyt would last four decades in the most dangerous of sports is remarkable considering he had enough serious injuries to fill a hospital ward. In 1959, a midget car crash left him with a brain concussion and a cracked back. In 1965, his stock car bounced end over end down a 35-foot embankment at California's Riverside 500. A doctor pronounced him dead at the scene, but Foyt was pried loose to nurse a broken back, a fractured ankle and severe chest injuries. In 1966, Foyt suffered second and third degree burns when his car burst into flames during practice in Milwaukee. Six years later, he was doused with burning fuel at a race in Illinois. As he jumped out of the car, it ran over his left leg. In 1983, he broke two vertebrae at the Firecracker 400, but he still won the Paul Revere 250 later that night.

He suffered perhaps his worst accident in 1990 at a race in Elkhart Lake, Wisconsin. He plowed into an embankment after his brakes failed, crushing his left foot, breaking a knee and dislocating a tibia. After being dug out by hand, he went through six months of grueling therapy. "If this had been just any old 55-year-old guy," said his doctor, "he'd probably never have walked again." The next year, he had the second-fastest qualifying time at Indy.

Foyt is ranked behind Richard Petty only because Petty's charisma was built around his driving and his accessibility. For Foyt, his driving did the talking because he rarely would—or when he did, you had to remove the expletives to quote him. "I'm just A.J., and you got to take me the way I come," he explained. And he came hot-tempered, with an ego said to be as large as his reputation. Even his stern father, perhaps the only man who ever got the better of him, remarked that getting too close too Foyt on a bad day was "about like trying to dance with a chain saw." He was often quick with a snarl—at the press, the pit crews, certainly his competition on the track. As fellow driver Bobby Rahal explained, it was understood that "you're nobody unless you've had a fist shaken at you by A. J. Foyt."

Before calling it quits, in fact, Foyt had told the media not to expect any theatrics when he closed out his career. "When I decide to retire," he said, "I'll just pull into the pits, jerk off my helmet, and tell you guys and everybody else to to go hell." He'd earned the right to say it.

97

Gilbert Patten

"Of all the athletic heroes who have appeared on the American scene," wrote Robert H. Boyle in *Sport: Mirror of American Life*, "probably none ever aroused the admiration or left so enduring an impression as one who never really existed."

Before television and newsreels and radio, before Nike created the athletic image of the '90s and Grantland Rice spawned the sporting giants of the '20s, before *Sports Illustrated* took shape and newspaper sports sections took the country by storm, before Jordan and Namath and Palmer and Louis and Ruth and Dempsey, there was Frank Merriwell, fictional character, bona fide sports hero.

Merriwell's career approximated a typical sustained athletic lifetime, beginning in 1896 and sliding from the spotlight some two decades later. But the pages of *Tip Top Weekly*, the nation's most widely read nickel novel, were his athletic arena, and his creator was a man named Gilbert Patten. Even Patten's pseudonym, Burt L. Standish, has been somewhat lost along the way to sports immortality. But the creator has been survived by his creation.

At what did Frank Merriwell excel? You name it. For twenty years he was the big man on campus at Fardale Academy and then Yale University, and he made Jim Thorpe look positively one-dimensional. He starred in baseball, football and hockey; golf, billiards and lacrosse; track, crew and bicycle racing. Merriwell wasn't quite perfect, but he was damn near close. According to Boyle, he simply stood for "truth, faith, justice, the triumph of right, mother, home, friendship, loyalty, patriotism, the love of alma mater, duty, sacrifice, retribution, and strength of soul as well as body."

Essentially, Patten planted in the minds of thousands, perhaps millions, of young readers the image of the ultimate athletic icon at the turn of the century. He created an ideal of honesty and modesty, courage and carriage—a standard met by only a handful of sports figures since, but a standard nonetheless. When subsequent athletes have failed to live up to it, it disappoints because the harsh reality of their humanity falls short of the superhuman expectations conjured up, to a large extent, by Patten and Merriwell.

Patten himself admitted, "I began to realize that I had about the biggest chance to influence the youth of this country that any man ever had," adding that "no boy, if he followed in [Merriwell's] tracks, ever did anything that he need be ashamed of." Through the first half of the century, outstanding athletes were constantly compared to Patten's fictional hero, most often at Yale, where particularly outstanding performances often elicited the question, "Who do you think you are, Frank Merriwell?"

Patten, as it turns out, was no Frank Merriwell. Born on October 25, 1866, in Corinna, Maine, he was gangling, insecure, a smoker at age fourteen, a runaway at age fifteen, never a college student, married three times. "It was natural," he said, "for me to wish to make Frank a fellow such as I would like to have been myself."

While still a teenager, he had two stories published—earning a total of $6. For the next thirteen years, he wrote largely forgettable westerns, and by 1895 he was struggling to make ends meet. He was saved by Frank Merriwell. In December of 1895, Patten received a letter from Ormond Smith, of Street & Smith Publishing, in which he explained his desire to begin publishing a weekly series. Wrote Smith, "The essential idea of this series is to interest young readers in the career of a young man at a boarding school, preferably a military or a naval academy." After a dozen stories about life at the academy, he would come into money, and he and a friend would travel the world. After another series of stories exhausted this theme, he would return home and attend college.

Patten signed a three-year contract for $50 a week, each weekly story consisting of 20,000 words. He figured it would take him just over half the week to write his story, while the remaining days could be spent chasing his ultimate dream: the great American novel.

The first story in the series appeared on April 18, 1896, under the title "Frank Merriwell; or, First Days at Fardale." In the story, Merriwell encounters a rival (his future best pal, Bart Hodge) and a love-interest (his future wife, Inza Burrage), whom he saves from a rabid dog while playing tennis. It was a harbinger of things to come. Merriwell could do no wrong, and the peripheral characters in the stories were largely there to serve as his foils or fawning friends.

The formula was a hit, and within a few months *Tip Top Weekly*'s circulation had risen to 75,000 copies. Eventually, some 300,000 youngsters each week were tracking the hero's adventures. For twelve episodes, Merriwell was introduced as Fardale Academy's shining star. Through the next twenty-seven episodes, Patten detailed his exploits roaming the globe after an uncle bequeathed Merriwell the money and the mission to do so. After that, it was off to Yale, where Merriwell overcame the jealousy of classmates and rival classes, not to mention just about any athletic challenge thrown his way.

A classmate challenges Merriwell to a dual with rapiers? Well, Merriwell just happened to be Fardale's fencing champion. Another muffs a grounder at third base, putting an end to Merriwell's perfect game against Harvard? The star pitcher turns to him and says, "You are all right. The best of us do those things occasionally."

Of course, Merriwell's greatest heroics were saved for Harvard. On one occasion, injuries left him on the sidelines for the first half of a scoreless football game against the Crimson. He could barely stand, let alone play, but—unable to ignore the exhortations of the crowd—he limped into the game. Naturally, he picked up a fumble with less than a minute remaining, dashed the length of the field and dragged a Harvard defender into the end zone for the game-winning touchdown as time expired. He was the first comeback hero. He was Joe DiMaggio and Ben Hogan and Willis Reed and Kirk Gibson before any of them were born.

Having churned out 20 million words about Merriwell, Patten asked that a fresh team of writers take over the saga in 1914. Once the new writers took over, the Merriwell stories lasted only another three years, their demise due largely to the advent of motion pictures, though they reappeared in the 1930s as radio programs.

Patten went on to publish more than two dozen boys' novels, several Hollywood scripts and a collection of adult adventure stories. On January 16, 1945, he died in his sleep, having never produced the great American novel but having created the blueprint for sport's great American hero.

98

Eleanora Sears

The image that may best describe Eleanora Sears is that of her walking. Not just a stroll: a sport. Long-distance walking was particularly popular in the heyday of this turn-of-the-century athletic pioneer, and she was one of its most well-known practitioners.

But when Sears walked, as was generally the case with all the sports she excelled in, she did so with a combination of ground-breaking aplomb and privileged arrogance. As she walked from, say, Newport to Boston, she would shock passersby with her attire, forgoing accepted feminine style for athletic comfort. Yet all the while parading slowly behind her would be her chauffeur-driven car, as if to say, "Shocking, isn't it? But who's going to stop me?"

Or perhaps the appropriate image is of her riding onto a polo field in Burlingame, California. Women traditionally rode sidesaddle; she would ride astride the horse. Women were expected to wear long skirts; she would be wearing breeches. Polo was a sport reserved for men; she would ask to play. And this at a time when women weren't even allowed to vote.

"When you really think about the women's movement, it has always been led by the privileged," explained Donna Lopiano, executive director of the Women's Sports Foundation. "The first group that started the women's movement was from Smith and Vassar and the exclusive women's schools. They had so much money and so much going for them that they didn't have to worry about retribution or backlash. They had independence born of wealth."

Such was the case with Sears, who has often been described as America's first true sportswoman. "Eleo" Sears was born on September 28, 1881, in Boston, a merging of two American royal families. Her father, Frederick Sears, was heir to a shipping fortune and a cousin of former U.S. senator Henry Cabot Lodge and former Connecticut governor John Davis Lodge. Her great-great-grandfather on her mother's side was Thomas Jefferson.

Blonde, blue-eyed, beautiful and fabulously wealthy, Sears grew up in a world of private tutors and debutante balls. She became a leader of the New England social set, ranked as one of the best-gowned women in America, a favorite dance partner of the Prince of Wales and a rumored love interest of Harold Vanderbilt. But luxury provides freedom, and Sears chose to flaunt convention and shock conservatives by using her freedom to satisfy her love of sport. In doing so, she merged her social standing with her athletic skill to make athletics a more acceptable diversion for women.

Sears was one of the first women to appear publicly in pants and short hair, to drive an automobile, to ride as an airplane passenger. Among her other pursuits were baseball, football, golf, boxing, field hockey, auto racing, swimming, skating, canoeing, trapshooting, polo, yachting and even speedboat racing. All in all, she accumulated some 240 trophies in her athletic career, but her most publicized accomplishments came in tennis, squash, walking and equestrian events.

A member of the International Tennis Hall of Fame, Sears was a three-time national singles runnerup (in 1911, 1912 and 1916), a four-time national doubles champion (1911, 1915–1917), a mixed doubles champion (1916) and, at the age of fifty-six in 1939, a women's veterans' doubles champion.

Sears took up squash in 1918, though there were no courts open to women at that time. In a typical mix of pioneering and privilege, she simply invaded the courts of Boston's Harvard Club, well before its courts were officially opened to women. A founder of the U.S. Women's Squash Racquets Association in 1928, Sears was also its first singles champion. She later served as president of the association and captain of the U.S. national team.

Though she had a chauffeur at her disposal, Sears had a consuming passion for walking, particularly as she closed in on middle age, and she became one of the country's most famous long-distance walkers. Her Newport-to-Boston walk was an annual news story, as were her record-setting paces.

As much as she liked to walk, however, she loved to ride horses. She showed horses, operated a full-scale stable of racing thoroughbreds, played polo, competed in equestrian events, and served as a financial benefactor to both the U.S. equestrian team and the National Horse Shows. Sears frequently wore riding britches, a practice considered so sinful that sermons were preached against her. She was elected to the Horsemen's Hall of Fame in 1977, nine years after her death on March 26, 1968, at the age of eighty-six.

By then, of course, Sonja Henie, Babe Didrikson, Althea Gibson, Wilma Rudolph, Billie Jean King and others had carried the torch for women's sports. But it was Sears who essentially lit the torch. Her social status gave her the freedom to do so; her love of sport gave her the will. Her accomplishments were often fodder for the society pages instead of the sports pages, particularly when the publicity surrounded her attire instead of her athleticism. But for a sportswoman at the turn of the century, any publicity at all was an achievement in itself. And anyway, who was going to stop her?

FAMILY AFFAIR

Three of Eleanora Sears's close relatives were among the most important people during the infancy of tennis in America. Sears's father, Fred, and his first cousin, James Dwight, claim to have played the first game of tennis in Nahant, Massachusetts, in the summer of 1875, organizing the first tournament in America a few weeks later. Fred Sears's younger brother, Richard, grew into America's first tennis star, winning the U.S. men's singles title from 1881–1887. He and Dwight became the first Americans to compete in the Wimbledon championships, in 1884, but it was Dwight who became known as America's "Father of Lawn Tennis."

Dwight served as president of the United States Lawn Tennis Association (USLTA), which standardized the rules of the game in America and organized the first national tournament, from 1882–1884 and from 1893–1911. Author of the sport's first authoritative book, Lawn Tennis, in 1886, he was one of the first seven men inducted into the International Tennis Hall of Fame.

99

Jacques Plante

The pitcher, the quarterback, the center and point guard, the goalie. By redefining those positions, several athletes have redefined their games, and so they have been included among *The Sports 100*.

Jim Creighton turned pitching toward its modern course in the 1860s by actually trying to make batters miss the ball. Two receivers, Knute Rockne and Don Hutson, are given credit for establishing and perfecting the passing game, and thus the role of the quarterback. George Mikan and Bill Russell transformed basketball's center position; Magic Johnson created a new prototype for the point guard. Which brings us to hockey's goaltender and the contributions of Jacques Plante, the man most responsible for giving goalies the freedom to move and, ironically, the freedom to stay put.

One Plante innovation, his tendency to roam out of the goal crease after the puck, brought goaltenders more into the flow of the game. Another Plante innovation, the goalie mask, brought goaltenders added confidence, the willingness to watch the puck *that much longer* in a game in which split-second timing makes all the difference. Because Plante was so effective, his methods and his mask soon became the standard.

Plante was born on January 17, 1929, in Shawinigan Falls, Quebec, but he truly *arrived* just south in Montreal. At the age of twenty-four, in 1953, Plante's first NHL appearance was a trial by fire as a member of the Montreal Canadiens against the Chicago Blackhawks in the semifinals of the Stanley Cup playoffs. He recorded a shutout, the first of 82 in his career, a total exceeded by only three goaltenders.

Plante would go on to spend ten seasons with the Canadiens, helping the team to five Stanley Cup championships and winning the Vezina Trophy as the NHL's top goaltender six times. Plante led the league in goals against average five straight seasons from 1956–1960, and after a one-year pause he did it again in 1962 and 1963. In the 1961–1962 season, he became one of only four goalies to earn the Hart Trophy as league MVP.

Plante's success, however, was not as influential as his style. Early in his career, he displayed a tendency to wander from the net. Plante's explanation was that he developed the style while guarding the goal for some amateur teams that were short on talent. "I was constantly having to chase the puck behind the net," he said, "and before long I realized that in this way—whether the team was bad or good—the goalie can often help himself." When other goaltenders realized the same, Plante's style became the rule.

That done, Plante went on to alter the game once more in his eighth season with the introduction of the goalie mask. Clint Benedict, of the Montreal Maroons, had actually been the first to wear a face mask during the 1929–1930 season, his final year in the NHL. After a shot by the Canadiens' Howie Morenz broke his nose, he donned a makeshift leather mask while it healed. But, claiming it obscured his vision, he soon discarded it.

Plante was barely one year old when Benedict retired, but he would eventually take over where Benedict left off. In 1959, Plante had begun experimenting with a goalie mask during practice scrimmages, but never in games. There was a stigma attached to wearing a mask, along with the widespread belief that it would hinder a goalie's effectiveness. It would take the league's most respected goaltender to turn the exception into the rule. Like Benedict, a hard shot off the stick of an all-star (Andy Bathgate, of the New York Rangers) made the mask a necessity. It happened on November 1, 1959, and Bathgate's shot broke Plante's nose. When he returned for the next period of play, he had dressed his wounds and covered his face.

"His whole face was a bloody mess and he went into the dressing room and told the coach [Toe Blake] he wouldn't play any more if he couldn't wear the mask," Plante's legendary teammate Maurice "Rocket" Richard recalled. "Blake didn't like the idea of goalies wearing masks; it just wasn't done in those days. But there was nothing Blake could do, and he let Jacques finish the game with that big thing over his face."

That "big thing," a cream-colored plastic mask, became a permanent part of Plante's equipment. When he continued to dominate, goaltenders throughout the league began to realize that he had introduced a means of protection without necessarily limiting production. Today, a goaltender without a mask is as rare as a quarterback without an arm.

How has the mask affected the game? "It was a revolutionary change," explained Fischler. "It gave goalies additional courage to do things, to look in places where they might not have looked or to look longer at the puck. They were less reluctant to go down and less reluctant to stick their head into scrambles. Now the mask is so strong that goalies will use it as a puck-stopping device."

Plante's career was long, indeed. Following the 1962–1963 season, he was traded to the New York Rangers, part of a seven-player deal. He was throught to be nearing the end of the line, and at first, that seemed to be the case. After two unspectacular seasons in New York, he retired, becoming a salesman for a Canadian brewery. But when the expansion St. Louis Blues offered him a $37,000 salary, Plante donned his mask once more. That season, he won the Vezina Trophy for a record seventh time, sharing the award with another ancient goaltending legend, 37-year-old teammate Glenn Hall.

After he was traded to the Toronto Maple Leafs in 1970, Plante topped the league once again with a 1.88 mark at the age of forty-three. He was sold to the Boston Bruins late in the 1973 season, producing two shutouts in eight regular season games before faltering in the playoffs. After the season, he signed a 10-year deal as head coach and general manager of the Quebec Nordiques of the World Hockey Association, but he broke the contract to play with another WHA team, the Edmonton Oilers.

Plante finally retired in 1975, nearly a quarter-century after his first pro game. In eighteen NHL seasons, he had recorded 434 wins, one less than Terry Sawchuk's record total. Adding in 15 wins from the WHA gives Plante the top spot in major league hockey. Among modern goalies (after 1950), only another Montreal standout, Ken Dryden, recorded a better career goals against average than Plante's 2.38 mark.

Plante died on February 27, 1986, just eleven years after retiring. He had lost his battle with cancer, but hockey's masked man had been the game's net gain.

Jim Bouton

There is a sign posted in major league baseball clubhouses. It says, "What you say here, what you see here, what you do here, and what you hear here, let it stay here." Jim Bouton ignored that sign, and because of the repercussions, he owns the final spot in *The Sports 100*.

In 1970, Bouton published *Ball Four*, a realistic day-by-day portrayal of life in the big leagues. For the most part, until then, the public had only been fed the positive side of sportsmen, or at least the public side. Bouton gave us the dark side, the childish side, the moronic side, the jealous side, the cheap side, the painful side. *Ball Four* turned the sports world on its head, aesthetically and commercially. It was, said one observer, "the diary that changed the way fans look at their baseball heroes and the way publishers look at sales charts."

Born on March 8, 1939, in Newark, New Jersey, Bouton made his mark in baseball as a righthanded pitcher for the New York Yankees. After going 7-7 as a rookie in 1962, he produced a 21-7 mark and a 2.53 earned run average in 1963 and then 18 wins, including two World Series victories, in 1964. Then he suddenly lost his fastball.

Bouton went 4-15 in 1965 and 5-9 over the next three years, becoming primarily a spot relief pitcher. He seemed to be washed-up, and on top of that, he was an outspoken liberal voice among Yankee-pinstriped conservatives. To no one's surprise, he was dealt to the expansion Seattle Pilots following the 1968 season. It was then that he decided to develop a knuckleball in an effort to keep himself in the game. He also kept a tape-recorded diary of the 1969 season to keep himself busy. The result: *Ball Four: My Life and Hard Times Throwing the Knuckleball in the Big Leagues*.

Bouton had the good fortune to chronicle an eventful summer. He was demoted to the minor leagues, made his way back to the majors, fought with his pitching coach over his ability to get by with just a knuckleball, and then was traded to the Houston Astros toward the end of the season. The heart of the book, however, was the story of the games behind the games.

"There's pettiness in baseball," Bouton wrote at the beginning of the book, "and meanness and stupidity beyond belief, and everything else bad that you'll find outside of baseball." Then he proceeded to document it.

Bouton's perspective, unorthodox at the time, seems rather tame by today's standards, but that is largely because his book opened the floodgates. Yet at first, Bouton's publisher, the World Publishing Company, had foreseen little interest in "a diary by a marginal relief pitcher on an expansion team." A printing of only 5,000 copies was scheduled, but after advance excerpts in *Look* magazine drew the ire of the baseball establishment, Bouton drew royalty checks as a best-selling author.

The commissioner hated the book; the owners hated the book; the players hated the book; many sportswriters hated the book. *Ball Four* was attacked because "it used four-letter words and destroyed heroes." It was banned in libraries and homes. Baseball commissioner Bowie Kuhn told Bouton he had done the game "a great disservice" and tried to get him to sign a statement saying the book wasn't true. Dick Young of the *New York Daily News* called Bouton a "social leper." The San Diego Padres burned the book. The publicity was a publisher's dream, and *Ball Four* became the largest selling sports book in history.

Another righthanded pitcher with a similar name, Jim Brosnan, had written a somewhat comparable book less than a decade earlier called *The Long Season*. But it was *Ball Four* that broke new ground. "Don't get me wrong. I think Brosnan's book was great," said Bouton. "But Brosnan was more detached. He was the guy sitting over in the corner sipping a martini. I wrote from the view of the guys sloshing the beer around."

What it was, quite simply, was real life: a glimpse at so-called heroes behind the scenes. Bouton talked about contract squabbles, dishonest negotiations, coaches' vendettas, intrasquad fights, pep pills, voyeurism. He badmouthed Ralph Houk and Carl Yastrzemski and Frank Crosetti and Roger Maris. Mickey Mantle, he said, shunned autograph seekers to the point that he closed a bus window on children trying to get to him.

"*Ball Four* is a people book, not a baseball book," wrote Christopher Lehmann-Haupt, in *The New York Times*. "He tells you gossip you wouldn't even know about your fellow workers around the water cooler."

The notoriety Bouton received, more than any he had found as a pitcher, ushered him into a new career. After retiring from baseball following the 1970 season, he spent five years as a sports broadcaster before working on a short-lived network situation comedy based on *Ball Four*. The following year, he mounted a comeback, pitching for three minor league teams. He started five games for the Atlanta Braves in 1978, going 1-3, which lowered his career record to 62-63. He has since embarked on a career in motivational speaking and product development, with Big League Chew bubblegum ranking among his most successful creations.

Bouton has also published two more books. In 1971, he wrote a follow-up to *Ball Four* called *I'm Glad You Didn't Take It Personally*. In 1994, he turned to fiction, co-authoring *Strike Zone*, a novel about an umpire fixing a baseball game, which took its place on the sports bookshelves alongside a parade of books spawned, to some extent, by Bouton's first. In fact, stores are now filled with tell-all memoirs, unauthorized biographies and "inside" accounts, each touted as more "shocking" and "outrageous" than the previous and each further demythologizing the sports hero. Bouton is reluctant to take credit for the trend, but he does admit that he prefers real people to fake heroes. "I think we are all better off looking across at someone," he claimed, "rather than up."

Critics knew this at the time and many considered *Ball Four* a valuable piece of literature. George Frazier of the *Boston Globe* called it "an authentic revolutionary manifesto." David Halberstam, writing in *Harper's*, explained, "A reporter covers an institution, becomes associated with it, protective of it, and, most important, the arbiter of what is right to tell. He knows what's good for you to hear, what should remain at the press-club bar . . . [Bouton staked out] a new dimension of what is proper and significant."

As might be expected, Bouton said much the same thing when discussing his legacy, but he said it with a little more earthiness. "By establishing new boundaries," he explained, "*Ball Four* changed sports reporting at least to the extent that, after the book, it was no longer possible to sell the milk and cookies image again . . . Besides, you can get sick on milk and cookies."

Appendix

What do the figures profiled in *The Sports 100* have in common? Most apparent is the amount of inherent contradiction in their various influences and personalities. Take prizefighter John L. Sullivan, for instance. He was a business failure, yet he heralded boxing and sport as big business. He is remembered as the last bare-knuckle fighter, yet 44 of his 47 bouts were with gloves. He overcame rampant anti-Irish discrimination, yet became a voice of racism. He was one of the sport's most public alcoholics, yet he later became one of the country's most persuasive temperance lecturers.

Muhammad Ali was the "greatest fighter of all-time," but he was vilified during the Vietnam War for refusing to fight. Jack Dempsey may have been the second greatest fighter, but he was charged with draft evasion following World War I. Jack Johnson was the first African-American sports hero, yet he may have hindered the progress of blacks in sports. Jesse Owens made one of sport's most symbolic statements against racism through his feats and then virtually avoided the civil rights movement.

Henry Chadwick was an Englishman, but he did more than any other person to make baseball America's national game. James Naismith, the only man to invent a major American sport, was Canadian. Walter O'Malley was a lifelong New Yorker who moved the Dodgers to Los Angeles. Red Grange put the NFL on the map in 1925 and then created a direct competitor, the AFL, in 1926. George Mikan, the player most responsible for the early survival of the NBA, became the first president of its biggest competitor, the ABA. Al Spalding created the National League as a rebellious player and then became a driving force in stifling player rebellions as an executive.

Michael Jordan, basketball's most transcendental figure, quit the game (temporarily) for baseball. Bill Tilden was adamantly against professionalism in tennis until the day he turned professional and became its biggest proponent. Avery Brundage preached separation of politics and sports, yet he came close to running for political office. Peter Ueberroth was a financial and public relations genius who then cost baseball's owners $280 million and some embarrassing headlines by orchestrating collusion. Curt Flood's loss in court may have been baseball players' most significant victory.

Ned Irish was a former newspaper reporter who couldn't deal with the press. Walter Byers was a college dropout who became the most powerful man in collegiate athletics. Vince Lombardi constantly preached the importance of family, but his own family came second to his football team. George Halas was ruthless toward his enemies, yet loyal to a fault; he was willing to risk big money, but frugal over small concerns. Branch Rickey was as much motivated by piety as a search for profits. Jim Creighton revolutionized pitching and then died while hitting a home run.

Certainly, the contradiction—sometimes even hypocrisy—evident in many of the above figures is a product of circumstance or even semantics. But it is also interesting to note the number of people in *The Sports 100* whose character may have been influenced by suffering severe childhood trauma of some kind. Among those who lost one or both parents at an early age (before age twenty) through death or abandonment are Jackie Robinson, Babe Ruth, Jim Thorpe, Red Grange, Knute Rockne, James Naismith, Ned Irish, Billie Jean King, Bill Tilden, Arthur Ashe, Martina Navratilova, George Halas, Roy Hofheinz, Tex Rickard, Bill Veeck, Peter Ueberroth, Harry Edwards, Jim Brown, Bill Russell, Larry Bird and Theodore Roosevelt. Perhaps these men and women learned a sense of self-reliance early on.

In addition, several of the figures profiled were married more than once—in some cases, several times. These include John L. Sullivan, Jack Dempsey, Jack Johnson, Joe Louis, Muhammad Ali, Jim Thorpe, Pelé, Walter Hagen, Avery Brundage, Sonja Henie, Theodore Roosevelt, Roy Hofheinz, Mark McCormack and Babe Ruth. What does it mean? Probably nothing, except that celebrity sometimes overwhelms priority.

Finally, while the 100 people in this book certainly represent some of sport's seminal figures, many of them might not have had the opportunity to influence the games at all were it not for the role played by a handful of bit players. For instance: the groundskeeper who kept Pelé from quitting soccer in 1954; the man who taught Babe Ruth how to play baseball in the orphanage at the turn of the century; the friend who convinced Joe Louis to drop the violin and take up boxing; Luther Gulick, the man who, in 1891, told James Naismith to devise a new game; the business school professor who assigned Phil Knight the task of writing a thesis about a small start-up business; the handful of players who chose Marvin Miller as the first executive director of the MLBPA; the Cornell football player who convinced Pop Warner to try the game; and Ron Charity, the tennis player who asked seven-year-old Arthur Ashe if he would like to learn how to play. Never underestimate the role of a supporting actor.

Following are some tables to determine the exact makeup of *The Sports 100*:

IN WHAT SPORT OR EVENT DID THEY MAKE THEIR MARK?

Sport	# On List	Sport	# On List
Baseball	21	Golf	6
Football	16	Tennis	6
Basketball	14	Olympics	6
Miscellaneous	13	Auto racing	4
Hockey	6	Horse racing	1
Boxing	6	Soccer	1

NOTE: The miscellaneous category includes figures who could not be pigeonholed into one sport, including Howard Cosell, Gary Davidson, Eleanora Sears and Charles McNeil. Jim Thorpe and Lamar Hunt were considered football figures. Harry Edwards and Peter Ueberroth were placed in the Olympics category.

WHAT IS THE RACE AND GENDER DISTRIBUTION IN THE BOOK?

Race	# On List	Race	# On List
Caucasian	81	Latino	2
African-American	16	Native American	1

Gender	# On List
Male	93
Female	7

IN WHAT CAPACITY DID THEY MAKE THEIR MARK?

Role	# On List	Role	# On List
Athlete	47	Chronicler	8
Executive	20	Innovator	4
Coach	10	Activist	2
Entrepreneur	9		

NOTE: Many of the figures were excellent athletes, but their most significant influence came in another capacity. For instance, Knute Rockne, Amos Alonzo Stagg, Lester Patrick and George Halas were placed in the "coach" category. Al Spalding and Branch Rickey were placed in the "executive" category, as were Matt Winn, Bill France, Sr., and Tony Hulman. Jack Kramer was considered an "entrepreneur" along with other promoters and businessmen, such as Mark McCormack, Tex Rickard, Ned Irish, Bill Rasmussen, Phil Knight, Abe Saperstein, Gary Davidson and Charles McNeil. The "chronicler" label includes Roone Arledge, Howard Cosell, Grantland Rice, Andre Laguerre, Henry Chadwick, William Randolph Hearst, Gilbert Patten and Jim Bouton. James Naismith, Walter Camp, Alexander Cartwright and Danny Biasone were considered "innovators." Harry Edwards and Marvin Miller were labeled "activists." (Obviously, many figures fit into more than one category.)

WHERE WERE THEY BORN?

Location	# On List	Location	# On List
New York	15	Colorado	1
Illinois	9	Connecticut	1
Canada	7	Iowa	1
California	5	Kansas	1
Ohio	5	Louisiana	1
Pennsylvania	5	Maine	1
Texas	5	Maryland	1
Alabama	4	Missouri	1
England	4	Nevada	1
Georgia	3	Oklahoma	1
Indiana	3	Oregon	1
Massachusetts	3	South Carolina	1
Arkansas	2	Virginia	1
Kentucky	2	Washington, D.C.	1
Michigan	2	Puerto Rico	1
New Jersey	2	Brazil	1
North Carolina	2	Czechoslovakia	1
Tennessee	2	Italy	1
Norway	2		

NOTE: The birthplaces of the 100 figures represent twenty-nine different states, Washington, D.C., Puerto Rico and six foreign countries. Interestingly, two figures on the list—Ban Johnson and Paul Brown—were born in the town of Norwalk, Ohio; two more—Babe Didrikson and Roy Hofheinz—grew up in Beaumont, Texas, at the same time.

WHEN WERE THEY BORN?

Decade	# On List	Decade	# On List
1820–1829	2	1900–1909	12
1830–1839	2	1910–1919	16
1840–1849	1	1920–1929	7
1850–1859	5	1930–1939	15
1860–1869	7	1940–1949	10
1870–1879	3	1950–1959	4
1880–1889	7	1960–1969	2
1890–1899	7		

NOTE: Three figures—Babe Ruth, George Halas, Bert Bell—were born in February 1895; Ruth and Halas were born four days apart. Gary Davidson and Roberto Clemente were born five days apart in August 1934. Sonja Henie and Roy Hofheinz were born two days apart in April 1912. Perhaps most striking, fifteen figures were born between the years 1937 and 1943.

THE DECEASED ON THE LIST: HOW LONG DID THEY LIVE?

Age at Death	# On List	Age at Death	# On List
20–24	1	65–69	6
25–29	0	65–69	6
30–34	1	70–74	6
35–39	1	75–79	12
40–44	2	80–84	6
45–49	2	85–89	7
50–54	3	90–94	0
55–59	5	95–99	0
60–64	7	100–104	1

NOTE: Baseball star Jim Creighton died at age twenty-one in 1862, three months after football legend Amos Alonzo Stagg was born. Stagg lived to be 102.

THE LIVING LEGENDS: HOW OLD ARE THEY?

Age as of Jan. 1996	# On List	Age as of Jan. 1996	# On List
30–34	2	60–64	6
35–39	3	65–69	4
40–44	0	70–74	3
45–49	2	75–79	4
50–54	5	80–84	1
55–59	9	85–89	1

NOTE: The oldest living figure in *The Sports 100* is John Wooden, age eighty-five. The youngest is Michael Jordan, age thirty-two.

WHEN DID THEY REALIZE THEIR PEAK INFLUENCE?

Decade	# On List	Decade	# On List
1840–1849	1	1920–1929	12
1850–1859	0	1930–1939	8
1860–1869	2	1940–1949	10
1870–1879	3	1950–1959	7
1880–1889	3	1960–1969	19
1890–1899	2	1970–1979	16
1900–1909	5	1980–	8
1910–1919	4		

NOTE: This table is probably the best indication of the diversity of *The Sports 100*, as well as the themes that run through it. After, all year of birth doesn't necessarily designate a person's span of influence. For instance, Don Hutson and Vince Lombardi were both born in 1913, but Hutson flourished in the '30s and '40s; Lombardi was a 1960s icon. Likewise, Red Grange and Walter O'Malley were both born in 1903, but Grange's most important moment came in 1925; O'Malley's came in 1958. It is interesting to note that the eras most repre sented in the book are the 1920s (the Golden Age of sports), the 1940s (the era of racial integration) and the 1960s and '70s (when television led to expansion and financial upheaval).

Bibliography

Anderson, Dave. *The Story of Basketball.* New York: William Morrow and Company, Inc., 1988.

Araton, Harvey, and Filip Bondy. *The Selling of the Green: The Financial Rise and Moral Decline of the Boston Celtics.* New York: HarperCollins, 1992.

Ashe, Arthur R., Jr. *A Hard Road to Glory: A History of the African-American Athlete (1919–1945).* New York: Warner Books, 1988.

Ashe, Arthur R., Jr. *A Hard Road to Glory: A History of the African-American Athlete (Since 1946).* New York: Warner Books, 1988.

Ashe, Arthur R., Jr., and Arnold Rampersad. *Days of Grace.* New York: Ballantine Books, 1993.

Astor, Gerald. *The PGA World Golf Hall of Fame Book.* New York: Prentice Hall Press, 1991.

Baker, William J. *Jesse Owens: An American Life.* New York: The Free Press, 1986.

Barkow, Al, David Barrett, et al. *20th Century Golf Chronicle.* Lincolnwood, Illinois: Publications International Ltd., 1993.

Bodo, Peter, and David Hirshey. *Pelé's New World.* New York: W. W. Norton & Company, Inc., 1977.

Bouton, Jim. *Ball Four: My life and Hard Times Throwing the Knuckleball in the Big Leagues.* New York: Macmillan. First published by The World Publishing Company, 1970.

Boyle, Robert H. *Sport: Mirror of American Life.* Boston: Little, Brown and Company, 1963.

Brondfield, Jerry. *Rockne.* New York: Random House, 1976.

Brown, Paul, and Jack Clary. *PB: The Paul Brown Story.* New York: Atheneum, 1980.

Cahn, Susan K. *Coming On Strong: Gender and Sexuality in Twentieth-Century Women's Sports.* New York: The Free Press, 1994.

Carroll, Bob. *When the Grass Was Real.* New York: Simon & Schuster, 1993.

Chaney, Lindsay, and Michael Cieply. *The Hearsts*. New York: Simon & Schuster, 1981.

Cohane, Tim. *Great College Football Coaches of the Twenties and Thirties*. New Rochelle, New York: Arlington House, 1973.

Creamer, Robert W. *Babe: The Legend Comes to Life*. New York: Penguin Books, 1974.

Daly, Dan, and Bob O'Donnell. *The Pro Football Chronicle*. New York: Macmillan, 1990.

Deford, Frank. *Big Bill Tilden*. New York: Simon & Schuster, 1976.

Durso, Joseph. *Madison Square Garden: 100 Years of History*. New York: Simon & Schuster, 1979.

Edwards, Harry. *The Revolt of the Black Athlete*. New York: Macmillan, 1970.

Evans, Richard. *Open Tennis, 1968–1988*. Lexington, Massachusetts: The Stephen Greene Press, 1989.

Falla, Jack. *NCAA: The Voice of College Sports*. Mission, Kansas: The National Collegiate Athletic Association, 1981.

Fischler, Stan. *Those Were The Days*. New York: Dodd, Mead & Company, 1976.

Fischler, Stan, and Shirley Fischler. *Fischlers' Hockey Encyclopedia*. New York: Thomas Y. Crowell Co., 1975.

Fleisher, Arthur A. III, Brian L. Goff and Robert D. Tollison. *The National Collegiate Athletic Association—A Study in Cartel Behavior*. Chicago: The University of Chicago Press, 1992.

Fountain, Charles. *Sportswriter—The Life and Times of Grantland Rice*. New York: Oxford University Press, 1993.

Gardner, Paul. *The Simplest Game*. New York: Collier Books, 1994.

George, Nelson. *Elevating The Game*. New York: HarperCollins, 1992.

Gilbert, Thomas W. *Roberto Clemente*. New York: Chelsea House Publishers, 1991.

Golenbock, Peter. *American Zoom*. New York: Macmillan, 1993.

Grange, Red, and Ira Morton. *The Red Grange Story*. Chicago: University of Illinois Press, 1993.

Gretzky, Wayne, and Rick Reilly. *Gretzky*. New York: HarperCollins, 1990.

Grimsley, Will. *Tennis: Its History, People and Events*. Englewood Cliffs, New Jersey: Prentice-Hall, Inc., 1971.

Guest, Larry. *Arnie: Inside the Legend*. Orlando: Tribune Publishing, 1993.

Gutman, Bill. *The Pictorial History of College Basketball*. New York: Gallery Books, 1989.

Guttmann, Allen. *The Games Must Go On*. New York: Columbia University Press, 1984.

Guttman, Allen. *The Olympics: A History of the Modern Games*. Chicago: University of Illinois Press, 1992.

Halas, George, Gwen Morgan and Arthur Veysey. *Halas By Halas*. New York: McGraw Hill, 1979.

Halberstam, David. *The Breaks of the Game*. New York: Ballantine Books, 1981.

Hanks, Stephen, Thomas W. Gilbert, et al. *150 Years of Baseball*. Lincolnwood, Illinois: Publications International Ltd., 1989.

Harris, David. *The League: The Rise and Decline of the NFL*. New York: Bantam Books, 1986.

Hauser, Thomas. *Muhammad Ali: His Life and Times*. New York: Simon & Schuster, 1991.

Hearst, William Randolph, Jr., and Jack Casserly. *The Hearsts: Father and Son*. Boulder, Colorado: Robert Rinehart Publishers, 1991.

Hobbs, Michael, ed. *In Celebration of Golf*. New York: Charles Scribner's Sons, 1982.

Hollander, Zander, and Hal Bock, eds. *The Complete Encyclopedia of Hockey*. Englewood Cliffs, New Jersey: Prentice-Hall, Inc., 1974.

Hollander, Zander, and Alex Sachare, eds. *The Official NBA Basketball Encyclopedia*. New York: Villard Books, 1989.

Isenberg, Michael T. *John L. Sullivan and His America*. Chicago: University of Illinois Press, 1994.

James, Bill. *The Bill James Historical Baseball Abstract*. New York: Villard Books, 1986.

Johnson, Earvin, Jr., and Roy S. Johnson. *Magic's Touch*. New York: Addison-Wesley Publishing Company, Inc., 1989.

Johnson, Earvin, and William Novak. *My Life*. New York: Random House, 1992.

Johnson, William Oscar, and Nancy P. Williamson. *"Whatta-Gal": The Babe Didrikson Story*. New York: Little, Brown and Company, 1977.

King, Billie Jean, and Frank Deford. *Billie Jean*. New York: The Viking Press, 1982.

King, Billie Jean, and Cynthia Starr. *We Have Come a Long Way*. New York: McGraw Hill, 1988.

Levine, Peter. *A. G. Spalding and the Rise of Baseball*. New York: Oxford University Press, 1985.

Libby, Bill. *Foyt*. New York: Hawthorn Books, Inc., 1974.

McCallum, John D., and Charles H. Pearson. *College Football U.S.A. 1869–1971*. New York: McGraw Hill, 1972.

McCormack, Mark H. *The Wonderful World of Professional Golf*. New York: Atheneum, 1973.

Mead, Chris. *Champion—Joe Louis, Black Hero in White America*. New York: Charles Scribner's Sons, 1985.

Metzler, Paul. *Tennis Styles and Stylists*. New York: The Macmillan Company, 1970.

Michelson, Herbert. *Charlie O.* New York: The Bobbs-Merrill Company, Inc., 1975.

Miller, Marvin. *A Whole Different Ball Game.* New York: Carol Publishing Group, 1991.

Miller, Nathan. *Theodore Roosevelt: A Life.* New York: William Morrow and Company, Inc., 1992.

Moldea, Dan E. *Interference: How Organized Crime Influences Professional Football.* New York: William Morrow and Company, Inc., 1989.

Namath, Joe Willie, and Dick Schaap. *I Can't Wait Until Tomorrow-'Cause I Get Better Looking Every Day.* New York: Random House, 1969.

Navratilova, Martina, and George Vecsey. *Martina.* New York: Alfred E. Knopf, 1985.

Neft, David, Richard Cohen and Rick Korch. *The Sports Encyclopedia: Pro Football (The Modern Era).* New York: St. Martin's Press, 1992.

Nickerson, Elinor. *Golf: A Women's History.* Jefferson, North Carolina: McFarland & Company, Inc., 1987.

O'Brien, Michael. *Vince: A Personal Biography of Vince Lombardi.* New York: William Morrow and Company, Inc., 1987.

Peper, George. *Golf in America.* New York: Harry N. Abrams, Inc., 1988.

Peterson, Robert W. *Cages to Jump Shots: Pro Basketball's Early Years.* New York: Oxford University Press, 1990.

Peterson, Robert. *Only the Ball Was White.* New York: Oxford University Press, 1970.

Petty, Richard, and William Neely. *King Richard I.* New York: Macmillan Publishing Company, 1986.

Porter, David L., ed. *Biographical Dictionary of American Sports: Football.* New York: Greenwood Press, 1987.

Porter, David L., ed. *Biographical Dictionary of American Sports: Indoor Sports.* New York: Greenwood Press, 1989.

Porter, David L., ed. *Biographical Dictionary of American Sports: Outdoor Sports.* New York: Greenwood Press, 1988.

Prendergast, Curtis, and Geoffrey Kolvin. *The World of Time Inc.* New York: Atheneum, 1986.

Reich, Kenneth. *Making It Happen: Peter Ueberroth and the 1984 Olympics.* Santa Barbara: Capra Press, 1986.

Sasuly, Richard. *Bookies & Bettors: Two Hundred Years of Gambling.* New York: Holt, Rinehart and Winston, 1982.

Seymour, Harold. *Baseball: The Early Years.* New York: Oxford University Press, 1960.

Seymour, Harold. *Baseball: The Golden Age.* New York: Oxford University Press, 1971.

Slater, Robert. *Great Jews in Sports.* New York: Jonathan David Publishers, Inc, 1992.

Steele, Michael R. *Knute Rockne—A Bio-Bibliography*. Westport, Connecticut: Greenwood Press, 1983.

Strait, Raymond, and Leif Henie. *Queen of Ice, Queen of Shadows*. New York: Stein and Day, 1985.

Sullivan, Neil J. *The Dodgers Move West*. New York: Oxford University Press, 1987.

Thorn, John, and John Holway. *The Pitcher*. New York: Prentice Hall Press, 1987.

Thorn, John, and Pete Palmer, eds. *Total Baseball*. New York: HarperPerennial, 1993.

Twombly, Wells. *200 Years of Sport in America*. New York: McGraw Hill, 1976.

Tygiel, Jules. *Baseball's Great Experiment*. New York: Oxford University Press, 1983.

Vass, George. *George Halas and the Chicago Bears*. Chicago: Henry Regnery Company, 1971.

Vecchione, Joseph J., ed. *The New York Times Book of Sports Legends*. New York: The New York Times Company, 1991.

Veeck, Bill, and Ed Linn. *Veeck—As in Wreck*. New York: Bantam Books, 1962.

Wallechinsky, David. *The Complete Book of the Olympics*. New York: Penguin Books, 1988.

Wheeler, Robert W. *Jim Thorpe: World's Greatest Athlete*. Norman, Oklahoma: University of Oklahoma Press, 1979.

Whitehead, Eric. *The Patricks: Hockey's Royal Family*. Garden City, New York: Doubleday & Company, Inc., 1980.

Wind, Herbert Warren. *Follow Through*. New York: Ticknor & Fields, 1985.

Wolff, Alexander. *100 Years of Hoops*. New York: The Time Inc. Magazine Company, 1991.

Wolff, Rick, ed. *The Baseball Encyclopedia*. New York: Macmillan, 1992.

Woolum, Janet. *Outstanding Women Athletes*. Phoenix: The Oryx Press, 1992.

Zimbalist, Andrew. *Baseball and Billions*. New York: Basic Books, 1992.

Photo Acknowledgments

We would like to thank the following for providing photos used in *The Sports 100:*

1.	Jackie Robinson	The Los Angeles Dodgers
2.	Muhammad Ali	Amateur Athletic Foundation of Los Angeles
3.	Babe Ruth	National Baseball Library and Archives
4.	James Naismith	YMCA Archives, University of Minnesota Libraries
5.	Albert Spalding	Sherry Group
6.	Walter Camp	Yale University
7.	Joe Louis	Amateur Athletic Foundation of Los Angeles
8.	Billie Jean King	TeamTennis, Inc.
9.	Roone Arledge	ABC News
10.	Branch Rickey	Los Angeles Dodgers
11.	Marvin Miller	AP/World Wide Photos
12.	Mark McCormack	Linda Dozoretz Communications
13.	Jack Johnson	Amateur Athletic Foundation
14.	George Halas	Chicago Bears
15.	Michael Jordan	copyright © Bill Smith
16.	Harry Wright	National Baseball Library and Archives
17.	William Hulbert	National Baseball Library and Archives
18.	John L. Sullivan	Amateur Athletic Foundation of Los Angeles
19.	Amos Alonzo Stagg	University of Chicago
20.	Red Grange	University of Illinois
21.	Arnold Palmer	Arnold Palmer
22.	Jim Thorpe	Amateur Athletic Foundation of Los Angeles
23.	Babe Didrikson Zaharias	Amateur Athletic Foundation of Los Angeles
24.	Henry Chadwick	National Baseball Library and Archives
25.	Pete Rozelle	National Football League
26.	David Stern	National Basketball Association

27. Bobby Jones	Amateur Athletic Foundation of Los Angeles
28. Knute Rockne	University of Notre Dame
29. Jesse Owens	Ohio State University
30. Kenesaw Mountain Landis	National Baseball Library and Archives
31. Lester Patrick	Hockey Hall of Fame
32. Magic Johnson	Los Angeles Lakers
33. Larry Bird	Amateur Athletic Foundation of Los Angeles
34. Ban Johnson	National Baseball Library and Archives
35. Lamar Hunt	Kansas City Chiefs
36. Arthur Ashe	University of Los Angeles
37. Walter Byers	National Collegiate Athletic Association
38. Wayne Gretzky	Los Angeles Kings
39. Curt Flood	Amateur Athletic Foundation of Los Angeles
40. Joe Namath	New York Jets
41. Bill France, Sr.	Daytona International Speedway Archives
42. Tex Rickard	Amateur Athletic Foundation of Los Angeles
43. Bill Russell	University of San Francisco
44. Jack Kramer	Amateur Athletic Foundation of Los Angeles
45. Avery Brundage	Amateur Athletic Foundation of Los Angeles
46. George Mikan	DePaul University
47. Jim Creighton	National Baseball Library and Archives
48. Bill Tilden	Amateur Athletic Foundation of Los Angeles
49. Roy Hofheinz	Houston Astros
50. Satchel Paige	Amateur Athletic Foundation of Los Angeles
51. Paul Brown	Cincinnati Bengals
52. Jim Brown	Cincinnati Bengals
53. Jack Dempsey	Amateur Athletic Foundation of Los Angeles
54. Wilma Rudolph	Tennessee State University
55. Jack Nicklaus	Golden Bear International
56. Andre Laguerre	Sports Illustrated
57. Bill Rasmussen	Intellinet
58. Ned Irish	New York Knicks
59. Hank Luisetti	Stanford University
60. Howie Morenz	Hockey Hall of Fame
61. Grantland Rice	Vanderbilt University Photographic Archives
62. Phil Knight	Nike, Inc.
63. Althea Gibson	International Tennis Hall of Fame
64. Bert Bell	Philadelphia Eagles

65. Theodore Roosevelt	AP/World Wide Photos
66. Walter O'Malley	Los Angeles Dodgers
67. Abe Saperstein	Harlem Globetrotters
68. Vince Lombardi	Green Bay Packers
69. Bill Veeck	Chicago White Socks
70. Pop Warner	Cornell University
71. Howard Cosell	AP/World Wide Photos
72. Francis Ouimet	Amateur Athletic Foundation of Los Angeles
73. Martina Navratilova	Linda Dozoretz Communications
74. Alexander Cartwright	National Baseball Library and Archives
75. Gary Davidson	AP/World Wide Photos
76. Julius Erving	Philadelphia 76ers
77. Bobby Hull	Chicago BlackHawks
78. Roberto Clemente	Pittsburgh Pirates
79. Tony Hulman	Indianapolis Motor Speedway Corp.
80. Walter Hagen	Amateur Athletic Foundation of Los Angeles
81. Bobby Orr	Boston Bruins
82. Don Hutson	Amateur Athletic Foundation of Los Angeles
83. Charlie Finley	AP/World Wide Photos
84. Red Auerbach	Naismith Memorial Basketball Hall of Fame
85. Danny Biasone	AP/World Wide Photos
86. Matt Winn	Churchill Downs
87. Sonja Henie	AP/World Wide Photos
88. Richard Petty	STP Racing–Bryant Murray
89. Cap Anson	National Baseball Library and Archives
90. Pelé	Amateur Athletic Foundation of Los Angeles
91. William Randolph Hearst	AP/World Wide Photos
92. John Wooden	UCLA
93. Harry Edwards	San Francisco 49ers
94. Peter Ueberroth	Amateur Athletic Foundation of Los Angeles
95. Charles McNeil	University of Chicago Library
96. A. J. Foyt	United States Tobacco Company
97. Gilbert Patten	AP/World Wide Photos
98. Eleanora Sears	International Tennis Hall of Fame
99. Jacques Plante	Hockey Hall of Fame
100. Jim Bouton	Jim Bouton